Monarch wing photo by Sharon Blaziak.

STORIES OF AMERICA

LIFE IN PACIFIC GROVE CALIFORNIA
BOOK 2

Personal Essays and Stories

DEEPER CONNECTIONS TO BUTTERFLY TOWN, U.S.A.

Patricia Hamilton, Publisher • Peter Mounteer, Photographer

PACIFIC GROVE BOOKS
Pacific Grove, California

**Life in Pacific Grove, California Book 1, Oct 7, 2017.
Book release at Chautauqua Hall, during P.G. Butterfly Days.**

Pictured: California State Senator Bill Monning, with a copy of *Life in Pacific Grove Book 1*; book Illustrator Keith Larson; and publisher Patricia Hamilton, with a Certificate of Recognition from the California State Senate; and Pacific Grove Mayor Bill Kampe. Senator Monning and Mayor Kampe were great supporters of our community effort to gather and preserve P.G. heritage and culture with the first printed book of personal stories. Photo Pacific Grove photographer Donna Kiernan.

Bringing People Together – Through the Power of Story

This book is the second editon of two community books with special essays and personal stories by residents and visitors to Pacific Grove. Each reflects the story writer's research, opinions, and present recollections of experiences over time—some names and characteristics have been changed, some events have been compressed, and some dialogue recreated. All text and photographs supplied by individual story writers (unless stated otherwise) and are used with their permission. Although the writers and publisher have made every effort to ensure that the information in this book was correct at press time, the writers and publisher do not assume and hereby disclaim any liability to any party for any loss, damage, or disruption caused by errors or omissions, whether such errors or omissions result from negligence, accident, or any other cause. Please send any corrections with documentation or personal affidavit to the publisher. All rights reserved. No parts of this book may be reproduced in any form or by any electronic or mechanical means including information storage and retrieval systems without permission in writing from the publisher, except for fair use or by a reviewer who may quote brief passages in a review. *Please send any corrections to Pacific Grove Books, P.O. Box 722, Pacific Grove, CA 93950.*

LIFE IN PACIFIC GROVE BOOK 2
  Softcover: ISBN 978-1-943887-73-6 • FIRST EDITION October 2018 Updated January 2019
  Hardcover: ISBN 978-943887-82-8
  Copyright text © Patricia Hamilton • Photographs © Peter Mounteer
  Editing by Joyce Krieg, Diane Tyrrel and William Neish

LIFE IN PACIFIC GROVE BOOK 1
  Softcover: ISBN 978-1-943887-36-1 • FIRST EDITION October 2017; Updated December 2017
  Hardcover: ISBN 978-1-943887-54-5 • E-book: ISBN 978-1-943887-55-2
  Copyright text © Patricia Hamilton • Illustrations © Keith Larson
  Editing by Joyce Krieg, Diane Tyrrel and William Neish

Published by PACIFIC GROVE BOOKS, KEEPERS OF OUR CULTURE, Imprints of Park Place Publications, P.O. Box 722, Pacific Grove, California 93950 • LifeinPacificGrove.com • KeepersofOurCulture.com • ParkPlacePublications.com • Printed in the United States of America STORIES OF AMERICA - *Building Community One Story at a Time* For all general information contact KeepersofOurCulture@gmail.com. Watch for the 2020 launch of StoriesofAmerica.us with an invitation to bring our communities together through the power of personal stories. Storytellers Rule the World!

A donation is made to the Pacific Grove Public Library for each book sold, specifically for the procurement and preservation of Pacific Grove stories, historic documents and memorabilia.

BE HERE NOW

The meeting of two eternities,
the past and future ...
is precisely the present moment.
— Henry David Thoreau

The moose, owned by Wm. B. Saleh Jr., decided the winters were too cold on the East Coast, and emigrated to the warmth of Pacific Grove on the Monterey Peninsula.

"The Butterfly Effect" Revisited

Note from the Publisher

Life in Pacific Grove: Book 1, published one year ago, was a leap beyond the concept of the "Butterfly Effect"—the idea that seemingly small and insignificant actions taken by one person can have a profound effect globally—that in sharing our personal stories with others, we not only affect the lives of people around us, but also have a long-lasting ripple effect on our entire community and outward.

No sooner did that collection of personal stories by more than 400 town residents and visitors hit the shelves than the feedback began to pour in. Neighbors who'd lived near each other for years and never did more than smile politely now knew each other's names and a little bit about their lives. "There's a warmth there now," one told me.

One resident concerned about the health of her lemon tree discovered an expert gardener living nearby. A tree was saved and another friendship took root. Over and over, we heard the sentiment: "I fell in love with Pacific Grove all over again when I read these stores." And "Who knew so many people love Pacific Grove as much as *I* do?" I was pleased by a recent remark from a colleague, "One thing I like about this book is it makes one curious to know one's neighbors … now I want to meet Vicki Pearse at the Farmers Market—as well as other contributors. I am just beginning to grasp that aspect of these books, rather than just looking at the words. :) It's a very special 'community building' gift!"

With proceeds from Book 1 sales, a down payment was made towards the purchase of a new microfiche printer at the Pacific Grove Public Library, making our town history available to everyone. Sales of all Pacific Grove Books will continue to support the library and the work of preserving our city's heritage and culture.

◉◉◉

Life in Pacific Grove: Book 2 makes deeper connections to our community through special essays by local authors, in areas of their own interests—plus personal stories.

With these stories, the "Butterfly Effect" continues to transform us, and as the monarchs make part of their transformation in our Butterfly Sanctuary, and as we write and share our stories with each other, we all become something more beautiful than before.

I hope you enjoy what we have put together—for you and for the generations to come. I'm a firm believer in the power of story to change our lives, the lives of people around us, and those of future generations. Thank you all for your story contributions to the Pacific Grove Books and to our beloved City of Pacific Grove, Butterfly Town U.S.A.

– Patricia Hamilton, 2018

Front Cover and page vi photos Peter Mounteer.: Pacific Grove Butterfly Sanctuary butterflies by Sharon Blaziak.

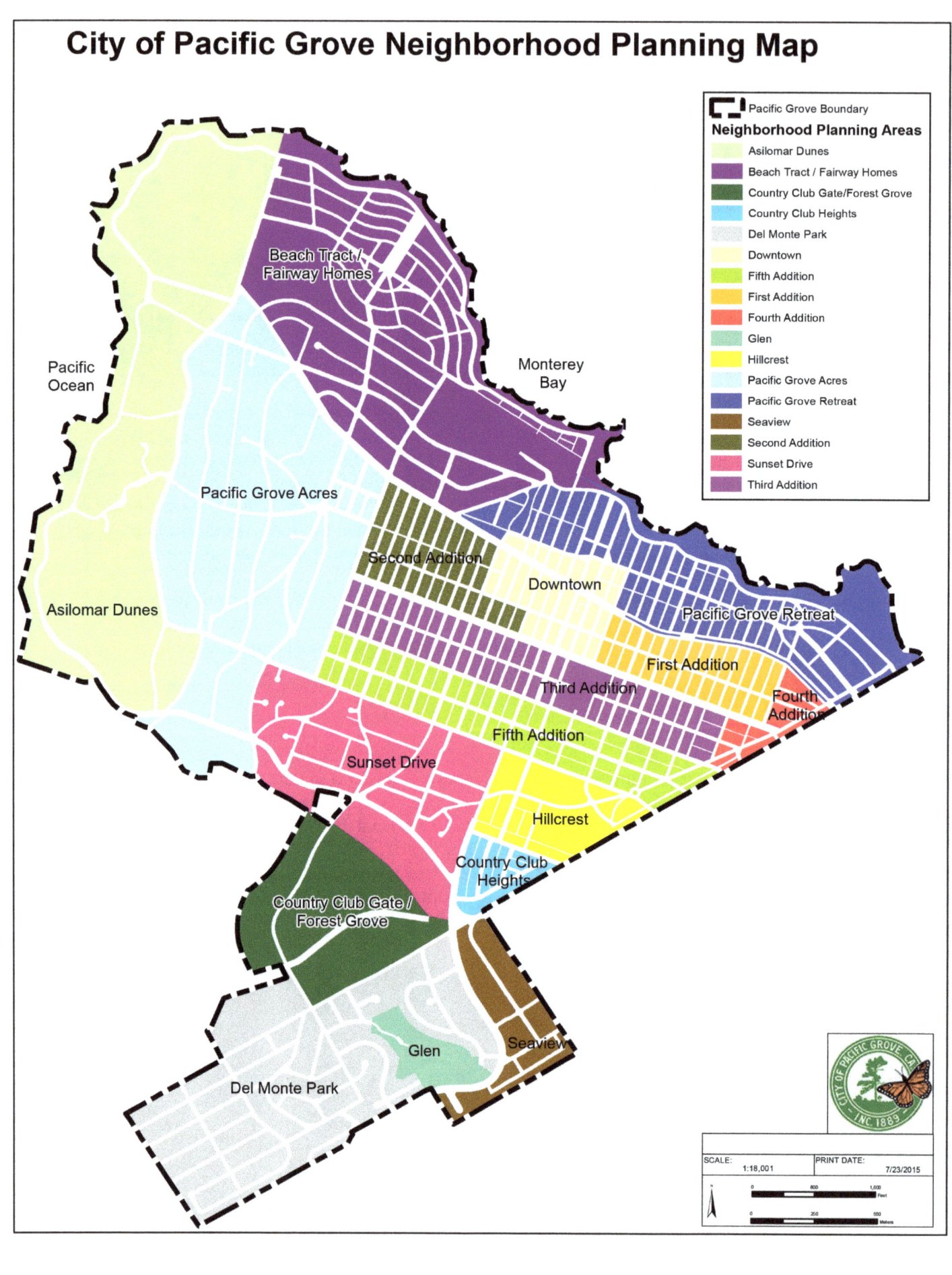

DEEPER CONNECTIONS TO BUTTERFLY TOWN, U.S.A.

"The Butterfly Effect" Revisited – Patricia Hamilton   vii

SECTION 1– SPANNING GENERATIONS   1

With our quaint Victorians and a major annual event called "Good Old Days," Pacific Grove is obviously a town with one foot planted firmly in the past. But we Pagrovians have always had the other foot just as firmly anchored in the now, facing the future. Explore a few of our beloved local traditions and institutions: the library, Feast of Lanterns, the real person behind Robert Down Elementary School, the night Paris came to P.G., and more.

    The Monterey Peninsula – Randall A. Reinstedt   1
    Pat Hathaway Collection – Dixie Layne   22
    Robert Down & Pine Schools – Dixie Layne   27
    P.G. High School Newspaper and Yearbook photos/clippings   31
    Personal Reminiscences – 32
        Becky DeSmet, Dawn Armstrong, Anne (Allen) Vucina, Bob Fisher,
        Sherry Lewis Howard, Keith Larson
    Pacific Grove Friends of the Arts – Nancy Jacobs   43
    Feast of Lanterns   48
        Interconnected Threads of Time – Kaye Coleman   50
        The Royal Court: Turning Young Women Into Leaders – Kaye Coleman   52
        Elmarie Dyke – Joanie Hyler/Dixie Layne   56

SECTION 2 – THOSE HIPPIE TRIPPY 1970s   62

Tune in, turn on and go trippin' for a heady look at the 1970s, when Pacific Grove boasted the largest collection of hippies between San Francisco and Los Angeles. From hootenannies to the Monterey International Pop Music Festival to the early days of Tillie Gort's, it's a groove, Daddy-o!

    Looking Back: P.G.'s Wild Hippie Days – Joyce Day Meuse   64
    A Head Start on 'California Dreamin' – John McCleary   72
    Pacific Grove 1974 – Bill Minor   90
    Pacific Grove Hootenanny Still Rockin' – Vic Selby/Joyce Krieg   94
    More From That Era   102
        Gary Kildall, The Asilomar Microcomputer Workshop–David A. Laws;
Del Monte Park – Mimi Sheridan

SECTION 3 – A WRITER'S DREAM TOWN 108

Beautiful scenery to tempt the muse … a good, dependable local bookstore and library … a lively coffee house scene … kindred spirits for support and encouragement … and a rich literary tradition. When it comes to meeting the needs of a writer, Pacific Grove is the ideal haven.

    P.G. The Perfect Retreat for Writers – Joyce Krieg   110
    CITY OF PACIFIC GROVE MAYOR'S PROCLAMATION   119
    An Author's Ode to Pacific Grove – Brad Herzog   120
    A Time of Magic with John Steinbeck – Phyllis Edwards   128
    Writing in P.G.: Lies, Big and Little – Diane Tyrrel   136
    P.G. and Steinbeck's Romance Novel – Diane Tyrrel   143
    The Editor is "IN" the *Cedar Street Times* – Diane Tyrrel   146
    Steinbeck: The Untold Stories – Steve Hauk   148
    Steinbeck, Pacific Grove and Me – David A. Laws   148
    Poetry in the Grove   152
        Joy Ann Fischer, Evelyn Kahan, Susie Joyce, Frank Pierce, Patrick Flanigan
    The Art of the Spec Script – Wolf Bukowski   154
    Flash Fiction "Bedtime Story" – Jeffrey Whitmore   156
    Central Coast Writers   158

SECTION 4 – CONNECTIONS AROUND TOWN 160

Where else but Pacific Grove could you find a falconer on the city payroll, or a life-size sculpture of a gray whale, or a business with a name that translates to "textile zoo"? All this and more to interest and intrigue you as we take a stroll around town.

    Five Women in Business – Rebecca Riddell   162
    P.G. Pride – Rebecca Riddell   171
    Kat, David, Mac and Me – Russell Sunshine   172
    Meet Sandy, the Whale – Elayne Azevedo   184
    Museum of Natural History Transformation   192
        John Pearse, David W. Greenfield, Geva Arcanin,
        Vicki Pearse, Betty Lou Young
    Dreams of Pacific Grove – William Neish   200
    City Hall and the Library   210
        Dionne Ybarra, Rudy Fischer, Bill Peake,
        Ken Cuneo, Donald Livermore and Bill Pagano
    The Heritage Society – Mimi Sheridan, Jean Anton   222
    The Farmers Market – Vicki B. Pearse and Maureen Mason   224
    Rotary Club Celebrates 70 Years – David A. Laws   226

Personal Reminiscences   230
> Judy Wills, Devora Stark, Judy Avila, Terry Piotrkowski,
> Mimi Sheridan, Helen Ogden, Barbara Kraus, Kaito Kraus,
> Ann Dee, Tania Panarello, Richard Jenson, Rosi Edwards,
> Cynthia B. Guthrie, Jim and Barbara Gianelli, Bob Fisher, Flora Anderson,
> Nancy Bell/Stan Countz, Annette Corcoran/Nancy Jacobs,
> Robin Aeschliman, Charlie Higuera/Katie Shain

SECTION 5 – ADVENTURES ON MONTEREY BAY   248

From a calm day on the rocky shores at Perkins Park to the panic on a stranded boat at the mouth of the bay, explore sea life in the depths of the Great Canyon, experience a life or death encounter with a sea lion, and cook up the tastiest fish you'll ever eat.

> Dropping a Line Into The Bay – Ken Rockefeller/Patricia Hamilton   250
> Personal Reminiscences   258
>> LeeAnn Stewart, Emily Miller, Rudy Fischer,
>> Sharon Law Tucker, Edward E. Jarvis, Evelyn Kahan,
>> Jim Willowby/Susan Goldbeck, Betty A. Sproule, Bonnie Sailer   258

SECTION 6 – SPIRITS IN MOTION   268

Feeding the soul, nurturing the body—Pagrovians find a balanced spiritual life through our many houses of worship, mindfulness of our origins, and this gentle and ancient movement.

> The Churches of Pacific Grove – Gary Baley   270
> P.G., Tai Chi, and Me – Jeffrey Whitmore   288
> Personal Reminiscences   296
>> Joe Neary, Joy Ann Fischer, Elizabeth Fisher, Keith Larson,
>> Dennis Trason/Deane Ramoni, Alexis Bunten, Kristina Kringle

WRITING PROMPT: MEMOIR MOVIE METHOD 314

INDEX TO WRITERS   315

Scenes from Butterfly Parade and Good Old Days Parade. Photos Peter Mounteer.

SECTION ONE

SPANNING GENERATIONS

"An enchanted land at the tip of the Monterey Peninsula."
– Randy Reinstedt

The Monterey Peninsula, An Enchanted Land – Randy Reinstedt

Ghost Town Publications, Pacific Grove, California, © 1995, reprints 2001, 2012.
Chapter Two, reprinted and used with permission of Randy and Debbie Reinstedt, 2018.

OTHER RESOURCES FOR PACIFIC GROVE HISTORY

Hamilton, Patricia, *Life in Pacific Grove, Book1*, Pacific Grove Books, Pacific Grove, CA, September 2017

Heritage Society of Pacific Grove, Ketcham's Barn:artifacts, docents, Laurel Street: and *Board and Batten,* newsletter mailed free to members of the Heritage Society of Pacific Grove, http://www.pacificgroveheritage.org/

Jaques, Louise V., *Story of Wilford Rensselaer Holman,* August 1979.

McLane, Lucy Neely, *A Piney Paradise by Monterey Bay*, 2nd ed. Fresno, Calif.: Academic Literary Guild, 1958. 2019 Reprint Pacific Grove Books, Pacific Grove, California.

Pacific Grove Public Library, Newspapers, Microfiche files and card catalog.

Reinstedt, Randy, *More Than Memories: History of Happenings of the Monterey Peninsula*, Ghost Town Publications, Pacific Grove, California.

Seavey, Kent and the Heritage Society of Pacific Grove, *Pacific Grove (CA), (Images of America)*, Arcada Publishing, San Francisco, CA, 2005.

Whitehurst, Patrick, *Pacific Grove Museum of Natural History (CA), (Images of America),* Arcada Publishing, San Francisco, CA, 2018.

More resources on pages 117–118.

Pacific Grove
"GOD'S KINGDOM BY THE SEA"

Excerpt compliments of Randy and Debbie Reinstedt.

In the early days the Pacific Grove Retreat was protected from outsiders, and all "modern" conveniences (which some considered "a work of the devil"), by gates and a fence. The entryway shown in this circa 1880 photo was not open to vehicular traffic, providing easy access only for those on foot. The gate was located near the intersection of Lighthouse and Grand avenues, in the heart of present-day downtown Pacific Grove. The buildings to the right housed a small provisions store and restaurant, where Ford's Department Store (formerly Holman's) is now located. The stout gentleman in the foreground is thought to be J.O. Johnson, one-time superintendent of the Pacific Improvement Company, and later the owner of the Mammoth Stable.

Photo by C.W.J. Johnson. Pat Hathaway Collection.

Text for this chapter is excerpted by permission of Randy Reinstedt.

The Grove's 30-by-60 foot tent lots sold briskly, and it was not long before tent-like structures were built—some right over the existing tents! A number of the Grove's early rules were reflective of the tent culture, such as a ban against smoking on the platforms (tent floors). This rule was especially important since there was no fire department in the retreat's early days. Photo by C.W.J. Johnson. Pat Hathaway Collection

LIKE THE OTHER COMMUNITIES ON THE Monterey Peninsula, Pacific Grove has a unique personality. It is known for many things, including its beautiful shoreline, Monarch butterflies, and Victorian houses. History buffs probably know Pacific Grove best as a seaside retreat, a "piney paradise" that, over a century ago, was referred to as "God's kingdom by the sea." It's Point of Pines (Point Pinos) is the site of the west coast's oldest continuously operating lighthouse, built in 1855 and still in use. The Point Pinos area has also been suggested as one of the landfalls described by the Portuguese explorer Juan Rodriguez Cabrillo. In 1542 while in the service of Spain, Cabrillo became the first European to sail up the rugged Alta California coast.

Even though Pacific Grove borders California's first capital city, its history is decidedly different. In 1873 Monterey County land baron David Jacks owned much of the property that was to become Pacific Grove. In the summer of that year, Jacks granted permission to a Methodist minister to build a small house on his holdings.

Completed in 1855, the Point Pinos Lighthouse is considered the oldest continuously operating lighthouse on the West Coast. The main structure is built of granite quarried near the site. After the 1906 earthquake damaged the tower, modifications were made to the structure, but the lighthouse still boasts the original lenses and prisms. The light source stands 89 feet above sea level, and when conditions are right it is visible from a distance of 15 miles. Pat Hathaway Collection

The Reverend Ross and his wife had exhausted all "modern" medicines in their search for relief from various ailments. They were advised to make their home in an area "where the fluctuations from heat to cold were merely nominal." After much research, they chose the Monterey Peninsula. After only a short time living "amongst the pines," they experienced a remarkable improvement in their health. With a new lease on life, Ross returned to his former home in the East and convinced his brother and sister-in-law (both of whom were suffering from pulmonary problems) to return with him to his pine-forested promontory. Settling in what is now Pacific Grove, the four of them ignored most indoor comforts and lived primarily on fish and game. They looked upon the improvement in their health as almost miraculous.

Rev. Ross entertained many visitors at his woodsy residence, and word of the benefits of his peaceful grove soon spread. Among his more distinguished guests was the Methodist bishop Jesse Truesdale Peck, a member of a group of Methodist clergymen who had been seeking a suitable California site to build a church summer camp. They needed an atmosphere conducive to religious meetings, for they wanted to establish a Christian seaside retreat similar to the one in Ocean Grove, New Jersey. Peck's stay with Rev. Ross in 1874 led him to convince the others on the committee that he had found just the place they were seeking. The Pacific Grove Retreat Association was

This photograph was taken in 1879, the year Robert Louis Stevenson visited the "dreamlike" Pacific Grove Retreat. Stevenson described this outdoor minister's pavilion, where many of the retreat's early gatherings were held, as an "open-air temple, with benches and soundingboard." Photo by C.W.J. Johnson. Pat Hathaway Collection

founded at a meeting in San Francisco on June 1, 1875.

When he heard about the project, David Jacks generously advanced a large sum of money and contributed 100 acres of prime land—a portion of downtown Pacific Grove now stands on part of this property. The bayside retreat got off to a fast start. In August 1875 the first in a long line of camp meetings was held. As the years rolled on, the fame of the Pacific Grove Retreat spread far and wide, drawing an ever-increasing number of people to the religious resort.

Visitors described this Methodist meeting place as "a little paradise," a place to "breathe the pure aroma of the pines" and "inhale the ozone from the broad Pacific." Its climate was said to be "the most equable in the known world," "so healthy that doctors scarcely make a living." Such descriptions induced even more people to visit the Grove, hoping to cleanse their bodies as well as their souls.

During the early years of the retreat, most of the activities took place during the summer season. Meetings were usually held outdoors or under a huge tent. Smaller tents served as accommodation for many of the people who attended the gatherings. The sale of 30-by-60-foot "tent lots" was brisk, and some came to look upon the Grove as a real estate venture. Soon small houses were built on the tiny lots, a limited number of stores opened their doors, and straight streets were laid out. Before long the Grove became a haven for conventions, catering to such groups as the Young Men's and Young Women's Christian Associations, the State Sabbath School, the Women's Christian Temperance Union, and (perhaps most important) the Chautauqua Society.

The Chautauqua organization began in 1874 at Lake Chautauqua, New York, as a summer training camp for Methodist Sunday School teachers. Chautauqua developed into a nationwide cultural and educational movement, featuring entertainment, concerts, lectures, and readings. In 1879, Chautauqua arrived at the Pacific Grove Retreat. At first the gatherings were held in temporary quarters, including a large tent. In 1881 the meetings were moved to a new wood building that is a Pacific Grove landmark to this day and is known as Chautauqua Hall. When Robert Louis Stevenson lived on the Monterey Peninsula in 1879, he visited the Point Pinos lighthouse. On the way there, he happened on the Pacific Grove Retreat, which was all but deserted in the off-season. Stevenson's description of this Methodist campground is one of the best that we have.

One day—I shall never forget it—I had taken a trail that was new to me. After awhile the woods began to open, the sea to sound nearer at hand. I came upon a road, and, to my surprise, a stile. A step or two farther, and without leaving the woods, I found myself among trim houses. I walked through street after street, parallel and at right angles, paved with sward and dotted with trees, but still undeniable streets, and each with its name posted at the corner, as in a real town. Facing down the main thoroughfare—"Central Avenue" as it was ticketed—I saw an open-air temple, with benches and sounding-board, as though for an orchestra. The houses were all tightly shuttered; there was no smoke, no sound but the waves, no moving thing. I have never been in any place that seemed so dreamlike. Pompeii is all in a bustle with visitors, and its antiquity and strangeness deceive the imagination; but this town had plainly not been built above a year or two, and perhaps had been deserted over-night. Indeed, it was not so much like a deserted town as like a scene upon the stage by daylight, and with no one on the boards. The barking of a dog led me at last to the only house still occupied, where a Scotch pastor and his wife pass the winter alone in this empty theater. The place was "The Pacific Camp Grounds, the Christian Seaside Resort." Thither, in the warm season, crowds come to enjoy a life of teetotalism, religion and flirtation, which I am willing to think blameless and agreeable. The neighborhood at least is well selected. The Pacific booms in front. Westward is Point Pinos, with lighthouse in a wilderness of sand, where you will find the light-keeper playing the piano, making models and bows and arrows, studying dawn and sunrise in amateur oil-painting, and with a dozen other elegant pursuits and interests to surprise his brave, old-country rivals.

The resort also attracted people bent on leisure activities of a wilder sort than worship. To combat these influences, the leaders of the Christian retreat (and in later years the elected officials of the town) enacted a code of blue laws. In the eyes of some observers, Pacific Grove remained an outpost of Puritanism well into the twentieth century. One ordinance read:

It shall be unlawful for every person wearing a bathing suit or portion thereof, except children under the age of ten years, to appear in or upon the beach or in any place open to the public—unless attired in a bathing suit or other clothing of opaque material, which shall be worn in much a manner as to preclude form. All such bathing suits shall be provided with double crotches or with skirts of ample size to cover the buttocks.

It was further stated:

Bathing without costumes, or in immodest bathing apparel, or passing through the streets to and from the beach without suitable covering, is prohibited at all times.

Bathing, fishing, and boating were prohibited on the Sabbath. Among the many other restrictions enforced on Sunday was the sale of all objects other than medicine. One druggist, who broke this law and sold a toothbrush to a visitor who had lost his, was forced to pay for his mistake with a fine.

What's more, there were curfew laws that required inhabitants of all dwellings to keep their shades up until 10 p.m., at which time the shades had to come down and all lights put out. Other curfew laws were aimed at young people. At certain times of the year no one under the age of 18 was allowed on the streets between 8 p.m. and daylight. Adding to the dismay of minors was an early law that prohibited dancing. As time went on the city fathers became a bit more open-minded, and a limited amount of social dancing was permitted. However, as late as 1920 an ordinance permitting dancing parties was issued with the following restrictions:

It is hereby declared to be unlawful for any person while dancing to assume or maintain any position which tends in any way to corrupt the good morals of any person attending said dance hall. Dances known as the tango, turkey-trot, bunny-hug, or shimmie, are hereby prohibited and declared to be unlawful.

This scene of perhaps a century ago depicts one of the Grove's earliest homes, as well as a number of carefully posed and very obliging residents and visitors. Photo by C.W.J. Johnson. Pat Hathaway Collection

Gambling of all kinds was forbidden, including games such as cards, dice, and billiard. Profanity was also prohibited, and all loud or boisterous talking and rude conduct was to be discontinued immediately, as it was not considered "in harmony with good order and propriety." As for liquor,

The buying, selling or giving away of any and all intoxicants, spirituous liquors, wine, beer, or cider, are strictly prohibited on any public or private property within one mile of the center of the original survey of the Retreat; and the Directors hereby request all well-disposed persons to promptly notify the Superintendent of any violations of this rule.

The sale of liquor within the city limits, as well as the establishment of bars or saloons, remained prohibited until 1969. For many years, Pacific Grove had the distinction of being the only dry town in California.

The preceding is only a partial listing of old Pacific Grove's blue laws, but serves as proof of the Puritan tradition and regulated way of life there. The following note from a visitor in the late 1800s perhaps sums up the frustrations and feelings of many of the people.

Pacific Grove is a pretty but queer place. The Methodistical rules are stringent and the newcomers are kicking. Business places are not allowed in residence blocks. Boarding and lodging houses are not "business" but the butcher and baker are . . . One can roller skate there but not dance, and croquet but no billiard, while nary a card nor a euchre deck is tolerated. A quiet private nip is frequently taken, but no public drinking. While the laws are not so stringent as the famous blue laws of Connecticut . . . their effect is deadening to visitors. Among a few of the forbidden fruits are waltzing, playing the zither, reading the great Sunday dailies, selling popcorn on the beach, and playing ten pins.

Some of the Grove residents began to balk at the blue laws, as well as at a fence that encircled the area. Built during the retreat's early years, the fence began near the

The Grove's first church building was this Episcopalian edifice known as St. Mary's-by-the-sea, located on the southwest corner of Central Avenue and Twelfth Street. English Gothic in design, the church was modeled after a similar structure in Bath, England. Except for an extension of the sanctuary, the church remains much the way it was when it opened in 1887. Its beautiful interior includes signed Louis C. Tiffany stained glass windows and natural woods of pine, cedar, redwood, and walnut. Pat Hathaway Collection

This Italian Villa-style house at 225 Central Avenue was built in 1884 by Senator Benjamin J. Langford, the man who "took an axe" to the retreat's gate. The house has long been a favorite of local history buffs. Photo by Chuck Scardina. Courtesy, Pacific Grove Tribune

In May of 1901 (only a few months before his assassination) President William McKinley visited the Monterey Peninsula, including Pacific Grove's flag-bedecked Methodist Church. In this photograph the presidential party is about to enter the twin-towered edifice. Completed in 1888, this imposing building was more to Pacific Grove than a church, serving as an assembly hall, a meeting place for Chautauqua gatherings, and the headquarters for several Methodist-related conferences. Due to "inadequacy and disrepair" the striking structure was torn down in 1964. Pat Hathaway Collection

Monterey land baron David Jacks was not only an important figure during the retreat's early days, but also the builder of these two houses. Built in 1881, the structures were located on the corner of Central Avenue and Fifteenth Street. Jacks is thought to be the man on the far left. Photo by C.W.J. Johnson. Pat Hathaway Collection

Chinese fishing village (near what is now the dividing line between the cities of Monterey and Pacific Grove) and extended around the entire community except for the waterfront. Among other reasons, the fence was erected to preserve the individuality of the area and to keep interlopers out. The stile mentioned by Robert Louis Stevenson provided access to the Grove for those on foot. Near the stile was a locked gate, which was the main entrance and exit for horse-drawn vehicles. The gate also kept "wagon merchants" out, so residents had to make a trip to the Grove's main entryway if they wished to purchase commodities from the peddlers who lined the Monterey side of the fence.

Another drawback to the gate, for residents as well as weekend visitors, was the bother of getting a key from the retreat office every time they wished to drive their wagons or carriages in or out of the enclosed area. This inconvenience is eloquently described by Lucy Neely McLane in her book *A Piney Paradise*. The gentleman she quotes is State Senator Benjamin J. Langford, who owned an imposing house near the waterfront and often visited the Grove on weekends. According to McLane's delightful book, the Senator said:

Every time that I pulled up to the padlocked gate with my family, I would have to dismount, go over the stile, hike about a mile to the Retreat office to get the key to unlock the gate, walk back to the gate, drive to the office to return the key in order that others might use it, unload my family and baggage, drive again to the office for the key, drive back to the gate, unlock it, drive through, tie my horses, walk back again on foot to the office to leave the key; then, no matter how late the hour or how fatigued I felt, I would have to walk back to my carriage, drive to Monterey to be stabled, hire some equipage to return me to the fence, climb over the stile and limp to my house.

Langford effectively put an end to the era of Pacific Grove's locked gates. Approaching the fence one evening, he took an axe from his carriage and, with a "senatorial swing," did away with the main gate. For all intents and purposes, this did away with all gate-related problems. After the gate was gone, the fence soon followed.

Soon the name of the retreat also changed. On July 16, 1889, the "kingdom by the sea" was incorporated as the City of Pacific Grove. Several other events of interest and importance took place during the 1880s, among them the building of two impressive and popular churches. Since Pacific Grove began as a Methodist retreat, one would expect a Methodist church to have been built first. Strange as it seems, it was the Episcopalians who erected the first formal church building. Organized within the confines of the retreat grounds in 1886, the energetic Episcopalians wasted little time in starting construction of their church. The striking structure was consecrated in July 1887. Modeled after the English Gothic design of a church in Bath, England, the Episcopal edifice became known as St. Mary's-by-the-Sea. In use to this day, the church is one of Pacific Grove's most prized and cherished buildings. Not long after its completion, Miss Harriet Hammond of Chicago visited and fell in love with the picturesque structure. She canceled her plans for a fashionable "windy city" wedding and arranged to be married at St. Mary's instead. The future Mrs. Cyrus H. McCormick and her husband-to-be, accompanied by approximately 40 friends and relatives in a private railroad car, returned to the Grove to be married in their adopted church.

As token of her thanks and as a memento of the occasion, the bride presented English embroidered white silk altar hangings to the church. Seven years later the happy couple returned to St. Mary's laden with gifts, including several large stained-glass windows, which can still be viewed near the entrance of the church. Many years later, after the death of his wife, McCormick commissioned the master craftsman Louis C. Tiffany to create a pair of floral glass windows for the church. Considered to be among Tiffany's finest works, the exquisite windows are treasured to this day by the congregation of St. Mary's; they add a touch of serenity to the Victorian interior of this beautiful sanctuary.

Following in the footsteps of the Episcopalians, the Methodists raised the twin towers of their church in 1888. Larger than St. Mary's and perhaps even more imposing, the Methodist Church was also used as an assembly hall and a meeting place for summer Chautauqua audiences, as well as church conferences. The impressive structure became "home" to the California Conference of the Methodist Church which was held there for 31 years. This Pacific Grove landmark (which was unfortunately torn down in 1964) also boasted an impressive list of guests and lecturers, including President William McKinley in 1901.

Several other churches were eventually attracted by the seaside resort's religious climate. Over the years, Pacific Grove has often been called a "city of churches." Two other houses of worship constructed before the turn of the century were the Congregational Church (1892) and the First Christian Church of Pacific Grove (1895).

Another important nineteenth-century event was David Jacks' foreclosure on a portion of the property in the Grove. The Pacific Grove Retreat Association did not make the improvements that had been agreed upon and had difficulty making payments on the money Jacks had advanced. Jacks regained control of a portion of the property and proceeded to sell individual lots. Eventually he sold the entire package to the Pacific Improvement company.

The Pacific Improvement Company agreed to honor the Retreat Association's goals and its deed restrictions. The community's success was ensured and important improvements began to be made. Numerous new homes were built on grand scale; some survive to this day as bed-and-breakfast inns. Also of importance was the construction of the impressive Hotel El Carmelo, which soon

This October 1887 view looking south from near the entrance of the Hotel El Carmelo (later known as the Pacific Grove Hotel) shows a portion of the hotel's recently planted park-like grounds. Across Lighthouse Avenue one sees the block bounded by Fountain (left) and Grand Avenues. The house facing Lighthouse Avenue, to the left of the Tuttle drugstore building and Ray's Hardware Store, is the home of J.O. Johnson, owner of the Mammoth Stable (the tower of which can be seen above Ray's Hardware Store). Photo by C.W.J Johnson. Pat Hathaway Collection

One of the Grove's most elegant lodging houses was the Pacific Grove Hotel, opened in 1887 as the Hotel El Carmelo. As the community of Carmel-by-the-Sea became better known, the establishment's name was changed to the Pacific Grove Hotel (and a Hotel Carmelo became a part of early Carmel). Like the Hotel Del Monte, it was owned and operated by the Pacific Improvement Company and thus became known as the "Del Monte" of the Grove. It featured elaborate gardens, an elevator of the "newest and most approved" design, superb cuisine and service, and views from all of its 114 rooms. The hotel was torn down in 1918. Pat Hathaway Collection

It's Feast of Lanterns time again and Pacific Grove's Centrella Hotel is decorated appropriately. Originally known as the Centrella Cottage and later as the Centrella House, this hotel was constructed in the late 1880s. Today the building has been completely restored and welcomes guests as a bed and breakfast inn. It is located at 612 Central Avenue, across the street from the original Chautauqua Hall. Pat Hathaway Collection

gained prominence as Pacific Grove's most elegant lodging house. Even though it was smaller in scale and not nearly as grand, its interior facilities were often compared to Monterey's Hotel Del Monte. Such comparisons were expected, since both hotels belonged to the Pacific Improvement Company. The *Del Monte Wave* newspaper wrote:

To some considerable extent the interior of "El Carmelo" reminds one of its sister, the beautiful "Del Monte" . . . there is the same breeziness of lobby, the same inviting influence of drawing rooms, and the same general permission for enjoyment—and freedom from metropolitan restraint.

Opened in 1887, the commodious El Carmelo enjoyed many years of success. As the community of Carmel made its presence known, the hotel changed its name to the Pacific Grove Hotel and continued to function as "Queen of the Grove." In 1918 the hotel was torn down, and much of its lumber was used in the reconstruction of the Pebble Beach Lodge, which had burned in 1917.

A second guest facility of note is the Centrella Hotel, also constructed in the late 1880s. Today, approximately one century later, the Centrella has been restored to its original splendor and caters to visitors as a bed-and-breakfast inn. The Del Mar was another prominent Pacific Grove Hotel. Built in the 1890s, this handsome structure was a part of Pacific Grove until 1953, when it was torn down to make room for a bank.

Boarding houses first opened in Pacific Grove in the 1880s. Among these Victorian structure was a building

Another of the Grove's popular pre-1900 hotels was the Del Mar. Standing on the southwest corner of Lighthouse Avenue and Sixteenth Street, the bay-windowed building served visitors until 1953, when it was torn down to make room for a bank and parking lot. Pat Hathaway Collection

Established in 1891, the Monterey and Pacific Grove Street Railway was a boon to the Peninsula, and gained even more popularity in 1903 when the line was converted to electricity. In this photo, a railway car stands in front of the Hotel El Carmelo on Lighthouse Avenue. Photo by C.K. Tuttle. Courtesy, Pat Hathaway Collection

owned by J.F. Gosby. It was rather plain in appearance upon its completion in 1887, but over the years the structure experienced many alterations and additions, and today is considered an excellent example of Queen Anne design. The building is now known as the Gosby House Inn. Like the Centrella, it is a popular lodging house that caters to those who appreciate the charm of yesterday, with many of the conveniences of today.

In 1894, just to the west of the Gosby House, Dr. A.J. Hart built a lovely house as his residence and office. Over the years this stylish structure (also of Queen Anne design) has become one of Pacific Grove's better known buildings, and has housed businesses of various kinds.

In addition to elegant lodging houses for people, a famous hotel for horses was built in 1884: the Mammoth Stable, owned by J.O. Johnson, one-time superintendent of the Pacific Improvement Company. For several years, passengers heading for the Grove disembarked from the train at the Monterey depot to be welcomed by Johnson, who directed them to his coaches. Besides large carriages and well-kept coaches, Johnson also offered one-man buggies and speedy horses for those who desired fast transportation.

Johnson's Mammoth Stable more than lived up to its name. The structure boasted an elaborate tower that rose 80 feet in the air, as well as facilities for nearly 100 horses. In addition to rooms for harnesses, grain, and so on, the stable contained bedrooms, an office, a kitchen and a dining room. Described as "one of the most extensive and complete stables in the state, and rated as "the largest,

Above: Built in 1884 by J.O. Johnson, the Mammoth Stable straddled Grand Avenue and could house nearly 100 horses. It added considerable prestige to downtown Pacific Grove. Pat Hathaway Collection

Opposite Top: By 1907 development had come to Lovers Point. In this view one sees the beginnings of the Grove's permanent rock pier, a small observation house (the building to the right), and a Japanese Tea Garden (the oriental-style building to the left.) Perhaps of most interest to Lovers Point visitors were the glass-bottom boat rides, as advertised by the sign on the pier. The swan-bedecked boats (foreground) afforded dramatic views of the point's marine life and underwater gardens. Pat Hathaway Collection

Opposite Bottom: In this circa 1910 view from the Lovers Point Promontory, the Del Monte express steams along the Pacific Grove coast and heads for the nearby depot. The run from Monterey to Pacific Grove was one of the most scenic in the state. Pat Hathaway Collection

handsomest, most costly, and best equipped on the coast," Mammoth Stable became a great source of pride for Pacific Grove residents.

Another important means of transportation before the turn of the century was the Monterey and Pacific Grove Street Railway. Beginning in 1891, its brightly colored horse-drawn coaches were a great success. The run from Monterey's Hotel Del Monte to Pacific Grove's Methodist Church was described as "among the grandest scenic roads on the Pacific Coast." It is true that the original route—leading from the opulent Hotel Del Monte, through California's romantic first capital city, along the picturesque Monterey shoreline, and on into the pine-forested grounds of old Pacific Grove—passed many historic sites and provided its passengers with numerous scenic vistas. In 1893 the line became known as the Monterey and Pacific Grove Street Railway and Electric Power Company. The name change hinted at things to come, and the line was eventually converted to electricity. By 1903 the communities of Monterey and Pacific Grove boasted a modern link in the form of an electric streetcar line. Through the early 1900s the line remained a popular mode of transportation for visitors as well as residents. However, as the automobile became more and more commonplace, the Monterey and Pacific Grove streetcar was used less and less, except for a sharp increase during World War I. In 1923 the line closed down, and the tracks were torn up.

Other tracks that led from Monterey to Pacific Grove

Above: These Pacific Grove ladies partake in tea and pleasantries at the Japanese Tea Garden on Lovers Point, circa 1900. Pat Hathaway Collection

Opposite Top: Faculty and students of the Hopkins Seaside Laboratory pose for a photograph during the summer of 1894. As the facility's reputation grew, it also outgrew its Lovers Point quarters, so in the early 1900s the station moved only a short distance away to Point Cabrillo, near the north end of Cannery Row where the Chinese fishing village once stood. The facility is now known as Hopkins Marine Station of Stanford University and has gained recognition and respect throughout the world. Photo by C.K. Tuttle. Pat Hathaway Collection

Opposite Bottom: An important part of the early Lovers Point scene were the buildings of Hopkins Seaside Laboratory. Established by Timothy Hopkins and funded by Stanford University, it was built in the early 1890s on land donated by the Pacific Improvement Company. The laboratory was the first marine station on the West Coast and offered research facilities for marine biologists, as well as programs for Stanford students and public school teachers who wished to increase their knowledge of marine life. The windmill to the right is thought to have pumped salt water to the facility. Also of interest is the wood pier, which, for a time, graced the Lovers Point Beach. Photo by C.K. Tuttle. Pat Hathaway Collection

in the late 1800s were those of the Southern Pacific Railroad. The Grove continued to draw many visitors from faraway places, and officials of the Pacific Improvement Company and Southern Pacific agreed that an extension of the Monterey Line was in order. Pacific Grove became a busy transit point for trains to and from the peninsula. Even more scenic than the route of the Monterey and Pacific Grove streetcar line, the Southern Pacific tracks hugged the Pacific Grove shoreline and passed several picturesque promontories, including Lovers Point.

Some say that Lovers Point was known as Lovers of Jesus Point. Before that, it was Point Aulon (an old Spanish word for "abalone"). Over the years this area has been the site of several important functions, including prayer meetings. Just why the promontory became known as Lovers Point is open to question, but the writer of the following quote from an 1880 issue of the Pacific Grove Review had a definite opinion.

It is not only among the stately solemn pines where a friendly bush invites lovers to exchange confidences and plight their troth, but it is on the beach, where the discreet sea would no more reveal the stolen trysts along its boisterous margin than it would give up its dead, that one can see visions and hear sounds that should make the outgoing tide linger. If that rocky headland, known as Lovers Point, which projects its solitude away from the shore had only kept a day book of notes, or rather a night book of observations, how sensational would be its chronicles.

A rendezvous for lovers and a gathering place for prayer meetings, Lovers Point and its adjoining beach have also played other important roles in the history of Pacific Grove. The sheltered cove and white sands of "Main Beach" (Lovers Point Beach) have served for over a century as a favorite gathering spot for sunbathers and those who enjoy frolicking in the sea. In its early years the Lovers Point area, including its beach, pier, and bayside buildings, boasted such things as a Japanese Tea Garden, band concerts, a photo gallery, a bowling alley, "Feast of Lanterns" festivals, community bathhouses, a carousel, glass-bottom boat rides, a marine laboratory, an ice cream parlor, and a skating rink.

Among the most popular of these early attractions were the glass-bottom boat rides. Aboard these small vessels visitors and residents alike thrilled to the sight of the remarkable underwater gardens and marine life of the Lovers Point area. The Japanese Tea Garden, housed in a building of oriental design, offered delicious cakes and teas served by ladies in traditional Japanese attire. However, the Hopkins Seaside Laboratory has perhaps evoked the most modern-day interest.

The marine laboratory was established by Timothy Hopkins in 1891. (Timothy Hopkins was the adopted son of Mark Hopkins, of San Francisco and Big Four railroad fame.) Inspired by Dr. Anton Dohrns' famous Zoological Station in Naples, Italy, Hopkins returned to America with dreams of a Stanford-operated marine research facility on the Pacific Coast. After presenting his plans to the proper authorities and consulting with selected Stanford professors, it was decided that Monterey Bay offered the type of environment and marine life they were seeking.

The Pacific Improvement Company donated land at Lovers Point. Enthusiastic help came from key Stanford personnel, including David Starr Jordan—noted ichthyologist and Stanford University's first president. A size-

able two-story frame building was constructed, and the marine station got off to a very promising start. Soon a second building was added, and the Hopkins Seaside Laboratory began to gain international fame.

In the early 1900s it became apparent that the Lovers Point site was not big enough for the expanding station. A new location was found at Point Cabrillo, near the bor-

After the turn of the century, with "Bathhouse Smith" in charge, Pacific Grove's Lovers Point Beach took on a new look. Smith expanded the concession, increased the size of the beach area, added a boathouse, and greatly enlarged and improved the bathhouse. Nevertheless, the bathhouse eventually fell into disrepair, and was condemned by the city. Pat Hathaway Collection

der of Monterey and Pacific Grove, site of the old Chinese fishing village. When the buildings there were constructed and put into use, the new facility became known as the Hopkins Marine Station of Stanford University.

The research laboratory has continued to expand. Today its neighbor is the Monterey Bay Aquarium (opened in 1984), and together these two unique facilities add to our knowledge of life in the sea and help us to understand the mysteries of Monterey Bay.

Back at Lovers Point, another continuing and colorful attraction was the bathhouse. The first of a long line of such bathing facilities was built on Lovers Point in 1875. Unfortunately for salt-water bath buffs, the facility left much to be desired: it was described as "cramped, cold, and decidedly inadequate." As so often happened when Pacific Grove was in need, the Pacific Improvement Company came to the rescue. In the early 1880s the company built a new and improved bathing facility, featuring eight private salt-water baths. The residents of the Grove flocked to the waterfront to partake of the pleasures of their new bathhouse. As time went on problems again began to plague the facility. The importance of the bathhouse to the pioneer residents of the Grove is indicated by the following account from an 1884 issue of the *Del Monte Wave*:

Salt water baths are the one principal attraction at a seaside resort, and Sandy Cove Lovers Point Beach where the bath house is located is admirably suited for the purpose, being well sheltered; but a new building with appointments for hot water is the ringing cry of the residents, that resounds and reverberates through the pine forest till all else is lost in that one appeal . . . When Pacific Grove can boast of good bathing facilities and suitable quarters to meet the demand, winter and summer, then she will "receive her share of the laurels that crown Monterey the Hotel Del Monte queen of watering places."

Through the 1880s and the 1890s, problems continued to plague the beachfront bathhouse, prompting additional comments from the *Del Monte Wave*:

Is it not about time that the miserable shell called a bathhouse . . . was replaced by one in which a person with the slightest degree of modesty might disrobe, without first stopping up numerous holes and cracks, to keep their next door neighbor from having a full view of the proceedings? The arrangement called by that name at present is a disgrace to the city, a disgrace to the owners and a standing opportunity for Peeping Toms.

By the turn of the century, the trials and tribulations of the bathhouse began to subside. William Smith acquired the waterfront facilities. With dynamite blasts, protested by various Pacific Grove residents, he proceeded to expand the beach. Smith also added a boathouse and enlarged and greatly improved the bathhouse. "Bathhouse Smith" (as he became known) has been credited with cre-

In this 1920s view, looking in a westerly direction from Grand Avenue, one sees the north side of Lighthouse Avenue. The buildings to the right (in the first block) still stand in the center of downtown Pacific Grove. The outlet with the extended awning was the B.F. Sowell and Son grocery store. To its right was the T.A. Work Co., a hardware outlet, and on the corner was the Bank of Pacific Grove. Across Forest Avenue was the Johnston Brothers store which specialized in drygoods.

Further down the block was the E.B. Lewis Jewelry store. All the buildings in this block have since been demolished. In the next block, the building shown is still standing and at the time of this photograph was known as the Winston Hotel. The twin-towered structure in the background was the Methodist Church. The flag-bedecked streets and cars are thought to have been in observance of the Fourth of July. Pat Hathaway Collection

ating a bathing resort for the Grove.

In time Dr. Clarendon E. Foster took charge of the Lovers Point facilities and continued to operate the concessions well and respectably. Unfortunately, Dr. Foster eventually left the Grove to continue his medical practice in another California community.

After Dr. Foster's departure, the previous problems of the bathhouse again began to surface. Things came to a head when neglect and disrepair prompted the city to condemn the facility. The concession was now controlled by Mrs. Mattie McDougall, who also claimed much of the property adjacent to the bathhouse. Upon word of the city's action, she erected a barrier, preventing public access to the beach. But Julia B. Platt, not content to let McDougall control the popular beach, suggested to the city council that they tear the barrier down. The city fathers chose to play a waiting game, seeking a more amicable solution.

Citing the Grove's original deed, stating that "the Pacific Improvement Company guarantees public right of way to the beach," Platt decided that more decisive action was in order. She made her way to the locked gate and proceeded to file off the padlock. Platt was applauded by several of her Pacific Grove neighbors, who delighted in her boldness and chuckled at the sign she is said to have displayed:

Opened by Julia B. Platt. This entrance to the beach must be left open at all hours when the public might reasonably wish to pass through. I act in the matter because the council and police department of Pacific Grove are men and possibly somewhat timid.

McDougall countered with a second padlock, which Platt again filed off. Workmen then securely nailed the gate shut from the inside. Public use of the beach was at stake, and Platt again made her way to the board barrier, with a crowd on hand to witness the event. She set to

Above: In 1924 Holman's Department Store opened on the block where the Pacific Grove Hotel once stood. The store is seen here from the corner of Lighthouse and Fountain avenues. During the Depression era a third story and a solarium were added, and the store gained fame as the largest department store between San Francisco and Los Angeles. Today the store is known as Ford's of Monterey Bay. Photo by D. Freeman. Pat Hathaway Collection

Pg 58 Below: Lodge Hall reveals architect Julia Morgan's distinctive blend of wood and stone, and the pleasing designs of the rustic original structures that are scattered about the Asilomar Conference Grounds. Seen here in 1934, the building today looks similar in most every way. Photo by Louis Josselyn. Pat Hathaway Collection

work with an axe; in the tradition of Senator Langford, she dutifully did away with the barrier. Although a battle of words continued to be waged and legal ramifications were yet to be worked out, Julia B. Platt is credited with having put the McDougall matter to rest.

In addition to her antics with an axe (and the fact that she was to become Pacific Grove's first woman mayor), Julia B. Platt spent much of her time raking, hoeing, planting, watering, and, in general, beautifying the Lovers Point area. This remarkable lady also spearheaded a successful drive to remove the aged bathhouse and replace it with a swimming pool.

Local residents knew Julia Platt as a lady to be reckoned with, and a bit on the eccentric side. She was also an accomplished zoologist who held a doctorate degree from Germany's Freiburg University and had served as a director of Italy's prestigious Naples Zoological Station. The talented Platt had a deep love for her adopted home town, and, according to historian Lucy Neely McLane, endeavored "almost single-handed" to make Pacific Grove a beautiful, progressive, and judiciously run city.

When she died in 1935, Pacific Grove lost a remarkable lady who was not afraid to fight for what she thought was right. Following her wishes, Julia B. Platt was buried at sea in a wicker basket. A gathering of city officials attended the ceremony on a boat. As the basket was slowly lowered into the sea, an airplane containing many of her friends circled the boat and dropped hundreds of roses upon the water. This grand lady is still remembered by those who know and love the history of the Grove. A marker in her honor has been placed at Lovers Point Park, adjacent to the beach she fought to keep open and upon the picturesque promontory she loved so much.

Before she died, Julia Platt worked with a second well-known Pacific Grove resident, Wilford R. Holman, to arrange for a road that would make Pacific Grove more accessible to Carmel and other outlying areas. Their efforts were successful, and the road is officially known as W.R. Holman Highway, part of California's Highway 68.

W.R. Holman was the son of R.L. (Luther) Holman, who came to Pacific Grove in 1888. R.L. Holman and J.W. Towle operated "The Popular" dry goods store, which more than lived up to its name. But the cry of "Gold!" lured Towle from the Grove; he pulled up stakes and headed for the Klondike. The partnership was dissolved, and the store took the name of R.L. Holman.

Over the years the store continued to expand, moving to a succession of Pacific Grove locations. In 1905 Luther Holman turned over the operation of the store to his two sons, Wilford and Clarence, who rechristened it Holman's Department Store. In 1914 Wilford R. Holman became

the full manager, and 10 years later he moved the store to a site it was to occupy (under the Holman name) for approximately 60 years. At this location—where the Pacific Grove Hotel once stood—a new two-story building was constructed. Holman's became known as the largest department store between Los Angeles and San Francisco.

The depression years brought additional expansion to the store. However, some people felt that the large establishment was out of character for the Grove and predicted a gloomy future for the energetic undertaking. Time proved the skeptics wrong: shopping at Holman's became a family tradition for residents of the Monterey Peninsula. In 1885 Holman's was purchased by the Ford's Department Store chain of nearby Watsonville. The store is now known as Ford's of Monterey Bay and continues to operate at the same location. Appropriately, the Ford name is well known in the Monterey Bay area; its Watsonville store is the oldest operation of its kind in California.

Built in 1889, the Holman house was one of Pacific Grove's early landmarks. Although the house still stands on the southeast corner of Lighthouse and Granite avenues, it is virtually unrecognizable. Its third story has been removed, a stucco exterior has been added, and parts of its roof have been hipped and covered with red tile. Standing to the left of the house is R. Luther Holman, the man who started the department store that was to take the Holman name. His son Wilford R. Holman, who developed the store into one of the most respected department stores in central California, is the lad sitting on the top step. After W.R. Holman's death in 1981, the house was given to the Monterey Peninsula Museum of Art. Pat Hathaway Collection

Members of the Holman family played other important parts in the community's development, bestowing many gifts on the people of the peninsula. Most recently the historic Holman house was donated to the Monterey Peninsula Museum of Art. Previously, they had given a collection of American Indian artifacts that are displayed in Monterey's historic, state-owned Pacific House. A collection of books about California donated by the Holmans is also housed in a state-owned facility, Pacific Grove's popular Asilomar Conference Grounds. It is most appropriate that these publications are housed at Asilomar, since this unique facility is used in part as a training center for employees of the California State Department of Parks and Recreation.

The Asilomar Conference Grounds are bordered on two sides by Pebble Beach and the Pacific Ocean, but the grounds are within the community of Pacific Grove. Beginning in 1913, when a YWCA group gathered there, this place of rolling sand dunes and picturesque pine trees has developed into one of the finest conference centers in the country. Asilomar's forest setting has been retained, and its natural wood and native stone buildings have been strategically placed within the contours of the land. The site has won praise by people from throughout the world as an example of human land use that respects the environment.

Julia Morgan, who is best remembered as the architect for the fabulous William Randolph Hearst Castle of San Simeon, California, developed the plans for the Asilomar grounds and its original structures. The Morgan-designed buildings form the nucleus of the conference center, but the overall grounds have grown to more than three times the size of the original 30-acre site (which was donated by the Pacific Improvement Company), and several additional structures have been built. Following the pattern set by Morgan, the new buildings were designed to fit in with the sea, the sand, and the pines that surround them and have won several major architectural awards.

Today the Asilomar Conference Grounds are busier than ever and help to stimulate the local economy. The center handles an estimated 200,000 people per year and plays host to more than 1000 organizations. Asilomar has truly become a refuge by the sea (as its name implies), and is a major drawing card for the visitor-oriented Monterey Peninsula. Besides its popular conference grounds, its mild climate, and its rugged coastline, several attractions draw people to Pacific Grove. The community-oriented Good Old Days is an annual event that boasts antique cars, an arts and crafts fair, live entertainment, a colorful parade, pie-eating contests, a firefighter's competition, and a pancake breakfast. *The most popular event of the fun-filled weekend is the Victorian Home Tour, in which residents open many Victorian homes to the public. People from throughout California and beyond flock to the Grove to view the carefully restored structures, beautiful both inside and out. A visit to these vintage buildings affords the opportunity to view old Pacific Grove and to appreciate the numerous architectural styles that help to make the community so appealing.

The Heritage Society of Pacific Grove can take much of the credit for renewing interest in the Grove's aged dwellings. It is a relatively young organization compared to Monterey's History and Art Association, but the Heritage Society has accomplished much in its existence. It has established an "old-time" museum which complements the Grove's outstanding Museum of Natural History, and it co-sponsors the Victorian Home Tour in conjunction with the local Chamber of Commerce and the Pacific Grove Art Center. The Heritage Society researches and records all information pertaining to Pacific Grove's old buildings and awards a special "Heritage Plaque" to the owner of each such dwelling. These green plaques are displayed on many of the town's historic structures, making it possible to tell at a glance when the old houses were built and who the original owners were.

Also drawing visitors to Pacific Grove is another event that has evolved from the area's unique history: the annual Feast of Lanterns Festival. The festival began in 1905 and continues to be a popular summertime activity. According to tradition, the Methodist-sponsored Chautauqua movement at Lake Chautauqua, New York, closed its season with fireworks and a lantern parade along the shores of the lake. Since Pacific Grove was considered the Chautauqua of the West, it was only natural that it would stage a similar event in the summer.

Various sources describe the festival's origin in different ways. It is safe to say that the pageant was of Methodist origin, combined with Chinese overtones and interspersed with local touches. The original story involves Chinese villagers searching for a Mandarin's daughter who has wandered off to drown herself rather than marry a nobleman chosen by her father. In the Pacific Grove pageant the search for the lovely Chinese maiden is re-enacted year after year, but not because she is a potential suicide. She succeeds in fleeing with her lover, managing to elude the lantern-bearing searchers sent by her father. The pageant is staged in the evening on the colorfully decorated pier of Lovers Point Beach. The sandy beach and the walkways and rocks around it are crowded with spectators of all ages; some hold paper lanterns of their own, in keeping with the occasion.

Nowadays the festival has other attractions, including the crowning of the festival queen (who plays the part of the Mandarin's daughter) and her court. Over the years the festival has included such events as barbecues, sailboat races, tennis tournaments, golf tournaments (held on the city's beautiful 18-hole course by the ocean), band concerts, pet parades, fireworks displays, and lantern-bedecked boats that parade back and forth in the dark waters of the bay. Homes along the waterfront and throughout the town display brightly lit oriental lanterns in their window and on their porches. No wonder Pacific Grove's Feast of Lanterns continues to draw spectators from far and near.

Another Pacific Grove attraction is its park system. Visitors and residents enjoy strolling through these public places and picnicking in picturesque settings. Adjoining Lovers Point is the best known of all Pacific Grove parks. Situated along the rocky coast, between the scenic shore drive and the blue waters of the bay, is a stretch of land known as Perkins Park. Just as the dedicated work of Julia Platt was instrumental in the beautification of Lovers Point, the history of Perkins Park also revolves around a dedicated Pacific Grove resident. Hayes Perkins arrived in the Grove in 1938 and rented a cottage near the waterfront. He watched with dismay as young people playing along the shore caught poison oak. Perkins was immune to the poison, so he began pulling poison oak plants from the ground. He noted the ugly holes that were left and began beautifying the area by planting shrubs and ground cover that he had observed in his worldwide travels. One that he had seen in South Africa, named mesembryanthemum, was effective at smothering weeds, and also proved to adapt well to the Pacific Grove shore.

As his garden grew, the shoreline became a sea of color. People began to take note, and admirers from distant places journeyed to the Grove (usually between the months of April and August) to view "Perkins' posies." Hayes Perkins died in 1964, but his work has been continued by the city and by interested residents, and his "magic carpet" continues to grow. Among the tributes to this dedicated citizen and to his love affair with the Pacific Grove shoreline are pictures of his park that have appeared in more publications than there is room to men-

As evidenced in this photograph, it takes more than rain, or a moist morning fog, to dampen the spirits of these "make-believe" monarchs as they prepare for a parade through the city streets. Staged on an annual basis and attracting hundreds of participants and spectators, the Butterfly Parade is held under the auspices of the local school district, and has been a Pacific Grove tradition for nearly 50 years. Photo by Pat Hathaway. Pat Hathaway Collection

tion. A 60-foot mural depicting Perkins' colorful garden of lavender and pink once graced the walls of New York's Grand Central station.

Another of Pacific Grove's beautiful gardens can only be viewed from underwater: the Pacific Grove Marine Gardens. This marine wonderland has become a popular gathering place for scuba divers from throughout the West. Almost any weekend of the year, numerous diving enthusiasts can be seen enjoying the wonderful underwater plants and animals off the coast around Lovers Point.

Pacific Grove may be best known for the thousands of orange and black butterflies that fly around the town. During the months of October and November—since before man can remember—countless Monarch butterflies have found their way to the Grove. Traveling from as far away as the *Rocky Mountains and perhaps beyond, these colorful creatures arrive every fall to make a small section of Pacific Grove their winter home. On warm sunny days during their stay, the monarchs awaken and flutter about—a delightful sight. However, when the days turn cold and fog envelops the Grove, clusters of butterflies can be seen clinging to the branches and leaves of their chosen trees.

Celebrating the Monarch's pilgrimage, Pacific Grove's schoolchildren honor the occasion with an annual parade. Dressed in colorful costumes, many featuring wings of orange and black, the children, along with their parents and throngs of local residents, celebrate the homecoming of the monarchs. "Butterfly Town, U.S.A." gets caught up in this occasion as only a small town can.

More and more people are discovering Pacific Grove, and some residents look upon this with disfavor. They have chosen to live there because of the small-town atmosphere and the unique beauty of the area, and they fear that too many people and too much development will ruin both. But these very same qualities of Pacific Grove still prompt others to move there. It is hoped that those who are arriving now will remember what attracted them there in the first place. If so, they in turn will strive to keep their town as it started out to be: a peaceful paradise by the sea.

CA VIEWS – THE PAT HATHAWAY COLLECTION

2000-023-001 Looking up Grand Ave. from across Lighthouse Ave. Circa 1885 CWJ Johnson

Minister Retirement Home 85-011-048 Site of Canterbury Woods

EAC-3258 LaPorte Mansion/March 12, 1909
EACohen/ Pinehurst 77-003-0620

cows6x8gl Dairy cows surrounding LaPorte Mansion Circa 1908

Views of California from Hathaway's Perch
Dixie Layne with Pat Hathaway

Pascal Hathaway, or Pat as he is known to friends and colleagues, has arguably one of the largest privately held collections of California photographs—81,000 in total. Hathaway's collection spans the 1800's to present day, and primarily consists of photos from California's Humboldt County to San Diego, and Yosemite—although his collection's focus is coastal California from Marin County to Santa Barbara.

Hathaway's interest in photography was inspired by a 12th birthday gift he received—a Kodak Brownie camera. This is part of a larger collection of cameras that lines the shelves in his home, along with hundreds of prints that adorn his walls and are meticulously filed in cabinets and bins that have taken over two rooms in his Pacific Grove home. Hathaway acquired his first professional camera when he was in high school, and became the yearbook staff photographer in his junior and senior years while Mr. Bruce Henderson was the yearbook advisor.

When asked what was next, he simply says, "I progressed from there." His progression followed into the Army where he was first stationed in Vietnam in 1968 and then Alaska in 1969, where he ran the craft shop photog-

raphy lab for leisure. During his tour of duty in Vietnam and Alaska, he carried his camera with him everywhere. After his service was complete in 1970, Hathaway came back to Pacific Grove and started looking for a job—and by happenstance, he came across Jan Josselyn who was getting rid of all her husband's photographic "stuff". It was one of those take it all or nothing situations. Josselyn told him the museums or libraries weren't interested in the collection, so she was happy to hear he was interested in it. Hathaway took it all.

Included in the "take it all" stuff was a collection of over seven thousand 5x7 glass and film negatives for photos of Monterey County taken over several decades by Lewis Josselyn, plus his photographic equipment. Pat made several prints of Josselyn's work and hung the photos on his walls—"friends wanted copies and it snowballed from there." This was the beginning of a long career for Hathaway as a photo collector, photographic historian, and archivist.

It was at this same time that Hathaway also started working for the legendary Elmarie Hurlbert Hyler Dyke as her chauffer and helping her with various projects at the P.G. Art Center. This position provided him an insight into the business end of the art world and he was happy to hold it until her death in 1981. During this same time

Lighthouse Avenue
Late 1880's

J.O. Johnson Home | C.K. Tuttle Drug Store | Looking up Grand Avenue at the Mammoth Stables | Hall & Wolf Avenue Store Groceries | D.W. Lloyd Wholesale and Retail General Merchandice | Pioneer Boot & Shoe Store J.F. Gosbey & E.C. Smith Real Estate Agent | Gale Bros Crockery Groceries | Grove Restaurant | Candy Kitchen

Pacific Grove Curio Store G.S. Gould | For Rent Candy Factory Hays Ice Cream Parlors | C.K. Tuttle Drugs | E.C. Smith Real Estate | Monterey & P.G. Street Railway tracks | Pacific Improvement Co Office | Ground of the Pacific Grove Hotel

Looking west down Lighthouse Avenue from Fountain Avenue, Pacific Grove, 9:00 A.M. June 4, 1901

Both photo by Charles K. Tuttle

PANORAMAZ PacificGrove1887-18 Pat Hathaway Collection

72-017-0047 Home of grandparents Marcus D Hyde on Forest Ave.in 1893 1885 CWJ Johnson

2000-005-0001 C.L.S.C Meeting (Chautauqua Literary Scientific Circle) looking down Grove St from Forest Ave.1885 CWJ Johnson

79-069-006 Outdoor alter Minister's Pavilion P.G. 1879 CWJ Johnson

period, Hathaway opened a studio in the P.G. Art Center, right next door to Elmarie's studio.

It was 1971, when the *Herald* did a story on Hathaway and his photography—and this story was the catalyst for people seeking Hathaway out to give him their photographic collections. It was also what led Hathaway to start browsing through old phone books to help him track down photographers who weren't working or living any longer in an attempt to acquire their collections. When Hathaway asked if they would like to donate or sell their work to him for his collection, well, "they were just happy someone wanted their work." Hathaway muses, "I have no idea how much stuff went to the dump before I came along."

Beyond the Josselyn collection Hathaway took possession of in 1970, he was gifted with a collection of photographs of Yosemite, Pacific Grove, the early California Missions, and the aftermath of the 1906 earthquake, all taken by Edgar A. Cohen from 1890 through the 1920's. A.C. Heidrick (b.1876-d.1955) took panoramic photographs from 1907 through 1940, and his children gifted those photos, happily, to Hathaway.

Hathaway was acquainted with Charles K. Tuttle's daughter, Winifred Beaumont, and when she began to distribute her father's photos to various organizations in the early 1970s she gave Hathaway a collection of his photos taken from 1880 through the 1920's. Hathaway also received C.W.J. Johnson's photo collection that consisted primarily of images of the Peninsula from 1880 to 1903. Hathaway's collection consists of, in total, some 70 photographers' work for whom he has at least 50 images are more, and another 1,000 photographers whose collections are less than 50 images each.

Hathaway kept his studio in the P.G. Art Center for 15 years, where during this time he kept expanding his studio into adjoining studios, and even after acquiring Elmarie's storage space in the P.G. Art Center, he realized he had outgrown it and relocated CA Views to New Monterey in 1985. He later moved his studio back to P.G., and finally to Monterey on Pacific Street, where he remained until 2015, when it felt like it was time for him to downsize his retail operation. He had a small showroom on Cannery Row in the Antique Mall until recently, and now his primary business location is a 21st century virtual showroom on the Internet—which is open 24/7, address: www.CaViews.com. Some 20,000 photographs are housed on Hathaway's website, organized by location. Copies of all his photographs are for sale through his website.

Over the years Hathaway's collection has been shown in a number of galleries and used to decorate the walls of restaurants, hotels, and other businesses. His first show was hung at the offices of the *Carmel Pine Cone*, his big-

74-021-0001 Methodist Church during construction 1888/CWJ Johnson

72-014-004 Demolition of P.G. Methodist Episcopal Church 1964

gest show was at the P.G. Art Center in 1973, and there have many others since then. Today you can find his photographs adorning the walls of many Pacific Grove businesses, including The Beach House at Lovers Point, Victorian Corner, and Monterey Bay Aquarium. His photographs can also be found around the Peninsula in any number of hotels, restaurants, and businesses. If you ever find yourself admiring photographs of California vintage scenes, there is a good chance they are from the Hathaway California Views collection.

One of the most interesting parts of Hathaway's vast knowledge about the visual history of California is that until recently he was not all that interested in his own family's history—he knew he had been born in Paris, to French parents. His father had been reported dead and after the war Pat's mother married a U.S. Army officer and adopted Pat. Pat and his mother moved with his adoptive father to Fort Ord where he was Deputy Post Commander from 1956 to 1958. The Hathaways moved to Pacific Grove when his adoptive father retired from military service; Pat was just 9. The same year the Hathaway family moved to Pacific Grove his adoptive father was asked to be a judge for the first Feast of Lanterns' Miss Pacific Grove pageant.

Hathaway's paternal grandmother, Mary Hyde Hathaway, lived in Carmel and told Hathaway stories of her playing in the early 1900's on the grounds of what is now called the LaPorte Mansion on Lighthouse Avenue. She told him how there were no other houses around, just a dairy farm. Hathaway also remembers visiting his great Aunt Polly (Patricia Hardwick Smith), a widow who lived at 609 Gibson Avenue. She had been married to E. Cooke Smith, who had owned E. Cooke Smith Bank in Pacific Grove, which was located on the corner of Lighthouse at Forest Avenues where the Chase Bank now stands.

Recently Hathaway has developed an interest in tracing his own genealogy, and has since learned quite a bit about the generations of his family who have lived in Pacific Grove for nearly 150 years. He learned his great grandparents, Marcus D. and Alice Hyde, once lived at 148 Forest Avenue about 1890—although the house was moved to David Avenue in the 1920's. He also found that he had a relative, a great grandfather, stationed at the Presidio of Monterey in 1902; one Lt. Charles Emery Hathaway, who was one of the white officers in charge of a company of Buffalo Soldiers stationed there.

Who knows, maybe Hathaway's great collection of photographs and his newly acquired knowledge of his relatives will inspire him to create another of his wonderful pictographic books on his family's Pacific Grove genealogy? In the meantime, Hathaway's collection can be viewed on and purchased through his website, www.CaViews.com, and he can be reached via phone at 831/373.3811

(831) 373-3811

Lighthouse and Forest Aves 79-010-001.

79-099-035 Lighthouse Ave. 500 block from P.G. Hotel ground 1900 CK Tuttle

89-023-Elk Elk near Point Pinos Elk moved to Yosemite 1920
Murray E White

14-022-0002 Southern Pacific Train Station in P.G.
AC Heidrick, his car to right

72-101-0007 Sand Plant at Moss Beach PB 1972 Pat Hathaway

84-003-0008 Police demonstrating new radar equipment at
769 Lighthouse Ave. to WR Holman, Judge Eldred 1956

1975-Pat Hathaway at work in his darkroom

83-100-011 Removing So Pac RR tracks to make way
for rec trail in P.G. 1983 Pat Hathaway

73-03-118-PH Pat Hathaway with
Elmarie Hyler Dyke at P.G. Art Center

ROBERT H. DOWN SCHOOL • PINE SCHOOL • HIGH SCHOOL

Robert H. Down aka "Fuzzy", with his infamous mustache 1917. Photo Pat Hathaway.

Pine Street School 1891. The one-room schoolhouse used for kindergarten classes utilized until 1921 can be seen adjacent and to the rear of Pine Street School. Photo P.G. Museum of Natural History.

Robert Hodge Down
By Dixie Layne with Pat Hathaway

Educator Robert Hodge Down moved to Pacific Grove in 1914 to begin his remarkable tenure as principal at Pacific Grove's public grammar school—Pine Street School. He retired as principal of Pine Street School in 1945 after 31 years. No one before or since has served as principal longer. Down had a genuine love for his adopted city and a deep pride in the part he played in educating its citizens.

Down was the fifth son born to English immigrant parents in the small mining town of Idria in San Benito County, and it was here his father worked as a superintendent at Quicksilver Mining Company.

Shortly after Robert's birth in 1882, the Downs moved to San Jose, where his father continued working for Quicksilver Mining Company and Down attended school, graduating from California State Normal School in San Jose, a teachers' college that eventually became San Jose State University.

After graduation, Down accepted a teaching position with Mount Jackson School, a one-room schoolhouse in Sonoma County, where he taught grades 1st through 8th. Next, Down accepted a position in New Almaden where he was paid $65 a month in 1904 for teaching at Hacienda Public School. Down's life soon met with many changes after he accepted a vice principal position in Los Gatos. Here he met Ethel Harriet Webster; they married in 1907 and started their family—three sons in four years: Webster Robert (1909), Kenneth Hodge (1910), and John Willis (1913).

Robert H. Down Elementary School, 1923. Photo: Monterey Public Library.

Interior of Pacific Grove Grammar School, the one-room schoolhouse built in 1887 for grades K-12. It was used for the kindergarten classes at Pine Street School from 1891 to 1921. Photo Pat Hathaway.

Robert Down was a tall, slender man with dark hair and a bushy black mustache—and a Methodist. He was a dedicated educator, and when offered the position of teacher and principal at Pine Street School in a fast-growing town that just happened to be the western branch for the Chautauqua Literary and Scientific Circle, well, it sounded like the perfect place for his family. So, in 1914 the Downs rented a home in Pacific Grove at 211 Park Street, just a short walk to school for him and his sons.

With the school year beginning, Down began preparing for his first term as a teacher and principal of Pine Street School. With his wife and sons ensconced in their new home, Down made his way up the hill to Pine Street to see his school, meet the school's eight teachers, and become familiar with its 200 students. In 1914, Pine Street School (built in 1891) was located along east side of 14th Street, facing Pine Street. The school was a two-story, four room facility with a third story bell tower and an adjacent one-room schoolhouse in the rear. The one-room schoolhouse that was built in 1887 for grades K through 12 became the kindergarten classroom in 1914.

As Down settled into his new position as teacher and principal, his life soon began to take-on many new aspects of an educator. As the population of Pacific Grove grew, so did the school's student body and the need for additional teachers, which created a need for a larger school. Between hiring teachers and working towards building a larger school, Down began graduate studies at Stanford and UCLA. It was the long road trips to Los Angeles—and one return trip in particular—that landed him on the front page of the *Pacific Grove Daily Review*. In his Ford, with its 20 horsepower engine and a top speed of 45 mph, he made the drive from Los Angeles to Pacific Grove in 16 hours and 11 minutes—quite a feat in 1919 California when the roads were nothing more than small country lanes that wound around and through the mountain ranges between Los Angeles and the Central Coast.

Perhaps it was his life moving at record speed into mid-life that inspired Down to shave off the dark, bushy mustache of his youth in hopes of losing the nickname "Fuzzy." So it was with a clean-shaven face he welcomed the birth of his only daughter, Ruth Mildred, in December 1920, purchased the family's new home at 211 13th Street in 1921, opened the new Pine Street School with its 16 classrooms in 1923, and accepted the appointment of Assistant Superintendent of Monterey County Schools in October 1922.

Life for Robert Hodge Down continued to be exhilarating, both professionally and personally. The 1920s continued with yet another new enterprise—he purchased a shoe store in downtown Pacific Grove at 591 Lighthouse Avenue, R.H. Down and Son. The "Son" was John Willis Down. The store thrived until the business was sold in 1927, and the building was razed just a few years later.

Pine Street School continued to grow under the watchful eye of Principal Down, and things certainly didn't slow down for him in the 1930s. He oversaw the purchase of the Bethlehem Lutheran Church chapel that sat adjacent to his school in 1939, and its subsequent conversion into a kindergarten classroom where Louise Oliver took up residence as the kindergarten teacher. Down was principal when the

Robert H. Down was "Fuzzy", no more, 1927. Photo Pat Hathaway.

R.H. Down & Son Shoe Store located at 591 Lighthouse until 1927. 591 is the first one story building to the far right of the photo. Photo Pat Hathaway.

first Butterfly Parade and Bazaar was held as part of the Butterfly Pageant in 1939. The Butterfly Parade and Bazaar was founded by Mildred Gehringer, a Pacific Grove resident and Recreation Chairwoman for Pacific Grove's Parent Teacher Association (PTA). Gehringer joined the faculty as a first grade teacher at Pine Street School in 1944, and the Butterfly Parade became a school project.

Down was elected president of the School County Board of Education in 1947.

Through Down's tenure as principal of Pine Street School, he oversaw the student population grow by 650%, the faculty by nearly 450%, and watched over the construction of a new Pine Street School (now Robert H. Down Elementary School). He marshaled his charges

Teacher Millie Gehringer and her first grade class 1944. Photo Pat Hathaway.

through a number of outside influences, from the Great War (WWI) and the supercharged Roaring 1920s to the depths of the Great Depression and into the face of World War II with Japanese submarines off our coastline. He was an educator who prepared his students for whatever the future might hold for them.

Robert and Ethel Down saw their children marry and give them eight grandchildren and one great-grandson. Webster married a Pacific Grove girl in 1928; Kenneth, a USPS employee, married Ellen, a Monterey High School teacher in 1937; John, a Pacific Grove High School teacher for 21 years, married Iris in 1936; Ruth married Arthur Oeser and taught elementary school for 28 years.

Down's last years were saddened by the death of his wife in 1947, and his son Kenneth's in 1950.

During his later years he found his greatest pleasure in reminiscing about his teaching days. He died March 9, 1952, and was buried in El Carmelo Cemetery. His 12 pallbearers were a who's who of Pacific Grove society: Robert Getz, Lee Weber, Corneil G. Culp, Ernest McAnaney, Reginald Foster, and Andrew B. Jacobsen. Honorary pallbearers were Paul Varien, Harold Harper, Judge Henry G. Jorgensen, Dr. J.J. Williams, Dr. Paul Hicks, and Thomas Turner. Pine Street School was renamed Robert H. Down Elementary School in 1953 to honor this man who touched so many lives through education.

"I've had a full and interesting life, have met lots of interesting people, and made lots of fine friends." RHD, 1952

© Dixie Layne 2018

Photo Pat Hathaway.

1911 New High School Building

Class Poem '05.

No seas were ever half so blue,
  No hills so fair as these,
And nowhere on the earth are found,
  Such matchless forest trees.

The voice of Nature grand or sweet,
  Is ever in our listening ear,
For here the surf is roaring loud,
  And whispering pines are near.

And may these voices through the years,
  In memory sound forever,
And may we loyal to the last,
  Forget our "Alma Mater" never.

Girls' Basket Ball Team

Alice Peebles, Edna Goldsworthy, Louise Sheppa, Elizabeth Bean,
Lois Salsman, Antoinette Guernsey.

Boys' Basket Ball Team

Back Row—R. Coe, M. Bertelson, J. Campbell, E. Goldsworthy (coach)
Front Row—R. Holman, H. McMahon, L. Sharp, T. Yahanda, V. Wood.

Images on this page were copied from high school yearbooks at the Pacific Grove Public Library.

THE CLASS

SENIOR CHARACTERISTICS

	Name.	Pastime	Appearance	Fault	Ambition	Expression
1.	Maud Hampton	gathering material	pleasing	teasing	to be a farmer's wife	O, pshaw!
2.	Claude Hayes	shaving	enormous	making speeches	to be a farmer	Nay, nay, Pauline.
3.	Georgie Douglas	keeping house	demure	blushing	to live across the street	By jinks!
4.	Rena Beverton	teasing the teacher	minute	innocence	to settle down to domesti	Ding bust it!
5.	Roy Meadows	ask Rena	dignified?	mumps	to be an athlete	Poolywah.
6.	Carol Moore	giggling	winning	studying	musician	O, jolly!
7.	Lewis Sheldon	going up to Maud's	smiling	too quiet	to be a parson	Angel!
8.	Sadie McGeorge	talking	stately	tardiness	to run like Tude	O, bother!
9.	Clarence Elliott	seizing rings	pious	too industrious	to graduate	Not so you could notice it.
10.	Helen Saxe	dancing	petite	"sassing	to go to Stanford	Bum! bum!
11.	Francis Hilby	making love	girlish	too obliging	to get a girl	O, Alexander.
12.	Reba Ballou	making eyes	attractive	gossiping	to marry a naval officer	Jerusalem!
13.	Mabel Berwick	laughing	charming	flirting	to be a teacher	O, My!
14.	Josephine Waggoner	running	cute	skipping class	to climb a tree	For the love of Mike.
15.	Kathleen Luke	studying	cheerful	too shy	musician	Goodness sakes.

STAFF

Images on this page and the top of page 33 are copied from a Pacific Grove High School yearbook, *The Sea Urchin,* Class of 1913, at the P.G. Library.

Saturday Night Blaze Razes Main High School Building

1946 High School Fire

---

49 Stars
Alyce Thompson

At Lovers Point in 1957, Girl Scout Troop 90 raised the first American 49 star flag commemorating Alaska joining the United States as the 49th state of the Union.

The recreation coordinator Mildred Gerhringer organized the event. Alyce Thompson was their troop leader. Troop members were Sandy Thompson, Marsha Maybe, Terry Weeks, and Sherry Bussey.

Submitted by Alyce Thompson.

PAINTINGS and FAMILY MEMORIES AT THE LIBRARY

Daddy Can I Go With You?
Becky DeSmet

I grew up a daddy's girl. Hector DeSmet owned some of the local bakeries in town and I was one of the five baker's daughters. He was busy growing his business when I came along. He opened his first bakery in 1951 and I was born in 1957. Of my earliest memories, the Pacific Grove Public Library visits were among my favorite. I was maybe 5 or 6 years old. I remember going in the evenings, and he went in some room children weren't allowed in. I was thrilled to look through all the books, time had no meaning as I was fully absorbed in choosing my selection to take home. Dad would come get me after he'd chosen his books. I can still hear the cards being slipped out of their pockets, replaced by one that told us when to come back and return the books, and the snap of the book being closed.

I still remember bits of the first book that enthralled me. I've often wished I had a copy of that book. I don't know who the author was, what the title was, and as the years have gone by the gist of the story is just a fog now. But I remember a faraway place under the sea. It was a story like nothing I could have imagined on my own! It took me away. It was the benchmark that I judged all future books by. After finding that fascinating, captivating book that opened my eyes to a whole new and curious world, I started looking at all the other books on the shelves with curiosity and hope. I looked but I never found that first book again. Years later, I found another book I absolutely adored, *Brighty of the Grand Canyon*. I was afraid that story would get lost, so I received the book for Christmas one year, I still have it. It's still a FABULOUS story.

Reading became an essential desire, something I have treasured my entire life. My mother always had a book going as well, usually a Zane Grey. I LOVE to go to the library to choose. I have library cards for all the Peninsula libraries and Salinas libraries to this day. I don't enjoy buying books near as much as I enjoy a trip to the library. It's a constant friend. Always there, dependable, with a guarantee I'll find something to enthrall me as much now as that first book thrilled me then. Dad took me everywhere he could, especially the bakery to work. While making deliveries, I often found myself on a bar stool next to him with a Shirley Temple! Tuesday nights (the bakery had a league) were for bowling. Thursday nights we made pies at the Forest Hill Location (next to Stone's Pet Shop). Wednesday nights after dinner was library night. It was a common phrase in our house, "Dad, can I go with you?" Books, bakeries, and my memories—life doesn't get any better.

From Hula Girl to the Rock Closet
Dawn Armstrong

The Pacific Grove Library I remember was a big place. It had high ceilings and multiple rooms. Each room had tall shelving crammed with books in Dewey Decimal System order. The rooms were labeled so that patrons were directed to appropriate selections. You had to be very quiet or you would be shushed.

Mom introduced me to the library when I was a second grader at Lighthouse School. Then, each of the three

Untitled by Louise McCaslin (White house on Congress Avenue. Current site of Gateway Center) cir. 1962. *Courtesy of the P.G. Public Library, where all four paintings are on view.*

Untitled by Louise McCaslin (Two homes on Lighthouse & Park—current location of Lugo's Shell Station) cir. 1962

times we moved back and forth to P.G., I was re-introduced, from the Children's Room to Young Adults. As I got older, I walked to and spent many hours exploring all the rooms looking on my own, carefully choosing which book to take home.

One summer there was a Hula Girl program to encourage reading. Supervised by the Librarian, each time a reader brought back a book she or he could color a designated part of their individual Hula Girl page. There were Hawaiian themed decorations, including a grass skirt, at the check-in desk. I don't remember the number of books required, but the idea was to complete coloring your page by summer's end. Mine was almost finished when dad got transferred. When we returned, there was no Hula Girl program, but I had outgrown that anyway. There was a competing, more age appropriate attraction across the street.

Kitty-corner from the library in this learning-and-culture corner of P.G. was the Pacific Grove Natural History Museum. For a young teen, the musty building housed dead, dusty, stuffed birds of little or no interest. The only plus was a display on the second floor. The inconspicuous rock closet exhibit provided a different kind of learning experience for a blossoming youth of mid-1950s P.G.

In my crowd of eighth graders, no one really cared about rocks that glowed in the dark. However, this irresistible exhibit was a key location for testing out new hormones. Many of us held our first sweaty hand and got our first tentative kiss in the rock closet. Sometimes we weren't exactly sure whose hand and whose lips were involved. We went as a group. Last one in slid the black curtain closed on its rod. We were all friends, and maybe one had a crush on you or vice versa. There could be surprises.

Thinking back, the museum staff must have heard giggles and whispers. But our daring encounters were brief. When one of us got nervous about getting caught, whoever was next to the curtain slid it open and we ran back down the stairs and out the front door into the daylight world of adults. No one but us knew what happened in the rock closet. It still happens I'm sure.

The Library, Saturday Matinees and Cooking Dinner for Elmarie Dyke
Anne (Allen) Vucina

My family moved to Pacific Grove in 1943 when I was 9 years old. The first thing we did was to get library cards. For 75 years our library has been an important part of my life. I might be one of the "oldest" patrons. I started with the Oz books, then on to the Nancy Drew mysteries. The mystery genre is still my favorite.

Back then, children walked everywhere in town, to school (Robert Down), the library, the Grove Theater (all the kids went to the Saturday matinee), the beach and the Lovers Point pool. We loved those great beach burgers! One of my favorite teachers was Herbert Wherley for seventh grade. I think we were his first class.

When I was 15 I got an afterschool job at Dyke's Drug Store at the soda fountain. Clyde Dyke was the pharmacist; Gladys Dean managed the store and at night I was alone at the soda fountain. I could make the burgers, milk shakes, etc., but I was in terror when Elmarie Dyke, wife of Clyde and "Mrs. Pacific Grove," came in, because she would drag me into the back kitchen and make me cook her dinner. I still scramble eggs the way she taught me.

So of course, my husband Mike and I bought our home here in 1963, one-half acre right in the middle of town. We raised five kids here and are still living in the same house.

Untitled by Louise McCaslin (Pacific Grove train depot at Ocean View) cir. 1962 Louise McCaslin paintings

Untitled by Louise McCaslin (Service station at SW corner of Lighthouse Ave. and Fountain Ave.) cir. 1962

History of Our Civil War Memorial
Bob Fisher

Just a few steps from my apartment on Lighthouse Avenue at the junction of 11th Street is a commemorative concrete bench inlaid with the five-pointed star crest of the Grand Army of the Republic (GAR), depicting a soldier and sailor clasping hands in front of a figure of Lady Liberty. This bench is a memorial to Pacific Grove's Lucius Fairchild Post #179 of the GAR.

The preeminent veterans' organization formed at the close of the Civil War, the GAR was based upon three objectives: **fraternity, charity, and loyalty**. The **first ideal** was encouraged through joint gatherings with members from other posts. Their "camp-fire" was the most popular activity. To promote its **second objective, charity**, the veterans set up a fund for the relief of needy veterans, widows, and orphans. **Loyalty,** the **third ideal**,

was fostered through constant reminders to those who had not lived through the war of the significance of the GAR in reuniting a divided nation.

Membership reached its peak in 1890, when over 400,000 members were reported. By then the GAR had well over seven thousand posts, ranging in size from fewer than two dozen members in small towns to more than a thousand in some cities. Post #179 had 72 members. The P.G. Museum of Natural History has a photo c.1905 depicting veterans of the GAR near the corner of Forest and Lighthouse during one of the annual reunions they hosted in Pacific Grove.

Almost every prominent veteran was enrolled, including five presidents: Grant, Hayes, Garfield, Harrison, and McKinley. In May 1901 a cheering crowd gathered on Lighthouse Avenue in Pacific Grove during the visit of President William McKinley, who visited this area during the 34th Grand Army of the Republic encampment. (He would be shot later that year in New York and soon succumbed to his injuries.)

Next to this bench is a small stone-mounted plaque that identifies J.H. King as the last member of Post #179 who died in 1935 at age 88. James Harvey was one of five King boys from Chautauqua county New York. He was only sixteen years old when the persuasive words of Lincoln's call set fire to his eagerness to "Join up."

J. H. King's service during the war was as a soldier aboard the blockade runners. Their job was to protect the troops being moved up and down the rivers and other waterways from rebel snipers. He came face to face with death when his ship was shattered and most of his comrades killed. Out of a crew of 126, only 25 survived the battle. One of them was young King who was forever after to carry as souvenirs scars on his right arm and right leg from shell wounds. He was moved to the Marine hospital at Memphis, where only the remarkable skill of his physician and the care of a nurse saved his life. He was to meet the nurse again 69 years later during special ceremonies at the University of California in 1934.

Comrade King felt that if our country should undertake a war as the aggressor, *do not enlist*; but if we are attacked by a foreign power, that is the time for you to shoulder a gun. As a conscientious objector during the Vietnam War, I appreciate the importance of the Civil War in preserving the Union and abolishing slavery, but am dismayed by the harshness of the "scorched earth" policies against the Confederate States.

During the time of the Civil War and following, there were other war efforts that were deeply troubling. Most prominent was the immoral *American Indian Wars* from 1860-1890 designed to force First Peoples onto reservations. For me, then, the GAR plaque and bench is a reminder to engage in war only as a last resort; to act humanly toward those who are affected adversely by conflict; and to be loyal to the call for unity while including diversity.

Nationally, the GAR's principal legacy is the annual observance of May 30 as Decoration Day, or more recently, Memorial Day. General John A. Logan, Commander-in-Chief of the GAR, requested members of all posts to decorate the graves of their fallen comrades with flowers on May 30, 1868. This idea came from his wife, who had seen Confederate graves decorated by southern women in Virginia. The flagpole at El Carmelo Cemetery with the cannon at its base is in honor of Pacific Grove's Lucius Fairchild Post #179 of the GAR.

—Sources for this information: From the May 25, 1935 *Tribune*, reprinted in the December 2001-January 2002 *Board and Batten*; and Library of Congress Reading Room.

Growing Up At The Seventeen Mile Drive Cottage Courts
Sherry Lewis Howard

Our family lived in West Los Angeles, five miles from the beach in Santa Monica. Every year from the late 1940s until 1985, we went to Pacific Grove several times a year for our vacations.

Every June, as soon as school got out for the summer, our parents packed our car and we drove to Pacific Grove for a few days on Daddy's first week of vacation. Again in August this was repeated, this time for ten days, and when Daddy had earned a fourth week of vacation time by the 1960s, we came up for a few days again in December. It was our second home.

It's funny, but every September, when I went back to school, my friends and I always shared what we had done during the summer and where we had gone for our vacation. I would tell them that we went to Pacific Grove, and every year they always would ask, "Where's that?" It always set me apart a little and made me feel different, although not in a good way back then. It was confusing when I was young, because they were going to places that were well known, like Yosemite or Chicago. I wondered why we always went to the same place, the little town of Pacific Grove, when it seemed like no one had ever heard of it and no one was interested in going, except our family. In retrospect, that was what made it the perfect place. It was unspoiled, and my parents liked it that way, and it wasn't anything like where we lived the rest of the year.

My sister and I always knew when we were almost at our destination, the 17 Mile Drive Cottage Courts in Pacific Grove, when we saw the red fence tipped in white paint along Highway 68 near Laguna Seca. We were almost there.

The 17 Mile Drive Cottage Courts was a magical place for my sister and me. It was an old-fashioned motor court, consisting of sweet little cabins encompassing the entire block bounded by 17 Mile Drive and Sinex, with a block of houses across the street starting at Sinex and going toward Pine Ave. At the entrance there was a gas station and a building that included the registration office, with lots of postcards to choose the perfect photograph to send to our grandparents on both sides of the family, and our cousins. Past the registration desk was a small restaurant, and best of all, there was a small grocery store in the back of the building. It was like a small town on a block of land.

When we first started going to the 17 Mile Drive Cottage Courts, I was in a crib. Then I graduated to Daddy's army cot with sheets, his army blanket, and a pillow. When my sister came along, they added a crib for her, and when she outgrew the crib, they added a roll-away bed and put it next to the cot, which was next to my parent's double bed. It was very cozy. There was no television, but we didn't seem to notice, because we had books to read and postcards to write.

We always had a cabin with a kitchen, which included a little table and chairs, and came complete with dishes, silverware, pots and pans. It also had a small stove and refrigerator, and Mom cooked most of our dinners there. The most interesting thing in the kitchen was a small door that had a latch on it that when opened, was exposed to the forest outside of the cabin and had wire on the sides forming a small square box. It was used to keep produce and fruit fresh, and I had not ever seen one before, or since. They didn't build them in post-war houses like we had at home. It just added to the fantasy world of the place that you could see outside through a door in the kitchen wall, and might even see a deer passing by.

Mom wasn't ever really convinced that the maids washed anything properly, so as soon as we got there, she re-washed everything from the dishes, silverware, pots and pans, to the kitchen sink and the bathroom, and when we were little, the kitchen floors had to be mopped. It was something that my sister and I couldn't understand, because we wanted our vacation to start but it was always delayed.

So, that would be when we would take our first outing to explore the property of our trip, and included walking up to the store to get our daily supply of about ten cents worth of penny candy, and possibly cat food to feed the feral cats that lived on the property, as well as postcards.

The owner of the 17 Mile Drive Cottage Courts was Fred Workman, and he lived in a sweet little house across the street at the corner of 17 Mile Drive and Sinex. He was a kind, older gentleman who always wore a brown suit with a shirt and tie, and walked with a limp. He was behind the registration desk himself for many years, but gradually turned over that position to kind, dependable men who stayed on for many years and became people we always looked forward to greeting every time we visited. When Daddy would write a letter to Mr. Workman requesting a reservation for a specific room, he would reply in writing with a typewritten letter of confirmation, including the price currently in place for that cottage. It was a very civilized way to do business, very proper and with no room for mistakes.

It smelled so different there. When the breeze blew through the pine forest, it was magical. The sound of the breeze was wonderful, and it brought with it an air of excitement of something familiar but at the same time, not the usual. The vacation we all waited so long for had arrived.

Pacific Grove was full of sounds that we didn't have at home. Our home in West Los Angeles where we grew up was a post-war house built in 1947 consisting of about 1,000 square feet and very little character, and the only sounds we heard were traffic noise and the sound of small airplanes as they traveled around the flight pattern over our house on their way to Santa Monica Airport. Our vacations in Pacific Grove were such a different world, like going to a foreign land. The 17 Mile Drive Cottage Courts were built in the 1920s I believe, and were charming and surrounded by forests and fog. The wind made an amazing sound as it blew through the pine trees, and the train whistle would sound as it passed a few blocks away on its way to the Del Monte Sand Plant in Pebble Beach to load the cars with fine grade silica sand that would be used to manufacture high quality glass in the Midwest. Then there was the sound of the crashing surf and of course, the sea lions and buoys. It was magical to us.

Then there was the foghorn. In the evening, after dinner, we would usually go for a drive and quite often, it was around Point Pinos. Daddy usually would park across the street from the lighthouse, and just wait. He would take great delight when the fog horn would blow and scare us so much that we would scream every time, even though we knew it was coming. The waves crashing against the rocks around Point Pinos were, and still are, unlike any other place on earth. We would fall asleep each night hearing the waves, the buoys, and the seals barking. It was heavenly.

My sister and I would go to the grocery store at the office every day. Our grandparents would give us vacation money, and although it was just a few dollars, it went a long way back in those days. The store was tiny but amazingly well stocked. It had at least one of everything you could need. It also had an incredible selection of penny candy. We would carefully choose ten cents worth of penny candy, and leave with our own little brown bag to enjoy as we walked the grounds of the Cottage Courts, as we called the place. We weren't allowed to cross the street, but we found breaks or bends in the wire fencing at certain places, and climbed outside and walked outside the enclosure, still on the block technically but feeling very independent. We loved seeing the deer, squirrels and birds. We didn't have those back home. In West Los Angeles, our parents rarely let us out of their sight, even in the 1950s, but in Pacific Grove it was different. We were allowed to wander around the grounds by ourselves, and I was in charge of my sister, who is five years younger than I am, and I learned responsibility and leadership. This was where we grew up.

The back half of the 17 Mile Drive Cottage Courts was like another world. It was an old-fashioned trailer park, complete with a tiny shed that housed a laundry room, which was something that we had not ever seen before. Most of the small trailers were owned by full-time residents, and many had put in short fences around their space so they could have their own yard, complete with beautiful gardens. My sister and I made friends with a few of the people who lived there, mostly little old ladies with a dog or cat, and we looked forward to seeing them each time we came to stay. I wanted to live there when I grew up. It seemed like paradise.

One of the best parts of our vacation each year was going to the beach, and our favorite beach was a secluded rocky beach across the road from a small red cottage next to Asilomar on Sunset Drive before Spanish Bay. Daddy would blow up a plastic air mattress with his hand pump, and stand in knee high water and push my sister and me, one at a time, in with the waves between a channel of rocks. Sometimes it was so cold, Mom would put a tee-shirt on us underneath our bathing suits. Those photographs are still amusing. We were pretty cold, but we always wanted to go in the water. Even though the water was unbearably cold, Daddy would put on a brave front for us so that we could have a good time, although I remember that his legs sometimes would turn blue from standing in the cold water for so long. In our adult years, this beach was the scene of birthday picnics and get-togethers with family and friends who came to town. It was, and is today, our family's beach.

◉ ◎ ◉

Our vacation days were filled with the things that became part of our routine when we were spending time in Pacific Grove, like going to the wharf in Monterey to get fresh fish from the beds of ice at the many stands that once lined the wharf, and as well as shopping for trinkets to take home at the gift shops, getting donuts from Hector De Smet's Bakery on Lighthouse Avenue for breakfast, and shopping for gifts to take to our grandparents at Holman's Department Store. We loved going on picnics to Point Lobos with things to eat that we would purchase at the Mediterranean Market on Ocean Avenue in Carmel, and we liked to window shop in Carmel and go for drives just to look at the beautiful scenery. If we were lucky, we were there for the Monterey County Fair. We always went out to dinner one special night of our vacation, and it was usually at Lover's Point Restaurant, later The Tinnery. If I remember correctly, spaghetti and meatballs cost 75 cents.

Daddy loved trains. He had grown up taking trains all around the country, and had his own HO layout in our home with six trains, with buildings and mountains, and scenery chosen from trips to the forest and beach. Starting when we were very small in the 1950s, after we finished dinner at our cabin, we would drive to the train depot in Monterey to greet the train as it arrived from its daily trip to San Francisco. The Del Monte Express took businessmen to work and ladies to shop in San Francisco each day. Daddy would get Mom, my sister and me aboard the train, and then hurry to his car, and race the train along the coast to Pacific Grove, where it turned around on the turnstile for the next day's trip north. My sister and I would search the streets for Daddy's car as it slowly made its way along the coast, trying to catch a glimpse of Daddy racing along the streets following the train on his way to meet us at the Pacific Grove station, and we would squeal in delight when we could spot him. There was always a very kind porter on the train to talk with, and they would let us ride for free because it was just a few miles to the last stop. When we got off the train, we would squash a penny under the train as a souvenir. I still have some of them.

In the early 1960s Mr. Workman sold the 17 Mile Drive Cottage Courts, and the name changed to The 17 Mile Drive Village. They remodeled the cabins and added beautiful tuberous begonias everywhere. They also put in a heated swimming pool and Jacuzzi, which was really nice on cold summer days, but by the late 1960s, the 17 Mile Drive Village had seen better days. My sister and I were teenagers and we needed a little more room as well, so our family changed to the Bide-a-Wee Inn and Cottages on Asilomar Boulevard, and became regular occupants there, still coming at least once and sometimes twice a year with our parents, long after my sister and I were out on our own. Just because we had grown up, we hadn't outgrown Pacific Grove.

Our parents finally decided to move to Pacific Grove in 1985, choosing a sweet little two-bedroom home on 17 Mile Drive at Short Street, ironically a block away from where we had spent so many years of our lives. Interestingly, they didn't ever go back to West Los Angeles, even to visit. That year, my sister and her husband moved north to San Francisco, and in 1986, my husband and I followed my parents to Pacific Grove. My parents owned that home until 2005.

Postscript

This memory is dedicated to our father, who we are forever grateful to for introducing us to Pacific Grove. We love it as much as Daddy and Mom did, and are so fortunate that they followed their dream of moving to Pacific Grove. It gave my sister and her husband and my husband and me an extension of that dream that we wouldn't have had if they hadn't made the move. We would still have been able to have childhood memories, but we are so happy to have adult memories and continuing experiences here in this amazing place. Daddy and Mom are resting now, where they wanted to be, at El Carmelo Cemetery, happy in knowing that the deer are grazing on their grave site, listening to the ocean and smelling the pines in the breeze. They are at home.

Note: Sherry Lewis Howard is a retired executive assistant who worked for Pebble Beach Company for fifteen years. During that time, she contributed articles to, edited and coordinated the production of the Pebble Beach Company newsletter SCOREBOARD for twelve years as the Company kept the community informed about what was going on in Pebble Beach, Pacific Grove and the surrounding cities, as well as sharing historical articles about the area. She was fortunate to work with many Pacific Grove locals, including Paul Finnegan at the Pacific Grove Museum of Natural History, and Moe Ammar of the Pacific Grove Chamber of Commerce, as well as the people at Colorgraphics typesetters and Rapid Printers.

A Lifetime of Nurturing a Creative Spark
Keith Larson

I was only three-and-a-half years old when I made a life-long connection with the graphic world of cartoons, the stories and characters presented in animated and print forms such as comic strips and comic books. Now they refer to these as graphic novels. All of my friends were captivated by these art forms. We would watch animated cartoons in the afternoon and Saturday mornings on local TV. *Tom and Jerry, Bugs Bunny* and *Daffy Duck,* the old Warner Brothers and MGM cartoons made to be shown before the main feature movie in the 1930s, 40s and 50s found their way to TV screens in the 1960s. We watched programs like Captain Satellite, a kiddie show host on KTVU who was always dressed like an astronaut. Every day he had a crew of children with him who had sent in their names so they could be on the show. Most of the time things went smoothly except once in a while as the captain would exclaim, "We're blasting off now," one of the crew would say, "No, we're not!" You could see Captain Satellite taking off into space every day, and once in a while, the real-life host inside the space suit, Bob March, could be seen forecasting the weather on the KTVU newscasts.

It was assumed if you were a kid you could pretend and most of us could do that without any hesitation. But when you hit a certain age and still want to play pretend games, it is just harder to find others who want to play with you unless you have small children of your own or grandchildren, as I do now. The structure of television has changed, too. All the local stations used to have their own kiddie shows, as I believe they needed to air a certain amount of children's programing. That is all history now.

Saturdays were ruled by the stable of Hanna Barbara cartoons, *Space Ghost, Milton the Monster,* and *Wacky Racers* to name just a few. I remember on a trip to Disneyland my dad pointed out the Hanna Barbara studio as we drove through Hollywood. It had a sign with a big "HB" in capital letters. These shows kept us focused on the small picture tube, small compared to the big screens we have today. Most of my friends stayed near the TV set, elbows on the floor and hands propped up under their chins. until around noon. I was always ready to head off into the woods for adventures long before this. But many Saturdays I could not pry my friends away from the TV until the last cartoon show signed off.

Hours of Fun for Just 12 Cents

We also collected comic books. Each grocery store had a display of comic books on a rack that you could twirl around to find your favorites. Most of my friends had a pile of Marvel, D.C. and Disney comic books stashed somewhere in their rooms, homemade places like tree houses, or up above the garage in rafters. Some of us liked to read the comics at the grocery stores without buying them, choosing to instead hang around the comic rack. That is, if the grocery clerk was too busy to pay attention to you. Sometimes a clerk would pass by and say, "You're planning on buying those, aren't you?" Hint-hint. I never liked reading my comics this way. I preferred the special time that I could spend with my favorite comic book heroes like Hulk, Captain America, Iron Man, Dare Devil and Spider Man. I wanted to read them by myself in my room or sometimes in the back of our old station wagon. Comic books sold for 12 cents, or 25 cents if it was a bigger issue. We traded comics with each other, a good way to be able to read the ones you hadn't seen yet. The times were very primitive, no tablets or smart phones. I suppose if we could have carted a portable TV around with us, we would have. I do remember being in a treehouse with a TV hooked up to it, a dream come true, but most of our forts and private spaces didn't come with this option.

I collected the comic strips in the newspapers by cutting them out and pasting them in a scrapbook my mother bought me at Holman's Department Store. The graphic worlds created in these little square boxes were special to me, like friends you could check in with every day to see what they were up to. *Nancy, Dick Tracy, Blondie, Gordo, Dennis the Menace* and *Peanuts*, each strip side-by-side. And when we took vacations my dad would pick up the local papers and I would see comic strips I had not read before, as each newspaper carried different ones that the editor hoped would please their current readers and bring in new ones. I loved them all.

Discovering Role Models
Right Here on the Central Coast

Around second grade I began to experiment with little squares and characters that talked using word balloons. Some of my friends did the same thing. Little did I realize there were some bigger "kids" who lived on the Peninsula who created some of the cartoons I saw in the papers every day. The Central Coast has always seemed to be a magnet for creative individuals including the cartoonists who live and work here. Then through various means of distribution, their work is seen throughout the world. Local artists included the likes of Eldon Dedini. who drew cartoons for the *New Yorker* and *Playboy* magazine, Gus Arriola, who created the syndicated *Gordo* comic strip, and Hank Ketchum of *Dennis the Menace* fame. It was years later that I started to get in touch with some of these

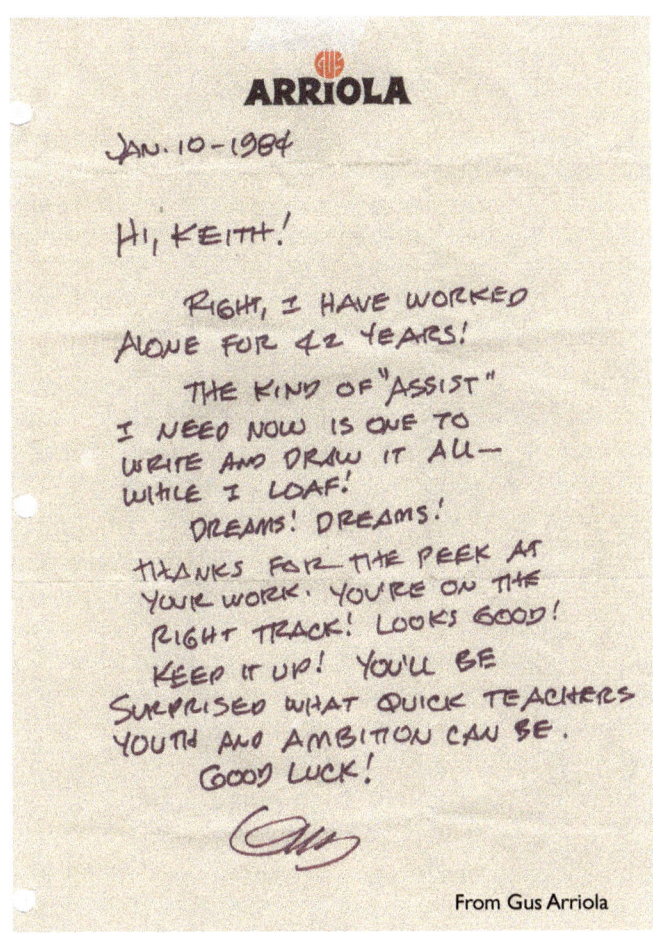

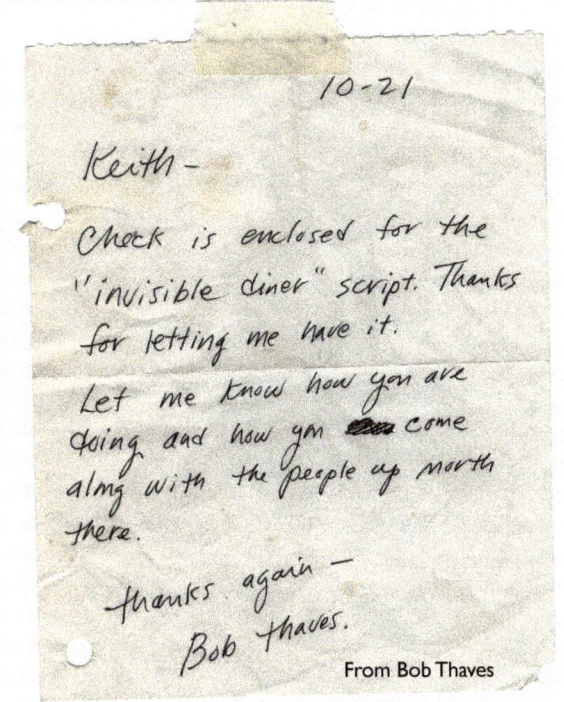

Correspondence Keith received from his role models on the Central Coast.

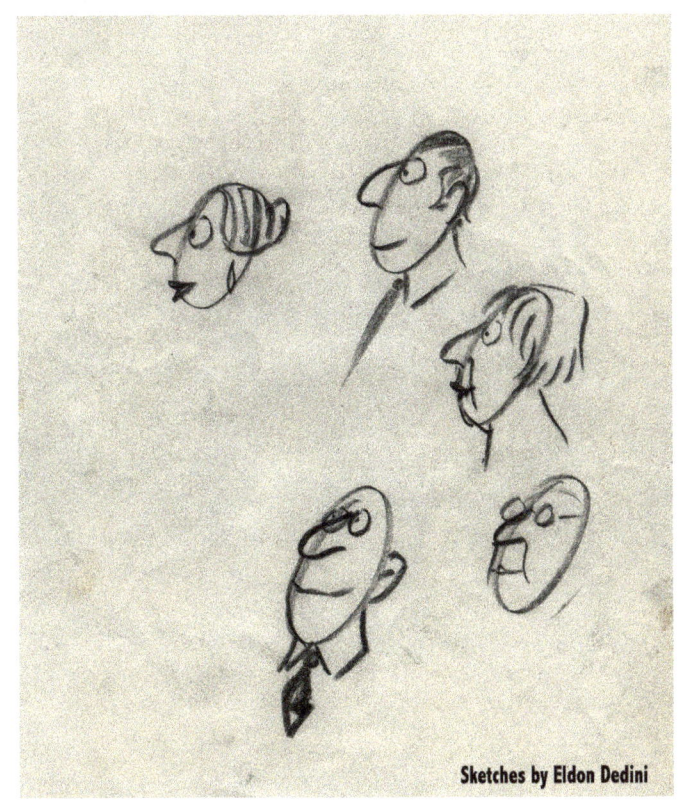

wonderful individuals who shared their talents with the local and larger world community.

I realized at some point that expressing myself in this graphic art form was not going to fade away like it did for many of my friends. I kept drawing cartoons and thinking up gag lines and stories no matter what my life situation might be. My art teacher, Nancy Johnson, a very fine local watercolor painter and art teacher at Sunset Center, knew I wanted to draw cartoons but always said it would be more exciting for me if I learned to draw well. I took her advice and I have been working on this ever since. I started drawing cartoons for magazines, newsletters, and writing some Sunday pages for the syndicated *Frank and Ernest* comic strip. I'd send a brochure out to editors to see if they used cartoons, and asked for a copy of their publication so I could read it and think up some ideas. I was in every kind of publication from the newsletter of The Brotherhood of Locomotive Engineers to *Cosmopolitan* magazine.

My friend, local artist Dick Crispo, introduced me to Eldon Dedini, who drew cartoons for the *New Yorker* and *Playboy*, two of the most prestigious publications for a cartoonist's work to appear in. I met Eldon on a day that he had just come home from the post office with a rejection letter for some ideas that he had sent to *Playboy*. One of the comments on the rough drawings was not very complimentary and had him a bit worried, yet I always remember Eldon putting that aside and giving me the grand tour of his studio. He was so gracious to me a newcomer. Later he framed this rough that had been returned by *Playboy* and displayed it in a show. Artists of any stature have to endure criticism from time to time. Eldon invited me to come over on Saturdays sometimes to talk cartooning and help me with any questions or drawing problems I was having. Around this time I got the idea of perhaps working as an assistant on a comic strip, something that never materialized, but the correspondence I received from Gus Arriola, Hank Ketchum and Bob Thaves are reprinted for this book.

Advice for Today's Young Cartoonists

I've had many different experiences in life including marriage, being a stay-at-home dad with my son Wesley, and now a grandfather to Mattias and Kaia. I worked as a freelance magazine cartoonist and also ran a 15-acre farm for a number of years. Perhaps this is all material that will find its way into ideas that I can express through the medium of cartooning at some future time. So you young cartoonists out there, if you are reading this and still drawing funny pictures with word balloons and expressing yourself in this way, even though Mom stopped taping your pictures to the refrigerator years ago, this little part of your childhood has somehow survived an onslaught of appropriate behavioral training and wants to stick around and be your friend. By all means do what you need to do to take care of yourself, but remember to also nurture and find outlets for this little spark of creative energy that survived. In fact, any creativity is a survivor left over from when life was as simple as reading comics with your friends and when thinking up stories and characters was just so much fun.

Row of tiny birdhouses on a fence in the P.G. Retreat illustrated by Keith Larson.

PACIFIC GROVE FRIENDS OF THE ARTS – NANCY JACOBS

Then-Mayor Sandy Koffman and her husband, Dan.

When Paris Came to Pacific Grove: Beaux Arts Ball
Nancy Jacobs

Give Me Women, Wine and Snuff

Give me women, wine and snuff
Until I cry out "hold enough!"
You may do sans objection
Till the day of resurrection:
bless my beard, they aye shall be
My beloved Trinity.

—*John Keats*

In 1889, two enterprising men, Charles Zidler and Joseph Oller, decided to build a cabaret in Paris, close to Montmartre in the district of Pigalle on Boulevard de Clichy in the 18th Arrondissement. They created an instant landmark by placing a red windmill—Moulin Rouge—on the roof. The location had a rural, village atmosphere, which proved good for attracting a diverse clientele.

The Moulin Rouge presented a variety of entertainment, attracting many artists like Toulouse-Lautrec and Auguste Renoir. They found inspiration at the Moulin Rouge. It also brought laughter and fun to the Montmartre district, which also includes the Basilica of Sacre Coeur. This area was designated a nightclub district. Artists and writers gathered there and they made the Moulin Rouge a huge success. A dancer known as La Goulue introduced the provocative can-can dance at the popular nightclub. The Moulin Rouge existed during the Belle Époque era when the French people became more liberal, with ordinary working people mingling with socialites and aristocrats. This is exactly what the founders had in mind when they created the nightclub. It was also during the Belle Époque period when the Eiffel Tower was built by Gustave Eiffel.

◉ ◉ ◉

No other establishment was quite like the Moulin Rouge. It was a mix of quirkiness, some elegance, plus unusual features. It provided an atmosphere where laughter, fun and euphoria came easily. Women might ride donkeys around the inside and aristocrats could enjoy the atmosphere that was created. Balls became well known. The balls ended with the can-can, a wild and naughty French dance where women pulled up their skirts and bent over to show their derriere. Essentially, the can-can was a new version of the old French quadrille. The daring French girls who danced the can-can were usually the models for the artists who came to the Moulin Rouge and were featured in many paintings. They were sketched by the artists as they sat and enjoyed their absinthe or, in other cases, coffee. La Goulue was immortalized by Toulouse-Lautrec. It was the place for many outrageous fun nights. And then, in 1915 disaster struck. A fire burned the Moulin Rouge to the ground.

The Moulin Rouge was rebuilt and reopened in 1921 and an entertainer with the stage name of Mistinguett became co-director of the cabaret. As a very successful songstress, she kept the club going by attracting many customers with her songs, many of which have become inseparable from the Moulin Rouge name. Mistinguett left in the 1940s and the place was turned into a dance club during WWII. Yves Montand and Edith Piaf performed there during this time. However, they were never as popular or profitable as Mistinguett. In the 1950s the Moulin Rouge underwent renovations and various artists have performed there ever since. It is one of the best known attractions in Paris to this day.

Meanwhile, Across the Atlantic …

Across the Atlantic and straight to the west coast, one finds the city of Pacific Grove. At just about the same time as the Moulin Rouge was opening in glamorous Paris, Pacific Grove had its humble beginnings as a Methodist summer retreat, complete with tent cabins. Still, it was enchanting. W.R. Holman, who was very young when he came to Pacific Grove in 1888 and who became manager of Holman's Department Store, found Pacific Grove to be beautiful, with trees and wild lilac everywhere. The lilacs gave off a lovely perfume-like scent. W. R. Holman was enchanted by the clouds of butterflies that took to the air. "The sky became a beautiful sight much like a painting covered with the blue background of the sky, the oranges and the black from the fluttering butterflies." This quote, attributed to W.R. Holman, comes from a 1975 lecture on Pacific Grove history that the author attended. W.R. Holman's father, R. L. Holman, founded the department store that was later run by his son. W. R Holman fought to have the Holman Highway built in the 1920s, which has become an alternate route out of Pacific Grove.

◎ ◎ ◎

In 1883, the Pacific Grove Methodist retreat published its rules and regulations, and most things that people love were prohibited. No alcohol, gambling, dancing, profanity, fast buggy riding, bathing at the beach without costume, dirty outhouses, firearms, and smoking in or near buildings. Inn 1885, a curfew was mandated. Those who were under 18 years of age could not be out after 8:00 p.m. in the winter and 9:00 p.m. in the summer. A fence was erected around Pacific Grove up to New Monterey.

Of course there were those who were not going to adhere to these rules so they found ways around them. Mariposa Hall in New Monterey was originally built as a dance hall built especially for those in Pacific Grove who wanted to dance. Those who wanted to gamble could do so by going to Hollenbeck's Cigar Store on Lighthouse Avenue between Forest and 16th streets. Hollenbeck's had two card rooms located in the back of the store that could be rented out for gambling. The hi-jinks, as Steinbeck referred to such goings on in *Sweet Thursday*, did not end here. A favorite pastime of those who'd had a drink or two at the Half Way Saloon was to rock the car of the electric trolley off its track. Electric lights came to Pacific Grove in 1895. The electric trolley de-railings happened between 1903 and 1923.

◎ ◎ ◎

Benjamin Langford, a former Nevada judge and California state senator, built a house just inside the fence and locked gate that separated Pacific Grove from New Monterey. He grew so annoyed at constantly being locked out of his own home after missing the nightly curfew that in 1885 he took an axe and chopped down the gate.

Or consider the story of Pacific Grove's town jail. The town fathers built the jail, but the citizens were so law-abiding the lock-up was always empty. So the story goes, the constable went to the Chinese camp, arrested a sleeping man and put him in jail for one night, then released him the next morning! Thus the lawman could say that the jail had been used, establishing the need and keeping his job.

◎ ◎ ◎

Visitors to Pacific Grove came by railroad, debarking at the depot just past Lovers Point. In the 1890s three passenger trains arrived daily in the summer. People were excited when they heard the train whistle and they often rushed to see it arrive. The trains with their tourists brought possible business for the drivers of surreys or wagons, which lined up at the train depot.

Fascinating characters peopled Pacific Grove in its early days, like "Whistling" Bob Mitchell, the town's first postman. Hattie McDougal who owned the bath house at Lovers Point, erected a barrier denying access to the beach to anyone but her customers. Julia Platt, Pacific Grove's first female mayor, like Langford before her took to the axe to get rid of the fence and restore beach access to all.

Cheers! Liquor Becomes Legal in P.G.

As the decades of the 20th century passed, the old slowly gave way to the new. In 1963 the old Methodist church was demolished. Pacific Grove has the honor of being known as the last "dry" town in California, not allowing the sale of spirits until 1969. The Pacific Grove Art Center opened that same year and its grand opening celebration was the first public event in Pacific Grove in which alcoholic beverages were served, at least legally. Silicon Valley came to Pacific Grovein 1974 with the founding of Digital Research by Gary Kildall. In 1975 the Heritage Society was founded and became incorporated the next year. In 1994 Pacific Grove passed the first historic preservation ordinance. The 1990s saw an incredible fight to preserve Rocky Shores. That section of coastline was saved from development thanks to the work of Bud Nunn, Annette Corcoran, Flo Schaefer and others. Flo Schaefer was elected mayor on a platform that included the idea that the city does not have an obligation to make room for everyone who wants to live in Pacific Grove.

The 1990s:
Britney Spears, Beanie Babies and 'You've Got Mail'

The 1990s are considered by some historians to be one of the greatest decades. The Cold War ended in 1991. The surprise ending to the OJ Simpson trial stunned many people. The death of Princess Diana in a car crash affected millions who loved her and still do. Sadly, John F. Kennedy Jr. died in a plane crash. Bill Clinton was president, and along with Bill Clinton came "Monica-gate," and then there was Clarence Thomas and Anita Hill. All this played out with the background music of Britney Spears, Christina Aguilera, Shania Twain, Whitney Houston and Celine Dion. Fashions were comfortable and people loved plaid. Favorite television shows included *Seinfeld*, *Law and Order* and *Dawson's Creek*. The silver screen featured *Independence Day, Saving Private Ryan, Schindler's List, Jurassic Park* and Disney's *Beauty and the Beast,* just to name a few. *The Bridges of Madison County* became a best-selling book Who can forget the romantic escapades of Julia Roberts and Lyle Lovett? Beanie babies, Tickle Me Elmo, Nintendo and Pokemon were really BIG! A new dance, the Macarena, hit the dance floor in the 1990s. Kids loved loud boom boxes but Pacific Grove found them less than acceptable. This is hard to believe, but the 1990s was when most of us first got internet service with the dial-up modems. Remember "you've got mail?"

Here in Pacific Grove, Les Reed constantly complained about sidewalk sandwich boards and had them removed. It was also the decade of Sandy Koffman. Sandy served four consecutive terms as Mayor of Pacific Grove. She loved her dogs, her friends and the natural beauty of P.G.

And it was the decade that Paris came to Pacific Grove in the form of the Beaux Arts Ball.

In the summer of 1993, after months of working on the bylaws, The Pacific Grove Friends of the Arts was formed as a nonprofit to help fund art projects in Pacific Grove. The officers were Eleanor Rogge, president; Nancy Jacobs, vice president; Angela Tyler, secretary, and Annette Corcoran, treasurer. Board members included Barbara Zito, Meg Manus, Canan Barriman, Karen Morgan and Shelley Sitzman. Eleanor Rogge, a member of the city council, felt that the arts were good for the economy and one of her campaign promises was to do something for the arts. Eleanor was a former arts and English teacher. She believed very strongly in the arts and understood that funding was always a problem. She was instrumental in organizing the Pacific Grove Arts Commission in 1991 with nine members, all with some involvement in the arts, who were appointed by the mayor and city council.

However, there were no funds available to support the work of the Arts Commission. So, Eleanor began the Pacific Grove Friends of the Arts. The first fundraiser event was a production of *Funny Girl*, presented on Aug 22, 1993, at Monterey Peninsula College. That gave the Arts Commission enough money to sponsor Sundays in the Park but not much else. Eleanor said that two things were apparent: One, Pacific Grove had quite a few artists, and two, there was very little money to support art in the schools.

Many fundraisers were sponsored by the Pacific Grove Friends of the Arts, from ice cream socials to theater productions, but none beat the popularity of the Beaux Arts Ball. This was the brainchild of former mayor and council member Flo Schaefer. Most members of Friends of the Arts had an arts background. Nancy Jacobs, for example, started out as an artist and gave it up to support her husband's efforts. He was a Navy pilot who attended Art Center College of Design in Pasadena and graduated as an illustrator. Flo Schaefer, meanwhile, had a career as an educational administrator.

Just Imagine the Moulin Rouge in Chautauqua Hall

When these forces came together—the arts and administration—Paris came to Pacific Grove with its wild and wooly Moulin Rouge! Two completely opposite cities were connected by this one event. Chautauqua Hall was chosen for the event.

Officers of Pacific Grove Friends of the Arts, an organization recently formed to help fund arts projects in Pacific Grove, met at the home of the group's chairwoman, Eleanor Rogge (back row, right). They are (clockwise, from Rogge) Angela Tyler, secretary; Nancy Jacobs, vice chairwoman; and Annette Corcoran, treasurer.

◉ ◉ ◉

Much time was spent in the planning of the Beaux Arts ball, with many details to be worked out. The sets were constructed and artists found to paint them. The Friends of the Arts and the Arts Commission, along with board members, turned Chautauqua Hall into the Moulin Rouge complete with the iconic red mill. Let's enter this magical world. Walking to the event treated you to the soft music coming from Chautauqua Hall. The first impression as you entered through the door was one of awe. The small round tables all had centerpieces which featured small battery-operated candles enclosed in glass coverings. The tables were located in one corner around the edge of the dance floor. It felt like stepping back to the original Paris Moulin Rouge, into another world.

Amazing is the word for the various costumes. A plastic box seemed to be floating around on the dance floor but when one looked closely one realized that two people were dancing in a beautifully constructed replica of a shower. It was mesmerizing and won best costume prize. Other impressive costumes included a man dressed as a locomotive engineer and his companion in a stunning silk navy skirt and white see-through top, with a one-sided hat that was dark navy as was the skirt. Sparkling lights seemed to be moving around. It turned out to be a man dressed in a matador costume with fancy decorative stitching. He sparkled as he walked. A second glance was not out of the question, he was so impressive. Spotted on the dance floor was Sandy Koffman and her husband Dan. Sandy came as a dance hall girl and her husband as Toulouse-Lautrec. They were joined by Nancy Jacobs in a 1940s dress and pillbox hat. The two dancers became a trio made all the more humorous being led by the short Toulouse-Lautrec. Some came as monarchs of the past such as Queen Elizabeth I, others wore costumes

as attendees of the Venice Carnival, complete with feathered hats and eye masks. Throughout the hall one could hear Barbara Zito's soft and sometimes loud laughter. Les Reed came as a Southern gentleman decked out in a period suit. Some of the hats were fascinators before fascinators were in style. The dance hall girl costume seemed to be the most popular, with even Flo Schaefer sporting the look. Eleanor looked like a monarch of old, perhaps a queen or one of Henry VIII's six wives.

The food was light and wine was served to those who wanted it. Les Reed walked around to make sure everyone enjoyed themselves. The artists loved this event. They came and gave it an authentic French atmosphere as they did sketches. Near the end of the event, one could hear the tempo of the music going faster. Suddenly the dance floor was filled with performers from the DiFranco Dance Company. Wearing 1880s French attire, they were on the floor dancing the can-can in its rousing authentic form! With this, the event became totally Paris style.

More Beaux Arts balls would be held. It was a fun event and seemed to be well liked as Chautauqua Hall was always full during the Beaux Arts events. Many well-known artists contributed their works to the auction, including ceramicist Annette Corcoran, stained glass artist Bud Nunn, cartoonists Gus Arriola, Eldon Dedini and Bill Bates, and sculptor Christopher Bell. Randy Chinn donated his father's work from their Carmel Gallery, while Nancy Jacobs donated her husband's award-winning "Desperate Trails" lithograph. The auction items were very eye-catching. In addition to works of art, prizes included vacation trips along with an assortment of other attractive donations.

◉ ◉ ◉

The money raised by the Friends of the Arts paid for several historical mural projects, including the mural by artist Jon Ton on the Recreation Trail as well as the popular, family-friendly Concerts in the Park. The "Butterfly Children" sculpture by Christopher Bell in front of the Pacific Grove Post Office was also funded by the Friends of the Arts. Money was allocated for art supplies in schools and for art scholarships

Unlike its counterpart in Paris, Pacific Grove's Moulin Rouge did not last a century and longer. Nancy Jacobs had to leave Friends of the Arts in 1999 to care for her brother, who was ill with cancer, and then split her time between Pacific Grove and Santa Cruz for some ten years. Sadly, Eleanor Rogge, Flo Schaefer, Sandy Koffman and Les Reed died. It was said that Les Reed was singing "There's No Business Like Show Business" as he waited for his last journey to end. The Friends of the Arts kept going until 2001. Sometime after 2001, the group disbanded, along with the Arts Commission.

Sponsored by Pacific Grove Friends of the Arts

Chinese Wedding Mural
Artist: Merlin Brown
Photo by: Alex Jacobs

Chalkfest

Scholarship Award 2000

Presented by Kimberly Herring
for Pacific Grove Friends of the Arts
at Pacific Grove High School

Fundraising Event

Gingerbread Contest
in December

Fun Time

Getting Ready
for a Fundraiser!

A Bygone Era Beckons

as seen through the eyes of artist Jon Ton.
This is one of the many projects funded by the
Pacific Grove Friends of the Arts.

PACIFIC GROVE FRIENDS OF THE ARTS
P.O. Box 1015, Pacific Grove, Ca. 93950
(831) 644-2549

FEAST OF LANTERNS

Painting by Cheryl Kampe. Marabee Boone Collection

"Perhaps it was the transformational power of true love that captivated the early Pacific Grove community …."

– Kaye Coleman

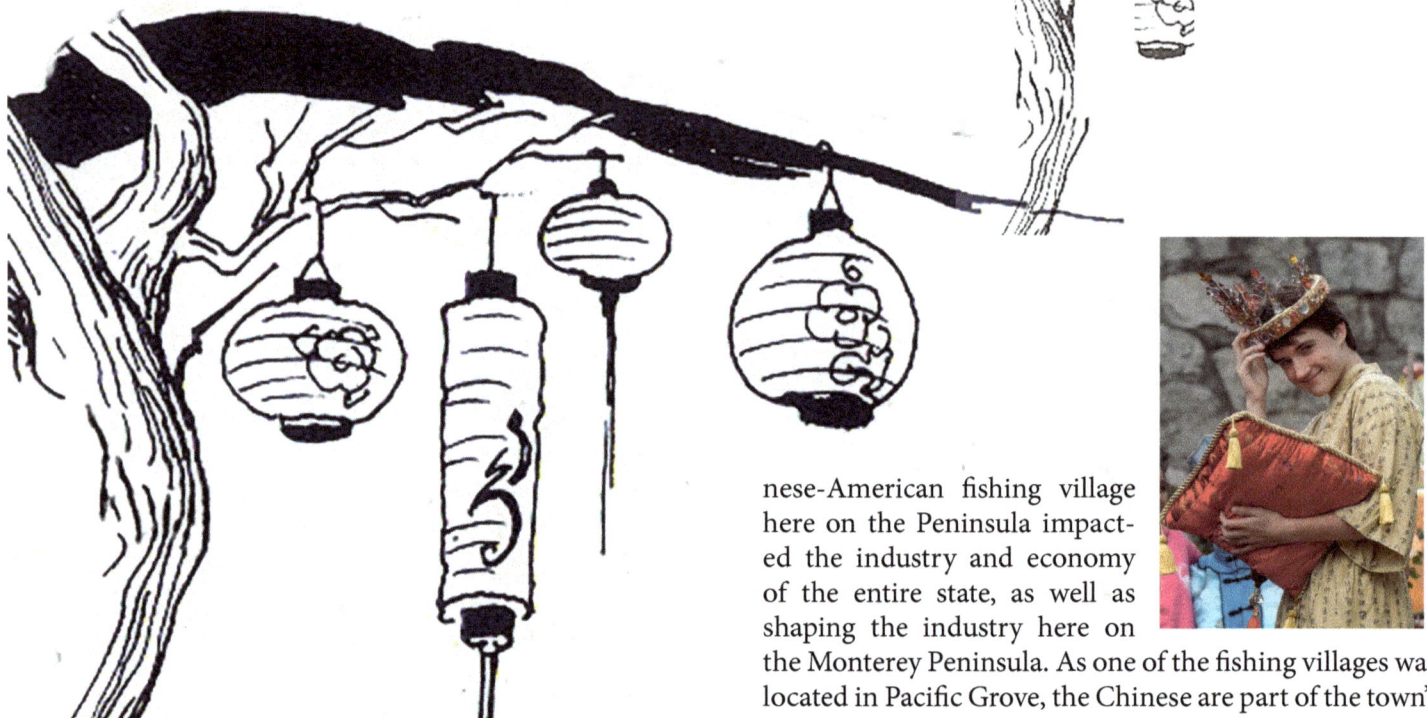

Interconnected Threads of Time
A History of Pacific Grove and the Feast of Lanterns
Kaye Coleman

President of the Feast of Lanterns and Queen Topaz 1993

In order to fully embrace the rich history of our hometown, it is important to dig deeper to discover the truths that shape this beautiful area. John Steinbeck helped popularize the myth that Chinese explorers planted the first cypress trees here on the Monterey Peninsula centuries before the Spanish first landed here. The Chinese often planted trees as a token of discovery and the cypress tree is unique to this area and to a single area in China. In my research, I have found that many of the early settlers in our area felt a strong connection because our coastline reminded them of their home coastlines in Asia and Europe.

Chinese fisherman settled between Cabrillo Point (China Point) and Point Alones (Point Almejas) in 1853. They moved their fishing village from Point Lobos to Pescadero in Pebble Beach, then to Point Alones in Pacific Grove and Point Almejas, where the Monterey Bay Aquarium now stands. The Chinese who settled here in California where amazing people who continued to innovate their craft of fishing even in the face of adversity. They created an international industry of squid fishing, sending their dried squid home to China, one of the few international industries created in this area. The Chinese-American fishing village here on the Peninsula impacted the industry and economy of the entire state, as well as shaping the industry here on the Monterey Peninsula. As one of the fishing villages was located in Pacific Grove, the Chinese are part of the town's history. The Point Alones Chinese fishing village burned down in a fire in 1906. The remaining Chinese-Americans relocated to McAbee Beach in Monterey or headed further north to pursue new beginnings.

The quiet town of Pacific Grove was not formally established until 1889, although the P.G. Post Office had opened three years earlier, in1886. The Point Pinos Lighthouse had been built in 1855 and today is the oldest continuously working lighthouse in California. Soon after that, Lighthouse Avenue was constructed to connect the lighthouse with the pueblo of Monterey. Downtown Pacific Grove would take shape around this important road and the Chautauqua Assembly. The First United Methodist Church was built on Lighthouse Avenue between 17th and 18th streets and it was the women of the Methodist Church, along with the Chautauqua Assembly, that organized and celebrated the first Feast of Lanterns in 1905.

'I Have Never Been in Any Place so Dreamlike.'

In 1879, Robert Louis Stevenson visited Pacific Grove at the end of the summer retreat for the Chautauqua Assembly. He wrote, "I have never been in any place so dreamlike. Indeed, it was not so much like a deserted town as like a scene upon the stage by daylight, and with no one on the boards."

Stevenson would not be the only famous writer to be drawn to Pacific Grove. John Steinbeck, Ed Ricketts and Joseph Campbell would all live here and be influenced by Pacific Grove and the Peninsula. The inspirations they gained here would shape each of their life's works. Steinbeck lived in a cottage on 11th Street during his early years as a struggling young writer, and went on to write lovingly—and sometimes with gentle mocking—about Monterey and Pacific Grove in *Cannery Row* and *Sweet*

Thursday. Marine biologist Ed Ricketts was the inspiration for the character "Doc" in Steinbeck's books and was the author of the influential work *Between Pacific Tides*. Joseph Campbell spent only one year in Pacific Grove and spent considerable time in the company of Ricketts and Steinbeck. During that year the clarity of his life's work on the Hero's Journey would take shape while he absorbed Rickett's understanding of the interconnected interplay within tide pools and the ocean at large. Our area has drawn amazing minds that shaped the world through innovative, big-picture thinking.

'The Most American Thing in America'

The Chautauqua movement in the United States was described by former President Teddy Roosevelt as "The most American thing in America." The Chautauqua Assembly sought to reach out to Americans and teach them about art, culture and science through public performances. Perhaps Roosevelt felt as he did because the Chautauqua movement celebrated America as the great melting pot, understanding that this country was born as a nation of immigrants who left home to find a better life for their families and that we can all learn from the different cultures that make this country their home. Making the journey to the West meant being open to adventure and new ideas, pushing people to expand beyond the limits of old thinking to find new opportunities. In 1874 the Chautauqua Assembly was established at a lakeside resort community in New York, a movement that brought culture and education to all who participated. The summer retreat concluded with a lantern parade and fireworks over the lake.

In 1875 the newly formed Pacific Grove Retreat Association initiated a three week summer camp meeting under the coastal pines. Pacific Grove housed the Literary and Science circle starting in 1879, and soon became known as "the Chautauqua of the West." The Methodist women studied to become Sunday school teachers and learned more about the diversity of the area. So from the Chautauqua movement in New York, we gained a summer festival that eventually became Feast of Lanterns, ending with fireworks and lighted lanterns over the water. Since we are blessed with a beautiful coastline, we get to have fireworks at the beach.

Captivated by a Story of True Love

The first recorded Feast of Lanterns took place in 1905 and was marked with a lantern parade in which the town's residents walked from Lighthouse Avenue down Forest Avenue to Lovers Point. A play told the story of forbidden love based on the Blue Willow china pattern, which had nothing to do with Chinese legend, but was a popular pattern from England. Perhaps it was the transformational power of true love that captivated the early Pacific Grove community and is a reason why this story has lasted as long as it has. The Pacific Grove version of the Blue Willow story was first told by Pauline Benton of the Red Gate Shadow Players in 1958 at Pacific Grove's Methodist Church. She changed the ending of the story to have the lovers fly away as monarch butterflies to return again every fall.

1875 was the first year on record that monarch butterflies were noticed in Pacific Grove during their migration. Pacific Grove became "Butterfly Town USA" and for many it is loved as one of the "last hometowns" in America. To be represented by the majestic monarch butterfly is truly a gift to our community. Monarch, of course, refers to royalty and the orange-and-black butterfly may have been named for King William III of England, also known as William of Orange. Since a royal butterfly is the symbol of our town, it makes sense that over time we would grow to have a historical and cultural event that features a royal court.

The butterfly is also a beautiful universal symbol of transformation, rebirth and the soul taking flight. So, in the Feast of Lanterns myth when Queen Topaz (Koong-Se) and Scholar Chang are changed into monarch butterflies by Guan Yin, it is about the transformative power of love. This story can also be seen as a hero's journey. Queen Topaz is brave enough to answer the call and be transformed. Each year the lovers return to the place where they fell in love, protected by all the monarchs who fly with them.

Celebrating the Potential Held in Our Children

As a small town we celebrate each fall the return of the monarchs with the historic Butterfly Parade and all those cute kindergarteners who march as butterflies. We celebrate the next generation and potential held in our children. The Feast of Lanterns also celebrates the next generation with middle school and high school students who serve on the Royal Court and the Royal Guard. Those who serve on the Feast are the best of our community. They are young women and men who are chosen because they are leaders, scholars, athletes, musicians and community-minded. Pacific Grove sends future leaders out into the world who understand the importance of knowing their local history and how to be a role model in everything they do.

Elmarie Hurlbert Hyler Dyke created the modern Royal Court of princesses named after birthstones in 1958. She served as the matriarch of the Feast until she passed in 1981. The Royal Guard was added in 2017 and they represent the elemental animals of the Chinese zodiac. Those young people who serve on the court and guard are part of Pacific Grove's living history.

The Royal Court: Turning Young Women into Leaders

Kaye Coleman

PGHS Class of 1995, President of the Feast of Lanterns, and Queen Topaz 1993

The Feast of Lanterns Royal Court has seen many evolutions through the years of this unique and historic event. The Feast of Lanterns first occurred in 1905, at the end of the Summer Retreat for the Chautauqua Assembly. In 1958, Elmarie Hurlbert Hyler Dyke revived the tradition and introduced the Royal Court. The young ladies who served on the court competed in the Miss Pacific Grove beauty pageant, with the winner crowned as both Queen Topaz and Miss Pacific Grove. In 1962, Pamela Gamble, Miss Pacific Grove, won the Miss California pageant and competed in the Miss America pageant.

Elmarie Dyke attended and was in the first graduating class of Pacific Grove High School in 1915. When she was a sophomore at PGHS, she acted in a musical called *The Little Feast of Lanterns*. This theater experience likely influenced how the feast would evolve under her guidance.

Elmarie, the wife of City Councilman Clyde Dyke, was the matriarch of the event until her death in 1981. She formed the Royal Court that we know today and personally selected the young women who served as royalty. Elmarie saw to it that these ladies were refined and were taught proper etiquette. Princesses of the Royal Court were named after the birthstones for each month of the year. There were years that Elmarie also selected a Princess Butterfly and a Princess Dragon. For the Diamond Anniversary in 1980, she selected twin queens (Topaz and Diamond) and twin sisters Wendy and Sylvia Junkin served as Queens Topaz and Diamond, respectively. For many years, the Royal Court was comprised of the daughters of the important families in Pacific Grove. In that regard, it was both an honor and part of your civic duty to serve your community as a member of the Feast of Lanterns Royal Court, especially if Elmarie asked you to participate.

A New Emphasis on Scholarship and Leadership

After Elmarie passed away, her family ran the Feast in 1981 as a tribute to her. After that year, the community members who stepped forward to keep the tradition alive would move the Feast of Lanterns through more transitions and evolution. In the 1980s, a formal Board of Directors was formed. The Board established that a panel of judges from the community and Feast of Lanterns would interview candidates and select eventual members of the Royal Court, rather than having one person choosing the young women who serve as princesses and Queen Topaz. After Elmarie's passing, the girls on the court themselves selected Queen Topaz by vote from the returning princesses. A third change occurred in 1987 in which the returning princess with the highest interview score would earn the title of Queen Topaz. Joni Coleman Birch was the first Queen Topaz selected by this more democratic process, effectively shifting the focus to selections based on academic records, public service and public speaking and writing skills. The board also established a scholarship fund in 1987 to give the members on the court financial support to further their studies after graduation from high school. To this day, the Feast of Lanterns continues to celebrate young women as leaders of our community. It is a long way from the days when the Feast was part of the Miss Pacific Grove beauty pageant and a huge step forward for our hometown!

In 1991, I had the honor of serving my first year on the Royal Court as Princess Jade. When I became Princess Jade for the Feast of Lanterns, I began a transformation. Being on the court shaped me into the leader I am today. It influenced me in more ways than I can describe. It was my great fortune to serve with Trisha Muench Randall, Queen Topaz 1991, and her mom, Joanie Hyler. Keeping Elmarie's legacy alive, they rekindled the general atmosphere of refinement, the lessons on etiquette and history that Mrs. Dyke had taught years ago when she ran the Feast. I remember learning about P.G.'s past as I became an "Ambassador of Pacific Grove's History." I took my role as Princess Jade very seriously. Joanie and Trisha were great mentors. I loved all the events we did as the Royal Court and I learned how to be of service to my community. I was so proud to be Princess Jade because this stone is found off our beautiful coast, unique to this area. I also had the honor of serving as Princess Emerald 1992, and was crowned Queen Topaz in 1993.

Discovering the Perfect Place to Settle Down

My family's history in Pacific Grove began in 1982, when my dad, Gordon Coleman, starting working at the Naval Postgraduate School. My parents had moved 13 times in their marriage and my mother, Virginia, felt that P.G. was the perfect place to settle down. I started Kindergarten at Robert H. Down Elementary School; my older brother Andrew was in 5th grade and my older sister Joni attended Pacific Grove Middle School as a 7th grader. We saw our first Feast of Lanterns in 1983 when Debbie Yingling Schugg was Queen Topaz.

My mother had owned a child's set of blue willow dishes and when we saw the Feast pageant, we all fell in love with Butterfly Town, USA. Joni and I both knew we wanted to be royalty one day. I marched as a butterfly in the Butterfly Parade, went through P.G. middle and high school. I feel blessed to have had the amazing opportunity to grow up in the best hometown, and to call Pacific Grove my home. During my childhood I was a musician, actor, singer, athlete, scholar and participant in student government. I was a bit of an over-achiever and loved all the positive reinforcement I received from my community. I served as drum major my senior year at PGHS and it was a huge honor to perform with the PGHS marching band. I can recall feeling so honored each time we were introduced as "The Pride of Pacific Grove." I wanted to be woven into the fabric of P.G. and be part of the town's legacy.

Serving the Feast of Lanterns as Queen Topaz was the ultimate crowning achievement for me. I will never forget that moment in the pageant when the spotlight was shining on me as I was crowned. I gazed out over the beach and wept. The Feast of Lanterns had polished me into a strong and elegant leader. The skills I learned serving on the Royal Court have helped me to create success in my adult life.

My parents served on the Feast of Lanterns Board of Directors for 26 years and my dad was president when I was queen. My mom served as secretary, keeper of the costumes and Queen Mom. They have since been named as Board Members Emeritus along with Marabee Rush Boone. They are collectively the longest-running volunteers, serving the Feast for decades. My older sister, Joni, was Princess Emerald 1985 and Queen Topaz 1987. Today she is the pageant director and has made a new

2018 Board of Directors.

2018 Feast of Lanterns Royal Court.

costumes for the new Royal Guard and my nephew, Thor Birch, served his first year as Master Rooster in 2017. I am currently president. I cannot tell you how proud I am to have three generations of my family serve the Feast of Lanterns and Pacific Grove.

More Change: Young Men on the Royal Court

Many have helped shape the Royal Court experience. In 1994, Lena Hakim Requist would serve as Queen Topaz and she introduced the illustrated storyboards, so that the Royal Court could tell the story of the pageant in greater depth. In 1998, the Royal Court trading cards, similar to baseball cards, were introduced. These collectible keepsakes, handed out at Feast events, allowed more people to learn about the meaning of the jewels on the court. In 2003, John Mothershead served as Chang and boldly printed his own trading card. Chang would be included in more events and on the trading cards in the years to come. In 2008, the Feast created its first Facebook page and joined the world of social media. In 2012, a community Facebook page was added so that more people could learn about the history and heritage of the event.

The Royal Court continues to evolve to this day. In 2016, the Board of Directors voted to add Chang as a formal member of the Royal Court. He is selected just like the young ladies are, in an interview process. In 2017, the Royal Guard was added. These young men attend all the events with the court and will receive a scholarship. Jason Kim made history in 2016 as the first official Chang. Thor Birch and Elias Yevdash became the first ever Royal Guards in 2017. Joni Birch made a new set of princess costumes a project that had not been completed at one time since Elmarie created the Royal Court in 1958. Joni also completed Elmarie's vision of the birthstone jewels with the addition of Princess Peridot. Serena Paci made history by serving as the first Princess Peridot in 2016.

In 2018, for the Diamond Anniversary of the Royal Court, Iva Heitz made a new set of costumes for the princesses and Queen Topaz. She had created new costumes

Serena Paci 2018 Diamond Queen Topaz.

Elias Yevdash Scholar Chang 2018.

Joni and Kaye Coleman 2005.

for the Feast in 1988 when her daughter, Sherry Heitz Sands, served as Princess Tourmaline. All the costumes are now fashioned out of coordinated butterfly brocade fabrics in tribute to Pacific Grove being Butterfly Town, USA. The Royal Court now has its full regalia, the traditional costumes that most people are familiar with. In addition to the new costumes, Iva made short coats to replace the old happi coats, purses to hold trading cards, and crowns out of the same brocade fabric. The costumes represent a blend of cultures just like the Feast of Lanterns itself. The main costumes are Chinese inspired while the crowns are European in heritage.

Elias Yevdash made history in 2018 as the first Scholar Chang who had also served on the Royal Guard, while Serena Paci was our Diamond Anniversary Queen Topaz. She wore a special diamond crown that was used only for this special anniversary year. Once her reign completes, it will go into the archive and will not be used again until 2033, the 75th anniversary of the Royal Court, which will be the diamond jubilee, just as Elmarie celebrated the diamond jubilee of the original Chautauqua-era Feast of Lanterns in 1980.

Celebrating the Cultural Diversity of Our Town

We are so lucky to have an event as rich in history, myth and evolution as the Feast of Lanterns. If you look at all the women who have served their community on the Royal Court, you will find leaders from different backgrounds who share the history of our area. It is rare to find an event that also celebrates and uplifts young women in the community as leaders. In this way, we are truly honoring the divine feminine and bringing greater balance to our world. I know that as the Feast of Lanterns continues to evolve, it will serve as an example for our country and the world on how we can celebrate our cultural diversity. The young women and men of the Royal Court and Royal Guard are the leaders of tomorrow, learning and teaching others about the interconnected history that we all share.

Feast of the Little Lanterns PGHS 1913, Elmarie Hurlbert, 17 years old.

Feast of the Little Lanterns PGHS 1913 Elmarie Hurlbert 17 years old.

22. co-exec directors Joanie and Becky with crown bearer Trisha and Royal Court 1981.

Serena Paci 2016 Princess Peridot.

Jason Kim 2016 Scholar Chang.

1967 Court with Elmarie Dyke.

Thor Birch and Elias Yevdash, Royal Guard 2017.

ALL PHOTOS from the Feast of Lanterns and the Hyler family archives.

Virginia and Kaye Coleman 1993.

ELMARIE HURLBERT HYLER DYKE

Ahree: How I Remember Elmarie
By Dixie Layne with Joanie Hyler

Elmarie Hurlbert Hyler Dyke with granddaughter, Joanie Hyler 1969.

The Hyler Five: Nelson William (Bill), Olive Dean, Deanna, Gail, and Joanie 1950.

Clyde and Elmarie Dyke the year of their 30th wedding anniversary 1963.

I don't believe there is a more idyllic place to grow-up than Pacific Grove—this heavenly place with its rocky coastline and abundance of flora and fauna. And tucked within this remarkable place that I considered just one big playground was my family, five generations of Hurlberts-Hylers and Ernst-Deans. It never occurred to me as a child how lucky I was to be surrounded by a family who is and was so much a part of the fabric that makes Pacific Grove our hometown.

My parents, Bill and Olive Dean Hyler, raised their three daughters, Deanna, Gail, and me, in the same house on 19th Street where my great grandparents on the Hurlbert side lived and raised their children, Elmarie and Elgin. My grandmother, Elmarie, also lived in this house with her two boys, Bill and Bob, after their father, Nelson Hyler, died. My earliest memory of my paternal Grandmother Elmarie was of her and Grandpa Clyde Dyke living in their home on Lighthouse Avenue. This house has since been moved to Surf Avenue—they used to do that back in the day, move houses when they wanted to use the lot for something else. My maternal grandparents, Ted and Gladys Ernst Dean (Gladys was Nana to me), lived

Elmarie and her granddaughters Deanna, Gail, and Joanie 1953.

in a large house on Forest Avenue, just a few houses up from Lovers Point. I was a lucky girl to be surrounded by so many generations of family—grandparents, uncles, aunts, cousins, and siblings—in this most remarkable small town.

My sisters were four and seven years older than me, which made them teenagers when I was a child and left me to have my own childhood experiences and memories. I remember spending the night at Nana's house and her tucking me into bed, our baking cookies, and her hugs. Then there was Ahree; I don't know why my sisters and I called our paternal grandmother Ahree, other than she didn't want to be called grandma. Maybe as toddlers Ahree was our best pronunciation of Elmarie.

'The Whirlwind Grandmother – a Force of Nature'

Anyway, as a child I remember Ahree was the grandmother who took me to concerts and the theater where we would go backstage and everyone knew her. We also visited museums and galleries, and then there was that most memorable trip to Yellowstone—just the two of us. She was always interested in what I was learning at school, and she gave me a Samsonite train case and suitcase for high school graduation. I don't remember that there were ever any family functions at her house, never a meal served—well, maybe she made us soup, simple things sometimes. She wasn't much of a cook. No, she was the whirlwind grandmother; she was always about something. Elmarie was a force of nature.

I was eight years old when my grandmother began working on the one thing for which she would be most re-

Costumes were a big part of Elmarie's life and here she managed to get her brother Elgin in this getup 1963.

Elmarie Hurlbert Hyler Dyke on the pier just before show time. 1967.

membered by generations of Pacific Grove residents who knew her then, and know of her now. My grandmother Ahree was Mrs. Elmarie Leslie Hurlbert Hyler Dyke—matriarch of the Feast of Lanterns.

You'd think there would have been quite a hullaballoo around the house when Mayor Frank Shropshire asked my grandfather, Councilman Clyde Dyke, to chair the city's revival of the Feast of Lanterns, but I don't remember anyone being all that excited about it. Grandpa Clyde was a smart man, and as committee chair he immediately asked his wife, Elmarie, to join the committee, and she agreed—for just this first year. Then the mayor suggested his wife, Helen, could also assist the committee as she just happened to be the director of the Miss Monterey County Pageant, which was part of the Miss America pageant. The original Feast of Lanterns committee was comprised of primarily city department heads, my grandmother, and the mayor's wife. I think we all know who ended-up getting the job done.

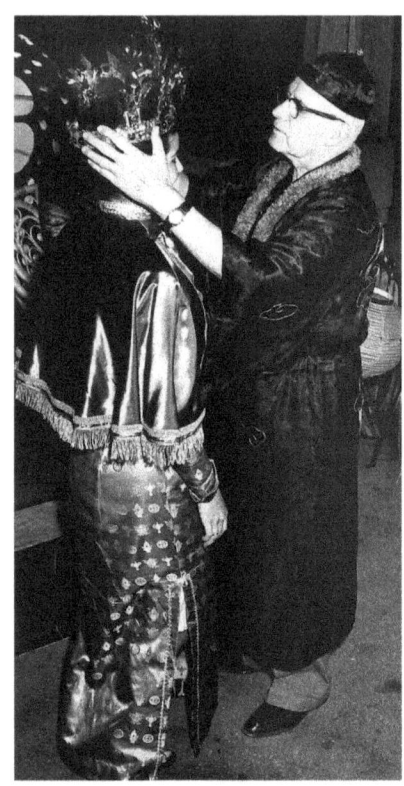

After receiving the coronation crown from the first crown bearer Joanie Hyler, Clyde Dyke gently sets it upon Queen Topaz's head. 1958.

A proud City Council with staff after voting to revive the City's Feast of Lanterns 1958.

Water Ballet in the salt water Plunge at Lovers Point 1958.

Feast of Lanterns Committee Meeting in Dyke's Drugstore. Who remembers the soda fountain? 1958.

As you'd suspect, my early memories of the Feast of Lanterns are limited, but there were some standout moments for this eight-year-old that are probably not much different from those of many young girls who attend their first Feast of Lanterns and meet their first Royal Court—I just happened to have a front row seat. I remember Grandpa Dyke asked me to hold the queen's crown; thus the tradition began—I was the first crown-bearer. I remember I was up on a balcony with the queen and there were lots of people below us. I was scared, too shy to say or do anything—just hold the crown. I was in awe of the queen; she was very nice and smelled good.

Elmarie ran the show from her make-shift desk on the pier. 19xx.

'Fully Immersed in P.G.'s Summer Festival'

The older I get the more I remember about the Feast of Lanterns, like the go-cart races down Alder Street and the synchronized swimming in the plunge at Lovers Point. By the time I was 11, I was fully immersed in P.G.'s summer festival. My oldest sister Deanna married in 1960, so she wasn't all that involved in it. I was in 7th grade the first time my sister Gail was a princess. I was a freshman at Pacific Grove High when she was crowned Queen Topaz in 1965. I was so excited and proud of her. I know now that from 1958 through 1964 the queen and princesses were selected from the Miss Monterey County contestants, but after the Miss Monterey County Pageant was moved to Fresno, Elmarie began selecting the Royal Court from P.G. High School students and recent graduates. Her criteria: their family must be actively engaged in the community. No one questioned her judgment.

Don Gasperson FDP.G. fire chief and firefighters are assembling the Torri Gate.

Elmarie, executive director of the Feast of Lanterns with future Queen Topaz 1965 Gail Hyler and future executive director 1981 Joanie Hyler posing inside Dyke's Drugstore 19xx.

I remember Herb Miller and his orchestra played music on Lovers Point beach with the great stone wall as their backdrop. Later that evening I went to Nana's house on Forest Avenue with my family. We went upstairs and from there we had a perfect view of Lovers Point. Until I graduated high school, this is where I joined my family to watch the pageant on the pier every year. Elmarie was always on the pier with the Royal Court. Then there were fireworks. I learned sometime later that my father had made the first mortar boxes for the fireworks. The P.G. Fire Department's Don Gasperson built the torii gate and Roger Brown of the P.G. Fire Department shot the fireworks off for many years. It was a hometown thing.

Go cart races down Alder Street.

Gail Hyler is crowned Queen Topaz 1965.

By the time I was in junior high, I had become quite a help to Ahree and I really loved being part of everything. Whenever my grandmother needed help, I was there to help her. Whether it was loading or unloading things for any of the many events, stuffing envelopes, selling lanterns, helping at the Lovers Point barbecue, or selling souvenirs and fireworks buttons, I was there to help. One year I even rode in the 4th of July parade as Princess Amethyst because my sister Gail couldn't make it. That was the year Vicki Samora was Queen Topaz.

Joanie Hyler recruited her friend Mary Opagh and cousin Ginny Edelen to help sell lanterns 1964.

As my high school graduation neared I began to wonder if I would get to be part of the Royal Court like my sister. I brought this up to Ahree one day and was surprised by her response. "You're not princess material." Her reply bewildered me; I wondered what she had meant. At first I thought it was because as a young girl I was such a tomboy and by the time I graduated high school I was a hippie. Nevertheless, until I graduated high school I was by her side, helping and volunteering. Even after I married in 1969, I continued to help.

I was so proud of my grandmother for all she accomplished. I was and am particularly proud that she was in charge of the Feast of Lanterns, that she had created this wonderful festival and managed it for 23 years. The community looked up to her. That's not to say I didn't take ad-

Joanie Hyler steps in as Princess Amethyst when her sister was unavailable to fulfill her duties. 1964.

Elmarie is delivering the Royal Court's chairs to the pier for Pageant Saturday.

vantage of her position in the community and mine as her granddaughter. I'd drop her name whenever it would take me where I wanted to go—like onto the pier during the Feast of Lanterns or backstage at a concert. "I'm Elmarie's granddaughter" was a fantastic VIP pass.

Elmarie's last hand-picked Royal Court 1980.

Joanie Hyler, co-executive director Feast of Lanterns 1981.

From 'Not Princess Material' to 'The Show Must Go On'

In 1981, just months before the Feast of Lanterns, my beloved grandmother died. This caused lots of discussions to take place in City Hall and throughout Pacific Grove: What do we do, cancel it? Who can possibly step up to manage this tiger? And this is when I began to understand—I was executive director material like my Ahree. I was her mini-me. I had been training for this most of my life. I was not princess material. I don't think she thought the handoff would be so abrupt—but here was my destiny.

Co-executive directors Joanie Hyler and Beck DeSmet with crown bearer Trisha Meunch and the 1981 Royal Court. Three of the princesses were selected by Becky and Joanie to complete the court that Elmarie had selected in 1980.

Bill Hyler, Elmarie's son narrates The Legend of the Blue Willow 1981.

#21: Becky DeSmet, Queen Topaz being escorted to the coronation on the pier by her father Hector DeSmet. This was the first time the Mandarin costume had been worn. 1975.

I called on my friend Becky DeSmet to ask her what she thought should be done, because she became Elmarie's Feast of Lanterns assistant after her reign as Queen Topaz 1975. We talked and decided we needed to do this to honor Elmarie. As Elmarie would have said, "the show must go on." So we picked up the torch, or in this case a lighted lantern, and began putting together the festival.

Jackie DeSmet, Princess Toumaline 1981 – she who would have made a wonderful queen.

As has always been the Hurlbert Hyler tradition, the family and extended family pulled together. Becky and I were named co-executive directors, my daughter, Trisha Muench, served as the crown bearer, my father, Bill Hyler, was the pageant narrator, and my mother, Olive, was the treasurer. And for all we did in 1981, I have but one regret—we did not name Becky's sister, Jackie DeSmet, Queen Topaz that year. We thought it best if we waited until next year, but next year never came.

The swan boat made it to the pier from the marina under the watchful eye of the Coast Guard. If anyone is wondering why there was a power outage and my dad, Bill Hyler, had to come to the rescue — check out the electrical wiring in the foreground. 1981.

I know Elmarie was with us every step of the way because there was definitely an angel riding with us that year. She was riding shot gun in my 1972 Chevy Blazer as I set out to deliver all the tabloids across the Peninsula. My poor truck almost collapsed under the weight; new shocks were required after all the deliveries were made. And then there was the near sinking of the swan boat. The swan boat was escorted to the pier by the Coast Guard from the Monterey marina with our honorable boat rowers, Franz Limper and Joe Krantz, at the helm. The swan boat served as a not-so-reliable mode of transportation for Queen Topaz and Chang's escape from the pier that evening—luckily they made it to dry land without incident. It was on the swan boat's return trip to the marina when the Coast Guard declared the swan boat "no longer sea worthy." I believe that was the last year the swan boat was used by the Feast of Lanterns.

Since 1981, I have continued to volunteer to help with any number of Feast of Lanterns activities, from selling lanterns and serving salads to acting as a Royal Court judge and serving on the Board of Directors in 2009, 2017, and 2018. I was Queen Mother in 1991 when my daughter Trisha Muench Randall was Queen Topaz. The Feast of Lanterns is in my blood.

I Remember Elmarie button 1981

Queen Mother Joanie Hyler with Queen Topaz Trisha Muench 1991.

The Mandarin, Bill Hyler, ready to make his entrance 1991.

THE LEGACY OF ELMARIE

Elmarie Hurlbert Hyler Dyke left quite a legacy. She served on innumerable committees and organizations, and received countless awards and citations for her decades of work and community service. My Ahree was named by the Chamber of Commerce the city's official Mrs. Pacific Grove and was named Honorary Fire Chief by the P.G. Fire Department in 1966. She was quite a woman, and her accomplishments legendary—she left us so much more than the Feast of Lanterns.

Elmarie was a member of and performer at the West Coast Chautauqua Assembly, president of the Pacific Grove Retreat Association, a 1915 member of the first graduating class from Pacific Grove High School (now P.G. Middle School), a 1918 graduate of the San Jose Normal School, now San Jose State University. She taught music and art at Pine Street School (now Robert H. Down Elementary School) and for 32 years she was superintendant of the Monterey County School District comprised of over 30 schools spread throughout the county.

Elmarie, Honorary Fire Chief with Don Gasperson, Fire Chief FDP.G. riding in the Good Old Days parade.

Elmarie dressed in costume for what is sure to be a festive occasion on the pier.

During WWII she started the local chapter of the American Red Cross and was the first councilwoman to serve on the council for the City of Pacific Grove. Elmarie was a member and president of the Native Daughters of the Golden West. During her tenure as president she created the official standardized design for California's state flag that was approved unanimously by the State Legislature in 1953.

She was director of entertainment for the Monterey County Fair and founder of the Monterey Concert Association. As its director she brought such performers as The Vienna Boys Choir, The Von Trapp Family Singers, The Robert Joffrey Ballet, and Metropolitan Opera baritone Robert McFerrin to Pacific Grove. In doing so, she broke many racial bearers and norms that performers of color experienced across the country. Elmarie worked with Rev. Nance of the First Baptist Church to remove the restrictions that limited homeownership to one neighborhood for the African-American community in Pacific Grove. She also hosted her own daily radio program, "Then and Now with Elmarie."

Elmarie with Vice President Gerald Ford 1974

Mrs. Pacific Grove lunched with presidents and governors and was a life-long friend with Chief Justice Earl Warren. She loved Pacific Grove and Pacific Grove loved her. Upon hearing of her death, her city ordered its flag lowered to half staff and the California State Assembly adjourned in her honor.

© Dixie Layne 2018

Elmarie Leslie Hurlbert performing at a Girl Scout Jamboree.

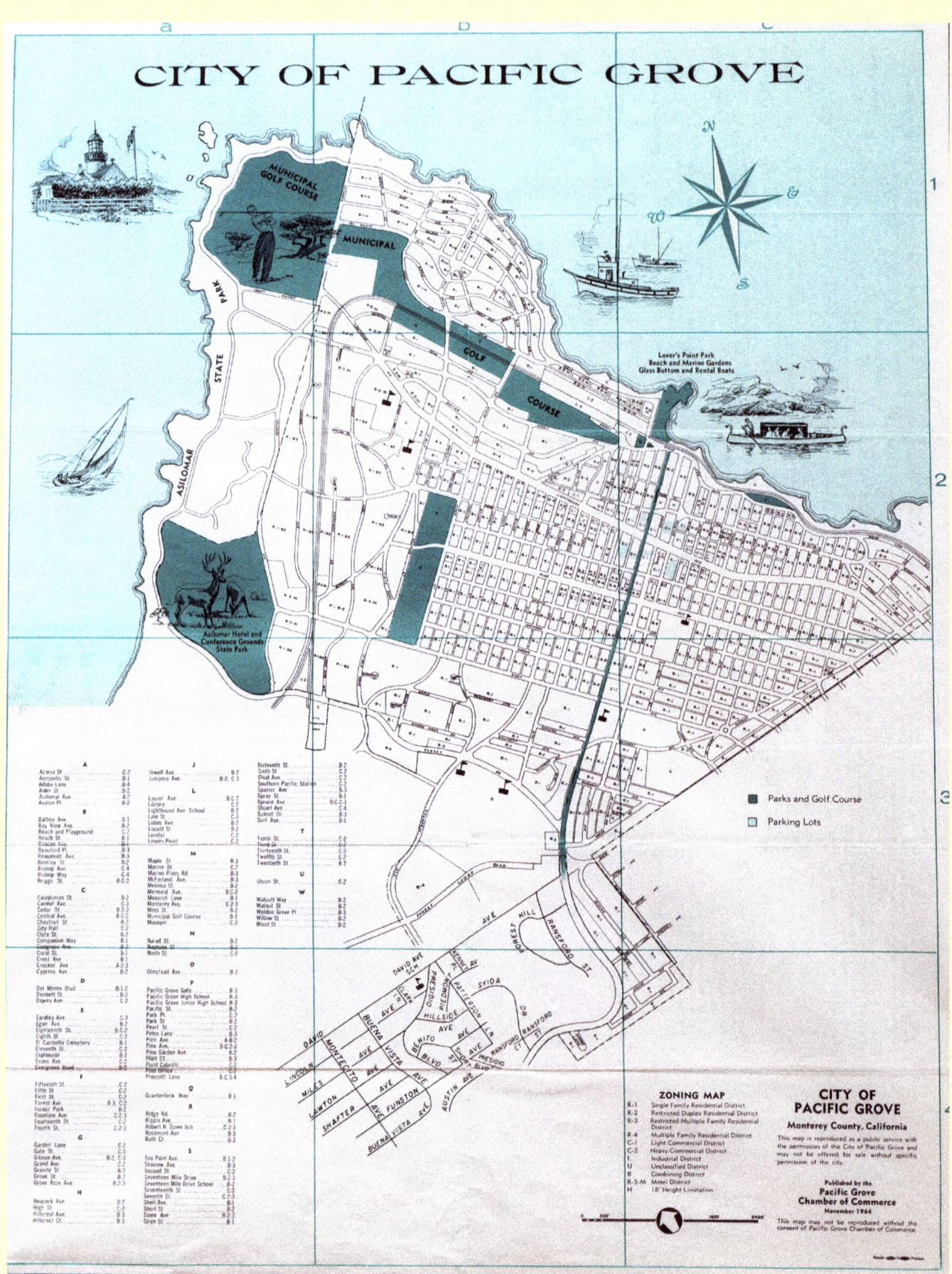

1964 Chamber of Commerce City map.

SECTION TWO

THOSE HIPPIE, TRIPPY 70'S

"Pacific Grove - P.G. - Pagrovia - and Pacific Groove."
– John McCleary

Photo Peter Mounteer.

LOOKING BACK: P.G.'S WILD HIPPIE DAYS – JOYCE DAY MEUSE

I found Pacific Grove in the early 1970s. My first trip here was in the spring of 1972. Some of my close friends with whom I shared a house in Maryland had come out to California earlier and landed in Pacific Grove. I had no idea how important this little town would become to me and what a significant role it would play in my life.

Much of what I fell in love with then still exists. The beauty of the coastline never ceases to inspire me. The weather changes often and we do have to put up with the marine layer more often than some of us would like. But it rarely gets too hot like almost everywhere else in the country. I wouldn't trade our fog for the heat and humidity the rest of the nation endures.

Life has changed so much. Back then we had no cell phones, no computers. Sometimes I am astounded that we were able to organize so many events, festivals and protests using the limited tools of the time. We had phones, of course. And local radio stations that played our music and publicized our events were indispensable. Word of mouth was always very important, as were posters and fliers on bulletin boards.

We were part of a divided nation then as now, but it was more along the lines of generations than by politics. You were either one of the normal people, or part of the counter-culture. I'm sure in many places there was greater variety of distinctions, but from my perspective you were either one of us, or a member of the clueless silent majority. There were so many of us who were young and rebellious and ready for big changes. We felt powerful and inspired to make a better world.

Finding Pacific Grove was a miracle to me. I didn't know the whole community, but finding so many of what we called "long hairs" in one place seemed outstanding. The place was incredibly beautiful with so many colorful flowers and lush landscapes, but beyond the physical beauty were many friendly, kind people. People would nod and say hello like they still do. If there is a problem most people will try to help.

It was easy to identify our soul group of hippies, as we were similar by age, dress, food and values in the seventies. Long-haired guys, often with beards, and long-haired women in loose-fitting blouses and colorful skirts. Bras were optional.

Although most in my circle were children of the middle class, mentally we embraced an idealistic, classless philosophy. We believed in equality and fairness. The military-industrial complex waging war in Vietnam was bad. Corporations were bad. Community was good. Sharing was valued. Support, love and affection for one another was indispensable. Being a part of something bigger was inspiring. Most of us were bonded through the wonderful music of the time. Crosby, Stills and Nash, Neil Young and Joni Mitchell and so many others spoke for us. That music still has the ability to transport me back in time to the wonderful days of being young. It really was the most fun decade that I have experienced. I'm glad I was there and often wish those times had continued.

My old friends from our original commune in Maryland had a house on David Avenue. In addition to Tommy and Carol, Sandy and Karl and Donnie from the old commune back east, there was new friends, including a young single mother named Wendy and her adorable toddler, Aaron. Most of us were totally enamored of that cute little guy. None of us had considered having babies as far as I recall until we met Aaron. He inspired many of us to have our own babies. I can count ten between the small group of us who started out together, including Wendy, who had three more after she raised Aaron.

One of our group, Karl, got an actual job as a janitor at the Pacific Grove Art Center. The rest of us did a variety of things to fill our time, including odd jobs like housecleaning, gardening and whatever came our way. With so many of us sharing the rent and expenses, it was easy to get by. Another of our daily occupations was what is now called dumpster diving. It seemed a shame the amount of good food that was just thrown away every day. We had a regular route to check the local dumpsters behind the grocery stores for still-good produce and other goodies. It sounds unappealing now, but we recovered food that was still good once we gave things a cleaning, trimming and cooking. Interestingly they just passed a law in France prohibiting the throwing away of good food, but instead donating it to those who need it.

In those early days we were one of many other communes that were sprinkled around town. There was a contingent of followers of a guy named Louie who lived in one. He had been a part of the Monday night class in San Francisco inspired by Stephen Gaskin. There were certain things that came along with that group like the staring thing, looking into someone's yes for extended periods without blinking. It was never comfortable to me.

Brown Rice, Whole Wheat Bread and Artichokes

So much of what began in the 1970s was a turning away from how we'd been raised surrounded lifestyle and diet. By the time I reached Pacific Grove, I'd discovered a new world of whole grains and vegetables. We usually had either brown rice or millet with a salad, rescued-from-the-dumpster vegetables, and whole wheat bread and butter. We embraced a vegetarian lifestyle but some of us were not too strict about it. If I was invited to dinner I'd eat whatever was being served. At the house, we had a long table where we'd sit cross legged on the floor to share our meal, beginning with an extended Om.

I still remember the first time I ate an artichoke. I had never seen one before. I pulled a leaf and started trying to chew it. That didn't work out so well. Tommy noticed my distress and kindly showed me how to scrape the artichoke meat off the leaf with my teeth. And I was shown how to get to the heart of the artichoke and devour the tasty center. Melted butter and mayonnaise added to the exotic thistle making them less healthy but much more delicious.

There were a couple of good health food stores in the area. Whole Family Foods and the Granary were my places to shop. The first one was a little shop near Cannery Row before the Aquarium made the area so congested. I met a woman, also named Joyce, who worked there. She and I were both pregnant with our first child when we met. She had grown up in Pacific Grove and had family and friends in abundance. We went on to be very good friends and she was my midwife when I had a home birth.

Buying groceries at the health food store was an adventure. There were bins of grains and beans to scoop into jars and bags. There was the world of herbs for tea and medicine that I was exposed to for the first time. Eventually I went on to work at the herb store in New Monterey originally called Feng Shui and I learned much about healing.

Baking bread was often a part of life in those days. Learning to use yeast and spending time making a sponge of dough, letting it rise, punching it back down, adding more flour and letting it rise again was very tactile and satisfying. Many of us had the *Tassajara Bread Book* guiding our early steps into the wonderful world of baking bread. *Ten Talents* was another vegetarian cookbook that explained how to make delicious and nutritious food without animal products.

Sandy and I were living with our guys in a tiny railroad flat on the bottom of a large, old Victorian home divided into apartments. We had the ground floor apartment. Sandy and Karl shared the living room as their bedroom, and Michael and I had the regular bedroom. Two doors led to the outside. We were only a half a block to the Monterey Bay. Sandy and I took walks along the still functioning railroad tracks for the train that traveled from Sand City to Pebble Beach to pick up the precious, fine grained white sand and take it back to go to places around the world.

That tiny kitchen was where I learned to cook. Sandy would encourage me with her kind and wise directions. "How big should I chop this?" I would ask. "As big as you'd like," she'd say, which blew my mind. I didn't realize how much choice went into cooking.

One of my first community feasts was at a potluck at Margot's house. For the party we made some very fancy loaves of whole wheat bread. We took the dough and rolled it out and filled it with nuts and raisins and cinnamon. Then we rolled the loaf back into shape and baked it. The bread turned out beautifully.

Margot asked us if we'd like to make pies for her restaurant, Tillie Gort's. Since we were earnestly trying to be vegetarians, we proceeded to make pies without eggs or dairy. One that I remember was a delicious date pie from the *Ten Talents* cookbook. We would spend hours making the crust with only whole wheat flour. We never used sugar; honey was our sweetener. We would take our pies over to Tillie's and get paid out of the till. At one point we sat down and figured out exactly how much we were making per hour. It came to about 25 cents an hour once we split the profits. That was the end of that project.

Karl ended up getting a job at Tillie's as one of the cooks. We shared our little apartment until I was nine months pregnant. Sandy and Karl moved out into their own place in the Wilson Hotel. My partner Michael and I rented a floor of a large divided Victorian house on Pine Avenue.

Having Babies the Natural Way

My first child was born in the hospital. I was in the pancake house with my close friend Sandy eating french fries and drinking Cokes in honor of my impatient frustration with still being pregnant after an endless nine-and-a-half months. I went into labor just as the noon whistle blew in Pacific Grove. Hurriedly I went home to get ready. I had learned Lamaze breathing patterns to ride the waves of contractions as they built up strength and frequency. It didn't take long for me to want to get to the hospital and settle in for the duration.

Michael and I headed up to the hospital in a borrowed VW bug. Every bump in the road triggered another contraction. When I arrived at my first-ever visit to a hospital, I told them that I wanted no episiotomy, no drugs, and don't give the baby a bottle. I wanted as natural a birth as possible. The nurse looked at me sternly and told me to just stop making demands.

Michael was a great coach. He knew just how to encourage me. I used the Lamaze breathing with every contraction. It was an earnest and challenging few hours. Sandy snuck into the room once or twice as I could only have one person with me. I had my peacock feather to use as a visual aid to focus on while breathing through the contractions. We went into the delivery room and I got down to real work. By the time I pushed the baby out, I seemed to be sitting over my body looking down at myself giving birth. I think the hours of deep breathing had put me into an altered state. My beautiful, wonderful son Orion was born.

In Pacific Grove a group of people had started the Birth Center to help folks deliver their babies at home. There were mostly women and a few men who trained to be lay midwives. Interestingly, that Birth Center is still operational and I see it on Facebook. They specialize in water births now. That hadn't yet become a thing when it was time to have my second baby. I had started to train to be a midwife but found myself pregnant again. My theory was that baby beings stay close to pregnant women and newborns. If you even have the thought that you might like to have a baby, it is easy to find yourself pregnant. I said a few times I'd like to have another baby someday. Well, someday came immediately.

I don't have the facts around the beginning of the Birth Center other than when I needed them they were there. I asked my friend Corina to be my midwife. They usually came in pairs to home deliveries, if possible. The pregnant moms would go to a meeting once a week and be checked by the midwives. I did get to attend a few home births other than my own.

At the first one, it was just the laboring mother, the dad and me holding the birth book wondering what to do. At the very moment the baby started crowning, the midwives walked into the room just in time to catch the baby. Another friend had the first water birth in Santa Cruz County and I got to attend it. It really was a profound and amazing experience. The mom had previously taken my psychic healing classes. At one point she said push it down, and the midwives started pushing on her belly and she said no, Joyce, bring the energy down. I visualized golden light surrounding the child and saw the whole golden ball of light coming down the birth canal, and the baby came with it.

I made it through my nine and a half months of pregnancy and, like my first birth, the baby took his time. I expected to give birth early in March, but it was a long wait until March 20. My first boy was an Aries, although I had wished for a Pisces girl. This time I really wanted a Pisces girl, like me. On the second to last day of Pisces I had a friend give me a polarity session. This was a form of energy healing and my hope was that it would start my labor. It did, but not quite soon enough. I went into labor the last day of Pisces. I had a half a dozen friends join me for the birth. My mother-in-law June drove in from King City to be there. She took it on herself to take care of the almost two-year-old Orion while I labored and her son,

Craig, the baby's dad, stayed with me through the endless hours. June would run in and out of the house since she was so freaked out by what we were doing without a doctor, but she couldn't leave.

I labored all night while my friends fell asleep. I remember poking Craig in the ribs when he would fall asleep. If I was awake he had to stay awake as well. A storm began with wind and rain blowing hard outside. The blustery storm outside finally ended and the sun came out at dawn. After almost 24 hours of labor I no longer cared if I gave birth to a girl or boy, Pisces or Aries. We finally delivered our new baby boy, who we named Shone. It happened to be dawn on the first day of spring. He's been a blessing to me and his family and friends every day since.

Blissed Out on a Spiritual Path

When I left the East Coast on the day after Nixon was re-elected for his second term after the Watergate break-in, I gave up on being a political activist. I decided that the better path would be to pursue a spiritual lifestyle.

The book *Be Here Now* by Ram Dass was my first exposure to the teachings of the east. He wrote about his own guru whom he had found on a trip to India. The book encouraged people to stay in the NOW, this present moment, and to stop living in their heads, in planning for the future or dwelling over thoughts of the past. The goal is to stay focused on this moment, this breath, what is going on in the surrounding universe. These teachings contributed to some of our most cherished practices, like chanting the Sanskrit word Om for long extended moments. When done in a group it was unifying and connected us with the present moment.

My next step on the spiritual path came through the inspiration of my long-time friends Sandy and Karl, who had moved to the desert in Palm Springs. They started taking the mail-order lessons composed by the Indian guru, Parmahansa Yogananda, through his organization, Self Realization Fellowship, based in Los Angeles. I picked up his book, *The Autobiography of a Yogi*, and devoured it cover to cover. As George Harrison famously said, "There is a miracle on every page." Just reading Yogananda's prose about his life and training in meditation opened my heart and transformed me into a spiritual seeker.

Just as I was about to sign up for the SRF lessons, Sandy contacted me again to let me know that they had been to see a teacher who represented Guru Maharaj ji, known at that time as the 13-year-old Perfect Master initiating people in what was called Knowledge. It just so happened on that same day one of Maharaj ji's Mahatmas was speaking at the local college. I went and watched a movie about the guru and his devotees at a festival who were blissed out after lining up and kissing the feet of the master. I decided I wanted what they were experiencing. I met some of his followers who had an ashram in Pacific Grove and I started attending their programs. I ended up in Felton where one of Maharaj ji's Mahatma's was initiating people in the practice of Knowledge. We promised to attend satsang, where devotees would take turns describing their experiences of being on the path. Satsang, service, meditation and darshan was the way to follow the path. He promised us the Peace Bomb. He would bring peace on earth. Still waiting.

The other thing I did was to attend the festivals that Maharaj ji would hold throughout the country. It was inspiring to be a part of thousands of people who sat and listened to various speakers and live music until the highlight of the event when Maharaj ji would speak. He would be dressed as Krishna, the hero of the Indian holy book the Bahagavad Gita, and would dance a bit before he left the stage. Everyone would be blissed out, our term for being in ecstasy, for the rest of our time at the festival.

At the very end of the 1970s I found myself learning psychic meditation as taught by the Berkeley Psychic Institute. This type of meditation focused on the chakras, the seven main energy centers in the body. We learned visualization to clean out the chakras, then how to use different colors to "run energy." I went on to teach classes in psychic healing and psychic meditation. Those classes were wonderful and former students continue to make up some of my closest friends. Having those high energy experiences really bond people together.

Love and Laughter

The first time I ever saw Josh Gogarty, my boys were going to school at Robert Down and the principal, Mrs. Holmquist, had a tradition of the fifth graders doing a May Pole dance every year. This year Orion was taking part and I went to watch. There were not an equal number of boys to girls, so one young guy, Josh, was dressed in a negligee and had a wig on his head and played the part of a girl. He was so high energy and all of us parents who were watching were greatly entertained by his wild and fun-filled antics. The laughter was uncontainable. Josh went on to become best friends with both of my boys at different times. He's become a successful actor, musician and an artist. His talent was obvious from the first time I set eyes on him.

I lived in a wonderful house in Del Monte Park in the mid to late 1970s with Craig and my boys. It was a ranch style, three bedroom, one bath home with a nice large living room and a yellow kitchen. The large yard had a white picket fence and a large acacia tree covered with yellow flowers that had a rope swing. We lived next door to the landlord, Father Charlie, a well-known figure in the alternative spirituality community. He had converted the garage into a modern and lovely home for himself. Charlie was a well-known and beloved person. He had performed my wedding to Craig and he was our landlord on Mermaid Avenue. He suggested we move into his rental house on Buena Vista. We had a great number of years there.

Dance, Music and Full Moon in Scorpio

Along with several friends I participated in a belly dance class once a week in the living room of our home. Marie, our teacher, was an excellent dancer and performer. We danced in a circle to lively Middle Eastern music on cassette tapes. We wore colorful scarfs and jingly belts as we practiced the energetic movements imported from an ancient culture. It was great fun and continued on at a couple of different locations throughout the years. We felt it was a life-affirming and women-supportive activity. This is when I met the two belly dancing Barbaras, tall Barbara and short Barbara, who were both accomplished performers and ended up being great friends.

One year I decided to have a music and dance party with the full moon in Scorpio. I welcomed the intensity and high spirits of that full moon. We had many musicians on guitars, congas and hand drums, plus a wailing female saxophone player as well as some other exotic instruments, like a bagpipe made from the body of a goat. The wine was flowing and the potent sinsemilla was freely shared. At that time I felt a spirit of camaraderie still left from the hippie era, enhanced by the beloved herb.

One guy who was happy to be there was Jose, a daily customer from Tillie's who also trained in the local Aikido dojo despite having a congenital heart defect. He was thin and slight and loved women, although he never had much of a chance with them. He was an artist, an aficionado of the mantic (secret) arts of magic and a devotee of Alistair Crowley, the famed, so called "beast" from the early years of the 20th century. Knowing that I was fond of tarot cards, he presented me with a copy of the Crowley deck, a colorful deck with astrological symbols. I still use that style deck now.

Many of the belly dancers wore their shiny costumes with their finger cymbals clanging to the beat of the music. Everybody seemed to be having a good time until one of the female guests pulled me to the porch to tearfully complain about catching her husband kissing another guest. I duly tried to comfort her the best that I could until I could return to the high spirits, loud music and frenzied dancing of my party.

Suddenly Jose collapsed on the floor. I thought he was dead. A friend, John, joined me at Jose's side. The chaos was intense. Over and over I kept yelling, "Stop the music!" John was simultaneously shouting, "Keep playing!"

Finally, the most gorgeous of the belly dancers, Chris, in her skimpy dance costume, dropped to the floor and grabbed Jose in her arms and held him close to her generous, sparkle-covered chest. Jose opened his eyes and came back to consciousness. I figured that being clasped to the breast of a gorgeous women was too good of a chance to miss. We helped him to his feet and gave him time to recover with a cup of coffee and some TLC. I still tread lightly when the full moon is in Scorpio.

Meeting Her Mock-up in the House on 17th Street

During the 1970s my boys were in grade school at Robert Down. We lived for a time in a beautiful old Victorian owned by the husband of a friend of mine. When I had gotten evicted from the house I lived in on Buena Vista, I asked Bob if I could rent an apartment. He said yes, and we moved into that great house on 17th Street. It had a side yard with a driveway and a garage, high ceilings, a stone fireplace and a kitchen with beautiful clay tiles. Bob was so kind. At one point he told me he was reducing the rent by $50 a month because he liked having us there. It was unheard of for a landlord to reduce the rent. He also never got freaked out by the activities of the wild pack of boys who were always around. One summer they spent their vacation digging a hole in the yard. They were so industrious and spent weeks digging that expanding hole. Eventually they filled it with water from a hose and it became a giant mudhole. I'm so glad my kids were free to express themselves, growing up natural and unhindered without the distraction of screens. We didn't even own a television for many years.

It was at this house where I met my soul mate and life partner, Peter. I used my new psychic skills of visualization to ask the universe to send the right partner to me. I had specifics that I wanted to assure astrological compatibility. I would meditate daily and send my wish list out to the universe. After this seven month-long ritual, I met Peter, a friend of my roommate, in my kitchen. I asked him if he were a Scorpio. He said, "Yes." I said, "You're my mock-up." He said, "I'm no mock-up, I'm Peter Meuse." After 38 years I'm still a believer in astrological compatibility. Peter is a talented musician, singer, teacher and performer. There is never a dull moment in our household.

Thanksgiving Family: A Circle of Love

One of the couples from Tillie's, Caren and Russell, hosted an annual Thanksgiving gathering every year for more than 30 years. The food was incredible with so many of us foodies preparing dishes to share. Beyond the usual traditional dishes like vegetarian-style gravy and dressing, we savored any dish you could imagine from salads to incredible desserts, especially Sweet Earth pies.

There were people of all ages, mostly boomers and their kids, but also a few older folks, parents of some of us. Before we ate, we held a gratitude circle outdoors. Everyone got a chance to say what they were grateful for as we went around the circle. It took a long time for everyone to speak, and meanwhile the food got colder and colder. We were all happy for the yearly chance to share in that circle of love.

The festivities didn't end on Thanksgiving. The party continued through Friday and Saturday with games, eating, chatting, hugging, laughter, and sharing of confidences throughout the weekend. The babies became kids, then teenagers, then brought their own sweethearts and eventually their own kids to the party. Even though the original hosts split up, Caren continued the tradition even up until now. Many of us have gone away, some have died, others have dropped off. But it is still a special feeling when we still get together and share that heart connection that began back in the wild and wooly days of the 1970s.

Preserving Memories with Photographs

The photography of John McCleary helped preserve our memories. He was the quintessential hippie and philosopher. He spent a lot of time at Tillie's working, playing and writing. He attended all the gatherings and was an excellent photographer. He did a yearly photo of the employees and friends at Tillie's. Those photos capture many of us at a pivotal time in our lives. If you ever ate at Tillie's I'm sure you saw some of his work on the wall. Tillie's closed its doors recently after 49 years as a cornerstone gathering place in our town. The memories from those times sustain me still. John McCleary has written several books, including the wonderful *Hippie Dictionary*, for which you can find a page on Facebook.

Some of the people I started out with in Pacific Grove who went back east have returned to the area and we have continued our friendships. Sandy, Carol, Wendy and I meet for coffee weekly at a local coffee shop. Margot, who was my first landlady and old boss at Tillie's, now owns the Bookworks with her daughters. It is a popular spot for locals, tourists and a place for old friends to gather and feed our souls with conversations and shared memories.

John looked at me recently and commented, "We're all starting to look alike." Scary thought. I hope we will continue to be here for each other through the years ahead. Once again we are gathering for protests against the current toxic political atmosphere, worse than anything we encountered in the 70s.

It comforts me to remember how lucky I am to have found my hometown, my paradise by the bay, Pacific Grove.

Photo Peter Mounteer.

A Head Start on California Dreamin'
John McCleary

I was born in California in 1943, so I had a head start on "California Dreamin'," the counterculture, and hippie ideals. After working in L.A. in the advertising and music industries, I "dropped out" in 1967 and soon moved back to the Monterey Peninsula, where I had grown up and gone to elementary, middle and high school.

When I came back to the Peninsula in 1972, I immediately found Tillie Gort's coffee house and restaurant right here in Pacific Grove. I worked there as a cook, dishwasher and wait staff.

During the years between 1967 and the mid-1980s, Pacific Grove could have been, technically, the largest hippie commune in California. We had our own coffee houses; our own radio station, KAZU; an organic grocery store, The Granary; the P.G. Art Center; a recycling center; and nude beaches. And if you counted the number of people living as hippies, albeit in separate and revolving houses and relationships, we would have constituted the largest population of the counterculture in the smallest space!

'The Johnny Appleseed of Hippie Businesses'

It can be argued that the ecology movement started here, and that the recycle logo was created here. Gil Tortolani is credited with creating it. He started a recycling center, Tillie Gort's and The Granary. He was the Johnny Appleseed of hippie businesses on the Monterey Peninsula.

The Monterey International Pop Music Festival itself was enough to make Monterey a center of hippie rock and roll. Joan Baez and Bob Dylan wrote songs in Sancho Panza coffee house in Monterey, and they lived together in the Carmel Highlands.

Tillie's, as we all called it, had the most beautiful waitresses, and so diverse, that any retail shop could boast. Margot, Jan, Rosie, Barbara, Blair, Candice, Jill and Mindy, to name a few. Guys came to Tillie Gort's to sit and drink a cup of coffee for hours while they watched and flirted with their favorite hippie waitresses.

Cooks and waitresses were often dating. On a slow Sunday with no customers, my girlfriend and I disappeared into the back for a while. As we came back into the coffee shop, straightening ourselves up, two tables full of customers, wide-eyed, waited to be tended to. A girlfriend and I were working a Saturday night; we were tired of the same ol' food we had cooked and served for months, so we ordered pizza. The guy came in with our pizza and an odd look on his face. The customers looked up with shocked expressions. We just smiled and said, "Over here, how much will that be?"

I posted a hand-written sign in Tillie Gort's only bathroom, a one-hole affair for employees and customers. The sign read, "Limit: 20 People!"

We actually believed that the old world had become a new world. A place where people were people, not numbers, not just "yes people," not resigned to mediocrity and a minimum wage life.

Finding a Home at Tillie Gort's

Tillie's served food as well as coffee, and in the early 1970s the menu was a mixture of vegetarian fare and roast beef, turkey or tuna melts in Arabic pocket, pita bread.

To answer the question before it comes up, as it did hundreds of time while I worked there: where did the name come from? Tillie Gort's was a take-off on an old nickname of the owner, Gil Tortolani. In high school, the kids called him "Gillie Tort," so when he opened the coffee house, he mixed that up and named it Tillie Gort's. I would love to have been there when that name was thought up. It must have been a real stony evening.

When I first walked into the place, I knew I had found a home. You had to have been there in the late 1960s and early 70s to know how comforting, and also stimulating, a good coffee house could be. You could sit there and be yourself alone. Or sit there and be yourself in the company of strangers, soon to be friends. Or friends, soon to be lovers. Or you could sit there and be somebody else alone.

The first woman who waited on me at Tillie's became my lover, and we eventually traveled to Mexico, Guatemala and Europe together. Later, after I became a regular customer, I once was served a sandwich with a bite taken out of it. The waitress said she was just sampling it for me. And she oddly enough was just a friend and never an intimate.

Coffee houses at the time were the gathering places for all the political dissidents, folk singers, poetry writers, astrologers and lovers. One guy used to come in and sit by himself with a cup of coffee every day for three or four hours. He did that for ten years. He may have read; I can't remember. He never made eye contact, he never bothered anybody, and he never drooled or talked to himself about little green men.

One day in year eleven, out of curiosity I said something to him. He answered me rationally; we had a conversation, and he turned out to be a very intelligent person. From then on, we acknowledged each other. He started coming out of his shell. He struck up conversations with people and even developed friendships.

When you walked into Tillie's, you could expect to have five or more sets of eyes turn to see who you were. Coffee shops were for the most part social gathering spots.

You went there to get out and see and be seen. You could sit at Tillie's for five hours and see all your friends. When I came back to P.G. after a trip of three to six months, as I did often, I would go to Tillie's to get reconnected to what was happening locally.

People played chess and painted on the paper plates; passing travelers would play guitar and sing for enough tips to buy a salad. There was always a dog or two waiting outside the door and several bicycles. I started my habit of writing in coffee houses at Tillie's.

I worked as a cook off and on for maybe two or three years. It was never more then subsistence living, but then, it was easer to live on four hundred dollars a month in the early 1970s. I once got a pay envelope with a note saying I owed Tillie's money because I signed for more food and beer than was covered by my pay.

The Changing Mood at a Coffee House

A coffee house is one of those places where the mood or tempo can change rapidly and often. If you work at a bank or gas station you know what to expect, that each day is going to be pretty much the same, except perhaps for the occasional robbery. When was the last time you were stimulated in an escrow office or enlightened by something while shopping at an auto parts store? Coffee houses create situations. Is it the caffeine? Is it the natural brown sugar? Is it the presence of chessboards, real art on the walls, or newspapers in more than one language? Is it the people who are working there, and who want to be there in spite of everything?

It's a bit of all of those factors. A coffee house is a milieu of spontaneity percolated by caffeine, and the social aspects of sitting and drinking a warm comforting beverage with friends. It is a petri dish of creativity germinated from a sophisticated and cosmopolitan atmosphere. It is a fermentation of political views gleaned from intellectual expression. It is a good place to learn new words like those in this paragraph. It is a good place to find a boyfriend or girlfriend.

When working in a restaurant and eating most of your meals there, as I did at that time, it doesn't take long before you get bored with the menu selections. So we started experimenting. These employee experimentations often eventually ended up on the menu. My contribution was a bagel and ham sandwich, which made it to the menu for several years. It was indeed a strange combination, considering the number of Jewish employees and customers who religiously ate there. As a goyim, I secretly called it the "Auschwitz Special," but only to my Jewish friends who would get the dark humor.

By the time I started working at Tillie's, it was owned by a lovely young woman named Margot. Much of the atmosphere of the place was created and maintained by her management technique and her attitude about service to the public. As a young single mother in need of help traveling across the United States, Margot had been befriended by a nameless waitress in a no-name cafe somewhere in the middle of nowhere. Margot remembered that warmth and friendship, and from that moment on, it was her desire to create that atmosphere for others who might need a bowl of warm soup or a person who would listen.

It is hard for me to fathom or to explain how someone who was so low profile could have such an effect upon the personality of a business, yet Margot made Tillie's what it was. She produced a space, set up a menu, hired good people, left them alone and created an icon. I often fearfully wonder what my life would have become had it not been for Margot Tegtmeier and Tillie's.

I am convinced that no other period of time created more interesting people or spawned more bizarre stories than the hippie era. This adventure into the life of a coffee house on the coast of California is by no means a diversion, for it brings this whole hippie culture into perspective. Whether it was Amsterdam, London, Moscow, Crete or San Francisco, the people who became hippies came from every culture in the world, and they met at tearooms, coffee houses, bars and restaurants to talk amongst themselves, read poetry, play music and concoct some form of revolution. For the most part, the hippie revolutions were meant to be non-violent.

Where Are All the Old Hippies?

The hippies of Pacific Grove have not all overdosed or died on the streets, as many people thought we would. As a matter of fact, percentage-wise they have exceeded expectations of other, more conventional populations. Aging hippies can be found in every segment of our society. There are many good lawyers, educators, medical doctors and practitioners, librarians, gardeners, retail workers and shop owners, local politicians, artists and writers, what I call the soft industries. Not many of them are in what I call the hard industries, such as military, law enforcement, venture capitalism, arms dealers and hit men.

If it weren't for old or nouveau hippies, we wouldn't have any astrologers, legitimate massage therapists or acupuncturists!

Throughout the 1970s, Pacific Grove was the home of many interesting people. Gordon Andrews, one of the most progressive humans to walk the earth, came to us from a commune he helped start in the Hot Springs area of New Mexico. Gordon was educated, I believe, as an urban architect, of all things. He brought midwifery to P.G., which became one of the largest and most active birthing communities in the state. At the time, hospitals were having a staph infection epidemic, and percentagewise more newborn babies died in hospitals than at home births. Gordon was an early ecologist, planting trees in our parks, and he talked-up water conservation and healthy eating habits. During all this he made his living as a city planning architect, designing downtown Monterey and Carmel parks, parking and street configurations.

We had many other interesting and progressive folks living among us: Don Mussell, the barefoot radio engineer who started KAZU, and helped build and maintain KRML, KUSP and KFAT, which became KPIG; Jeff Helwig, a music and vinyl expert who also drew some of the finest hippie art for posters and newspapers; Joyce Meuse, our astrologer; Jay Chaffin, our spiritual muse; "Digger," our historian of Native Americans; and "Digger," our beach boy/volleyball player. We also had our Cannery Row luminaries, such as Kalisa Moore at her namesake restaurant. You haven't lived until you've had Kalisa's coffee at three in the morning. John Harris and Alan Weber at the 812 Cinema; artists Art Guerra and Bruce Ariss, and too many more special people to fit in this short story.

Beach volleyball was happening in P.G. in the 70s just as it was taking off in Manhattan Beach and Santa Barbara. I thought I was going to teach the locals a few things when I came back to P.G. after my ten years on the Southern California beaches, but they were already well-versed in this leisure sport.

Soviet Hippies Then and Now
When the Russians Came to Town

Back in the 1970s we sometimes called it Pacific Groove, our little town on the tip of the Monterey Peninsula. The word "pacific" in Spanish means peaceful or calm, and, of course, "groove" is an old jazz term meaning good. As "groovy," it means something to be appreciated.

This area of the Pacific coast attracts many people for its beauty, but through the decades it also drew many others as a center of music and the hippie culture.

And then in May of 2018, the Russians came to Pacific Grove.

They were not the first Russians, the last, or the most numerous, but they may have been the most interesting. They were Russian hippies.

In the 18th and 19th centuries, the Russians competed with the Spanish and English for control of the western edge of the North American continent. The Russians came specifically to hunt for adventure, sea otter pelts, trade routes, and new lands to settle.

This time, in 2018, the Russians came looking for their heritage, but not from the 1700s and 1800s. They came looking for their 20th century hippie history. California is to millions of people around the world a spiritual and cultural center, and these travelers were looking for the home of the hippie culture.

I happen to be part of that cultural history, so they contacted me and asked if I would join them on their pilgrimage through California. They were planning to fly into San Francisco, tour the Haight–Ashbury district, and drive down the coast to Culver City for a conference and an exhibit on Soviet hippies at the Wende Museum of The Cold War.

Why me? In 1972, I had published a photographic essay of counterculture people in California, as well as across the United States and in Europe. Called simply *The People's Book*, it was released by Celestial Arts of San Francisco, also the publishers of twelve of my posters.

Influencing an Entire Generation of Soviet Hippies

Imagine my surprise when on May 18 of 2018 I received, quite out of the blue, an email from one Juliane Fuerst, a sociology professor at Bristol University in England. She introduced herself as a historian of the Soviet Union who had been researching the Soviet hippie community for many years. She wrote:

"You might not have known that there was such a thing as Soviet hippies, but they knew quite a bit about you. One of the *People's Books* you produced in the early 1970s made it in a mysterious way to Leningrad and caused a whole generation of Soviet hippies to imitate its style."

She invited me to come to the opening of the Wende Museum exhibition and participate in a panel discussion with one of the Soviet hippies—all expenses paid—and finished with, "My Soviet hippie friends would be thrilled."

Of course, I responded right away: "I would love to attend your gig in L.A.!" I also told Juliane about my later publication, *The Hippie Dictionary: A Cultural Encyclopedia of the 1960s and 1970s*, published by Random House.

More emails flew across the continent and the Atlantic, details of time, place and accommodations. When I told Juliane that I was now living in Monterey, site of the groundbreaking 1967 Monterey International Pop Music Festival, she became very interested in having the delegation make a stop here on their way from San Francisco to Culver City.

Little did the Soviet hippies know that they were soon to visit a place where the dream of social order was almost, and mostly, achieved. They were coming to Pacific Groove!

Few hippie communes are left intact in California or elsewhere. Yet the philosophy, attitude and hope still exist in many of us. We are not commies or pinkos like we were accused of being when the hippie movement was new 40 and 50 years ago. We are patriotic Americans, yet we are liberals, intellectuals, free thinkers and humanitarians. Welcome to the coast of California.

The Russian Hippies Arrive in Pacific Grove

On May 30, 2018, the Russians arrived in Pacific Grove. I showed the Soviet hippies the stage at the Monterey Fairgrounds where so many legendary acts performed, and then took them to Tillie Gort's restaurant for lunch and to see the photos on the walls of 46 years of hippie culture in Pacific Grove.

The stage at the Monterey County Fairgrounds is arguably as prestigious as the Palais Garnier in Paris, Carnegie Hall in New York, and the Tropicana in Las Vegas. To begin with, it is home to the longest continuously running jazz festival in the world. Almost every jazz, blues, country, and rock & roll artist has played there. Billie Holiday may not have performed on that exact stage, but she did sing at the Jazz Festival prior to the existing stage being built.

Then on a magical weekend in June of 1967, the Monterey International Pop Music Festival came to the Monterey Fairgrounds. The Mamas and Papas, The Who, Jefferson Airplane, Grateful Dead, Simon and Garfunkel, Buffalo Springfield, Otis Redding, and more legends performed on that stage. Jimi Hendrix famously burned his guitar, and Janis Joplin was introduced to the world that weekend.

California is the melting pot of the melting pot of the world, and the Monterey Peninsula is the melting pot of California. Add to that, California is one of the most productive and creative places in the world. Add to that, the Monterey Peninsula is one of the most beautiful places in the world. Add to that … well, you get the picture. The California air is most beautiful here!

We, that is, some of us, have a tendency toward a superiority complex. But on the other hand, because of our liberal status as a blue state and a higher than average IQ, we are at least philosophical about our status.

Californians are not openly arrogant. We actually tend to be even more welcoming to tourists, new residents and new ideas than we should be for our own good. But we also know that diversity of thought and of ethnicity is good for us as a community!

The thing that was most enlightening and precious about my meeting with the Russians was the verification, confirmation, justification and ratification of the spirit of peace and freedom, which is found in all countries and in all people. Too often, it is hidden underground by necessity. I also learned that persecution has no boundaries.

When I was told that my first book, *The People's Book*, released in 1972, had helped generate a freethinking counterculture in the Soviet Union, I was first "blown away!" Then I recognized how appropriate it was.

Author's Note: Tillie Gort's coffeehouse/restaurant closed on Sunday, June 1, 2018, at 3:00 p.m. It was more than the end of an era, and yet it was not the end of anything. So many searching souls, lost souls, and new souls found their future within its walls, with the help of its coffee and friendships.

Some of this piece is excerpted from *Common Sense Again*, one of John McCleary's new books in The Hippie Trilogy.

Front cover of *The Peoples Book*, by John McCleary, published in 1972. Blueprint and influence for the hippie movement in Soviet Russia in 1976.

Peace sign of people in Russia, 2015.

A hand made peace sign created for the Hippie Dictionary by John Ramsden (Random). 2002.

Peace sign of people in Russia, 1980.

76 *Life in Pacific Grove, California Book 2* STORIES OF AMERICA

Joan McCleary, Alik (a Soviet hippie), and John McCleary at a conference about Russian hippies at the Wende Museum of the Cold War in Culver City, Los Angeles area, June 1, 2018.

PHOTO ESSAY

1970s P.G. Hippie Community and Local Festivals

2018 Russian Hippies Visit

JOHN MCCLEARY, photographer
JOAN JEFFERS MCCLEARY, editor

A Soviet reproduction of the John and Yoko photo, 2015.

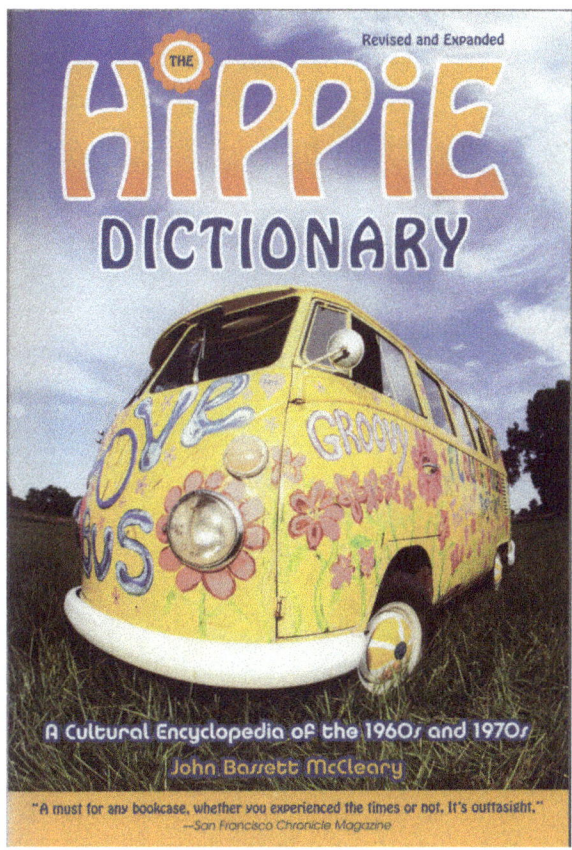

Front cover of the *Hippie Dictionary,* by John Bassett McCleary, published in 2002, revised and expanded in 2004. A cultural encyclopedia of the 1960s and 1970s.

TILLIE GORT'S RESTAURANT
"The place to be in Pacific Grove"

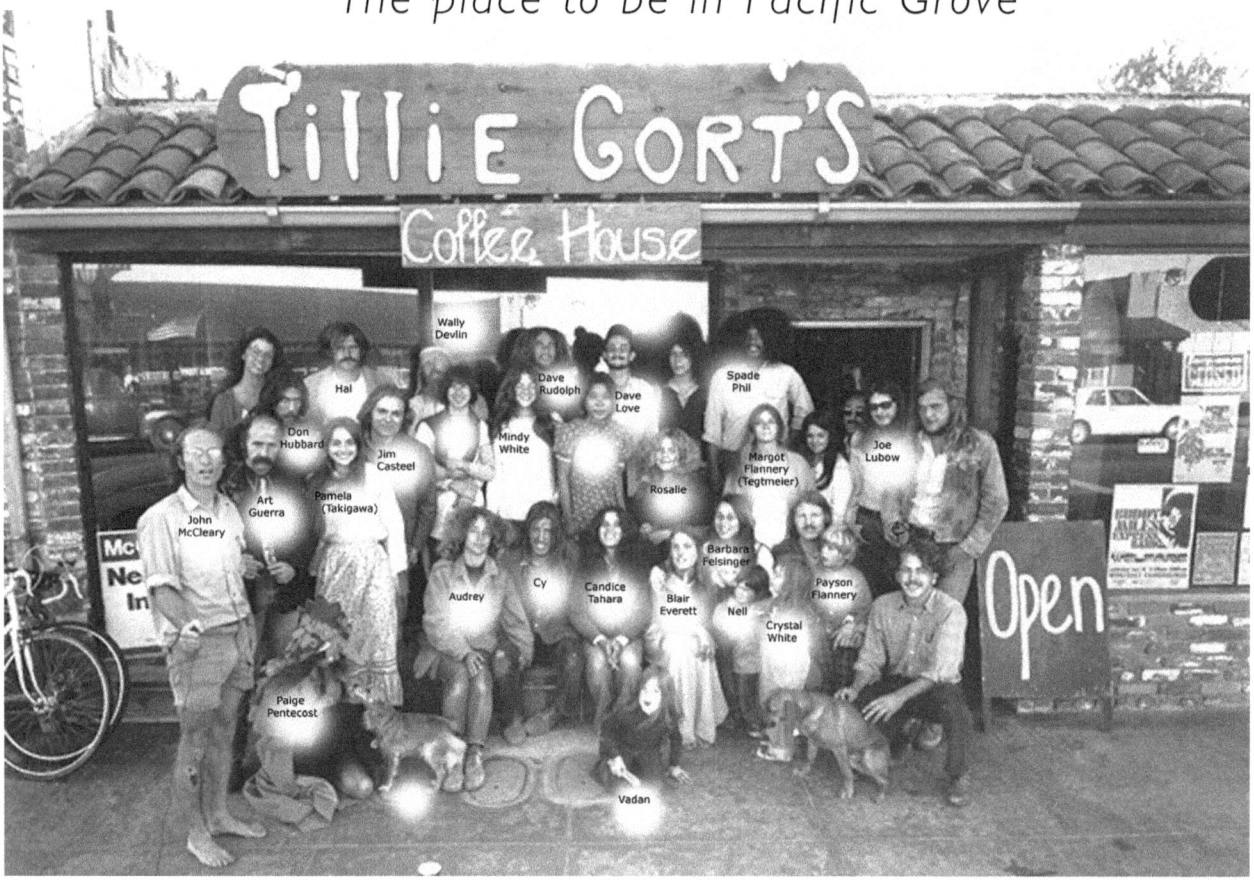

First Tillie's photo, 1972.

The first Tillie Gort's and New Family Breakfast on Asilomar Beach, 1971-72. Lisa Miller and Blair Everett are in this photo.

Self-portrait of photographer John McCleary as a cook at Tillie's, 1974.

Anniversary reunion of Tillie Gort's staff in Carmel Valley, 1999.

John Random and Tillie's first owner, Gil Tortolani. John made most of the tables for the new Tillie Gort's in 1969, and they were still in use in 2018.

Tillie Gort's 2009, the 40th anniversary photo of many old and new friends.

A POPULOUS CALIFORNIA HIPPIE TOWN

Party at Ellen Brownstein's house, 1974-76. These people were the foundation of a family, a commune, a human element that cannot be classified.

The Granary workers standing at their images in the mural. Granary was pre-Whole Foods co-op grocery.

Some of the "Row Rats," 1971-72. Some lived in abandoned canneries.

John Miller, John McCleary, and an unknown boy with the Salvation Navy truck in 1972.

Party of related and unrelated sisters and brothers in P.G. Marie O'Rielly, Valerie Dallas, Peter Meuse, Joyce Meuse, Sherard Russell; Shirley Polovy, Unknown, John McCleary; Russell Hicks, Caren Hicks, Aaron Hicks, Mike Hicks

Paige Pentecost and her daughter Vaden, at home. Vaden is one of the Peace Kids.

Dave Love and Karl Dobbratz, impromptu music at Tillie Gort's, 1972-74.

Peace Card, photographed in one of the abandoned canneries on Cannery Row. The small blonde girl in the middle is Vaden Pentecost.

Michelle Barrett and Sally Higgins planting trees in Washington Park, during a reforestation project started by Gordon Andrews: midwife advocate, urban architect, and psychedelic aficionado.

Staged photo of "Mexico City – 1935". Taken at 135 19th St. in P.G., with a nude girl wearing bullets, Bob Divale, and other unrecognized people, 1960s-70s, unknown photographer.

Art Guerra behind the Boat Works, our favorite nude beach in P.G., 1972. Art is now a well-known artist and character Back East.

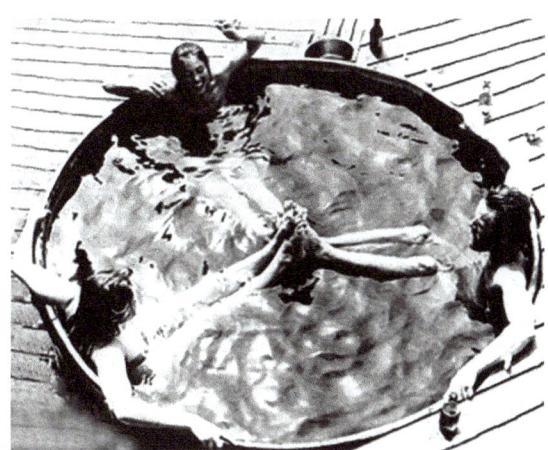

Mary's hot tub—a place to be yourself! Upper 19th St., P.G., 1980-84.

STORIES OF AMERICA

Life in Pacific Grove, California Book 2   83

editorial

In a grand philosophy, the world is filled with beings learning to be creators. Artists in evolutionary stages of development. Beings constantly experimenting with various forms of expression, using their means and talents in the painting of their realities. → Page 3

THE STUDIO
Composition Compliments of Catherine Holliday & Anne Johnson

KEEP THIS COUPON 295807

"A generation that ignores history has no past—and no future. You live and learn. Or you don't live long."

PRINCIPLES:

Julian C. Bartee
Marti Kirby
Kirk D. Osgood

OUR STAFF

PUBLISHER . . . . Kirk D. Osgood
EDITOR . . . . Marti Kirby
CO-EDITOR . . . . Julian C. Bartee
ASSOCIATE EDITORS:
COMPOSITION . . . . Catherine Holliday
ENTERTAINMENT . . . . Shoshana Rene
SPACE, TIME and
  BEYOND . . . . . . Mary Ann Stacy
ART and CULTURE . . . . David Thomas

PHOTOGRAPHIC and LAB WORK by:
                          John Turek

CONTRIBUTING WRITERS:

    Kirk D. Osgood
    David Thomas
    Karen Celso

The PAGROVIAN TIMES is printed by:
   THE PACIFIC GROVE PRESS GROUP

            PAGROVIAN TIMES
            Box 931
            Pacific Grove
            California 93950

            408/373-6510

MANY OF THE FINE PHOTOS IN THIS
ISSUE COURTESY OF THE:

PAT HATHAWAY COLLECTION

CONTENTS

LETTERS	16
COMMUNITY BILLBOARD	14
EDITORIALS	3
NINA CATRINA	
ART NEWS	6
RESTAURANT REVIEW	15
MENU OF THE MONTH	

PLEASE LET US KNOW IF THERE
IS AN EVENT YOU WISH PUBLISHED:

WRITE TO:

   COMMUNITY BILLBOARD
   PAGROVIAN TIMES
   Box 931
   Pacific Grove 93950

Information page of the *Pagrovian Times*, newspaper of the Pacific Grove hippie community, early 1970s.

.One of the gardeners at the community garden between 18th and 19th Street and Lighthouse and Central, late 1960s-early 1970s.

Cannery Row graffiti, a P.G. alternative high school photographic project, 1972.

The garden was once a church, which was once the Garden of Eden.

Communal household on David Avenue, 1971-72. Top, Sandy Dobbratz, Karl Dobbratz, Gail, Wendy Logan, Tom Berg, Joyce Meuse. Don Gray, Patrick, Aaron Erwin, Carol Berg, Laurie Patton.

House on 19th Street in P.G., what we called Tortilla Flats back then, in the 1970s. J. B. Rose, on the right, was our most popular local rock 'n' roll star for years, who played and sang at the Halfway House and other bars on Lighthouse Ave., New Monterey. JB could drink a can of beer in under four seconds.

The Heritage Corner
For a few, where it all began...

For a few long time residents, this building on the corner of Union and 16th is where it all began. For T. A. Work Jr., Miss Virgin's Sanitarium, as it was known then, was a birthplace. While home-birth was most common in the early 1900's, with the assistance of a mid-wife a few deliveries were made in Miss Virgin's Sanitarium, although sanitariums were usually centers for recuperation and healing of breathing ailments. At a time when business was slow, Miss Virgin must have branched out.

Photo by Lance Iversen

A famous house on lower 19th Street in P.G. Home of many artists during the 1960s and 70s, the place were the Mexico--1935 photo was taken. T.A. Work of Work Lumber was born here early on.

Community Center High School's geodesic dome near the playing field behind the Middle School, 1972-73.

Monterey State Theatre poster 2007.

Gene Elmore, creator of the original Monterey Jazz Festival chair and trumpet logo.

Top tunes of the era—KLRB in Carmel.

MONTEREY POP, JAZZ & BIG SUR FESTIVALS

One of D.A. Pennebaker's five portable 16 mm, sound-synchronized cameras that made the Monterey Pop movie possible. They were technology that D.A. created himself, which contributed to all future music videos and made MTV possible. Used with permission JM.

D.A. Pennebaker, director of the Monterey Pop Festival movie, accepting his Oscar from Al Franken, 2016. D.A. earned his Oscar for his life's work, for his revolutionary sound-sync cameras, and for creating the music festival genre, thus creating the music video phenomena. Photographed by the Oscars' photographer. Used with permission JM.

Joan Baez and a young boy at the **Big Sur Folk Festival**, late '60s to early '70s. John Jeffers, photographer. Used with permission JM.

Photographers and friends at the P.G. Art Center for a Weston Family Retrospective, 1999. Henry Gilpin, Janet Gordon of Gold Leaf Frame Design, Will Wallace, Cole Weston, and John McCleary. Unknown photographer.

Jimi Hendrix and girlfriend just outside Monterey Pop Festival buying flowers at The Flower Market on Fremont, 1967. Photographed by Elaine Mayes, who didn't know who he was. She thought he was an interesting looking person. Used with permission JM.

PACIFIC GROVE 1974 – BILL MINOR

My Pacific Grove: Here We Find Both Our Food and Love Pleasant

1. MY PACIFIC GROVE

I think of the writing that follows as an entertainment of sorts: a sweet and sardonic summer (even in winter) joy ride, a homage. In the year 1971, when my family (my wife Betty and two boys, Tim and Steve) and I arrived to live in Pacific Grove, California, my life became merry and mad in a way I'd never quite experienced before. I had a job teaching at the local college, and I took delight in riding my bike around the coast to and from work. I enjoyed the peace of mind and the calm those journeys provided: the "Pacific part" of our new home. To heck with the Grove, at least for the moment. Let's start with the ocean.

That is what brings one here. Peaceful, peacemaking, provoking or tending to the making of peace leading to peace—yes, my O.E.D., I've found my conciliatory place and like others, came to this by U-Haul after, in my case, five brutal winters in Wisconsin: a snowbound brandy lad once singing the blues: "Midwestern people, poor, decided, pure/—opposed to travel anywhere—/never go crazy, they just stay there." That work was mine. But no more of it. Goodbye hard truth. I'm all set now for small town tradition and tourist dreams and illusions. Hello Chautauqua! Attend the convention—sing psalms of praise! To this pacific place I've packed the kids, cat, wife and books, and arrive now like a lover at .005 cents a foot, U-Haul ...

2. GOOD HEALTH

Like the Beach Boys I behold in love, or sex, or merely pretty girls—an appropriate fiction, a metaphor for universal flux and California. I flux, you flux, everybody flux flux. The girls on the beach all jog within reach. Here, we are all quite obnoxious in our health. Philosopher George Santayana was struck, while living in California, by the deep and nearly religious affection which people had for nature, and the athletic rightness of their response: living as nature does.

However, he also found us emptier than the Sahara where the Arabs, he understood, had some conception of Fate or God. So he left. Comparisons are odious. Besides I'm not a stranger here. I've been here before—years ago, on my way to go camping in Big Sur. The difference I now find is a nuance, a color. We can't always count on the sun and, despite what others may think, we're often obliged to wear clothes. I like my body here. I like the subtle threat of miracles. Who watches your life? No lifeguards, no nose cone attendants with obedient knees. No Band-Aids, salami sandwiches, or stolen bread disallowed once you enter the water. Aside from a leash law pertaining to dogs, I have yet to find a discouraging rule ...

3. FAMILIES

"An olive leafe he brings, a pacific signe." The O.E.D. again. Not belligerent, peaceable. Of peaceful disposition. This "Pacifick and harmless temper ... an ocean relatively free from violent storms." Matthew Fontaine Maury, the father of modern oceanography and a relative of mine, spoke of "a dry season on the pacific slopes."

I take to sand. Asilomar. It isn't Coney Island nor even Santa Cruz, but we fill the space on fog-free days. The families. Mothers wear yellow and white. Fathers all have sallow beards. There are exceptions. This man in a cowboy hat and bright vermilion pants. His hip hugger wife has a push button navel. Both their bellies are round as globes, and oceanography. A two foot halfback cuts wide, into the ocean. "Out of bounds!" his father screams. His mother, a lady with pale blue legs, watching, interrupts the rhythms of her T'ai Chi dance. Hand in hand, a woman with turquoise hair, cerise pantsuit and heels, comes up the beach with her granddaughter, who wears the same.

They've come from a torte in Carmel and stopped here for a whiff of the ocean ("Would you believe I'm eighty-two?" "Hell yes."). A Coors commune, a family. The males all look as if they'd just come down from the Yukon. The women look as if they'd waited. A teen mother with snarled braid and baby sits in fatigues and pared jeans, a poodle tied to her foot. She has a Chuck Atlas husband, so perfect he nearly goes unnoticed, aside from the tattoos.

In the sand plant sewage, unknowing, kids play. Dogs wallow, knowing exactly what is there. It's hard to tell who loves that shit the most. "Git out," the mothers yell, and fall asleep. Here come the warriors! A band of brats with pails on their heads, Saran Wrap shields, robes that look like stolen green peignoirs, and black capes. They perch on dunes. The battle begins—to the crunch of ice plant (that peach and elephant flesh stuff, each blade an erection, pea pod, a man's unsharpened knife).

In a field all things are jealous. The kites! High in the air, from the hands of fathers and children, they spring. Black, with large yellow bulging eyes. Purple, with flower petal points. One is transparent, braless. Another is shaped just like the shield of a Japanese policeman. There a triangular goldfish flushed with stars. I send our own kite up--an endless three spool flight that rises in great blue yelps of air, in a hurry, I think, to free itself from us. Both boys run off to play.

Later, on my knees, I reel in string. The knot that tied the first spool comes, with mocking ease. The second knot takes centuries. The kite comes: a small bright yellow handkerchief snotty with sky and perfection. The spool grows larger than vision. The kite dips, stutters, and stands … Seven feet left, at the end of string, it crashes on its own into a dune. My sons run back, for pieces. "What happened?", they ask, in chorus. "A kite," I say, and rise from more than knees, a pound of prayer in hand—and all that string.

4. THE GROVE

The beach is where we eat tacos and refried dreams. The beach is where we watch and dream, too much. But I'm sick of this beach—Pacific. I've got nothing but sand in my hair, wind in my ears, and flesh on my mind. I need a Grove. The Grove is where we all go home. Help me O.E.D., complete my whatever poem. Graf. Grot. Grave. Grawe. Groave. Grove. A small wood. A group of trees affording shade or forming avenues or walks, occurring naturally or planted for a special purpose. There, deities were honored by a heathen people. We, instead, believe in telephone poles. We love our out-of-ground wires. 'The birdes may them hiding in the grawes Wel frome the halk.'

We took a home on Funston Street. It's a small affair, pre-fab, put up in no way, perhaps, a home should ever be. But it does afford shelter from wind and sand and flesh. The landlord lives next door. He is generous and kind and brings zucchini, trout, venison, large humps of lettuce, baseball tomatoes, even wood—at welcome intervals. Most perspicacious of all: he leaves us alone! For neighbors: an electrician, butcher, greens-keeper, carpenter, retired Army, computer salesman, a stripper who (each Thursday morning) empties her garbage in the nude, a Scotsman who (on Sundays in his bathrobe) plays bagpipe out on the front lawn.

Our area, our Grove, our turf, is largely concrete. The driveways are crammed with second and third and fourth cars, campers, boats, partially dismantled motorcycles, large retirement dreams. Windows are filled with empty Michelob bottles, bowling trophies and nervous daughters. Each garage is a shrine: lined with power tools, canned goods (for the apocalypse), plumbing fixtures, abandoned plants, dirty rags, nail jars, electrical wire, abandoned hi-fi and TV sets, garden shears, gargantuan grills, lawnmowers, family photographs and other forgotten memorabilia, grease-encrusted fathers and sons who kneel before engines. "They who live sheltered and flourish in a little grove of their own kindred."

My wife has a green thumb but doesn't need it. Whatever wishes to grow does so here, even near the ocean (that foggy residue of Steinbeck's fertile valley). Along the fence, in pots sometimes sunning are: geraniums, Marguerite, hydrangea, jade plants, chrysanthemums, poinsettia, nasturtiums, and tough strange and vaguely obscene succulents, each looking as if it were a refugee from the New Mexico desert. These and other sturdy things grow in our blue collar grove …

5. THE SAGE KIT

This is California, so I've decided to settle in and become a sage. I found a sage kit in a small shop in our neighboring place, Cannery Row—for just five bucks. For some reason it seemed largely made of ferro-cement boat fragments. And little cards. The cards were like those you use in Monopoly. You turn them over one at a time and they tell you what to do with your life—maxims. Here are some sample items:

ITEM #1:	Be a forester, alert on light soil, Abraham beneath an oak, a man aware of his girth and needs.
ITEM #2:	If that doesn't apply to you, then be a woman.
ITEM #3:	Eat sea otter; they're cute.
ITEM #11:	The sea doesn't wish to change, it simply has to.
ITEM #13:	The world is God's own teat; chomp on it.
ITEM #36:	When you go to an aquarium, take a skillet.
ITEM #69:	The quality of change is equal to the verve dispensed at birth.
ITEM #72:	Appease yourself with vermouth and yoga.
ITEM #73:	Self-loathing can be assuaged with aspirin.
ITEM #74:	Turn both left and right.
ITEM #75:	Go straight ahead—but be alert for deer crossing.
ITEM #83:	Good ladders have no rungs.

6. MY PACIFIC GROVE

Tide pools, and household heaters. They're all the same to me. I'm not a sage, so I shall settle for my human beach and home. I settle for where I am: Pacific Grove. I choose both synergy and the right to be alone. The ocean sounds like a snarl of foam, a freeway. A seal's shadow speeds through waves. The sea at night is filled with green neon. A phosphorescent glow. Girls on the beach play skip rope with a long loose love muscle of kelp. Sand plants and Indian red algae. Sardine tins. Molecules of cement and fog. The ghost of Ed Ricketts, laughing. Gulls eat Golden Bear potato chips ... What surrounds us is complex enough.

We're only as much, or as little, of it as we need. Praise for the village I carry in my head! It is a good one—Pacific Grove. It's filled with everything I've filled these pages with. Here we find both our food and love pleasant. We crack, like otters, shells on our bellies. Like sea lions we flop on the rocks and sun. We honk our human horns at night and make noise. We trouble no one with what we know, not enamel birds or tire-gray seals. We have few skills, but those we have are fully possessed. We make bean bag chairs and music. We are not obstinately attached to either success or error. We seldom, if ever, check the mail.

When we walk, we seldom ask where. We have not yet learned about weight and measure. We have no truck with conventions or congress or conspiracies. We know that one system of nonsense is the same as another. No laws. No money. No plumb lines. No tallies or official seals. One pot, one lawn, one barrel holds as much as another and if not, who cares? We've heard of villages beyond our own and look forward to meeting with them, but not with envy. We like ourselves and our neighbors. We love natural eccentricities. We like to look at our own, and other's spouses.

As for myself, I walk through this village dispensing stories and songs and poems, but I am not the only bard. My stuff is well received, though no one sees fit to praise me for it. I am one of those necessary happy mad persons who pays taxes and dues but forgets how much. And I get paid too, although I cannot remember that sum either and haven't checked my salary since 1936, the year of my birth. I tell people what they already know. Their souls and bellies being full, they tend to forget. They are my audience, I am theirs. I find in myself what there is in them. What we use seems sufficient ground for our own two feet.

This is the first place in my life I do not wish to move from: Pacific Grove.

PACIFIC GROVE SONG
by Bill Minor

(1)
Something familiar brought us together
In this quaint small place we call
The last home town in America.

We cherish the weather and trees in a grove
And peace our ocean bestows—
Plus daily bread Grove Market provides.

We are only as much of what surrounds us
As we truly need; so praise for the village
We carry in our hearts and heads.

(2)
Embracing like otters the shells on our bodies,
We find the life we have enough
To keep us continuously in love.

Slick as seals, we honk our horns at night
And make joyous music—but alert
To curfew time, we seldom go too far.

Not overly attracted to wanton success
Or failure, we simply abide within this
Pacific place, to savor the sea and trees nearby.

(3)
We flit about like Monarch butterflies
On streets named Laurel or Walnut or Pine,
Learning to be at home with ourselves.

Here, we ride bicycles, floating contented,
Or hike down a trail embraced by the sea.
For this is the very first place in our lives

We never wish to move from.

Pacific Grove, poems, drawings, woodcuts and prose by William Minor

Story below from 2018 reprint of Bill Minor's 1974 book (Pacific Grove Books):

TWO TALL SEA TALES

St. Francis comes down to the beach. He's dressed in natty threads, a fine brown reincarnationist.

Nine minutes of prayer then back to the car? He lasts longer. Robe to the ankles. The ancient cowl. A face as wasted as Grape Nuts. He folds his hands and squats before some imagined, or real, station of the sun. He commences canticles, and draws the sign of Jonas in the sand.

But the beach is a very carnal place today. Much physiology of the near naked. A low slung girl, bikini buttocks down by her knees. One with no butt at all but knees like breasts and breasts like yogurt, very loose and out to please. Many transparent blouses. But why go braless if only to disclose, now, those four sad eyes instead of two? Here's a girl so skinny one is tempted to pick her up for kindling. But not St. Francis. He pays them no prayer.

Can anyone break him? A girl just got off her motorbike.

Sniffing a prey, she saunters by with three large dogs. She has lank brown legs, a crotch as clean as cheese, shorts rolled tight as a compress. She wears no blouse. Just an outsized cowboy vest. Everything a masochist could ask for, and definitely after St. Francis. She winks, wiggles, and stops. He won't look at her.

He seeks not so much to be comforted as to comfort, to be loved as to love. He's also a little weird on the sun. When he fails to respond the girl cries 'sic him' to the dogs, which they do. Furious and unforgiving, they attack. They rip his cowl to pieces and then molest his person ...

Such a thing could never happen here. At least not on a public beach. But then, did this? The same girl, ignoring St. Francis, walked up to a child who'd just made two round firm holes in the sand with a little bucket. God knows what he dreamed for them. The girl was intrigued.

Pushing aside her vest, she lay down and loosed two large milky buff breasts into the holes, which were completely filled by them. The child of course began to cry (he certainly hadn't dreamed that use). Now the girl was not a bad sort but she was chock full of exuberant, excessive flesh and that too great enthusiasm which William Blake and others had commanded of her in a dream a few nights ago, and she was sorry.

She stood up. She apologized. Her belly was rich as sandpaper and the child dried his tears upon it. She asked if he'd like to bury her. He nodded yes and she was out of her clothes in a flash and lying, face down, in the sand. The young boy covered her completely. When he was through he slipped a long stemmed iris in her ass and departed for home on his ten speed bike.

So much goes on at the beach. And much of it is fit for children.

P.G. HOOTENANNY IS STILL ROCKIN' – VIC SELBY with JOYCE KRIEG

2016 - Hootenanny's 50th Anniversary at the Pacific Grove Art Center

"With anywhere from 30 to 70 singers attending the Saturday night song-fests, the **Pacific Grove Hootenanny** has become the largest community sing-along in continuous operation on the West Coast. – Vic Selby

Sixty years have gone by since the folk music craze swept the nation's college campuses, but the hootenanny spirit—and the sound—remains alive right here in Pacific Grove.

Those readers too young to recall pop culture of the late 1950s and early 1960s will find it difficult to imagine the huge impact of folk music and the hootenanny. A folk music revival, led by Pete Seeger and Woody Guthrie, had actually been brewing for the previous ten years, with The Weavers' version of the blues ballad "Goodnight, Irene" reaching the number one spot on the 1950 record charts. But for the most part, folk music bore the stigma of the scruffy beatnik and left-wing politics, and was pretty much confined to obscure nightclubs and coffeehouses in Greenwich Village during the buttoned-down Eisenhower era.

It took the arrival in 1958 of three clean-cut young collegiate types wearing striped shirts, playing guitars and a banjo, and calling themselves The Kingston Trio to break through to a general, mass audience as they topped the record charts with an old North Carolina folk ballad, "Tom Dooley." Their meteoric success encouraged dozens of other folk acts and individual artists such as The Limelighters, Peter, Paul and Mary, The New Christy Minstrels, Joan Baez, and Bob Dylan. At the height of the craze, folk music singalongs were regular and popular events on the nation's college campuses, and a weekly television show—named, appropriately enough, *Hootenanny*—was airing on the ABC network.

What, exactly, is a hootenanny? The origins are fuzzy and depend on the sources one consults. It could trace back to a hillbilly term for an item the name of which you can't quite remember, like a thingamajig or a whatchamacallit. It could be an old slang word for a party, similar to a shindig. In some circles, it referred to a conference or gathering of like-minded individuals for a sharing of ideas. But since the 1950s, it's most commonly been used to refer to a folk music party, an informal gathering of musicians featuring an open mic and group singalongs. Joan Baez was quoted in *Time* magazine in 1962 as saying that a hootenanny is to folk singers as a jam session is to jazz musicians.

From $20 a Week to $3,000 per Night

Speaking of Joan Baez, the singer with the pure, angelic voice may not have a direct connection to Pacific Grove, but she comes close. In 1961, all of twenty years old and with a second record album that had just achieved gold status, she and her then-boyfriend moved into a cabin at the corner of Highway 1 and Corona Road in Carmel Highlands. A few years later, she bought property in Carmel Valley and opened the Institute for the Study of Nonviolence in an abandoned schoolhouse. In the mid-1960s, students paid $20 a week to sit on the floor of the old adobe and "rap" about Ghandi, King and Thoreau. Today, the structure (extensively remodeled and improved) is part of the Stonepine Estate resort and, according to its website, rents for a cool $3,000 per night.

Just about the same time that Joan Baez was delivering the message of peace and love in Carmel Valley, Pacific Grove resident Vic Selby was hired as a math teacher at Carmel High School. He recalls, "I was given the choice of either chaperoning the rooters' bus to out-of-town games, or be the faculty advisor to an after-school club." Thus the Carmel High School Folk Singing Club was born.

The craze eventually faded, as most fads do. In this case, folk music got swept away by the triple threat of the British Invasion, Motown, and Psychedelic Rock. Strains of folk continued to in-

fluence the world of pop music, though, and can definitely be heard in late 1960s acts such as The Lovin' Spoonful, The Byrds, and The Mamas and Papas, as well as 1970s hit-makers like John Denver, Gordon Lightfoot and Joni Mitchell. At Carmel High, the Folk Singing Club evolved into the Country, Blues and Rock'n'Roll Club, also known as CBR-squared.

Fast forward some thirty years. Vic Selby has retired from teaching and has authored the book *Mathematics and the Human Condition*, which integrates math with cultural evolution. But he'd never lost his love for those old hootenannies, the informal congenial gatherings of kindred spirits whose only agenda is the raising of their voices in song. In 1996, he organized what was to become the first in a series of bi-monthly "Hoots" at the P.G. Art Center.

On October 20, 1997, Vic issued the first of what he then called "Hootenanny Newsletter" and which has evolved into "Hoot News." He reported, "We have tentative commitment from a great bass player and a conga player to provide a rhythm section, not that we were slack on rhythm but we'll keep working on that 'perfect' sound."

A typical grassroots special interest group newsletter, it included a plea for participants to bring music stands, and gave thanks to all who brought potluck snacks to share. "So bring some chips, dip, a 6 pack of soda or beer, a bottle of wine or maybe those great home baked chocolate chip cookies (a local favorite)." Vic further reported that the songbook had been expanded by 19 new songs and encouraged singers to bring their home collections for possible additions. He finished with an invitation to bring singers or players "who would enjoy the experience" to the next Hoot on November 11 of 1997.

Lest you conclude these sessions are one long rendition of "Kumbaya," consider that the "Hoots" are now based on a 235-page songbook featuring blues, rock, country and jazz and, yes, folk. Most of the evenings are themed around a specific artist, musical style or event: from Chuck Berry to Paul Simon, to the 50th anniversaries of the release of *Sgt Pepper's Lonely Hearts Club Band* and the Monterey Pop Music Festival. As Vic puts it, the goal is to feature tunes most people already know, and "to have fun with few musical 'rules' to dampen enthusiasm"

A perusal of the "Hoot News" over the years is a great way to get a feel for the spirit of hootenanny and a crash course of the musical styles and artists over the past century. The newsletters often include fascinating tidbits of trivia, and are brimming with Vic's quirky wit.

'The Chocolate-Chip Cookie Throw-Down'

A classic example comes from the September 2006 "Hoot News": "It is not one of our regular practices to enter the political debates which swirl around this time of year, but Hootenanny warmly endorses Kinky Friedman for Governor of Texas. I'm sure the debate during our break will be lively, but will not interfere with the chocolate chip cookie throw-down."

Another example: In February of 2007, the newsletter included a report on the group's "reach out" program at the Carmelo Child Development Center and how the kazoos seemed to be a hit with the kiddies. Vic concluded, "Remember our creed: if you can hook 'em on kazoo by age four, they will hoot forever!"

In a later "Hoot News," Vic explored the history of the kazoo: "… invented in the 1840s by Alabama Vest, a former slave from Macon, Georgia. The origin of the name kazoo is unknown, but the 11,000 kazoos made yearly are from the original factory (The Original Kazoo Co.), and is owned by the Suburban Adult Services Inc. that seeks to make life better for physically and mentally challenged individuals."

The P.G. Hoot went electric in April of 2007 with the introduction of a Fender "Hot Rod Deluxe" guitar. This added many new tunes to the songbook, including Chuck Berry's "Memphis," Van Morrison's "Bright Side of the Road," Little Eva's "Loco-Motion" Fats Domino's "Ain't That a Shame" Elmore James's "Rollin' and Tumblin'" and two versions of "Over the Rainbow."

July of 2007 saw the group celebrating not one but four 40th anniversaries in the world of pop music: The Monterey Pop Festival, the release of The Beatles' *Sgt. Pepper* album and Aretha Franklins' iconic single, "Respect," and Elvis Presley's wedding to Priscilla Beaulieu.

In December of 2007, the theme was country music, as well as the group's 62nd hoot, "featuring county favorites from Burl Ives through Johnny Cash, Willie Nelson, and Hal Laughlin doin' his imitation of Waylon Jennings."

In April of 2008, the P.G. hootenanny celebrated the 45th anniversary of The Freedom Singers and the Civil Rights movement. "By leading a dramatic singalong to accompany Martin Luther King's amazing speech in Washington D.C., the power of collective song became a major political force. So join us to sing classic folk songs and songs of freedom. With the electric guitars turned down, we will have an evening dedicated to vocal harmonies and the sound of teeth crunching through chocolate-chip cookies."

Folk-rock was the focus of the July 2008 Hoot. "It's said that the 12-string guitar riffs on 1964's 'Mr. Tambourine Man'" became the jumping-off point for the Folk-Rock explosion, so we will do our best cover of The Byrds along with some favorites, e.g. 'Rock Island Line,' 'Peggy Day,' 'Monday Monday,' 'Sweet Baby James,' and many other folk-rock standards."

Name That Rock'n'Roll Tune

Quick, who was the first musician to record a rock 'n 'roll song? If you guessed Elvis Presley or Bill Haley, you haven't been reading the "Hoot News." As Vic informs us, that honor goes to a Texas musician named Smokey Hogg who combined country with the blues to record and release "Penny Pinching Mama" way back in 1952. This factoid comes amidst the announcement in September of 2008 of an upcoming Hoot featuring crossover hits (blues, doo-wop, boogie, R&B and rock) from the 40s, 50s and 60s. Vic advised, "Dancing shoes are recommended, along with White Sport Coats and Pink Carnations along with those famous chocolate-chip cookies."

In May of 2009, the P.G. Hootenanny celebrated the birthday of folk pioneer Pete Seeger by having what Vic described as "as close to an acoustic evening as we can get (that means the electric instruments will be on low volume), and we will be having a 'Classic Hoot' by singing American folk songs from Leadbelly, Burl Ives, Sonny Terry and Brownie McGee, The Tarriers, Libba Cotton, Harry Belafonte, Woody, The Weavers, Joan Baez, Bob Dylan, Judy Collins, Josh White, and ... you get the point."

"It looks like we lost out for the Guinness record for the World's Largest Music Lesson," Vic reported in September of 2009. "That is now held by the 8,000 folks who showed up at Red Rocks Amphitheatre in Colorado last July 28. They learned two simple songs and sang and played them together. So it goes! We will continue in our quest to set the world record for Longest Continuing Hootenanny."

The December 2009 "Hoot News" played off the crossover theme, with the assertion that the most influential cross-over hit of all times was the release of "I've Got a Woman" by Ray Charles. Vic reported, "He found his own style in 1955 and virtually invented soul music when he changed the lyrics of a hard driving gospel tune and contributed greatly to the birth of Rock-n-Roll."

The roots of country music took center stage in March of 2010, with Vic promising a song set "where we conjure up the sounds of Ferlin Husky and Webb Pierce, Doc Watson, Waylon and Willie. If anyone knows 'The Gal Who Invented Kissin' we would shore 'preciate hearin' that one! Western wear is optional, but always fun."

By April of 2010, the Hoots had been going strong for fourteen years, and as Vic reported, "It took all those years to somewhat settle in" to a format of acoustic and "voice-featured" tunes during the first hour, while plugging in to electric and rock favorites in the second hour.

The October 2010 session featured the music of The Staple Singers, whom Vic described as, "the first family of gospel music in the late 50s and early 60s when Pop Staples, who died in 2000, got frustrated singing with the Trumpet Jubilees in the 1940s. Pop bought a guitar in a pawnshop, developed a reedy tremolo sound that would characterize the sound of the group, and taught his four children 'Will the Circle Be Unbroken.'"

"It was one great night singin' da blues and moving on to some early rock tunes at our November (2010) Hoot. With 50 or so folks singing in perfect harmony, some slick guitar work by 10 players, and many, many hand-clappers, it was impossible to keep the smiles from lightin' up the joint!!"

The April 2011 Hoot was dedicated to blues and R&B great Etta James, giving the group the opportunity to explore the progression of American Music from gospel, to blues and R&B, and on to early rock-n-roll.

In the August 2011 "Hoot News," Vic reported, "The fantastic sounds of more than 70 folks singing and playing at the July Hoot made for one of the most amazing and electrifying sessions we have ever had."

Vic's humor definitely comes to the forefront of the November 2011 "Hoot News," as he reported, "It was strange that nobody showed up with a 35,000 year-old flute to solo at our last Hoot, but we had plenty of soloists using the 150,000 year old instruments (hand clapping). We will now invite anyone with a Neolithic-era (7,000 B.C.E.) conch shell, to play along with our 'primo' guitarist, Bob 'Flash' McClaren as we move from 'da blues' to R&B and the blues rock tunes of the 1950s and 60s."

April of 2012 was dedicated to what Vic terms a "classic hootenanny, featuring mostly acoustic instruments, tight harmonies, and the philosophies of Woody and Pete. We will be singing songs of the people and songs of social justice. How loud must people sing to drown-out the political babble that deafens us to the real problems of the world?"

Vic advised in November of 2012, "Next time you find yourself wandering around the Mission District in San Francisco you might just check out the Rite Spot Cafe and see if Toshio Hirano is performing his two-hour homage to country singer Jimmie Rodgers. This wonderful dude has spent the last 40 years learning to yodel and sing 55 of the songs by the Mississippi troubadour known as the father of country music. He shares the essence of what we 'hootsters' are up to as he insists he is not trying to impersonate Rodgers but rather interpret and share the musical vision of an American legend."

January of 2013 saw a session dedicated to the combined forces of Gospel and Motown, the synergistic combination of church music and blues. "For those of us who got caught up in this during the early 60s, remembering stars like Fontella Bass who hit the top of the charts in 1965 with 'Rescue Me,' we have to show RESPECT," Vic said.

The Flip Side of 'Boogie Woogie Santa Claus'

The P.G. Hoot entered its seventeenth year in 2013 and Vic noted, "We have covered the mountain folk, early blues, the great folk movement of the early 60's, and had a great time singing our favorite gospel tunes in January. This 93rd Hoot will focus on the spectacular transformation of popular music in the 50s from the pop sound to rock 'n' roll. This will include a tribute to Patti Page and her wonderful career. From her start in 1947 she released 15 gold records, 24 songs in the top ten, and four number one hits. The biggest hit happened to be the flip side of 'Boogie Woogie Santa Claus' and we will surely do our best version of 'Tennessee Waltz.'"

The new year of 2015 started out with a Hoot featuring the songs of Joe Cocker, Willie Nelson, Bob Dylan and The Beatles, and with Vic noting, "The last Hoot was truly one of the best in years with 75 folks raising the roof. We will be having another session of our 'favorites,' as we will try to finish the set list from November and polish off the chocolate-chip cookies and other treats."

"Hoot News" readers received an introduction to the blues pioneer known as Leadbelly in April of 2015 as Vic wrote, "It seems wherever you look, the influence of Leadbelly is amazingly clear in the history of many forms of American music. His unique style of play on the 12 string guitar (it was a Stella) was picked up by Pete Seeger, and influenced the sound of Roger McGuinn (The Byrds), Bonnie Raitt, Judy Collins, and Van Morrison. Also inspired was Lonnie Donegan, the founding father of British pop, who had a big hit with his sped-up version of 'Rock Island Line.' Donegan inspired British teens to form skiffle groups, including 15-year-old John Lennon, who founded the Quarrymen in 1956 and later added Paul McCartney and George Harrison to the band. Harrison once said, 'No Leadbelly, no Lonnie Donegan. Therefore, no Leadbelly, no Beatles.'"

The September 2015 "Hoot News" was dedicated to Johnny Winter, who had died on July 16 of that year. Vic wrote, "In the 60s he was the most visible blues guitarist from East Texas. His avowed disciples were Jimmie and Stevie Ray Vaughn. He and his onetime lover, Janis Joplin, helped drive the boogie rock movement and celebrated the raw, imposing sound of electrified Texas blues of Freddie King, Gatemouth Brown and Johnny 'Guitar' Watson." Also honored was jazz and country bass player Charlie Haden, " … who, with Omette Coleman started the 'free jazz' movement in one of the seminal moments in jazz history at their 1959-60 engagement at New York's Five Spot Club. Mr. Haden saw the link between jazz and country with both being poor people's music related to the struggle to be recognized. He released *Rambling Boy* in 2009, playing songs of the Carter family and other country musicians."

The hootenanny enthusiasts kicked off 2016 with a session dedicated to the early years of rock-n-roll, "including the songs of Buddy Holly, The Five Satins, Chuck Berry, Elvis, The Stray Cats, and many others. There will be a doo-wop session, and, as always, we will be singing many of our favorites including show tunes and mountain folk."

Medgar Evers and the Blues

Medgar Evers is a name associated with the Civil Rights movement of the 1960s, one of its martyrs when he was assassinated in the driveway of his home in Jackson, Mississippi, in 1963. But as Vic points out in the January 2016 edition of "Hoot News," Evers was also an important figure in the local blues scene. In 1954 he became one of the first African-American radio disc jockeys in Mississippi, and later became manager of WMPR in Jackson. "In 1973 B. B. King encouraged Mayor Charles Evers of Fayette to found the annual Medgar Evers Homecoming concerts to commemorate the tenth anniversary of the murder of Medgar Evers. These events featured several days of concerts, parades, and other activities in Fayette and Jackson in honor of the slain civil rights activist. Dozens of blues, soul, and gospel acts performed at the annual festival during subsequent decades." Vic's office in the Giles Building on Lighthouse Avenue includes a rare framed poster of the 1975 festival.

Drawing by Keith Larson 2017.

2016 was the 50th anniversary of a number of significant events in music, and these were celebrated at the September Hoot. The Beatles performed their last live concert at Candlestick Park on August 29 of 1966. "That year produced not only the great *Revolver* album, but also Dylan's expansive double album *Blonde on Blonde* and the anarchic, boundary-bending of Frank Zappa and the Mothers of Invention's *Freak Out!*"

The Doors recorded their debut album in 1966. Vic quoted drummer John Densmore: "I always say the '60s, they didn't start until '65, and they ended after '67. Before '65, it was the end of the '50s; by '68, pop music was going to cocaine and heroin and burnout and the dream was getting a little ragged."

The Rolling Stones also stretched their creative wings in 1966 with the release of their album *Aftermath*, as Vic wrote, "… moving beyond their core sound of guitar, bass and drums in such future Stones standards as "Paint It Black," "Under My Thumb," "Lady Jane" and "Stupid Girl." Among the Stones' 1966 hits were "19th Nervous Breakdown" and "Mother's Little Helper," both exploring dysfunction and anomie lurking beneath the surface of carefully polished middle-class veneers."

1960s rock star Janis Joplin was the honored artist for the January 2017 Hoot. "She attended University of Texas and listened to and sang blues and early R&B by her influences: Ma Rainey, Bessie Smith, Otis Redding, and Tina Turner," Vic wrote. "She left Texas in January 1963 ('Just to get away,' she said, 'because my head was in a much different place'), moving to San Francisco's North Beach and later the Haight. In 1964, Joplin and future Jefferson Airplane guitarist Jorma Kaukonen recorded a number of blues standards, which incidentally featured Margareta Kaukonen using a typewriter in the background. This session included seven tracks: 'Typewriter Talk,' 'Trouble in Mind,' 'Kansas City Blues,' 'Hesitation Blues,' 'Nobody Knows You When You're Down and Out,' 'Daddy, Daddy, Daddy,' and 'Long Black Train Blues,' and was later released as the bootleg album *The Typewriter Tape*. We will sing some of these and many of our favorites, so come on along, share some snacks, and let loose!"

Inspiring the Lonesome 'Shower Singers'

March 2017 featured "classics" from the Hoot's 235 page songbook, with Vic penning in the newsletter, "Just as the works of Mozart and the ragtime music of 100 years ago have inspired many generations of composers, musicians, and lonesome 'shower singers,' some of the music of today will not only survive, but will bring the messages and spirit of our generation into the future. We will be singing and playing Folk, Blues, Country, Motown, and Rock classics as we remember the words of Al Jarreau: 'I grew up in Milwaukee and I took it all in. I want it all. Don't cut me off at the pass and say I can't listen to Muddy Waters because I'm a jazzer. Or I can't listen to Garth Brooks because I'm a jazzer. Get out of here.' Indeed, Hootenanny tries to mix it up as Ray Charles did. We will be paying tribute to Leonard Cohen, Percy Mayfield, Butch Trucks of the Allman Brothers Band, as well as Mr. Jarreau. The most amazing aspect of Hootenanny is that it is a truly synergizing experience. It combines the opportunity to read some great poetry, keep rhythm, satisfy the longing for harmony, and dance—all in one package. So come on along, share some snacks, meet some new friends, and keep the great music of a generation alive and well."

The May 2017 Hoot focused on two major forces in American music, James Cotton and Chuck Berry. "The Grammy award winning Cotton was born July 1, 1935, on a Mississippi cotton plantation and began playing the harmonica at age 9. Starting at the age of 20, Cotton spent 12 years on the road with Muddy Waters and was featured on Waters' record, 'At Newport 1960.' Cotton formed the James Cotton Band in 1966, eventually drawing him into the orbit of the new era through collaborations with, among many others, Janis Joplin, The Grateful Dead, and Led Zeppelin. Chuck Berry, who with his indelible guitar licks, brash self-confidence, and memorable songs about cars, girls and wild dance parties, did as much as anyone to define rock 'n' roll's potential and attitude in its early years. While Elvis Presley was rock's first pop star and teenage heartthrob, Mr. Berry was its master theorist and conceptual genius, the songwriter who knew what the kids wanted before they knew it themselves."

On September 9, 2017, the Pacific Grove Hoot celebrated its 20th anniversary, with Vic writing in the newsletter, "For over 100 years the emergence of Americana Music has transformed the ideals of our country and has played a major part in defining who we are and explaining our culture to the rest of the world. Like the folk and classical music that has been handed down and treasured for thousands of years, there is great power in the songs that will be played for the next hundreds of years."

The 20th anniversary also saw Vic reflecting upon the emergence of electric music at the 1965 Newport Folk Festival. "With the addition of the Chambers Brothers playing electric gospel, and the Paul Butterfield Blues Band, with Mike Bloomfield on electric guitar, the folk music world expanded and merged into a new age. Alan Lomax was stunned as he had to give the introduction, and wound up in a physical altercation with Albert Grossman. This was also the first time Bob Dylan played electric and it shocked Pete Seeger. The crowd and most of the other musicians loved it and a new age was born. This was taking the old music like 'House of The Rising Sun' up to a new level. It was reaching the back porches of America, and it had finally caught up with the folk world. Woody Guthrie had said it: 'Don't like dictators not much, myself, but I think the whole country ought to be run By e-Iec-tri-ci-ty!' Music changes but but the best music endures and is passed down as a part of the cultural evolution of our species. Like science, literature, and art, it completes the expression of who we are as humans ('nuf said)!"

November 2017 honored Fats Domino, "The founding star of rock 'n' roll, putting dozens of songs on the R&B and pop charts and paving the way for Bill Haley, Chuck Berry, Elvis Presley and the rest. Though he is usually filed alongside Berry and Presley as a teen idol, he also paved the way for Ray Charles' crossover success with songs like 'Blue Monday.' Like Ray Charles, he was comfortable with the old big band styles, with blues, with pop and even with country music. In the early 1960s, he preceded Charles' groundbreaking country-soul fusions by cracking the pop top 40 with R&B re-workings of 'Jambalaya' and 'You Win Again.'"

'Sittin' on the Dock of OUR Bay'

The P.G. "hootsters" started out 2018 with a tribute to Otis Redding and Hank Williams. In Vic's words: "Otis Redding was born on September 9, 1941, in Dawson, Georgia. He was discovered after recording 'These Arms of Mine.' Known for his sincere emotional delivery, Redding became the voice of soul music. As his career was taking off, he died in a plane crash on December 10, 1967. The song '(Sittin' on) The Dock of the Bay' became his first and only No.1 hit in 1968. Aretha Franklin's rendition of his song, 'Respect,; became legendary. Widely considered country music's first superstar, Hiram 'Hank' Williams was born September 17, 1923, in Mount Olive, Alabama. Picking up the guitar for the first time at the age of eight, Williams was just 13 when he made his radio debut. A year later he was entering talent shows and had his own band, Hank Williams and his Drifting Cowboys. He had his first #1 song in 1949 with the release of 'Lovesick Blues.' On New Year's Day 1953, he died in the back of his 1952 powder blue Cadillac. So come on along as we sit by the dock of OUR bay singing 'Jambalaya,' 'Hey Good Lookin',' 'Your Cheatin' Heart,' and many more classics."

The hootenanny of March of this year paid tribute to *Sgt. Pepper's Lonely Hearts Club Band,* rated by *Rolling Stone* as the number one rock album of all time. Vic noted, "It has been described as one of the first art rock LPs, aiding the development of progressive rock, and credited with marking the beginning of the album era. An important work of British psychedelia, the album incorporates a range of stylistic influences, including vaudeville, circus, music hall, avant guard, and Western and Indian classical music."

Vic Selby, founder of the Pacific Grove Hootenanny with a prized possession, a rare poster from the 1975 Medgar Evers Homecoming Concert.

And so it has continued throughout the years, a tapestry of tunes, with tributes to Pete Seeger, Theodore Bikel, Little Richard, Bob Dylan, Ronnie Gilbert, Johnny Cash and Patsy Cline and many more—all chased down with the Hoot's legendary homemade chocolate-chip cookies.

Throughout the years, the P.G. Hootenanny has entertained at Monterey's First Night New Year's Eve celebration, and offers a special edition of the Hoot during Feast of Lanterns.

Today Vic continues as Hoot coordinator and editor of the "Hoot News," with a mailing list of approximately 300. With anywhere from 30 to 70 singers attending the Saturday night song-fests, they've become the largest community singalong in continuous operation on the West Coast. While admission is free, the group encourages donations and has raised some $16,000 for the Art Center.

Since day one, the P.G. Hoots have found a home at the Art Center. In one issue of the Hoot News, Vic paid tribute to the group's home thusly: "We sincerely want to thank the folks at the Art Center who have made us a part of the art scene and continue to bring the community together with all forms of artistic experiences. We are honored to be in the company of the great painters, potters, dancers, professional musicians and those who work to bring beauty to us all, and give us all a chance to express our talents. It is indeed a wonderful 'down-home' venue."

The Enduring Appeal of a 'Synergizing Experience'

But what, exactly, is the appeal of these group singalongs?

Vic calls hootenanny a "synergizing experience," explaining, "it combines the opportunity to read some great poetry, keep rhythm, satisfy the longing for harmony, and dance—all in one package. This expression of all four great human symbol systems (language, mathematics, music and art) at one time is rare indeed!"

Vic notes that with the emphasis on individual creative effort—"go ahead and let loose"—combined with a congenial social effort—"at least we tune up"—hootenanny becomes "a complete uplifting human experience."

So if on a Saturday night you happen to be walking along the 500 block of Lighthouse Avenue and you hear voices from above belting out a familiar tune from long ago, pause for a moment and let yourself drift back sixty years, to those smoky nightclubs and campus social halls, and savor the feeling of being young once again.

Good Old Days 2017

Photos by Peter Mounteer

STORIES OF AMERICA

Life in Pacific Grove, California Book 2   101

MORE FROM THAT ERA

Gary Kildall, Pacific Grove's Forgotten Computer Genius– David A. Laws

The first volume of Life in Pacific Grove contained a story about the installation of a historic plaque in the sidewalk outside 801 Lighthouse Avenue to honor "Gary Kildall: The Father of PC Software." In response to interest for more information on this largely forgotten, local computer genius, the following is adapted from an article published on the Computer History Museum website in 2014.

Late one afternoon in the fall of 1974, in the California seaside town of Pacific Grove, computer science professor Gary Kildall and electronic engineer John Torode "retired for the evening to take on the simpler task of emptying a jug of not-so-good red wine ... and speculating on the future of our new software tool." By successfully booting a computer from a floppy disk drive, they had just given birth to an operating system (OS) that, together with the microprocessor and the disk drive, would provide one of the three fundamental building blocks of the personal computer revolution. While they knew the software was important, neither realized the extraordinary impact it would have on their lives and times.

Early Days: Repairing Automobiles, Having Fun

Gary Arlen Kildall was born to a family of Scandinavian descent in Seattle, Washington, in 1942. His inventive skills flourished in repairing automobiles and having fun, but suffered in scholastic pursuits. He qualified for admission to the University of Washington based on his teaching experience at the family owned Kildall Nautical School, rather than on his high school grades.

In 1963, Kildall entered college and married his high school sweetheart, Dorothy McEwen. He was one of 20 students accepted into the university's first master's program in computer science. Here his mathematical talents were applied to a subject that fascinated him, all-night sessions programming a new Burroughs B5500 computer. To avoid the uncertainty of the draft at the height of the Vietnam War, on graduating he entered a U. S. Navy officer training school and was posted to serve as an instructor in computer science at the Naval Postgraduate School (NPS) in Monterey.

Consultant to Intel: 'A Beautiful Rat's Nest'

Kildall remained at NPS as an associate professor after his tour of duty ended in 1972. He became fascinated with start-up chip company Intel Corporation's recently introduced 4004 microprocessor chip and simulated its operation on the school's IBM mainframe computer. This work earned a consulting relationship with Intel that included writing PL/M, a high-level Programming Language for Microcomputers that served the company for decades.

Gary Kildall. Photo Tom O'Neal 1988.

To enable software development for Intel's second-generation microprocessor, the 8080, Kildall needed to connect the chip directly to an 8" floppy disk-drive storage unit. As no commercial solution existed, he wrote code for his Control Program for Microcomputers (CP/M) in a few weeks but his efforts to build the complex electronic circuitry required to physically transfer the data failed and the project languished for a year. Frustrated, he called John Torode, a college friend then teaching at U.C. Berkeley, who crafted a "beautiful rat's nest of wire wraps, boards and cables" for the task.

"One of the Most Exciting Days of My Life"

Working in a tool shed behind his home at 781 Bayview Avenue, in mid-1974 Kildall "loaded my CP/M program from paper tape to the diskette and 'booted' CP/M from the diskette, and up came the [asterisk] prompt: * This may have been one of the most exciting days of my life, except, of course, when I visited Niagara Falls," he exclaimed, "We now had the power of an IBM S/370 [big mainframe computer] at our fingertips." This is going to be a "big thing," they told each other.

Intel expressed no interest in CP/M, so Kildall was free to exploit the program on his own. Torode refined the "rat's nest" and produced a complete floppy disk controller system. Kildall continued teaching part time at NPS and in 1976, with his wife Dorothy as co-founder, they started a company called Intergalactic Digital Research at 716 Lighthouse Avenue to promote sales of CP/M as an operating system for small business and personal computers. They shortened the name to Digital Research Inc. (DRI) after a couple of years.

Glenn Ewing, a former NPS student, approached DRI with the opportunity to license CP/M for a new family of disk subsystems for a hot new San Francisco Bay Area microcomputer maker, IMSAI, Inc. Reluctant to rework the code for every new controller, Kildall worked with Ewing to change the design of the software so that it could work on a wide variety of computer hardware.

According to John Wharton, Intel's technical liaison to DRI and a friend of Kildall, this was "perhaps Gary's most profound contribution ... All previous computer software had targeted specific hardware environments ... This idea created the third-party software industry by expanding the potential market several orders of magnitude."

Selling Floppy Discs via the 'Grassroots' Effect

Articles such as "Upgraded CP/M floppy disc operating system now available," published in the magazine *Dr Dobbs' Journal of Computer Calisthenics and Orthodontia* in late 1976, generated a steady stream of customers. Each day Dorothy walked to the Pacific Grove Post Office to pick up mail order checks for CP/M disks at $70 per copy. According to Kildall, "In the months that followed, the nature of the computer hobbyist became apparent ... CP/M gradually gained popularity through a 'grassroots' effect."

CP/M became established as a standard OS and was offered by most early personal computer manufacturers, including pioneers Altair, Amstrad, Kaypro, and Osborne. With a special add-in card built by Microsoft, it also ran on the Apple II to enable popular applications such as Word Star that were originally written for CP/M. Microsoft licensed CP/M from DRI to re-sell with the card.

In 1978 Dorothy and Gary purchased the house at 801 Lighthouse Avenue and converted the Victorian two-story residence into their company headquarters. One of their first recruits, Tom Rolander, joined from Intel in 1979 and immediately set to work writing enhanced versions of CP/M.

By 1980 DRI had opened an engineering office at 734 Lighthouse Avenue, today occupied by the *Carmel Pine Cone* newspaper, employed more than 20 people and *Fortune* magazine reported that the company generated revenue of $3.5 million. The same article noted that Microsoft earned about the same total over the prior five years combined, some of these sales being derived from reselling CP/M licenses. By 1982 DRI disclosed annual sales in excess of $20 million and that "More than a million people are now using CP/M controlled systems."

Meanwhile, in Seattle ...

Seattle Computer Products developed a system using the 8086, a powerful 16-bit microprocessor from Intel in 1980. Impatient for an update of CP/M to work with the new chip, programmer Tim Paterson filled the gap by writing an operating system known initially as QDOS (Quick and Dirty Operating System) to emulate the "look-and-feel" of CP/M. According to Paterson, "If there had been a CP/M for the 8086 microprocessor, QDOS would never have been developed."

Also in 1980, IBM decided to develop a desktop computer for the mass market. To introduce the IBM PC, as it became known, as quickly as possible, the engineers used commercially available software and hardware. An IBM procurement team visited Bill Gates in Redmond, Washington, to license Microsoft's BASIC interpreter program. Not having an OS to offer, Gates referred them to DRI.

IBM Comes to Pacific Grove

When the IBM team arrived in Pacific Grove they met with Dorothy and worked with company attorney Gerry Davis to settle the terms of a non-disclosure agreement acceptable to both parties. Gary, who had flown his personal aircraft to Oakland to meet an important customer, returned in the afternoon to discuss technical matters. The meeting ended in an impasse over financial terms. IBM wished to purchase CP/M outright, whereas DRI sought a per-copy royalty payment in order to protect its existing base of business. With some alternative approaches in mind, Kildall tried to renew the negotiations a week later but IBM did not respond.

In the meantime, Gates, who was anxious to sell his BASIC program to IBM, had negotiated the purchase of QDOS from Seattle Computer Products to consummate the deal. He then sold a one-time, non-exclusive license to IBM but retained the right to license the product as MS-DOS to others. When Kildall discovered that the application interface was identical to that of CP/M he threatened IBM with a lawsuit.

Kildall and Davis negotiated a resolution that required IBM to market an updated CP/M alongside the Microsoft offering and allow customers to choose their preferred OS. However the list price differential, $40 vs. $240 for the DRI product, discouraged consumer interest in the latter. Davis says "IBM clearly betrayed the impression they gave Gary and me."

Aftermath: 'A Little Company Called Pixar'

DRI continued to develop new software products and thrived for several years. Many of these programs continued in daily use worldwide for years, including a version embedded in IBM's operating system for point-of-sale terminals. DRI also introduced operating systems with windows and menu-driven user interfaces long before Apple and Microsoft. Some observers claim that IBM's promotion of MS DOS over the DRI product delayed progress on personal computers by as much as 10 years.

In other pursuits, Kildall founded KnowledgeSet with Tom Rolander in which they created the first CD-ROM encyclopedia for Grolier. Beginning in 1982, he also served as co-host with Stewart Cheifet on the popular PBS TV program *The Computer Chronicles*. Seen across the U.S. and in over 100 other countries, it continues to be viewed at online sites by millions of people across the world.

Brian Halla, Intel's technical liaison to DRI, recalls that Gary "showed me this VAX 11/780 that he had running in his basement and he was so proud of it and he said, 'I figured out a way to have a computer generate animation,' and he said, 'Watch this.' And he runs a demo of a Coke bottle that starts real slowly and starts spinning and so as maybe several months went by, he lost interest in this and he sold his setup to a little company called Pixar."

At its peak DRI employed over 500 people and opened operations in Asia and Europe. However, by the mid-1980s, in the struggle with the juggernaut created by the combined efforts of IBM and Microsoft, DRI had lost the basis of its operating systems business. Dispirited, Kildall, who never enjoyed the responsibility of managing a large company or displayed the business acumen of Gates, and the other investors sold the company to Novell Inc. of Provo, Utah, in 1991.

After leaving DRI, Kildall continued to innovate. He moved to Austin, Texas, where he founded a company to explore wireless home networking technology and participated in charitable work for pediatric AIDS.

Gary Kildall died at age 52 following an accident in Monterey in 1994. His ashes were buried in Seattle, the hometown that he shared with Bill Gates.

The Legacy of Gary Kildall:
'He Saw the Future and Made It Work'

In 1995, the Software and Information Industry Association presented a posthumous Lifetime Achievement Award to Gary Kildall, citing eight significant areas in which he contributed to the microcomputer industry. Despite these widely recognized technical accomplishments, his legacy remains mired in a tangle of myths and conspiracy theories. The most persistent is driven by a 1982 comment attributed to Bill Gates and published in the *Times of London* newspaper that "Gary was out flying when IBM came to visit and that's why they did not get the contract."

The former editor of the *Times*, Sir Harold Evans atoned for that story in a PBS documentary and in his book, *They Made America: Two Centuries of Innovators from the Steam Engine to the Search Engine*. The subtitle of the chapter on Kildall, "He saw the future and made it work. He was the true founder of the personal computer revolution and the father of PC software," offers a sympathetic telling of the life and times of the man who helped give birth to the modern PC operating system.

In April 2014, the Institute of Electrical and Electronic Engineering "The world's largest professional association for the advancement of technology" installed a bronze IEEE Milestone in Electrical Engineering and Computing plaque outside the former DRI headquarters at 801 Lighthouse Avenue. The Milestone program honors important events in electrical engineering and computing. Achievements such as Thomas Edison's electric light bulb, Marconi's wireless communications, and Bell Labs' first transistor are recognized with a plaque in an appropriate location. The NPS also dedicated a "Dr. Gary A. Kildall Memorial Conference Room" containing a replica IEEE plaque on the campus in 2017.

Note: Much of the information above is derived from a draft memoir written by Gary Kildall in late 1993. With permission of the family, portions of the manuscript, *Computer Connections: People, Places, and Events in the Evolution of the Personal Computer Industry*, were published on-line by the Computer History Museum in 2016.

The Asilomar Microcomputer Workshop
"Celebrating Microprocessor Technology Since the Dawn *of Sand!*"

David A. Laws

The ability to put thousands of transistors on a single silicon chip had made the microprocessor computer-on-a-chip a practical system component by the early 1970s. In 1975, a group of "movers, shakers, nerds, and greybeards" from the burgeoning semiconductor and personal computer industries of Silicon Valley organized the Asilomar Microcomputer Workshop (AMW) at Pacific Grove's Asilomar Conference Center. Their goal: to explore the unique characteristics of microprocessors and identify ways of enhancing their capabilities.

As the microprocessor emerged as an essential building block of the digital revolution, their deliberations over the succeeding decades proved fruitful beyond their wildest expectations. The first popular microprocessor squeezed a couple of thousand transistors onto a piece of silicon a fraction of the size of a fingernail. Today manufacturers routinely put more than one billion transistors in the same space.

In contrast with other technical gatherings, the organizers of the Asilomar conference intentionally eschewed written proceedings and excluded press representatives through an invitation-only attendance policy. This encouraged scientists and engineers from competing companies and institutions across the world to discuss and debate freely issues facing microprocessor designers. Architectural features were born and others aborted during sessions that stretched into the early hours.

Many attendees at the early meetings went on to play important roles in computer technology. Ed McClusky founded the Computer Science program at Stanford University. Justin Rattner led the Apple iPod development team. Jim Clark founded video graphics pioneer Silicon Graphics and Netscape.

Gary Kildall, who lived within walking distance of Asilomar, had recently founded Digital Research Inc. to promote commercial sales of his ground-breaking CP/M microcomputer operating system. DRI's first employee, programmer Tom Rolander, who later helped create the first commercial CD-ROM, the Grolier encyclopedia, continues to ply his trade in town. Representatives from competing microprocessor vendors AMD, Fairchild, Intel, National, Rockwell, TI, and others rubbed shoulders for intensive off-the-record discussions.

As microprocessors grew to play a dominant role in the personal computer business and the succeeding digital revolution, larger, more corporate-driven, technical conferences took over many of the original goals of the AMW. Session topics became focused on applications enabled by the newest generations of processors, rather than features of the chips themselves. By the 30th anniversary, one of the founding organizers, suggested that the gathering could be more aptly described as the "Asilomar Workshop on Neat Stuff."

Some attendees disparaged the transition from a specific technological focus to a more socially-oriented gathering. Others felt that this change facilitated exploration of the wider implications of technology and has allowed the conference to continue to attract new generations of attendees. If heeded, calls at this year's 44th meeting (2018) to make the sessions more welcoming to a diverse audience could help the AMW tradition survive into the second half of this century.

Del Monte Park: A Bohemian Enclave
Mimi Sheridan

Erik Nelson's 2018 exhibit on the artists and houses of Del Monte Park, shown at the Pacific Grove Art Center, inspired this essay. Erik and Amanda Chaffin, who both grew up in the neighborhood, generously provided invaluable details and insights. July 2018

Carmel is known as the Monterey Peninsula's art colony, but in the years following World War II another, more progressive, art colony developed between Pacific Grove and Pebble Beach. A group of about twenty families discovered a wooded hillside where they could shape their own community.

What Made Del Monte Park Different From Other Post-war Suburbs?

It was a place and a time in which, at least for a while, these families could be creative and live with a sense of freedom. They had diverse backgrounds but shared a sense of independence and creativity, seeking individual expression rather than conformity. Their lifestyles and their houses were a direct reflection of their personal interpretations of art and architecture, shaped by both financial necessity and their own talents.

These early residents were attracted by the natural beauty, with stately trees and dramatic views toward Spanish Bay. But they were also attracted by the cheap land. Wooded lots could be had for $150-$200. Until development began in the late 1940s, the area had been the Pine Ridge Dairy and, before that, a portion of the Felipe Gomez Ranch. The land was in unincorporated Monterey County (roughly between Montecito Avenue and Patterson Lane, Funston and Lincoln avenues). It was still fairly rural with few amenities—no paved roads and limited sewer availability. Since there were no building codes, owners could build as they wished—to express their own design ideas or simply to save money.

Children were free to wander, going down to the beach, exploring the many vacant lots and wooded ravines and walking to the David Avenue School or the little store on Shafter Avenue. Families knew each other, and children were welcome to visit and hang out, just as their parents gathered together and shared their lives and ideas.

Bill and Amy Nelson were among the first to discover Del Monte Park, in 1949. They were seeking a place to settle down after an extended European camping trip following Bill's discharge from the Navy. They didn't want a typical suburban life, but a place where they could be independent and creative. The couple designed and built a unique house and enjoyed the neighborhood's Bohemian social life. Bill taught at David Avenue School, but also blossomed as a ceramist, sometimes bringing his students to his studio to make pottery.

Among the best-known artists of Del Monte Park was Joan Savo (1918-1993). She and her husband, George (1923-1993), moved from San Francisco to the Monterey Peninsula in the late 1940s. While camping at Garrapata Beach along Highway 1, they met Jay and Nikki Chaffin, and they bought adjoining lots in Del Monte Park. Jay opened a tailor shop in Carmel, but their real loves were music and books. They often entertained friends from San Francisco at lively parties with wine, jazz and conversations, with no shortage of strong opinions.

Joan Savo opened a shop in Carmel—The Garret—selling hand-painted gift items. After a few years, they and their two children moved back to San Francisco, so George could earn his teaching credential. Joan's career flourished, with a show at City Light Books. Back in Pacific Grove, they built a new house and George began his 25-year career as a popular social studies teacher at Pacific Grove High School. Joan's large canvases, both figurative and abstract, brought her fame and are still highly valued in private and public collections. The Monterey Museum of Art had a Savo retrospective in 2018.

Another prominent couple was Victor Di Gesu (1914-1988) and Janet Ament de la Roche (1916-2000), who met while attending art school in Los Angeles. He had been stationed at Fort Ord during the war and was attracted to the Bohemian culture of Monterey Peninsula. They left Del Monte Park in 1952 to study art in Spain, France and Italy. Not only did their artistic talents develop, but they discovered another passion, flamenco dance and music. After their return in 1956, their home was filled with flamenco guitar music and students learning to dance. Both Victor and Janet belonged to the prestigious Carmel Art Association and their paintings are widely collected today.

The artistic pursuits were not limited to painting. Russ Eddy acted in numerous local theater productions including "Death of a Salesman," Waiting for Godot," and "Tobacco Road." His son Roger went on to form a well-known jazz band, while another son, Glen, a dancer, has performed and taught throughout Europe and is on the faculty of the California Institute of the Arts.

A part-time resident was Hazel Dreis (1891-1964), an internationally-renowned bookbinder. Her deep connections in the literary world brought visitors such as James Baldwin, Laurence Ferlinghetti, Philip Glass and John Steinbeck, adding to the community's Bohemian character.

Many residents expressed themselves in their handmade houses, some of which remain today. The houses were influenced by popular mid-century designers such as Joseph Eichler, Richard Neutra and Frank Lloyd Wright. They featured natural materials such as Carmel River stone and redwood, purchased from the local sawmill for only ten cents a board foot. Most were small cottages at first, enlarged over time, tucked away among the trees and native shrubs. Flat or shed roofs, board-and-batten cladding, wide eaves and clerestory windows to bring in light were common features. Because of the number of artists, many houses had studios, either separate rooms or free-standing structures. Most had stone or locally-made metal fireplaces, as their single-wall construction, lack of insulation, and leaky roofs and windows made the houses quite chilly.

Bill Nelson designed and built one of the first structures, using redwood and adobe bricks. It has a striking appearance, sitting on a pentagonal lot with large angled windows facing south for light and warmth. Jay Chaffin built a cabin like those he had seen in his native Great Smoky Mountains of Tennessee. Using only hand tools, he positioned redwood blocks for the foundation and fashioned the interior and furniture from discarded materials like scrap tiles.

Paul McReynolds (1903-1978) and his wife, Helen, built an L-shaped structure with radiant heating. Their "living room" was a studio filled with wood sculptures in progress, as Paul was becoming a successful sculptor. His popular image of a pelican sits near Fisherman's Wharf in downtown Monterey.

The community's Bohemian atmosphere was relatively short-lived. By the early 1960s, residents and their children had grown older, and some sought more middle-class jobs to support their families. As the Monterey Peninsula grew, more "ordinary" families built houses in Del Monte Park. By 1954 the center of the subdivision was built out and by 1960 it was almost completely developed. The area was annexed by the City of Pacific Grove in 1972.

Today, 1950s-60s Ranch and Modern Contemporary houses, interspersed among large oaks and pines, line the curving streets and cul-de-sacs. But if you look carefully, you can still see the more exotic houses that express the spirit of the early years.

Holiday Tree Lighting Ceremony, 2016. Photos Peter Mounteer.

Indie Author Day 2018

Saturday, Oct 13 • 11am – 5pm
Pacific Grove: Central Ave. btwn Fountain and 17th St.

HOSTED BY
Pacific Grove Public Library
Pacific Grove Museum of Natural History
and the Centrella Inn
Sponsored by Pacific Grove Books
and Central Coast Writers

William Neish & Wolf Bukowski
Script Reading & Writing

Heather Lazare
Consultant

Patricia Hamilton
Life in P.G.

Joyce Krieg & Jeffrey Whitmore
Mystery Writers & Editors

More Speakers – program details at lifeinpacificgrove.com

Join us for Q&A, talks, readings - Meet authors, buy books - and more!

Programs and talks convey deeper insights into the craft of writing about "place," or "setting." Presenters use select Pacific Grove locations to illustrate writing tips and techniques.

A Mayor's Proclamation
Mayor Bill Kampe and Scott Bauer
P.G. Public Library Director
proclaim: *October 13, 2018 as "Indie Author Day" in the City of Pacific Grove.*

Writing Productivity Challenges
David Rasch, PhD, lecturer in Stanford's Continuing Studies Program.

Mystery Writer/Editor Collaboration
Joyce Krieg and Jeffrey Whitmore
Editors, Authors, Mystery writers
A Quaint Town for a Killing

Screenwriter/Scriptreader Conversation
Wolf Bukowski and William Neish - The Story Tailor
Spirits in the Mist P.G. Screenplay release 2019

Importance of Place -Tea at the Centrella Inn
Heather Lazare, Editor, Consultant

Memoir "Movie" Method Class
Patricia Hamilton, Publisher *Life in Pacific Grove 1 & 2*

Conversations in the Garden Brad Herzog, Luke Herzog, John McCleary, Bill Minor, PLUS members of the Screenwriters Forum.

30 Authors selling and signing books

Indie Author Day — October 13, 2018 — New Pacific Grove Books Releases

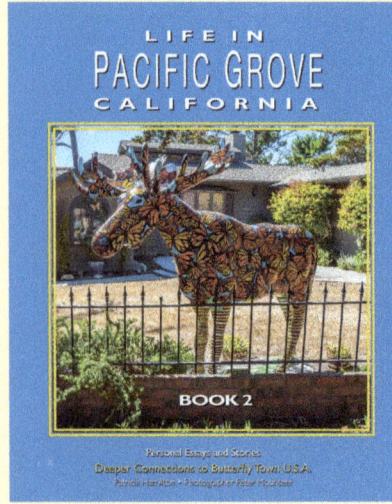

Life in Pacific Grove: Book 2
Personal P.G. Essays and Stories
Color photos Peter Mounteer

A Quaint Town for a Killing
A mystery set in Pacific Grove,
by Jeffrey Whitmore

Pacific Grove
1974 Poems, Drawings,
Woodcuts and Prose
by Bill Minor
REPRINT

A donation is made to the Pacific Grove Public Library for each book sold, specifically for the procurement and preservation of Pacific Grove stories, historic documents and memorabilia.

SECTION THREE

A WRITER'S DREAM TOWN

Centrella Inn at Christmas. Photo Peter Mounteer.

"Pacific Grove is an ideal blend of history, scenery, and community;
Victorian charm coexisting with California whimsy …."

– Brad Herzog

P.G.: The Perfect Retreat for Writers
Joyce Krieg

Pacific Grove is known as Butterfly Town, USA, and The Last Hometown. *Life* magazine has called us "the most romantic city in the U.S."

With all due respect to tradition and *Life*, we'd like to propose another descriptive image for Pacific Grove: the perfect town in which to be a writer. A literary landmark. An author's haven. A publishing paradise.

Pacific Grove: A Retreat for Writers …

Just look at all P.G. has to offer: a gorgeous natural setting sure to charm the muse … plenty of coffee houses ideal for hanging out with a laptop or notepad and pen … a thriving independent bookstore … a beloved public library … a branch of California Writers Club offering free monthly talks to educate and inspire … editors and publishers to lend a helping hand … and a literary tradition that features one of the great authors of the 20th century.

Any claim that a town might have as to its merits as an ideal home for writers would have to start with the library, and here the **Pacific Grove Public Library** exceeds expectations. Just being surrounded by all those books—some 99,000 volumes!—creates an atmosphere that invites the creative gears to begin turning.

Two key events back in 1886 brought this treasure to our community. P.G.'s first public library, known as the "reading corner," opened in a building called The Old Parlor at 165 Fountain Avenue. And, the Pacific Grove Library Association had its first meeting. In 1906, the city received a Carnegie Grant, enabling the construction of a permanent public library on a lot on Central Avenue donated by the Pacific Improvement Company.

The building has been enlarged and remodeled over the years, but you can still find traces of the original Carnegie library in the arches and windows in the Reading Area. The library is currently undergoing what is termed a "Renewal Project" with the goal of revealing and restoring more of the original architectural features, providing space to display historical archives, as well as updating restrooms, carpeting, shelving, lighting, technology and more.

Today, a writer will find quiet carrels perfect for tapping on a laptop or hunkering down with notebook and pen. Log on to one of the library's computers or bring your own device and hook into the library's free WiFi. Head over to the magazine area to read the latest issue of *Writers Digest* for informative and inspirational articles about the craft of writing, and stay up-to-date on the publishing industry. And if you need a break from the world of words, take a look at the library's community jigsaw puzzle table where you can engage other brain cells with challenges related to colors and shapes.

The Pacific Grove Public Library is located at 550 Central Avenue. Hours are Monday through Thursday from 10:00 a.m. to 7:00 p.m., Friday and Saturday from 10:00 a.m. to 5:00 p.m. Library cards are free for California residents, a mere $4.50 for out-of-state residents, and as an added bonus, the P.G. card may also be used at the Monterey Public Library.

Also vital to any town making a claim to be a writer's paradise is a good independent bookstore, and once again, Pacific Grove delivers. A bookstore called **Bookworks**, or variations thereof, has occupied 667 Lighthouse Avenue under a variety of owners for at least 25 years. The current iteration, operated since 2014 by Margot Tegtmeier and daughter Nell Flattery Carlson features some 5,000 volumes. Emphasis is on best-sellers and new releases, children's books and Steinbeck/Monterey Peninsula history. Special orders are welcome. You'll also find a selection of greeting cards, journals, puppets and games. Bookworks sponsors a book club that meets the second Wednesday of the month at 5:00 p.m. The popular Bookworks coffee house is located at the front, giving the writer the best of all worlds: browsing and brews. The bookstore is open daily from 10:00 a.m. to 6:00 p.m.

More than Steinbeck: P.G. Authors Past …

Of course **John Steinbeck** (1902-1968) must be acknowledged in any discussion of Pacific Grove's literary heritage. The future Nobel Prize laureate occupied his family's modest summer cottage on 11th Street with his first wife, Carol Henning, from 1930 to 1936. While there he penned several of his early novels, including *The Pastures of Heaven, Tortilla Flat* and *In Dubious Battle*. The unwanted attention caused by his increasing fame prompted the couple to move to Monte Sereno. But Steinbeck continued to make occasional stays in the Pacific Grove cottage until 1955, when he relocated permanently with his third wife, Elaine Scott, to a similar unpretentious cottage by the sea in Sag Harbor, New York.

⊙ ⊙ ⊙

Ed Ricketts (1897-1948) is best known as a pioneering marine biologist and the model for the fictitious character of "Doc" in his pal Steinbeck's *Cannery Row* and *Sweet Thursday*, as well as the Christ-like former preacher Jim Casy in *The Grapes of Wrath*. More than a literary inspiration, Ricketts was himself an author with deep P.G. connections. A native of Chicago, he moved to Pacific Grove in 1923 and set up Pacific Biological Laboratories at 165 Fountain Avenue, before the move to the more famed site of "Doc's Lab" on Monterey's Cannery Row. Ricketts is revered in the world of marine biology for his 1939 book *Between Pacific Tides,* one of the earliest published studies of intertidal ecology. He collaborated with Steinbeck on a chronicle of an expedition to Baja California, published in 1951 as *The Log from the Sea of Cortez.*

◉ ◉ ◉

Joseph Campbell (1904-1987) is another literary giant who briefly made his home in Pacific Grove. Years before he published the seminal *Hero with a Thousand Faces,* Campbell spent a year or so in our town in the early 1930s. As good fortune would have it, he moved right next door to another significant Pacific Grove literary figure, Ed "Doc" Ricketts. Though his stay in P.G. was brief, Campbell was a key member of the informal collection of poets, musicians, artists, philosophers and street people who hung out at the lab. His ideas about the universality of myth and the human experience greatly influenced the writings of Ricketts and Steinbeck.

◉ ◉ ◉

Clark Ashton Smith (1893-1961) penned hundreds of fantasy, science fiction and horror short stories in the golden age of "the pulps." He is considered to be one of the "big three" of *Weird Tales* magazine, along with Robert E. Howard and H.P. Lovecraft. He spent most of his life in the California Gold Country town of Auburn, but moved to a home on Ninth Street in Pacific Grove in 1954 when he married Carolyn Jones Dorman. After a series of strokes, he died in his sleep at age 68.

◉ ◉ ◉

Another science fiction writer to make a home in P.G. late in life was **Ward Moore** (1903-1978). He is best known for the 1953 alt-history novel *Bring the Jubilee,* which speculates what our nation might be like had the South won the Civil War. After spending most of his adult years in San Francisco, he moved to Pacific Grove in 1965 when he married fellow writer **Raylyn Moore** (1928-2005). Among her published works is the 1978 time travel novel *What Happened to Emily Goode after the Great Exhibition.*

Intriguing that a small, placid seaside community such as Pacific Grove would draw an unusually large number of creators of downright gruesome tales, but such seems to be the case. A further example is **Arthur Porges** (1915-2006). A native of Chicago and a one-time mathematics teacher at Los Angeles City College, Porges left teaching in 1957, moved to Big Sur, and devoted himself to writing. His output in the 1960s proved to be prodigious, with over 200 stories appearing in popular publications of the day: *The Magazine of Fantasy and Science Fiction, Fantastic, Amazing Stories, Alfred Hitchcock's Mystery Magazine,* and *Ellery Queen's Mystery Magazine.* Porges moved to Pacific Grove in the late 1960s and, with the market for pulp fiction drying up, began publishing essays and poetry in the *Monterey Herald.* He spent his final years at Forest Hill Manor.

Dianne Day (1938-2013) moved to Pacific Grove in 1993 after raising a family in Chapel Hill, North Carolina, and here began working on a cozy mystery series featuring amateur sleuth Fremont Jones, set in San Francisco in the early years of the 20th century. *The Strange Files of Fremont Jones* won the Macavity Award in 1996 for best first mystery novel, presented by Mystery Readers International. Five more Fremont Jones adventures followed in the series, praised not only for their clever plots, but also their historical accuracy and atmospheric sense of time and place. Ms. Day later relocated to Eureka, California, where she died from complications of rheumatoid arthritis and congestive heart failure.

... and P.G. Authors Present

Randall A. "Randy" Reinstedt: This Pagrovian's prolific writing career began when he was teaching fourth grade at Patton Elementary School out at Fort Ord. As every child who has gone through California public school knows, fourth grade is the year that focuses on California history. Randy quickly became disenchanted with the uninspiring required textbooks and, instead of simply complaining, wrote one of his own. *More than Memories: History and Happenings of the Monterey Peninsula* came out in 1985 and was an instant hit with both children and adults. A cottage industry—Ghost Town Publications—was born, with more than 20 titles that have sold some 400,000 copies. Many focus on the supernatural, with titles like *Ghosts, Bandits, and Legends of Old Monterey, Carmel and Surrounding Areas.* But as Randy explains it, the spooky stories are merely a hook, a device to draw readers in and then fill their minds with authentic, solid history.

◉ ◉ ◉

Peter Koper: Born in British-occupied Germany in 1947, Peter Koper's parents immigrated to the United States in 1952 and lived for a time in Pacific Grove, where young Peter attended local schools. The family relocated to Washington, D.C. in 1958. Peter Koper is a journalist, screenwriter and film producer. He has penned articles for the Associated Press, *Rolling Stone* and *People.* His film and television credits include working with John Waters on his early films and writing and producing *America's Most Wanted.*

◉ ◉ ◉

Laurence Yep: A prolific children's book author, Laurence Yep spent his childhood in San Francisco, where he felt "too American to fit into Chinatown and too Chinese to fit in anywhere else." He is best known for the Golden Mountain Chronicles, a ten-book series that documents the history of a Chinese-American family from 1849 to 1995. Two books in the series are Newbery Honor Books. In 2005, he received the prestigious Laura Ingalls Wilder Medal (now the Children's Literature Legacy Award) from the Association for Library Service to Children for making a substantial and lasting contribution to children's literature.

◉ ◉ ◉

Joanne Ryder: She has authored dozens upon dozens of picture books for children, most of them themed around animals, science and nature. The numerous awards for her work are a testament to the fact that young children can become interested in science and nature if the topics are presented in a distinctive, interesting and compelling way. Calling herself a person who thinks in images and who loves writing poetry, she describes writing picture books for children as "a joyful way to make a living." Early in her career, she worked as a children's book editor at Harper and Row, where she met her future husband, Laurence Yep. When the two writers married, they moved to Pacific Grove.

◉ ◉ ◉

Paul Fleischman: Another author of numerous books for children, Paul Fleischman was born in Monterey and lived in Pacific Grove in the 1980s and 90s. In 1989, he won the Newbery Medal for *Joyful Noise: Poems for Two Voices*, only two years after his father, Sid, also a children's book author, achieved the same honor. Paul Fleischman has won pretty much every major award offered for children's literature, and in 2012 was the U.S. nominee for the international Hans Christian Anderson Award, honoring his body of work. Paul Fleischman currently lives in Santa Cruz.

◉ ◉ ◉

Brad Herzog: He writes for both adults and children and is best known for his trilogy of travel memoirs: *Turn Left at the Trojan Horse*, *Small World* and *States of Mind*. The latter book was an Amazon best-seller and was named one of the top ten books of the year for 2000. *States of Mind* grew out of a cross-country journey that he and his wife, Amy, made in an RV in 1995-96, visiting all 48 states in the continental U.S. At the end of the adventure, the couple realized that of all the places they'd visited, they liked Pacific Grove best and have called it home ever since. Brad Herzog has penned numerous books for children, most with sports themes, through Sleeping Bear Press and Sports Illustrated for Kids. His son Luke is following in his father's footsteps, writing and publishing fantasies for middle school readers.

◉ ◉ ◉

Robin White: This Pacific Grove resident authored eight techno-thrillers, most of them themed around submarine warfare in the Tom Clancy mode, between 1991 and 2006. Drawing from his own experiences living in Russia and his background as a pilot, engineer and science writer, the titles include *The Flight from Winter's Shadow*, *Siberian Light*, *The Ice Curtain*, and *Typhoon*.

◉ ◉ ◉

Diane Tyrrel: She is the author of three romantic suspense novels published by Berkley (Penguin Group): *The Inn at Half Moon Bay*, *On Winding Hill Road*, and *On the Edge of the Woods*. She now lives in Pacific Grove and offers her services as a freelance editor and ghostwriter.

◉ ◉ ◉

Sharon Randall: Her heartwarming, homespun newspaper column, "Bay Window," began in 1991 in the *Monterey County Herald* and is now syndicated in more than 400 newspapers across the nation, with an estimated readership of over six million. She describes her column as "everyday people and ordinary things." A collection of her columns, *Birdbaths and Paper Cranes*, was published in 2002 by Plume Penguin. Sharon Randall has lived off-and-on in Pacific Grove for 35 years.

◉ ◉ ◉

Peter S. Fischer: A prolific screenwriter, Peter S. Fischer is best known for his work on the television series *Murder, She Wrote* and *Columbo*. He has also penned a series of mystery novels, each themed around the filming of a classic Hollywood movie such as *The Treasure of the Sierra Madre* and *Some Like It Hot*. He moved to Pacific Grove 12 years ago and concedes that P.G. does bear a passing resemblance to the fictitious Cabot Cove, Maine, the setting for Jessica Fletcher's crime-solving adventures in *Murder, She Wrote*.

◉ ◉ ◉

Steve Hauk: Art gallery owner, playwright and now novelist, Steve Hauk's latest project is *Steinbeck: The Untold Stories*, sixteen tales based on real events in the author's life, each examining the emotional and psychological issues Steinbeck struggled with as he attempted to write the truth as he saw it. Steve Hauk wrote the script for two award-winning documentaries, *Roots of California Photography: The Monterey Legacy* and *Time Captured in Paintings: The Monterey Legacy*. He has written plays on such varied topics as early California Impressionist artist E. Charleton Fortune and computer pioneer (and onetime P.G. resident) Gary Kildall.

◉ ◉ ◉

William Minor produced his first book containing poems, prose and woodcut prints, *Pacific Grove*, in 1974, reprinted by Pacific Grove Books 2018. Other poetry books include *Some Grand Dust* (for which he was a finalist for the Benjamin Franklin Award), and *Gypsy Wisdom: New & Selected Poems*. Bill has also published three books on music: *Unzipped Souls: A Jazz Journey Through the Soviet Union*, *Monterey Jazz Festival: Forty Legendary Years*, and *Jazz Journeys to Japan: The Heart Within*. He is currently writing his final book of his memoirs.

◉ ◉ ◉

Jeffrey Whitmore: He has extensive credits as a freelance writer and editor, including a stint as a columnist for the *Monterey County Herald,* but Whitmore's greatest claim to fame arrived in the form of a short-short story. Just 53-words long, "Bedtime Story" was originally written in 1990 as an entry to a writing contest sponsored by a weekly community newspaper in San Luis Obispo. Since then, the story has "gone viral," appearing in publications as varied as *Cosmopolitan*, *The Globe* supermarket tabloid, and the Cambridge University Press *Introduction to Narrative*, and has been read on NPR and the BBC. Under the pen name of Sterling Johnson, Whitmore has published a manual on effective swearing, *English as a Second F*cking Language*, and a mystery novel, *Dangerous Knaves*. His latest project is another mystery featuring a private eye in Pacific Grove, published by Pacific Grove Books 2018.

◉ ◉ ◉

Wolf Bukowski: He is a veteran of the television industry who now hosts a weekly screenwriting group called The Screenwriters Forum. As television director, producer, editor, and writer, he has been involved in countless projects: live broadcasts, talk shows and documentaries in studios or on location. He has received three Emmy awards and various other honors for his work. Theatrical plays and screenwriting have always been his real interests. In Los Angeles, he was a long-time member of the New Playwrights Foundation writers group, which generated original stage and screenplay material. In the 90s, the group operated a theater in Hollywood that produced its own original plays. One of them was Wolf's *Headgames, Tales from the Id*, which he is now adapting into a shooting script for a video production. One of his current projects is a screenplay entitled *Spirits in the Mist*, a tale which takes place in Pacific Grove in the 1940s. It deals with witchcraft and human passion and a young refugee child who has a special gift that malevolent forces desire.

◉ ◉ ◉

Joyce Krieg: Author of three mysteries published by St. Martin's Press: *Murder Off Mike, Slip Cue* and *Riding Gain. Murder Off Mike* was the winner of the St. Martin's Press "best first traditional mystery" contest. She is a past president of Central Coast Writers and is currently president of its parent organization, California Writers Club, overseeing a century-old nonprofit with 22 branches and some 2,000 members throughout the state. Joyce is a freelance editor through Park Place Publications. She is currently working on a mystery novel based loosely on her memories of growing up in San Jose in the 1960s, "before it became Silicon Valley."

Hart Mansion, Lighthouse Avenue. Photo Peter Mounteer.

The Hallowed Coffee House Tradition

When J.K. Rowling was a struggling single mother, she scribbled the first Harry Potter manuscript in The Elephant House coffee shop in Edinburgh, Scotland—or so legend has it. When Malcolm Gladwell launched his freelance career, he so missed being in a newsroom, he began hanging out at coffee houses. He said they provided the next best thing when it came to "the right kind of distraction," what he described as "random active social space." For most writers, there comes a time when one simply must emerge from the creative cave and engage with the world. For many, the coffee shop is the ideal setting, one of the few social venues where it's acceptable to arrive solo and monopolize a table for one, and where, for the price of a caffeinated drink, you have implied consent to linger for hours.

Fortunately for writers, Pacific Grove offers a variety of coffee shop experiences to choose from. Many have their cast of "regulars," walking and cycling buddies who drop in for a treat after a work-out, support and special interest gatherings for a variety of needs and interests, and in some cases, writing critique groups. All offer what you'd expect from a well-equipped coffee house: free customer WiFi, electric outlets, chairs and tables with flat work space, outdoor seating for writers whose creativity requires a canine companion, the usual coffee house fare of muffins, scones and cookies, and of course, plenty of caffeine.

Juice n' Java: 599 Lighthouse Ave. Open daily 7:30 a.m. to 6:30 p.m. Vibe: 21st century hippie/beatnik, complete with homey, cushy couches. You'd never guess this joint used to be a bank. Sponsors Curated Words, a series of poetry readings, on the last Thursday of the month at 7:00 p.m.

Bookworks: 667 Lighthouse Ave. Open daily 7:00 a.m. to 6:00 p.m. Vibe: Cozy, crowded, with an adjacent bookstore as an added bonus.

Carmel Valley Coffee Roasting Company:

510 Lighthouse Ave. Vibe: Modern, bright, serving sandwiches and Marianne's Ice Cream.

Crema: 481 Lighthouse Ave. Open daily 7:00 a.m. to 4:00 p.m. Vibe: Fun and friendly, shabby chic goes trendy in an old Victorian loaded with nooks and crannies. Offers a full service restaurant serving brunch and lunch daily.

Starbucks: 1212 Forest Ave. (inside Safeway). Open daily 5:30 a.m. to 8:00 p.m. Vibe: If you require a lot of background noise to get your writing done (cash registers, PA announcements, foot traffic, supermarket Muzak), this is the place for you.

Starbucks: 100 Country Club Gate Center. Open daily 5:00 a.m. to 8:00 p.m. Vibe: If only a classic Starbucks experience will do, then we've got you covered.

No, J.K. Rowling never did any writing in a Pacific Grove coffee house—at least, as far as we know. In fact, the legends swirling around her having created Harry Potter in a coffee house have gotten to the point where at least one Edinburgh establishment has installed a prominent sign proclaiming, "J.K. Rowling never wrote here."

Beyond the Coffee House

Of course, you don't *have* to write in a coffee shop to consider yourself an authentic writer. As fortune would have it, Pacific Grove offers a variety of alternatives to the writer who needs to get out of the house and into the wide world. The options described below will require a degree of flexibility—WiFi and electric outlets will probably not be available—but they definitely offer a much-needed change of pace.

◉ ◉ ◉

The Great Outdoors: Take notebook and pen (or a fully-charged tablet) to one of the many benches lining the Pacific Grove Rec Trail. If you set up shop near Crespi Pond, you'll also have access to a restroom. Spread a blanket on the beach at Lovers Point and take advantage of the casual food and drink available at the Grill or the Beach Café, as well as the new restrooms next to the Children's Pool. Head west and let your imagination loose at the gazebo next to Rocky Point at sunset. If the latter doesn't get your creative juices flowing, there may be no hope for you.

◉ ◉ ◉

The Parklet at Happy Girl Kitchen: If you drive in and out of P.G. on Central Avenue on a regular basis, you've undoubtedly noticed the blocky wooden structure extending out into the road in front of 173 Central.  Perhaps you've wondered what it is and why it's there. It's a parklet, a concept that debuted in 2010 in San Francisco in which the sidewalk is extended into the street and public amenities like benches, tables, and sometimes gardens and artwork are offered. In 2014, Jordan Champagne of Happy Girl Kitchen brought the idea to P.G., obtained city approval, and conducted a successful Kickstarter campaign to raise the money to have it built. Today, the parklet offers benches, tables, shade, and a place to hang out and watch the passing panorama of foot and automobile traffic—and to write.

The café serves breakfast and lunch, while coffee, tea, baked goods, and the Happy Girl's signature jams and pickles are available whenever the shop is open. "As long as you see a light on, you can come into the shop," they promise. Open daily from 7:00 a.m. to 5:00 p.m., with café service from 7:30 a.m. to 3:00 p.m.

◉ ◉ ◉

The Pacific Grove Museum of Natural History: Taxidermy animals, dioramas, oddball personal collections and Sandy the Whale may spring to mind when one thinks of this P.G. landmark. But the hidden jewel for writers is the back patio. On days when the rests of town is chilly and windblown, this space is sheltered, warm and cozy.  Several wicker chairs offer seating and a place to soak up the winter sun while finishing a poem or writing the next scene in a novel. Admission is free for Monterey County residents. Open Tuesday through Sunday from 10:00 a.m. to 5:00 p.m. at 165 Forest Avenue.

◉ ◉ ◉

Hearst Social Hall at Asilomar Conference Grounds: A personal favorite of this writer. No, you do not need to be attending a conference to take advantage of this beautiful and inspiring setting! In warm weather months, relax on the outdoor deck and let the combined aromas of salt air and the pine forest stimulate your creative senses. When the weather turns unbearably chilly, windy or foggy, cozy up to the roaring fireplace inside the historic craftsman-style lodge. There's something about being around people who have traveled from across the nation and around the world to attend a conference that makes being there feel as if you, too, have undertaken a journey, a mini-writer's retreat without ever having to your own hometown.

◉ ◉ ◉

Phoebe's Café, located in Hearst Social Hall, offers coffee, tea, beer, wine, and "grab-and-go" sandwiches, pastries, cookies and related snacks. Open daily from 6:30 a.m. to 9:00 p.m., Fridays and Saturdays to 10:00 p.m. Address: 800 Asilomar Avenue.

Photo Peter Mounteer.

Meeting Up with Kindred Spirits

Writing is undoubtedly the most solitary of all the professions and hobbies. Yet even the most hermit-like of wordsmiths cannot deny the longing to commune with others who pursue the same passion—those individuals whom Anne Shirley of *Anne of Green Gables* spoke of as "kindred spirits."

◎ ◎ ◎

Central Coast Writers, a branch of California Writers Club, has been meeting continuously since its founding in the summer of 2002. Several Pagrovians were key figures in the early days of the club, including Ken Jones, Anita Alan, Laura Emerson, Kerry Wood, and our own Patricia Hamilton.

The club meets at Point Pinos Grill at the P.G. Municipal Golf Course. The beautiful locale, with the view of the sea, the cypress, and the setting sun, the hip, trendy décor, and the friendly, accommodating staff make it the ideal venue for a gathering of creative folk. Meetings take place on the third Tuesday of the month, except for August and December, and feature a guest speaker on a specific topic relating to the craft of writing or the publishing industry. Guests are welcome at no admission charge. Doors open at 5:30 p.m. for optional dinner (ordered off the menu and paid for individually) or guests may come just for the meeting and speaker, starting at 6:30 p.m.

Today Central Coast Writers boasts 170 members and then some, ranging from authors with multi-book contracts with major New York houses to newcomers who just "always wanted to write." In addition to the monthly meetings, the club sponsors a booth at Good Old Days, encourages young writers with a high school short story contest, and hosts social events just for members.

CCW members who live in Pacific Grove and have published books include: John T. Blossom, *Trespassing*; Patrick Flanigan, *Surviving the Storm* and other books of poetry; Laura Hamill, *Writing Evolution: Cosmic Explorations*; Patricia Hamilton, *Life in Pacific Grove*; Ken Jones, *Monterey Shorts*; Sam Kier, *Two Centuries of Valor*; Jeanne Olin, *Dear Jude*; Russell Sunshine, *Far and Away*; Nancy Swing, *Child's Play*.

◎ ◎ ◎

The Sally Griffin Active Living Center offers a free creative writing class Tuesdays from 1:30 to 3:30 p.m. Location: 700 Jewell Avenue.

◎ ◎ ◎

At the other end of the age spectrum, P.G. High School offers a **Young Writers Club.** Led by faculty advisor Larry Haggquist, this dynamic group of teens has been publishing an annual literary magazine for eleven years. This year's issue is 20 pages long, in full color, featuring short stories, poetry and student artwork. Works by these talented young people also appear on a regular basis in the *Cedar Street Times*.

◎ ◎ ◎

Poetry in the Grove is a monthly gathering of Pagrovians interested in poetry or who want to learn more about it. Each month, the group selects a well-known poet whose work will be shared and discussed at the following meeting. The group meets the first Saturday of the month from 3:00 to 5:00 p.m. at the Little House in Jewell Park. Free admission.

Stocking Up: Goods and Services for Writers

Putting aside all jokes about writers and their booze and cigarettes—or Red Smith's famous "just open a vein and bleed"—the fact is, writers need stuff. The basic tools of trade are easily found right here in Pacific Grove.

Office Supplies: As tempting as it may be to stock up from an online source or to visit a big box chain store, a case can be made for shopping local when it comes to basic office supplies like notebooks, pens, envelopes, staplers, and sticky notes. The Grove Market (242 Forest Avenue), Safeway (1212 Forest Avenue) and Lucky California (200 Country Club Gate) all feature an office supplies section. Rite Aid (160 Country Club Gate) offers the usual office supplies, plus flash drives, cables and connectors, and a selection of ink jet cartridges for the most common HP printers.

Upscale Goods: If your creative soul cries out for a journal, notecards or planner that's beautiful, blingy, or both, try Bookworks (667 Lighthouse Avenue) or The Quill (552 Lighthouse Avenue).

Computer Help: When it comes to all the machines, gizmos and gadgets of the modern world, it often feels like a case of "can't live with 'em, can't live without 'em." At some point, every writer who is doing anything more than personal journaling is going to need to use a computer. And at some point, that rig is going to slow down, freeze up, or present the dreaded Blue Screen of Death. Moranda Minds at 223 Forest Avenue offers drop-in computer assistance Monday through Friday from 1:00 to 5:00 p.m. Bay Tech Repair is a P.G.-based business that specializes in mobile "house call" service, with phone lines open from 8:00 a.m. to 11:00 p.m. 831/200-6855.

Editing Services: They say every good writer needs a good editor. If you are planning to break into the world of traditional New York publishing, the major houses will insist that your manuscript be error-free before they will even consider accepting it. If you're planning to go the self-publishing route, the Amazon reviewers will skewer you mercilessly if your book is riddled with typos, grammatical errors and spelling mistakes. Fortunately, there are excellent professional editors right here in Pacific Grove. A few to consider: Heather Lazare, heatherlazare.com; Diane Tyrrel; dianetyrrel.com; and Joyce Krieg, joycek.com.

Getting Your Work Out There:

Few events in the life of a writer are more satisfying and exciting than the moment when they first hold a book in their hands with their name on the cover. Patricia Hamilton of Park Place Publications has been making that dream come true for local writers since 1991. Park Place is a full-service book publisher every step of the way, from editing a first draft to layout and printing. Patricia calls her business one of the first "indie publishers," and says, "Our niche is personal, creative and dependable service and products with a smile." Located at 591 Lighthouse Ave. #10, 831/649-6640. *Patricia is now accepting on-line queries for a new imprint,* **Pacific Grove Books**. *Fiction and non-fiction—the story must be inspired by or take place in Pacific Grove. Details: www.pacificgrovebooks.com.*

Books Inspired by Pacific Grove

We shall conclude this look at Pacific Grove as the ideal Retreat for Writers with an overview at books that are either about Pacific Grove or are set in our town. Some of the older titles may be available only as reference copies at the library, or possibly found by doing some serious searching with antiquarian book dealers. Other, newer volumes are readily available at our local bookstore, or can easily be ordered if they're not on the shelf.

Children's Books:

Cameron, Eleanor: *The Wonderful Flight to the Mushroom Planet* (1954: Little, Brown) was one of the first outer space adventure stories written for young readers and remains in print sixty-plus years later. As the title would suggest, most of the action takes place on the Mushroom Planet, but when young heroes Chuck and David return to earth, home is right here in Pacific Grove. Author Eleanor Cameron (1912-1996) barely missed making our list of Pacific Grove authors, as she lived not in P.G., but next door in Pebble Beach.

Cleary, Beverly: *Strider.* (1991: Harper Collins). Though best known for her Ramona Quimby novels set in Portland, Oregon, Beverly Cleary of Carmel Valley has penned dozens of other novels for children. *Strider* is about a 14-year-old boy living in Pacific Grove who rescues a dog on the beach—and about how the new pet ends up emotionally rescuing the boy.

Politi, Leo: *The Butterflies Come* (1957, Scribner). Another prolific writer for children, Leo Politi tells the tale of a little girl who visits the Pacific Grove Butterfly Sanctuary and learns all about butterflies and the celebrations surrounding their return to California.

Weintraub, Aileen: *Point Pinos Light: The West Coast's Oldest Active Lighthouse.* With more than 50 titles for children to her name, Aileen Weintraub published this fact-based story of Pacific Grove's Point Pinos Lighthouse in 2003 through PowerKids Press.

History:

Breene, Rose C.: *The History of the First Baptist Church of Pacific Grove.* (1995).

Breschini, Gary: *Archives of California Prehistory: An Off-ramp on the Kelp Highway* (2006: Archeological Consulting).

Butner, Evelyn, et al: *The Chautauqua Connection.* (1980: Pacific Grove Heritage Society).

Chrisman, G.H.: *Beautiful Monterey by the Sea.* (1906: Monterey Daily Cypress).

Dyke, Elmarie Hurlbert: *Pacific Grove, California: Butterfly Town USA* (1958).

Hamilton, Patricia: *Life in Pacific Grove, California Vol.1 and Vol.2* (2017-18 Keepers of Our Culture, Pacific Grove Books.)

Hanson, Earle C: *Monterey and Pacific Grove Street Car Era.* (1990: Interurban Press).

Howard, Donald M.: *The Old Pacific Grove Retreat: A Business Biography 1875-1940.* (1999: Monterey Peninsula Historiography Press).

Howard, Donald M.: *Rancho to Retreat: A Complete Guide to Pacific Grove Land Titles, 1830-1930.* (2000: Monterey Peninsula Historiography Press).

Howe, Wendy Salisbury: *Pacific Grove: An Early Seaside Retreat Revisited.* (1978, City of Pacific Grove).

Jaques, Louise V.: *Story of Wilford Rensselaer Holman.* (1979).

Jochmus, Augustus Carlos: *The Circle of Enchantment.* (1931: Pacific Grove Chamber of Commerce).

McCaffery, Jerry: *Lighthouse: Point Pinos, Pacific Grove, California.* (2001).

McLane, Lucy Neely: *A Piney Paradise by Monterey Bay.* (1958: Academy Library Guild). (2019: Fourth Edition Reprint by Pacific Grove Books, Pacific Grove, Calfiornia)

Miller, Evelyn Grantham, et al.: *Pacific Grove, California: The First 100 Years.* (1975).

Minor, William: *Pacific Grove 1974, poems/drawings/woodcuts/prose* (Pacific Grove Books reprint 2018)

Platt, Julia: *The Holy City.* (1922).

Seavey, Kent: *Pacific Grove.* (2005: Arcadia Publishing).

Semones, JoAnn: *Pirates, Pinnacles and Petticoats: The Shipwrecks of Point Pinos and Monterey Bay.* (2015: Glencannon Press).

Straley, Janice M., et al.: *Ed Ricketts: From Cannery Row to Sitka, Alaska.* (2015: Shorelast Editions).

Stumbo, Jean Serpell: *Emily Fish: Socialite Lightkeeper of Point Pinos Lighthouse.* (1997: Pacific Grove Museum of Natural History).Writers Program: *Monterey Peninsula.* (1941: Work Projects Administration.)

Travel and Special Interest

Burness, Tad: *The Vintage House Book* (2003: Newton Abbott). This look at classic American homes from 1880 to 1980 includes several examples of Pacific Grove's beloved Victorians.

Cort, Daniel: *Downtown Turnaround: Lessons for a New Urban Landscape.* (2010: Park Place Publications). Former Mayor Cort shares his vision as to how local governments can help downtown districts recapture their historic and cultural souls.

Courses and Links: *Golf on the Peninsula.* (1973: Courses and Links, Inc.). Includes a section on the "poor man's Pebble," the Pacific Grove Municipal Golf Course.

Crouch, Steve: *Fog and Sun, Sea and Stone: The Monterey Coast.* (1980: Graphic Arts Publishing). The classic coffee table book features scenes of Pacific Grove and surrounding communities.

Evans, Nancy M. and Neil: *Exploring the Monterey Peninsula.* (1994: Worldview Associates). Travel guide that includes a section on Pacific Grove.

Meursault, Martin: *Martin Meursault's Enjoy! The Authoritative Guide to the Restaurants of the Monterey Peninsula.* (1998: Stanford Frederick Press). Restaurant guide that includes a chapter on Pacific Grove. Fun to see how many are still in business, or to rekindle memories of favorite dining places that are long gone.

Riddell, Craig and Rebecca: *Pacific Grove Architecture and Anecdotes.* (2016: The Bookworks). Photographs of Pacific Grove's famed Victorians and the stories behind the homes.

Shugart, Alan F.: *Fandango: The Story of Two Guys Who Wanted to Own a Restaurant.* (1993: Carmel Bay Publishing Co.). Legend and lore surrounding one of P.G.'s favorite restaurants.

Vokac, David and Joan: *Carmel, Monterey and Pacific Grove: Getaway Guide to California's Monterey Peninsula.* (2016: West Press). Another general travel guide to our region.

Fiction, Personal Essay and Poetry

Breen, Elaine: *My Peaceful Forest: Reflections on Life in Pacific Grove.* (2001: Gallagher Press).

Houy, Julie: *Specific Grove: Some Poems about Pacific Grove and Some Specific Grovians.* (1979).

Minor, William: *Pacific Grove: Poems, Drawings, Woodcuts, Prose.* (1974). Reprint 2018 Pacific Grove Books.

Nielson, Fred Norris and Suzanne: *Chauffeur's Gold: Farm Boy Finds Treasure in Retirement Community.* (2014: Amazon Digital Services). Promises "a lot more going on in retirement homes than you'd ever imagine."

Whitmore, Jeffrey: *A Quaint Town for a Murder.* (2018 Pacific Grove Books). Mystery novel set in P.G.

Writers Group of Canterbury Woods: *Pacific Grove, California: This is Our Town.* (1968: D'Angelo Publishing Group).

More resources on page 2.

◉ ◉ ◉

We started our discussion of authors who have lived in Pacific Grove with John Steinbeck, so it is only fitting that we conclude our look at works set in or about P.G. with more reflections on Steinbeck's work. Though *Cannery Row* and *Sweet Thursday* are closely associated with Monterey, each contain scenes set in Pacific Grove, most notably Doc's collecting trips to the Great Tide Pool, located just west of the Point Pinos Lighthouse. *Cannery Row* is the novel that features the famous scene concerning the flag-pole skater atop the Holman Department Store building, while *Sweet Thursday* includes several of the author's wry observations about P.G. eccentricities: the laws protecting butterflies, the Methodist Church's forbidding of all "hijinks" and The Great Roque War.

Nearly 90 years ago, a struggling young writer found Pacific Grove to be his perfect writer's retreat. Perhaps the next Nobel Prize-winning novelist is just now making the same discovery about the special, magical quality of Pacific Grove, putting pen to paper and creating prose that will one day change the world—and future generations will look back and realize it all started right here in our little corner of the coast.

An Author's Ode To Pacific Grove
Brad Herzog

"It is a fabulous place: when the tide is in, a wave-churned basin, creamy with foam, whipped by the combers that roll in from the whistling buoy on the reef. But when the tide goes out the little water world becomes quiet and lovely."—John Steinbeck

In *Cannery Row*, arguably the most lyrical creation by America's finest writer, John Steinbeck reserves some of his most evocative prose for a description of the Great Tide Pool at Point Pinos. That place, a window into a microcosmic universe at the northernmost tip of the Monterey Peninsula, is where Doc Ricketts used to gather specimens for his laboratory. So let's begin with that: When an unparalleled writer at the top of his game chose to marvel at a near-perfect example of the interconnectedness of a place and its inhabitants, he was describing Pacific Grove.

We locals call it P.G., but that's largely just to save energy. The Chamber of Commerce touts it as "Butterfly Town, USA" in reference to the monarch butterflies that winter here, their numbers dwindling, if not their majesty. For them, at least, it actually may be "America's Last Hometown." Back in 2002, *Life* magazine referred to Pacific Grove as America's "Most Romantic City," offering a cover photo of a pink blanket of ice plant blooming along the coast, like a love letter from Mother Nature. A few years later, a writer for *Via* magazine referred to this tranquil hamlet, where sidewalk smiles are still in fashion, as something akin to the "Mayberry of the Monterey Peninsula."

Fine descriptions all, but not quite enough to capture my hometown in full.

An old college pal of mine came close. Not long after my wife and I first moved here a couple of decades ago, this friend visited for a spell, briefly shedding his big-city Midwestern existence for a respite on the Central Coast. He arrived at his epiphany one autumn evening as we sauntered into town to enjoy some local seafood specialties. Maybe it was the lemon butter sanddabs at Fandango, or possibly some carrot-ginger oysters at Passionfish. It was the Magic Hour, a cinematographer's favorite time of day. The soon-to-be setting sun cast a warm glow on the century-old Victorians, while the chimes from the City Hall clock tower began a serenade amid the serenity. My friend could only shake his head and chuckle. "It's like you live in that town from *The Truman Show*," he said, and then he added, in mock director's voice, "Cue the bells!"

Too good to be true. That's what he meant.

Still, for the best description, I'll return to the Peninsula's most eminent author, who worked on many of his masterpieces from his family's cottage, which still stands on 11th Street in P.G. In Steinbeck's examination of intertidal ecosystems, we can find not only limpets and hermit

crabs and waving algae, but also a universal metaphor. In *The Log from the Sea of Cortez*, he further expounded on "the brilliant colors, the swarming species" of tide pools. A simple study of a "small and perfect pool," he concluded, offers an understanding that "all things are one thing and that one thing is all things."

So there you have it: Pacific Grove is a Great Tide Pool—dense with history but alive in the moment, a great sum of its disparate parts, a little world of 2.7 square miles teeming with wonders both obvious and overlooked. And everywhere I look, I see a writer's inspirations.

> *"Nature gives to every time and season some beauties of its own; and from morning to night, as from the cradle to the grave, it is but a succession of changes so gentle and easy that we can scarcely mark their progress."—Charles Dickens*

During Christmas at the Inns, when much of the town seems to be dressed up in holiday light, Pacific Grove does seem rather like a Dickens village come to life. But the natural beauty hardly needs seasons to be spectacular. And believe me, I've seen America's most spectacular places—many times over. While researching and writing three travel memoirs about my journeys through small-town America, I have been able to (as Walt Whitman put it) "inhale great draughts of space." Or, if you prefer, I'll quote Johnny Cash: "I've been everywhere, man"—the rolling fences and perfect landscapes of Kentucky's horse country, the jaw-dropping wonderlands of southern Utah, the towering sand dunes of northwestern Michigan, the picture-postcard places in Vermont. Ours is truly a beautiful country—well beyond purple mountain majesties and amber waves of grain.

But for me, one of the great pleasures of going places is simply this: I get to tell people where I'm coming from. And no matter where I travel, much the same conversation occurs. I'll be chatting with a newly met acquaintance, and it will go something like this:

"So where do you live?"

"California."

"Oh? Where in California?"

"The Monterey Peninsula."

Pause. Heavenward glance. Groan. "Ohhh! That's paradise!"

It happens every time. Sometimes the reaction is slightly different. Maybe an earnest "I love that place!" Or an envious "I'm soooo jealous!" Or a sarcastic "Oh, poor you!"

Although I revel in the envy, I try not to smile too broadly. Then I return home, and maybe I take a stroll along Ocean View Boulevard in Pacific Grove. Perhaps it's spring and the ice plant is blooming in a great frenzy of those pink explosions, and I make my way along the dirt trail, past the Seuss-like aloe plants that always seem like vegetation from another planet. And there I spot an artist, brush in hand, peering toward Lovers Point and putting the finishing touches on a colorful canvas celebrating the rocky coastline.

And I think, *This isn't only a place that draws artists; it's a place that artists draw.*

My hometown is a dreamscape. Either folks are smiling because they're on vacation or they're grinning because they live here. We get to enjoy paradise fluidly, and we're not bound by the edges of a canvas. That goes for writers, too, of course. You can never run out of words about a setting that makes your jaw drop.

Yes, the four-mile recreational trail alongside Ocean View is a picture-perfect snapshot of wonders along the water's edge. But there are a whole bunch of wonders in our little world. What about the stroll through the forests and dunes at the Asilomar Conference Center? Or Asilomar State Beach, particularly at low tide, when the sea reveals what it has been hiding? How about the back nine at the Pacific Grove Municipal Golf Links, designed by Jack Neville, better known as the original designer of the links at Pebble Beach? Or the six-block-long trail through George Washington Park, occasionally under a canopy of visiting butterflies? Or the Butterfly Sanctuary itself? Like the often-unnoticed frenzy of activity in the gaps and crevices of the rocky shore, there are underappreciated gems within this underappreciated gem.

"Follow your bliss, and the universe will open doors where there were only walls."

—**Joseph Campbell**

Come to think of it, the town itself is a bit of a hidden treasure, at least in comparison to its neighbors. Monterey, Carmel and Pebble Beach are each internationally-known. Pacific Grove? It is the Zeppo Marx of the Peninsula. But history will note that the Marx brothers insisted Zeppo—not Groucho or Harpo or Chico—had the most natural good humor.

And actually, a poster of the Marx brothers long graced a wall of one of my favorite Peninsula places. Technically, it's not located in Pacific Grove (it's maybe a few hundred feet over the Monterey boundary). The tourists don't stop at 800 Cannery Row, and the marketers don't much tout it. It is, one might say, an unidentified icon amid a touristified stretch of coastline. But to me, it is analogous to P.G.—a scene often overlooked by visitors but brimming with historical significance and countless tales worth telling. In fact, if you're looking for a place that best captures the idiosyncratic charm, creative spawn, and ocean-sprayed saga of the area, look no further than this tiny, two-story building where a couple of Depression-era dreamers used to end their days by swapping philosophy and swigging beers.

Both Ed Ricketts and John Steinbeck made a living studying life's quirky interactions. Ricketts did it by combing tide pools to fill the shelves of Pacific Biological Laboratories; Steinbeck directed his attentions to the lovable and flawed denizens of his hometown. Cannery Row was his tide pool, and lyrical prose was his laboratory experiment. But his muse was Ricketts, and Doc's Lab—an anomaly even back then as a scientific repository among brothels and flophouses—was where the muse sang loudest.

Because it is open to the public on only a handful of occasions each year, a peek into the lab is a rare treat, and it must be approached with proper reverence and whimsy. Standing inside the wood-paneled set of rooms, with a second-floor view of the street on one side and the sea on the other, one is transported to a time when the bay was brimming with sardines, the town was awash in characters, and a motley crew of artists, writers and scholars would gather to get metaphysical over a batch of homemade brew. Not only Steinbeck, but Joseph Campbell, too—the myth-maker and the mythologist, both inspired by a fellow who became immortal as "Doc" without so much as a PhD.

In 1957, nine years after Ricketts was fatally struck by a Del Monte Express train at the other end of Cannery Row, his laboratory was sold to a group of 14 locals, several of them Doc's old friends, and it became an exclusive club of sorts. Every Wednesday for years, the men enjoyed cold drinks and cool jazz, occasionally to be joined by the likes of Dizzy Gillespie and Louis Armstrong when they were in town. Even though they deeded the building to the City of Monterey in 1992, the surviving members continued the Wednesday night tradition, a celebration of artistry and informality. Indeed, the photos and posters on the former lab's walls—of not only the Marx brothers, but also Albert Einstein and Charlie Chaplin—seem to represent a Steinbeck-Ricketts kind of genius, the kind that understands both humor and humanity.

So while the old canneries have become restaurants and malls or have been incorporated into the aquarium inspired by Doc's efforts, the historically preserved building at 800 Cannery Row retains the whiff of originality. It is an antique among extreme makeovers. And it is a monument to an original friendship—between a biologist-philosopher who found life teeming in the strangest places and a writer who found much the same thing.

"Probably nothing in the way of promotion Holman's Department Store ever did attracted so much favorable comment as the engagement of the flagpole skater ..." —**John Steinbeck**

So begins Chapter 19 of *Cannery Row*, my favorite section of the book. Based on a real event in Pacific Grove, when a performer known as The Mysterious Mr. X broke his own record by staying aloft 120 feet above the street for more than 50 hours, the chapter is a rather tangential diversion amid the narrative of Doc Ricketts and friends. But I prefer to think of it is as several hundred words of whimsy with an acute observation at its core. The story of the flagpole skater is an examination of perspective.

"Everyone in town," writes Steinbeck, "was more or less affected by the skater." Henri the painter vowed to build himself a skating platform and try it at home. Old Doctor Merrivale started shooting at him with an air rifle. Mack and the boys reacted with a shrug and returned to the Palace Flophouse. And high-strung Richard Frost ... well, he had a question that he couldn't quite get himself to ask.

The former Holman's Department Store is currently in the process of being reinvented, described in decidedly less lyrical terms as a "modern-day, mixed-use property." What was once a view reserved for the flagpole skater will be enjoyed by the residents of high-end condominiums and penthouses. But the century-old building still stands—squarely in the center of town on Lighthouse Avenue—as a lesson in point of view. Depending on one's outlook, it is either a piece of property with great possibilities or a piece of history bearing treasured memories. Or, perhaps, both. They are not mutually exclusive.

Like most anything, the point of view depends on one's perspective. And that describes one's point of view of Pacific Grove. For me, it was a carefully considered destination—a choice made after a 48-state home search and a sincere examination of criteria regarding where we wanted to live. For many—far more people than I realized when I first moved here—it is a lifelong home, a why-would-I-move-anywhere-else conclusion. For others, it is temporary good fortune. Maybe they're spending a couple of years at the Defense Language Institute, or they snagged a job in the hospitality industry. Pacific Grove can be retirement nirvana, a sort of senior sigh of relief. Or an experiment. Is small-town living for me? Is this the right place and climate? Can I survive occasional fog if I see daily friendly faces?

So yes, we can extrapolate from the *Cannery Row* characters. Some of us are Henri the painter, easily and often inspired. Some are surely like Mack and the boys, wondering what all the fuss is about. And some are like Richard Frost, unable to get beyond practical considerations. You see, thanks to some liquid courage, Frost finally got the nerve to pose the question that had been nagging him and more than a few other observers. "Hey!" he shouted up to the skater. "How—how do you—go to the toilet?"

Someone had to ask.

"I can think of no other edifice constructed by man as altruistic as a lighthouse. They were built only to serve." —**George Bernard Shaw**

My absolute favorite thing about driving through South Dakota—yes, South Dakota—is the series of upright images rising from the plains every six or ten miles like pegs on a cribbage board: the old country grain elevator. In towns with names like Faulkton and Redfield and Zell and Clark, they serve as a structural metaphor for the Heartland—no unnecessary decoration, just perfect functional simplicity. For these hamlets, the elevator stands as a sort of exclamation point, reminding passersby that a town still exists. But in recent years, the emergence of mega-farms has created a demand for the efficiency of massive concrete and steel elevators, making the old versions increasingly old-fashioned.

Fading icons ... you can find those, too, on the sides of old barns. I recall cruising past the fields and farmhouses of northern Indiana and coming across an old brown barn with a painted advertisement on the side. It was supposed to say "CHEW MAIL POUCH TOBACCO," one of many such barn-side ads created by crews in the mid-20th century in exchange for a farmer's choice of cash, magazine subscriptions or, yes, chewing tobacco. But the lettering on this barn had faded to such an extent that only three of the twenty letters now stood out clearly. So it said only "AIL."

How appropriate. There were once more than 10,000 Mail Pouch barns dotting rural America, particularly in the Midwest. But time and the elements have reduced those numbers considerably, and as the letters fade so too does a little history. It is an ailing piece of Americana and just one of various vanishing architectural archetypes.

Lighthouses beckon, too—and they serve as both a warning and a beacon, a sign of danger and of safety, a reminder of nature's power and a symbol of humanity's attempt to control it. If it has been around for more than 160 years—like Pacific Grove's Point Pinos, the oldest continuously operating light station on the West Coast, still utilizing the original building and lenses and prisms—well, then it is most assuredly a treasured icon. But like an old-fashioned grain elevator in the Heartland, historic lighthouses seem to be teetering on the edge of obsolescence in these days of global positioning systems.

With this in mind, I decided long ago not to take the remnants of yesteryear for granted. Outdated or not, these structures call to mind simpler times, when sailors looked for a light in the darkness and tiny hamlets painted their names brightly on prairie skyscrapers. So when I'm rumbling down the road and I spot a rusting grain elevator or a fading lighthouse or a tilting covered bridge or an abandoned one-room schoolhouse, I'll spend a moment musing about what a local treasure it must have been in its day and about the effort once needed to keep a whale oil lantern burning or teach a gaggle of homesteaders' kids. I'll remember that the march of progress must be tempered by a regard for the past—an appreciation of the journey, as it were.

There is certainly a sense of antiquation at Point Pinos, as if one is stepping into a bygone era. Run your fingers over the rusted anchor inside—a relic from the *Gipsy*, which met its demise in the bay more than a century ago—and you can almost feel the years at your fingertips. Climb the circular stairway to the restored bedroom on the second floor, and you can almost hear the sound of famed lightkeeper Emily Fish sighing as she fell into bed after a hard day's work.

But there is also a sense of the march of time—toward a world that is faster-paced, more vigilant, offering a continuous stream of information. Consider the light itself: The first light source was a whale oil lantern. Today, it is a 1000-watt electric bulb. The light used to be snuffed during daylight hours; now it is permanently beaming. Or consider that Punta de los Pinos, named by Spanish explorer Sebastian Vizcaino in 1602, translates to "Point of the Pines," so named for the trees that crowded the shores at the northern tip of the Monterey Peninsula. Point Pinos Lighthouse was once described by Robert Louis Stevenson as standing amid "a wilderness of sand." These days, it overlooks the largely treeless fairways of the P.G. muni golf course. Once a guide to occasionally wayward vessels with names like *Celia* (wrecked in fog off of Point Joe in 1906) and *Aurora* (stranded on Del Monte Beach in 1935), it is now more likely to attract wayward shots from Big Bertha.

But I prefer to think of Point Pinos as attracting something much more, beckoning not only sailors to the Peninsula, but also scientists and soldiers and merchants and tourists and immigrants. And purveyors of the written word. After all, a blank page is like an endless sea. You can launch a journey and not quite know where you going. So it's nice to have a beacon to guide you back.

So a lighthouse like Point Pinos is all things to all people—a signal, a sentinel, an announcement of civilization, a historical touchstone, a vacation snapshot, a conduit to distant places, and (maybe most of all) a welcome home.

"Why is it that when one man builds a wall, the next man immediately needs to know what's on the other side?" —George R.R. Martin

I would argue that much of Pacific Grove's foundation was constructed out of curiosity. P.G.'s gorgeous paths and grand edifices recall the genesis of this place. Consider, for instance, the Gosby House Inn on bustling Lighthouse Avenue. The street was originally simply a trail cut through the forest by the Point Pinos lighthouse keeper. The inn was built as a boardinghouse for Methodist ministers who came to preach to the hundreds of people assembled for a summer church retreat amid rough tents. That's how the community began in 1875—as a tent city of sorts on the shores of Monterey Bay. A few years later, it emerged as a West Coast branch of the Chautauqua Literary and Scientific Circle. So Pacific Grove was birthed as a place promoting intellectual curiosity (well, along with stern moral values, including prohibitions against "immodest bathing apparel").

Today's dress code is determined by the whims of the breezes and the coast-hugging fog. The intellectual curiosity? I see it in the Friends of the Pacific Grove Library … and in the Central Coast Writers group that meets monthly in town … and, most adorably, in each Little Library that has sprouted up in many Pagrovians' front yards. Intellectual curiosity, of course, is the whip that drives the writer. As I always say, it's fine to write what you know, but I often prefer to explore what I *don't yet* know. Writers, as observers of the human condition, treat the undiscovered as a call to adventure.

Pacific Grove's tents were soon replaced—often on the very same tiny plot of land—by charming cottages and stately Victorian homes. Rumor has it, in fact, that P.G. boasts more Victorians per capita than any city in America. So Steinbeck's description of a tide pool dweller searching for a new home—"And now one, finding an empty snail shell he likes better than his own, creeps out, exposing his soft body to the enemy for a moment, and then pops into the new shell"—might well describe the evolution of P.G.'s humble abodes. Indeed, rumor has it that modern contractors burrowing into the walls of these turn-of-the-century residences have discovered a surprising reminder of origins—tent canvas.

Hundreds of homes throughout town are adorned with green wooden plaques denoting the first assessed owner of the property and the first year of record. So a stroll through town can feel like an anachronistic amble. On Forest Avenue, you might find a plaque ("Annie L. Clayton 1891") alongside a window containing an "I Support Military Women" ribbon. On Chestnut Street, you might spot a metallic green VW bug in front of an even more boldly painted, bright yellow home. "Nancy Houghton 1899," the plaque announces.

Pacific Grove has found a way to hold onto its past, while making it currently functional, turning it into a communal celebration. So history comes alive in contemporary forms. Chinese immigrants first settled the area in 1853, maintaining a fishing village for more than half a century at China Point (now known as Cabrillo Point, the site of Hopkins Marine Station). These Cantonese fishermen are remembered annually in July with the Feast of Lanterns, when (weather permitting) we decorate the city with brightly colored lanterns, enjoy a Saturday pageant-and-picnic, and ooh and aah at fireworks. Every April, too, the late 19th century is reborn as the Good Old Days celebration featuring an old-school parade, but also a street fair offering everything from bounce houses to blues bands.

P.G. places evolve and adjust, as well. Lovers Point was once a flurry of activity back in the city's infancy. There was a Japanese tea garden, a merry-go-round, and a concession of glass-bottom boats decorated to look like Venetian gondolas. Eventually, the focus of this community park was simplified to its natural core—the leaning cypress trees, the rocky outcrop, the beach tucked away like a secret escape. But in recent years, much of the bustle has returned. What was once old is new again.

The residents of a tide pool, too, are constantly adapting to a change in environment, spending part of their time under water and part of it exposed to the air. Steinbeck: "A wave breaks over the barrier, and churns the glassy water for a moment and mixes bubbles into the pool, and then it clears and is tranquil and lovely … again."

So it is in Pacific Grove, where the weather can change in an instant and where the most celebrated nonhuman residents are the sea otters gamboling in the bay and the butterflies that arrive en masse each October from as far north as Alaska and take up residence in the pine and eucalyptus grove ("one of those happy accidents of nature that gladden the heart," Steinbeck wrote in *Sweet Thursday*). The temptation is to compare the orange-and-black-winged beauties with the tourists who come and go, but really the butterflies tell a tale of generations and return. These monarchs are the offspring of last year's crew, having never visited the Peninsula before, yet somehow knowing exactly where to point themselves.

In P.G., generations are revered as cornerstones. This is particularly evident in the school system and its remarkable number of local teachers were once local students. Only recently, I attended the 29th annual "Spring Fling" celebration. The P.G. Co-Op Preschool was honoring Jennifer Ross and her 43 years of launching the education of three- and four-year-olds in Pacific Grove. That's a stunning amount of show and tell—and generations of influence.

Small wonder, then, that every October the entire community gathers to watch the Butterfly Parade, a celebration of its children, in which each elementary school class dresses in its own historical or ecological costume. When the kindergartners march through town adorned in brightly-painted orange-and-black wings, as if just escaping their cocoons, the smiles on their faces as wide as their wingspans. All of which makes it more profound that in P.G., according to a city ordinance, it is illegal to harm a Monarch butterfly.

"It is advisable to look from the tide pool to the stars and then back to the tide pool again."
—**John Steinbeck**

Quite often in Pacific Grove, there is a stillness, a quietude that inspires. You can ponder life's riddles without the obstruction of background noise. It is like peering into a tide pool of the mind. *That*, I would argue, is a writer's paradise.

Despite all the remarkable sights and scenes and senses—the Asilomar Beach sunsets and ice plant displays, the cypress canopies and kelp dances, the fireplace at Asilomar Conference Center and bonfires at Asilomar State Beach, the chiming of the bell tower and the shining of the lighthouse—my favorite P.G. experience happens to take place in my backyard.

It's not a large backyard (it is, after all, in Pacific Grove), nor is it by any stretch a fancy one. Actually, it's little more than a small deck, a walkway, a few lawn ornaments, and a handful of flowering plants. But it's not really the amenities and shrubberies that make the yard. It's the sounds.

When the night grows dark and the wind is right, I can hear the waves crashing rhythmically against Asilomar State Beach. When the breezes shift slightly, I can listen to the sea lions bellowing to each other and the foghorns calling from Monterey Bay. Often, at precisely 10:00 p.m., I can make out the notes from "Taps" being played at the Defense Language Institute. On Friday evenings in the fall, I can follow the high school football game by simply listening to the P.A. announcer from several blocks away.

Still, my favorite sound of all is silence.

I've roamed the country enough to know that this is an unusual commodity. In the Midwest, where I grew up, the crickets at dusk sound like a symphony orchestra—or at least, the part where they all tune their instruments simultaneously. The locals there don't seem to hear it anymore, but when you haven't heard it for a while it can be nearly deafening. I spent enough summers driving an RV around the country to know that a campsite without a nearby early morning train whistle is actually an anomaly. And, of course, I have plenty of city-dwelling friends who swear they don't hear the honking horns and car alarms and ambulances anymore. But that's only because it is so loud that you have to retreat into yourself, and that can't be the way it's supposed to be.

In my backyard, however, there is a tranquility. As the saying goes, you can hear yourself think. And I think that's what a backyard is supposed to be. Of course, Pacific Grove is my backyard.

Many years ago, I embarked on a cross-country exploration for the second of my three U.S. travel memoirs. I called the book *Small World*, and the premise was simple: "There is a world of stories along the American highway, so I decided to embark on a microcosmic global expedition. My itinerary included visits to hamlets with names like Cairo and Calcutta, Athens and Amsterdam, Paris and Prague ... My hypothesis is that one can find the fascinating, the curious, the exotic, the eccentric and eclectic in one's own backyard."

My contention is that the United States is less a melting pot than a masterpiece of pointillism, a dot painting. The colors blend from a distance, but they stand out boldly from up close. If you want to understand America, you have to connect the dots. That means exploring the nooks and crannies of the nation, but the notion can be reduced in scope: It also means discovering the undiscovered wonders in the little dot that constitutes your local backyard.

What I have discovered is that Pacific Grove is an ideal blend of history, scenery, and community; Victorian charm coexisting with California whimsy; a tradition-bound place with a talent for adaptation; a town defined so much by its natural environment, but even more so by the people who call it home.

Here's how I concluded the first chapter of *Small World*:

"Geography is the residue of time, and every small town tells a story. The towns come and go, their stories often fleeting and easily lost, like candles flickering in the wind. If I could save a few flames still smoldering in the nation's nooks and crannies, all the better. Of course, every tale is at the mercy of the teller's state of mind. Or as Mark Twain put it following his final global excursion, 'The very ink with which all history is written is merely fluid prejudice.' Let this be mine."

Photo Peter Mounteer.

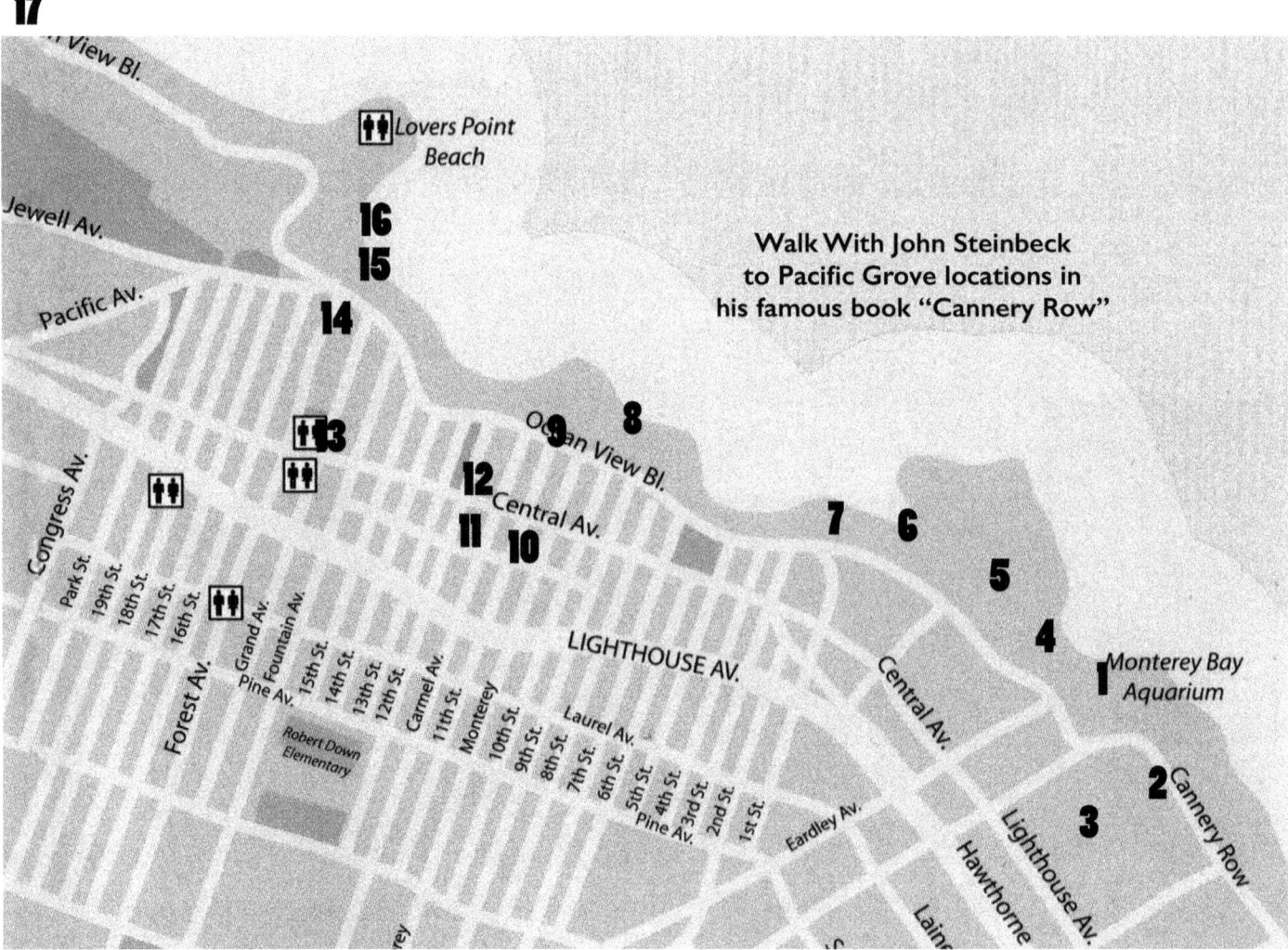

Map courtesy of the Pacific Grove Chamber of Commerce.

A 3-mile walk to #15, and a 7-mile walk to completion.

1. Start by parking near the Monterey Bay Aquarium and walking to Cannery Row.
2. Find the Pacific Biological Laboratories at #800 Cannery Row.
3. Walk up the stairway south across from #800 Cannery Row to see the cannery worker's houses, then return north down the stairway to Cannery Row.
4. Walk west past the Monterey Bay Aquarium and turn south uphill beside it.
5. Turn west to continue west along the Recreation Trail across Ocean View Boulevard from the American Tin Cannery Outlets.
6. Continue west along the Rec Trail to pass the Hopkins Marine Station on the right.
7. Walk west past the large beach on the west boundary of the Hopkins Marine Station where harbor seals hang out a good part of the year.
8. Continue west along the Rec Trail until you reach Berwick Park, south of the Trail.
9. At Berwick Park, cross Ocean View Boulevard, walk west two blocks, and turn south up 11th Street.
10. Continue south along 11th Street to the Steinbeck Family Cottage at #147, just past the intersection with Ricketts Row.
11. Follow Ricketts Row west to Carmel Avenue.
12. Turn north on Carmel Avenue and continue to the intersection with Central Avenue.
13. Turn west along Central Avenue and continue through the center of town along Central Avenue between Fountain and Forest Avenues.
14. Turn north onto Forest Avenue and follow it to reunite with Ocean View Boulevard.
15. Cross Ocean View Boulevard to find the continuation of the Rec Trail.
16. Decide whether to walk two more miles west to the Great Tide Pool or return east along the Rec Trail to reclaim your vehicle for the remainder of the trek.
17. Walk or drive west along Ocean View Boulevard to the end of the Pacific Grove Municipal Golf Links and the Point Pinos Lighthouse on the south and the parking area for The Great Tide Pool on the north.

A Time Of Magic With John Steinbeck
Phyllis Edwards

1 To start our walk through John Steinbeck's Pacific Grove and Monterey, it seems only fitting to recall the first lines of *Cannery Row*. He described the industrial area as he encountered it in the 1930s and 40s as " … a poem, a stink, a grating noise, a quality of light, a tone, a habit, a nostalgia, a dream...."

Of course, much has changed with the passage of three quarters of a century. Today one might say that Cannery Row is a story, a hum and a motor's roar, a shop's bustle, (still a quality of light and bit of a stink when the tide is low) and always a dream. Today's denizens of the Row share dreams as energetic shopkeepers, busy restaurant servers, speeding truck drivers, eager children, cautious parents. Workers of all types converge on the area and go through their day, not unlike Steinbeck's day when the sardine boats came into the bay with their catch and "cannery whistles scream and all over the town men and women scramble into their clothes and come running down to the Row to go to work..."

To share the flavor of Steinbeck's time, it's best for us to start our walking tour early in the day. At that hour many locals arrive to begin their work days: restaurant servers wearing sparkling aprons, shop clerks in cheerful-yet-comfortable attire, Monterey Bay Aquarium docents clad in rust-colored blazers, and visitors garbed in layers to accommodate rapidly changing weather conditions. Brightly decorated shops offering candy, sandwiches, pizza, and souvenirs line old Ocean View Boulevard, re-named in honor of Steinbeck's famous novel.

2 Today we'll park our autos or bikes within walking distance of the aquarium and proceed across the border into Monterey to 800 Cannery Row. This simple, rustic structure is the site of Pacific Biological Laboratories, the marine lab run by Steinbeck's friend, Ed "Doc" Ricketts. Called Western Biological in the book, Steinbeck wrote that it dealt in "strange and beautiful wares" and that "You can order anything living from Western Biological and sooner or later you will get it." Miraculously, this building survives despite the fires that leveled the canneries in the 1950s and 60s, and the tremendous demolition and rebuilding the area saw in the last decades of the 20th century. Inside, the lab is remarkably unchanged, even including some original specimens on dusty shelves in the basement rooms. The lab is open for tours only occasionally during specified times.

Even without a tour, it is possible to see a bit more of the lab than is visible from the street by venturing down the narrow sidewalk that runs perpendicular to the street, between the lab and the next-door Intercontinental Clement Hotel. This offers an excellent view of the back of the lab. Interpretive signs on the chain-link fence point out the concrete tanks where Ricketts kept his larger specimens, with fresh seawater available from the bay just beyond the lab's back door.

All photos Phyllis Edwards, unless stated otherwise.

Directly across the street from Pacific Biological is the Wing Chong Market, re-named Lee Chong's in *Cannery Row*. Behind that structure was an empty lot and beyond that the derelict structure known as the Palace Flophouse, home to Mack and "the boys." Steinbeck wrote, "The boys could sit in front of their door and look down across the track and across the lot and across the street right into the front windows of Western Biological."

3 Steinbeck's characters struggled up the hill from Ocean View Boulevard up to the Palace Flophouse on a muddy, rickety path known as the "chicken walk." Today, a stairway makes our journey easier. To visualize the area that once housed the Palace Flophouse, ascend the stairway up the hill across from 800 Cannery Row, passing workers' cabins that remain from the sardine canning days. A tiny park may be all that remains of what Steinbeck called "the empty lot." The stairs take us to the Recreational Trail that has replaced the railroad bed that once supported the Del Monte Express trains that ran from San Francisco to Monterey from the early 20th century until 1971.

From the top of the stairway beside the Rec Trail, pause to appreciate evocative views of the stairs themselves, Cannery Row, Ricketts' lab, and a snippet of the Monterey Bay far below. As you make your way back down the stairs, try to imagine a steep path with no stairs, and beyond, the sprawling wooden cannery buildings, the noise and the smell.

4 If we have undertaken this part of our walk in the cool, fresh morning hours, we will experience what Steinbeck called "the time of magic in Cannery Row" and "the hour of the pearl" and enjoy scenes very similar to those he described in *Cannery Row*. Even today, few automobiles or tourists are out and about in the early morning hours and it is possible to appreciate this area as Steinbeck saw it: the bay waters washing along the rocky shores behind Doc's lab, the perennial squawking of sea gulls and other marine fowl (especially when the fishing boats offer scraps from their night's catches), cats and dogs continuing their nocturnal explorations for a few moments before the sunlight of the day offers warm, comfy nooks for siestas.

5-6 To continue our Steinbeck tour into Pacific Grove, head west on the Rec Trail. On the land side, just across the border into P.G., you'll encounter a long, low building that once served as factory to supply the canneries with tin cans. It now houses the American Tin Cannery outlet mall.

7 On the bay side of the Rec Trail, directly across from the American Tin Cannery building, you'll see Monterey Boat Works with a couple of handsome, old, deteriorated fishing boats in the yard. Just beyond is Hopkins Marine Station, established in 1892 by Stanford University for the purpose of advancing marine science. Intriguing, given the hometown location, is the fact that neither Steinbeck nor Ricketts attended any university-level classes at Hopkins, although Steinbeck and his sister did take in some enrichment-type programs at Hopkins as children. Ricketts was educated at University of Chicago, while Steinbeck briefly attended Stanford at the main Palo Alto campus and is known as the university's "most illustrious drop-out." Hopkins does pay tribute to the pioneering marine biologist by maintaining an extensive collection of Ricketts's scientific studies and papers, available online at https://seaside.stanford.edu.

Harbor seal pups with mothers at Hopkins Marine Station.

During the months of April to June, strollers on the Rec Trail have the rare opportunity of observing harbor seals and their newborn pups residing on the beach on the western edge of the Hopkins property. The harbor seal pups weigh between 17 and 35 pounds at birth. Their mothers feed them rich, nutritious milk and carry them on their backs in the water until the pups are able to survive on their own after about six weeks.

8 Continuing west on the Rec Trail, we arrive at Berwick Park, a small, but very inviting section of lawn featuring the bronze Christopher Bell sculpture of a mother otter and her pup floating atop a bed of kelp, and a pair of breaching whales "repurposed" from a dead cypress tree by a local artist. We might even encounter a wedding or a Quinceanera party, a young guitarist playing and singing in celebration of the beauty of the day, or couples or family groups reclining or picnicking on the soft grass.

9 From Berwick Park, locate the sidewalk across Ocean View Boulevard between the otter and whale sculptures. Head west on Ocean View two blocks and turn left on 11th Street. Keep your eyes out for a deer or two taking advantage of a shady, empty lot beside the first house on the right. Squirrels skittering up a tree trunk to locate carefully hidden acorns for a meal or two are a common sight. While tourists often screech to stops in the center of the street to leap from their vehicles and take photographs of deer, squirrels, Canada geese, and various other critters, we local residents know better and simply slow down.

As we continue along 11th Street, I am reminded that in the 1930s when Steinbeck lived in Pacific Grove, he would have made this walk along the railroad tracks and through a well-established neighborhood. Some streets would have been paved and included sidewalks; others were less developed.

As a lover of residential and other architecture, the author of this work will thank you for your forbearance as she shares her appreciation of the wide variety of styles that grace the residences of Pacific Grove as we transverse this well-populated part of town. Houses we see today reflect the styles that were popular before and during Steinbeck's lifetime, so that as he walked the neighborhood around his family's summer home, he may have treasured them as well. For example, on 11th Street, we will see several Craftsmen styles of the early 1900s, such as the home at 113 with its front gable roof, tapered porch columns, and geometric division of window upper sashes.

At 11th Street and Central Avenue, the home on the eastern corner exemplifies a Colonial Revival American four-square style residence with a hip roof, a prominent entry porch with a wide pediment, and a small dormer window above the top floor. On the west side across 11th Street, #422 presents a home in a similar style with an interesting small chapel in need of TLC lest it lose its charm entirely. As we cross Central to its south side, #411 Central is a third home in the same period style. Its drought-tolerant landscaping includes netting to prevent deer consumption on a plant climbing up the wooden arbor, a common practice throughout Pacific Grove. We love our deer but still undertake efforts to control their attempts to consume all our hard-earned landscaping.

On the west side of the intersection, #134 11th Street offers an excellent example of the clean-cut Prairie style with its horizontal emphasis, low-pitched roof with broad overhanging eaves and a side entrance. Meanwhile, #141 on the east side exhibits a simplified Craftsman style that could also be called a vernacular style with geometric windows. Some of them have been replaced, providing evidence of several remodeling efforts over time.

10 Crossing Central on 11th, we soon reach the intersection with Ricketts Row, named, of course, in honor of Steinbeck's pal, Ed Ricketts. The Steinbeck family cottage is at #147 11th Street, colored a dark red that Steinbeck called "stud red" in honor of his status following his second divorce. Its hip roof, small French door-enclosed porch, and lovely cross-mullioned windows place it in the vernacular style. The author's father built this cottage in 1903 as a vacation retreat from the summer heat in Salinas. The elder Steinbeck offered it rent-free to the young writer and his first wife, Carol Henning, in 1930.

In this modest cottage, Steinbeck penned several of his early works, including *The Pastures of Heaven, To A God Unknown, In Dubious Battle, Tortilla Flat,* and *The Red Pony,* until the couple left for larger quarters in Los Gatos in 1936. Steinbeck returned to the cottage from time-to-time in the 1940s, but never again lived there on a full-time basis.

Today, the home remains in the Steinbeck family. A small deck and second French-doored entrance extends the width of the home to a section opposite the street side along Ricketts Row, revealing a fairly roomy home. Its tidily landscaped yard dotted is with trees Steinbeck planted in 1948. The home was remodeled in 2015 and drought-tolerant landscaping added. *Please note that this is a private residence and is not open to the public.*

11 From the Steinbeck family cottage, continue west on Ricketts Row. Like many smaller streets in Pacific Grove, it has the appearance of an alley with uneven paving and lacking sidewalks. At the intersection with Carmel Avenue, look for two large Craftsman style houses framed by gnarled, outstretching, and elegant oak trees and each bearing front and side gable roofs, shiplap siding, and windows with geometric divisions in the upper sashes.

Each also has its own porch boasting a comfy rocker to enjoy the outdoor life on a warm day. The home on the south at #151 Carmel Avenue has very tidily straight-lined porch-roof edges and is a slightly larger version of #145 on the north.

12 At the intersection of Carmel Avenue and Ricketts Row, turn north to find your way back to Central Avenue. According to some historic documents, Central was once considered "the more typical route into the heart of P.G." Today, it remains one of P.G.'s major thoroughfares.

Carmel Avenue on the way to Central Avenue presents additional examples of classic architecture popular during Steinbeck's time in Pacific Grove. Number 143 exhibits a simple bungalow form with a hip roof, beveled exterior finish, and a recessed porch. Three lovely examples of Spanish Colonial Revival style, in numbers #141, #139, and on the corner of Central Avenue, feature flat roofs, stucco exterior finish, and clay accents over the porches and front doors of two of the houses. Number #450 at the

intersection with Central Avenue provides another view of the vernacular style with its hip roof and wood beveled exterior finish.

As we turn west onto Central, directly across the street is the beautiful Christian Church (Disciples of Christ), built in 1895. Continuing a block or so west along Central at 12th Street, we find St. Mary's By-The-Sea Episcopal church, a large, dark-red structure built in 1887 with an imposingly tall and sharp steeple crowning its Victorian style. On the far side of Central is an example of one of Pacific Grove's lovely smaller parks. Greenwood Park boasts gigantic eucalyptus trees and shelters a creek that is fed by the Carmel River aquifer south of Pacific Grove, running through a steep ravine under the town of to the bay, readily visible in the distance. While the creek is nearly dry in the summer, its bed remains green and fresh-looking even then, with grasses thriving on the dampness of the creek banks and forming a beautiful path to carry the stream to join its companions in the Bay.

13 As we continue westward along Central Avenue and cross 13th Street, we greet the Wellspring church on the south side. This intersection marks the end of a series of historic churches along Central Avenue, a kind of "church row" reflective of Pacific Grove's heritage as a religious retreat. In the Victorian era, some of these churches enacted "blue laws" that discouraged many frivolous activities on Sundays and prohibited sale of alcohol at any time. The town was "dry" during Steinbeck's era, but even so, his books' characters, companions and acquaintances managed to buy, sell, and consume large quantities of intoxicants. When Steinbeck was a small child, summering with his family in Pacific Grove, he may have encountered a few remaining white tents left over from when P.G. was a summer Methodist Resort, a seaside haven as free as possible from the follies and vices of the fashionable watering places. Even today, throughout the Retreat area, roughly between Grand Avenue and 19th Street, small, rectangu-

lar-shaped houses were built either in place of the earlier tents or from the actual canvas tent walls surrounded by wooden surfaces.

As we progress toward the intersection of Central and Fountain Avenues, at #522 Central Avenue is another church called The Center for Spiritual Awakening. The architectural style from the 1950s seems out of place amidst the earlier styles of the Retreat area. Once we have crossed 15th Street, we will have arrived at what was considered the very center of the non-commercial part of Pacific Grove during Steinbeck's time. On the north side is Pacific Grove Public Library, built from a Carnegie grant in 1906 (when Steinbeck was a toddler) in the Mission style, with lovely arches and windows for the Reading Area.

Just past the library on Central Avenue's north side, we will enjoy an ideal resting spot under the trees of Jewell Park with its open space. During the Retreat days, the

Methodists used this space for an enormous prayer meeting tent. Today it boasts a beautiful gazebo and a small meeting room, known appropriately enough as "The Little House" for local gatherings. Directly across Central Avenue is the Pacific Grove Museum of Natural History. Its collection includes specimens donated by John Steinbeck and Ed Ricketts. The museum offers a living field guide to its native plant garden, presents exhibits about animals, geology, and cultural history, and even a native branch chair that, according to recent lore, once seated St. Junipero Serra. It also features a model of the Chinese

fishing village that once existed on the site of Hopkins Marine Station and brings to mind the fictitious character of Lee Chong in *Cannery Row*.

To continue the tour after visiting the museum, backtrack to Grand Avenue and make a right turn. Walk south one block to find the Holman building on Lighthouse Avenue between Grand and Fountain. Built in 1924, for decades it housed the landmark Holman's Department Store, for years the largest independently operated department store between San Francisco and Los Angeles. Steinbeck was a regular shopper at Holman's, as was practically everyone who lived on the Peninsula in the 1930s through the 1970s, and one of the most beloved scenes in *Cannery Row* takes place at Holman's—or, more accurately, on top of Holman's. Steinbeck regaled us with the true story of a publicity stunt that featured a man roller-skating on a small platform on the roof of the building for 51 hours, attracting visitors from far and wide to witness the phenomenon. Today, the Holman building is being remodeled as luxury condominiums and can only be viewed from the outside.

After visiting the Holman building and admiring a few stunning examples of Victorian architecture across Lighthouse Avenue, such as Aliotti's Victorian Corner Restaurant and Marita's Boutique, we will retrace our steps downhill on Grand Avenue to Central Avenue. Turn west (left) and then north (right) at the intersection of Central and Forest Avenues to follow this main artery downhill toward the bay. Before we cross Ocean View Boulevard at the north end of Forest Avenue, we will pass four little Spanish Colonial Revival style houses flanking the east and west sides of Forest Avenue and boasting bright color schemes, charming arched openings, asymmetrical facades, and stucco-enclosed front porches.

From this viewpoint on Forest Avenue we can also see the rocks of Lovers Point Park towering over the surrounding marine waters where Doc Ricketts and Steinbeck often searched for ocean critters to study and display at Pacific Biological. Today visitors and locals alike spend leisure hours on sunny days at the little beach on the warmer, east side of the park.

At Lovers Point, we are faced with a delightful dilemma: either we may energize for an additional 2-mile walk, continuing along the rustic footpath from Lovers Point to the Great Tide Pool (where Steinbeck and Ricketts enjoyed many an hour scavenging for more specimens for the lab) or we may return via the Rec Trail to Cannery Row, where we began our walk earlier today, to reclaim our vehicles and make the trip to the Great Tide Pool by car or bike.

14 Option #1: To proceed to the Great Tide Pool, use the marked crosswalk to enter Lovers Point, stroll through the park, and continue west on the dirt path that begins on the western side of the park. During this sojourn, we will revel in the crashing waves, diving seabirds, and sun-soaking harbor seals reclining in the sunshine on dry rocks above the bay waters, and may get occasional peeks at cavorting whales in the distant waters of the bay. Continue on the dirt path until it rounds the tip of the bay.

15-17 Option #2: To return to the starting point, use the marked crosswalk to cross Ocean View Boulevard and then turn east (right) onto the Rec Trail. Walk back to Cannery Row, enjoying the stunning rocky shores and imagining Steinbeck walking this very path as he created his memorable stories.

The walk on the Rec Trail from Lovers Point back to Cannery Row offers a very different experience heading in this direction The trail at the Lovers Point end is some-

what less crowded than near Hopkins Marine Station and consists of mostly serious striders, runners, pet walkers, and bikers for purposes of fitness. The closer one gets to Cannery Row, the people on the trail seem to be less interested in exercise and more captivated by taking in the sights. The offshore scenes at the two ends of the trail have much in common, however. Both are serenaded by squawking gulls and other seafowl and graced by fishing boats in early mornings, daytime yachts, whale-watching boats, kayakers, and even surfers on days with high waves. We may even see a deer or two stepping out from 11th Street to cross Ocean View Boulevard, despite the danger of heavy traffic that always seems to stop just in time.

When we are able to tear ourselves away from the sights on the fresh bay waters, we might want to pause from time to time to take in the views on the south. Across Ocean View Boulevard, between the intersections of Forest and Grand avenues and Forest and Fountain avenues, we encounter one of the most magnificent accommodations for travelers in Pacific Grove along the bay: the Seven Gables Inn, built in 1886, features lush landscaping with huge succulents. Every room has a view of the bay. Additionally impressive sights are offered by other remarkable structures along Ocean View Boulevard: some similarly grand hotels, some comparatively simple private homes and others more luxurious, some apartment and condo complexes—all tempting us with visions of life along the beautiful Monterey Bay.

Whether we arrive by car, bike or on foot, Pacific Grove's Great Tide Pool offers one of the richest marine shoreline habitats in the world once explored by John Steinbeck and Ed Ricketts and immortalized in *Cannery Row*: " ... when the tide goes out the little water world becomes quiet and lovely. The sea is very clear and the bottom becomes fantastic with hurrying, fighting, feeding, breeding animals ..."

To reach the Great Tide Pool, walk, bike or drive west along Ocean View Boulevard. If you can tear your eyes away from the foamy, crashing waves along the bay and its curving western shore, it is worth a glance or two to observe the architecture on the south side of the boulevard. The section nearest Lovers Point exhibits a string of rather predictable beachy houses on fairly small lots, some more awe-inspiring than others. As we move further and further westward, away from Lovers Point and past the Esplanade greenway, we will see modern homes that sit on more capacious lots, until we reach the large Pacific Grove Municipal Golf Links and the Point Pinos Lighthouse, both on the south side of the roadway.

Point Pinos Lighthouse.

Look for the house covered in Carmel stone on the beach side of the walkway, and a parking turn-out. This spot marks the westernmost point of the Monterey Peninsula. Here you will find a sign identifying the Great Tide Pool Trail. (If you pass the stone house on the beach side and reach the intersection of Ocean View Boulevard and Lighthouse Avenue, you have gone too far.)

As we walk along the trail with its new boardwalk, we will encounter several well-marked exits from the walkway that allow us to descend from the path without damaging the native plant growth and, assuming a low tide, wade among the creatures that live in the pools. Be aware, however, that we should never turn our backs to the ocean; it is unpredictable and the rocks are slippery! Keeping that caution in mind, we can splash to our hearts' content as we browse through an extensive exhibition of green anemones, sea urchins, sculpins, bat stars, turban snails, sea slugs, and other shallow sea critters. Note: Monterey Bay is a marine sanctuary and it is strictly forbidden to disturb or take any living creature. Resist the temptation to collect specimens as Steinbeck and Ricketts did during their day, leaving them instead for future visitors to enjoy, and instead "collect" with your eyes or camera.

As the sun drops to its resting place at the end of our day's venture into the Great Tide Pool, in clear weather we may be treated to a phenomenal view of one of the most beautiful sunsets on the California coast. This is the time to relax and reminisce about the pleasures of today's walk—the adventure we and Steinbeck and Ricketts and other walkers have shared. Before retracing our steps to our vehicles, either close at hand in the Great Tide Pool parking area or at our original starting spot near the Pacific Biological Laboratories on Cannery Row, let us truly crown our day reading a portion of a favorite ancient poem that Steinbeck used to bring *Cannery Row* to a conclusion:

Even now,
I mind that I loved cypress and roses, clear,
The great blue mountains and the small gray hills,
The sounding of the sea. Upon a day
I saw strange eyes and hands like butterflies;
For me at morning larks flew from the thyme
And children came to bathe in little streams.
— from "Black Marigolds" by Bilhana Kavi

Phyllis Edwards, our dear friend and colleague, singer, gardener, and social activist made her transition shortly after contributing this piece—and we miss her already.

Phyllis in the Community Garden. Photo Heidi Feldman.

◉ ◉ ◉

Other Steinbeck/Ricketts resources in Pacific Grove:

The Monterey Bay Aquarium includes a small exhibit about Ricketts and his work, including artifacts from the lab. 886 Cannery Row, Monterey. Open daily from 9:30 a.m. to 6:00 p.m. (hours may vary depending on the season). montereybayaquarium.org

Trotter Galleries has a section devoted to Steinbeck that includes letters by his third wife, Elaine Scott Steinbeck, first editions, and works of art inspired by the settings, characters and situations in his novels. 301 Forest Avenue, Pacific Grove. Open Thursday, Friday and Saturday from noon to 5:00 p.m. trottergalleries.com

A driving tour of Steinbeck's Pacific Grove was put together several years ago by former Pagrovian Esther Trosow, a helpful tool for any reader who would like to explore the sites mentioned in *Cannery Row* and *Sweet Thursday*. The tour is available online with a downloadable PDF. 93950.com/steinbeck.

Photo Joyce Krieg.

Writing in Pacific Grove: Lies, Big and Little
Diane Tyrrel

On Location

Late afternoon, early April, 2018. 17th Street slopes toward Lovers Point a few short blocks from the Victorian storefronts of downtown Pacific Grove. As I walk the narrow street I see below, through the trees, a weathered shingle roof. *Weird. I don't remember seeing that building in the middle of the little park on the bluff above the ocean.* And I'd been here just yesterday.

Lots going on at Lovers Point this afternoon. Bright jackets against the vivid blue of the Monterey Bay. Box vans lined up along the street from the Beach House restaurant to the parking area. It's an unusual level of activity even for this small but well-used shorefront park.

I walk down the hill, cross the street and approach the park, and—yes, there *is* a brand new building in the middle of the lawn. I'm still new in town, but I come here a lot to Lovers Point, to walk the Recreation Trail along the edge of the water, to wander up and down the narrow streets lined with little beach cottages, or to visit the park itself and say hello to the little boy with his sailboat; he's made of bronze and stands in the grass on the promontory, pointing off over the cliffs across the bay.

The structure, having sprung up overnight like a mushroom, is a charming gazebo of dark wood—a café, apparently, with a few tables and chairs beneath a pergola, on a deck overlooking the water. It's surrounded by pots of flowers, hand-painted signs, and lots of people. No customers, though. And I don't know why exactly, but these guys don't look like locals—or tourists, either. Maybe because they're working. Fiddling with bundles of cables running across the lawn from the gazebo out to the trucks at the curb. Wearing windbreakers, holding clipboards.

This whole scene—these trucks and these workers, the cables and the sudden appearance of the building—this is no ordinary construction project. This isn't your average construction crew wrapping up after a day of work. A café doesn't just magically appear in one day. Not on the California coast, anyway.

And yet this one did.

It's strange. The walls of the quaint little building are weathered. Like it's always been here. But the vibe around here is like … a celebrity wedding. An expensive party rental set-up.

Wait. That's it. They must be getting ready for the Good Old Days festival this weekend in Pacific Grove. Pretty elaborate for all that. But I've already found out they don't fool around here in P.G. Shortly after I moved to this town they put on the yearly Feast of Lanterns festival—colorful paper orbs appeared on houses and trees all over town. On Halloween, the quiet street in front of my house came alive with costumed hordes—the most adorably profligate, creative, and *polite* trick-or-treaters I've ever had the pleasure to encounter. At Christmastime, Lighthouse Avenue in the evening was transformed into a living version of downtown Bedford Falls, as in *It's a Wonderful Life*. All that was missing was the snow and George Bailey running down the street, shouting for joy.

There's always something going on here in Pacific Grove, and whatever they do, they do in a big way—for a small town. Looking forward to the festival this weekend!

But later that evening when I'm talking to my husband Jon, he tells me no, the gazebo at Lovers Point isn't for the Good Old Days festival—it's a set for *Big Little Lies*, the HBO series with Nicole Kidman and Reese Witherspoon.

I am aware of the show and several facts about it. *Big Little Lies* is set here on the Monterey Peninsula. The new season of filming started recently, and Meryl Streep is joining the cast. I read that in P.G.'s local paper, *The Cedar Street Times*. A few weeks ago there was a casting call for locals to be extras in the show—and a lot of them showed interest, judging from the long line of hopefuls out the door at the hotel where they held the auditions.

It does seem fitting that the imaginary world of TV should find its way here to P.G. There's something about this place ... sometimes I feel like I'm wandering through some fantasy world from a tale of adventure and magic. It isn't just the misty landscape, the otherworldly rock formations scattered along the beaches, the fog blowing through the strange Perelandra forests of improbably leggy pines and wind-bent Monterey cypress. Or the mists parting to reveal splendid blue skies and the vibrant light on the land, like a kingdom that comes and goes in the clouds, or is seen only once every seven years. It's also this sense I get that here: serendipity rules. The magic isn't just in the land, it's in the people.

And this enchantment goes along with the hidden quality of Pacific Grove. Though its shy beauty is known throughout the world, it remains a country hidden in plain sight. A mystical land, like Shangri-la. A Fata Morgana.

Pacific Grove was literally left off the map when a promotional campaign touted the virtues of Monterey, Pebble Beach, and Carmel-by-the Sea. According to a local woman with generations of Pacific Grove relations, P.G. refused to pay for the advertising, so when the map was printed, you had all the surrounding communities, and a blank space where Pacific Grove should have been.

All the while Pacific Grove was there, nestled between Highway 1 and the Pacific Ocean: Monterey on one side, Pebble Beach and Carmel on the other, a strange, lovely, and unique combination of forested hills, windswept dunes, rocky beaches and tide pools. P.G.'s disappearing act may be the reason the town has kept its sweetness, its sleepy, quiet attitude, even as giant tour busses skirt the area on their determined course from San Francisco, through Monterey, Carmel, and beyond.

Pacific Grove can be found on the tip of the Monterey Peninsula on the southern end of the big bay. It's a Victorian town that grew up from a Methodist tent camp on lands once claimed by the Spanish. And inhabited, of course, long before that. Taking a walk around Lovers Point months ago after a storm, not far from where the gazebo is currently standing, Jon and I came across a bare patch of ground studded with broken shells and roped off with yellow caution tape. It was an ancient shell midden, likely used by people of the Rumsen tribe of the Ohlone-Costanoan-Esselen Nation, uncovered by the rains.

P.G.: The Stand-In

So of course I have to check out *Big Little Lies*, whose target demographic, according to Emily Nussbaum in a *New Yorker* piece on the show, is hers—women who crave beachfront property and murder mysteries.

That's me, too, incidentally. My idea of happiness is any piece of real estate with a slice of ocean view. And a liking for murder mysteries led me to write a few of my own.

I turn on the pilot episode, settle back in my chair, and immediately I'm pulled into the gorgeously filmed and stylish production. From the opening credits, the show lives up to its hype (the imagery and music, enthralling!) and so does the local setting, familiar and yet exotic, like an aging movie star who is still beautiful and mysterious on camera. Dreamy music video-editing flashes images of the local scene in no particular geographically consistent order—the foggy coastline of Big Sur, the iconic Bixby Bridge, the Monterey harbor. And the *houses. Beach houses*.

The houses, and the way they mirror the characters living in them, are evocative, exquisite—and they're actual houses, not something built in a day like the gazebo. But only one of them is actually here on the Monterey Peninsula. The others are down in Southern California. And it turns out a lot of the locations that look so familiar aren't really around here, either. A café on Fisherman's Wharf, where the women sit outside, drink, and chat—I swear I know exactly the place—turns out it was created on a stage, with the Monterey harbor background digitally dropped in.

But there is one scene I'm pretty sure is filmed in a real location. It's in the beginning of the show. Two women are meeting for the first time on a street alongside the ocean—and I know that street. I drive it all the time. I recognize the trees, the spikes of orange flowers, and the houses there—and that particular view of the ocean.

It's Pacific Grove.

Well! So you're supposed to think this was all happening in Monterey. They're not even headed in the direction of Monterey.

But who cares? When you act in a movie, you can pretend to be someone you're not. You're supposed to, in fact. When a geographical location is used in a movie shoot, it, too, can pretend to be something it's not.

And yet I find myself wondering if Pacific Grove, sly celebrity, could use a good publicist.

◉ ◉ ◉

P.G. is like one of those unsung heroes who hustle behind the scenes while others take all the credit and get the glory.

The stand-in for the movie star.

Our Enchanted Land

I came to discover Pacific Grove like a wanderer in one of those old tales I mentioned earlier. Searching for a fabled place, stumbling across it unwittingly. While living in Santa Cruz for six years, I discovered one of its perks was having the Monterey Peninsula as an easy day trip. One afternoon I ventured upon downtown Pacific Grove by accident, driving along Lighthouse Avenue in Monterey, going a little too far.

Curving toward the tip of the peninsula, the streets become residential, old wooden cottages and prim Victorians with views of the vivid blue waters of the bay. Elegant Craftsman beauties, Painted Ladies and summer cottages gave way to the charming storefronts of yesteryear, and narrow side streets with tiny wooden beach houses in pastel colors stepped down to the ocean.

I must have missed the sign "Welcome to Pacific Grove," because I was thinking I was still in Monterey, wondering why they never mentioned *this* in the travel literature. Marveling at the old-timey hometown feel of the broad and gracious main drag, the quaint architecture, the restaurants and shops, coffee houses, boutiques—and a real bookshop. The tree-lined streets, the ocean views—it was like Carmel, except with fewer tourists and more parking.

And even after I blundered into town unawares, Pacific Grove remained hidden in plain sight, like any proper enchanted realm. Because all the things you're supposed to see and do when visiting Monterey and Carmel left little time to explore this unexpected gem of a place. There's the Aquarium, of course. Cannery Row and Fisherman's Wharf. Carmel and all its adorable hobbit houses and restaurants and shops and art galleries, Carmel Mission and the beaches. Pebble Beach's golf courses, Seventeen Mile Drive and the Lone Cypress. Big Sur to the south with some of the most spectacular stretches of scenic highway in the world. And Santa Cruz to the north: beachside amusement park, and its crazy-unique, buzzing-with-life downtown. The mountains, forests, farms, and orchards—all these small collections of interesting towns.

And hidden right in the heart of all this—Pacific Grove.

Pacific Grove as Muse

Before it was a real place for me, Pacific Grove was a place of the imagination, an inspiration. Long before I came here to live, before I came to visit—or even knew it existed—I had been traveling to Pacific Grove in my imagination. It was a place that inspired my creativity, though I didn't know it by name then. I bought a painting years ago in Cambria, from an artist off the street. It was a small oil on canvas—a dark pathway through a pine forest leading up a hill into the sunlight, and beyond the ridge, a bright wedge of a house overlooking the ocean. I looked at that painting every day, wishing I could be there, walking up that path. One day the frame fell off the painting and I found the artist had written "Asilomar" on the back, with his signature and the date, 1980.

I knew of Asilomar because of my admiration for the architect Julia Morgan, and the photos I had seen of the conference grounds complex she designed between 1913 and 1928, the Arts and Crafts-style redwood and stone buildings, a place for people to gather in the pines by the ocean.

In my first novel, I set a love scene at Asilomar. Because I had never actually been there, I followed the advice of novelist Nora Roberts, who said if she hasn't been to a place she's writing about, "I have to go there in books. … or I make it up." Of course now we can use the internet to pan around streets and neighborhoods, anywhere in the world.

Anyway, despite my fandom for the Asilomar Conference Grounds, I didn't realize Asilomar was in a city called Pacific Grove. It seemed so funny to me when I moved here and discovered Asilomar was here!

I somehow magically found my way into that painting, and I live here now.

It's not like I had never heard the name Pacific Grove, but I had a vague notion that it was somewhere near Los Angeles. If you're into culture, you've heard of Carmel, as well as historical Monterey— made even more famous by the fruits of its inspiration, the novels of John Steinbeck, or old episodes of Disney's *Zorro*. But think of all the creative people, particularly writers, who have been inspired by Pacific Grove! Robert Louis Stevenson wandered the beautiful and bleak rocky shoreline and some say it was this place that inspired him to write *Treasure Island*. Many of the scenes in John Steinbeck's novels take place in Pacific Grove. The model for Steinbeck's "Doc," Ed Ricketts, marine biologist and early environmental prophet, was himself a writer—check out his classic marine biology text *Between Pacific Tides*. He used to inhabit the Great Tidepool by the Point Pinos Lighthouse and hang out with Steinbeck when the two of them lived in Pacific Grove.

Someone sets off on a journey. A stranger comes to town. There is a saying that all stories fall into one of these two plots. Absolute statements get me scrambling to find the exception, but there is no denying the significance of *place* in fiction. Not only fiction, but other kinds of writing as well. Whether it's true crime or a cookbook, the regional setting of a piece of writing is intrinsic to the character of the piece. Often it's even a character in its own right. Michael Pollan says, "You can't tell a story without place, time, and character."

This idea of *place* and its power fascinates me. It's one of the reasons I got my degree in interior design, and studied Feng Shui, the ancient art of placement. And it's one of the reasons I became a writer. I loved books that evoked a *place*. At the age of twelve I was reading the popular gothic romance writers of the 60s, with their naïve heroines who find themselves in melancholy locations of great natural beauty, where getting to know the lay of the land was as important as divining the motivations of the broody hero, or solving the mystery as to why a certain faceless monk keeps appearing in strange locations. To get at the secrets of the moors and crumbling old mansions was to get at the secrets of the heart as well. Talk about metaphorical possibility!

So as artists and writers we are often drawn to a place because of the art created there, and the place itself inspires us to create. *Place*—as an idea, as an experience—has always enlivened the impulses of creative people, and the Monterey Bay area is extraordinary in this regard. It's no wonder that Carmel came alive with artists and writers in the early 1900s. Or that Cannery Row in Monterey inspired fiction so beloved by its readers that tourism generated by Steinbeck's stories helps to sustain the area even now, decades after the demise of the sardine canning industry of which he wrote.

Place in Art

"Where do you get your ideas?"

Writers get this a lot. It's not a bad question. It's something you have to ask yourself, if you're in the business of ideas. Where *do* I get my ideas? Ideas come from everywhere. Personal experiences. News stories. Overheard conversations. Ideas bump into other ideas and stick, creating new ideas. *Where do you get your ideas?*

"Where" is a place. Places I've lived. Places I've left. Places I've traveled. Or visited in my imagination. In books, in movies, and Google Maps. Visit a gallery in Big Sur and you will see how a trip along California's Highway 1 from the Monterey Peninsula to Cambria has been responsible for a myriad of artists' fantastical images, rendered in oils and acrylic, watercolor, textile art, photography, jewelry—improbable roads cutting through mystical landscapes, and seascapes of staggering scale, unending horizons, precipitous cliffs, psychedelic skies.

One night I was driving down from the high Sierra on Highway 120, and right about where the road leaves the steepness of the mountains and enters the undulating foothills, the idea for a story came to me. Images from the time I had spent in the mountains had fertilized other longer-held ideas, and a new creative project was conceived. It became my first published novel, *On the Edge of the Woods*.

As a writer, I am aware of a precarious balance. The right touch of *place* in a piece can give the reader that sense of *being there*. To experience the sights, sounds, and smells of a place. The feel of what it's like. To *be there*. It can give your writing not just physical grounding, but metaphorical grounding as well.

But let's be real: too much of that and, I don't know about you, but I'll begin to skim over the clustered words of description. Might even put the book down.

Paul Theroux, whose writing is inextricably tied with place, says, "Don't go into great detail describing places and things, unless you're Margaret Atwood and can paint scenes with language. You don't want descriptions that bring the action, the flow of the story, to a standstill." I'd say keep it to a minimum even if you are really good at it. Times change and so do styles and fashions in literature.

The popular novels I grew up on used description sparingly. In the best hands, a few choice words could convey an entire world. I was astonished when I delved into the history of the genre I loved—the gothic romance novel—and discovered the enormous 18th century bestsellers, like Ann Radcliffe's *The Mysteries of Udolpho*. Page upon page of description, the hapless heroine traveling through primeval forest—I wanted so badly to finish but after awhile it almost killed me to read it.

And I *like* descriptions of forests and castles.

Elmore Leonard said: *Try to leave out the part that readers tend to skip. Think of what you skip reading a novel: thick paragraphs of prose you can see have too many words in them.*

I have to admit I love that quote.

⊙ ⊙ ⊙

It's late April now and the fog rolls in from the ocean outside the windows of the Point Pinos Grill, across from the old lighthouse, where local author Brad Herzog is giving a talk at the monthly meeting of Central Coast Writers. He's generous in sharing his answer to the age old question—where does he get his ideas for his books and articles? He talks about this process of joining ideas to other seemingly unrelated ideas to come up with a writing project with a twist. During Q&A someone asks about his literary influences. He tells us, almost by way of confession, that he was drawn to the Monterey Peninsula by the books of John Steinbeck. And I feel a sense of kinship.

The stories that draw us forth into our destinies....

⊙ ⊙ ⊙

Jump back a couple years. I'm still living in Santa Cruz. Just finished reading Steinbeck's *Sweet Thursday*, which is a sort of sequel to his famous farce *Cannery Row*.

So now I have to go to Cannery Row. I've been there, but that was before I read the books. One afternoon I get in my car and drive the forty miles to Monterey. Of course, Monterey is a huge draw for Steinbeck fans. Many of the scenes in Steinbeck's books are places you can just go and walk around yourself.

Wandering through the area with the aftereffects of literary immersion still strong in my psyche, I'm charmed to see that something still remains of the era that inspired the stories. The inspiration for Doc's lab—the real-life laboratory of Ed Ricketts—it's still there. It's this modest wooden shack wedged incongruously between the aquarium, shops, and a large hotel. There's Lee Chong's store, across the street. A walk up the hill, and there's a huge old rusty cylinder rising up from the weeds in a vacant lot, like the boiler turned domicile in Steinbeck's quirky imagination. It's big enough that I can imagine it lying on its side, decorated with curtains purchased at Holman's Department Store.

It wasn't until later, when I moved to the area, that I discovered many of the scenes in this odd little book that had found its place in my heart weren't just in Monterey. Lots of the action takes place in Pacific Grove. The Holman building, where Suzy got her curtains, is still there on Lighthouse Avenue in downtown P.G. Cannery Row doesn't end at the border of Monterey—in fact, Cannery Row in Steinbeck's time was called Ocean View Avenue, and it extended into Pacific Grove. It still does.

Steinbeck spent time writing in his family's cottage on 11th Street, not far from Ed Rickett's home and first lab in P.G. Imagine the conversations that took place when their neighbor, mythologist Joseph Campbell, joined the party. There is a painting by Judith Deim that depicts a bohemian group—Steinbeck, Ricketts, and friends—gathered under a full moon on the beach in the shelter of a strange rock formation, like a landscape on another planet. The unusual and striking setting in the painting is familiar. The inspiration for the location has to be Pacific Grove.

'You've Got to have *Some* Progress'

Thursday afternoon in Janet's fitness class at Sally Griffin, one of the ladies says the Hollywood people offered to let the city of Pacific Grove keep the gazebo from *Big Little Lies*. But nobody knows where the structure would go once the filming is done. Not Lovers Point. The building is pretty cute, and it almost looks like it belongs there, though it crowds out the statue of the boy with the sailboat. But citizens of P.G. would surely resist any new building in a park, especially a tiny park like Lovers Point, with its pride of place overlooking the bay.

And yet Lovers Point has seen many structures come and go—a succession of bathhouses, a Japanese Tea Garden, an ice cream parlor, a carousel. The Hopkins Marine Station, now located just this side of Cannery Row, got its start at Lovers Point and was there until it outgrew the location.

Change happens!

Up the street in a little shop on Lighthouse Avenue, an overheard conversation: a young woman complains bitterly about a new building project happening a few blocks away. Something old is coming down, something new is going up. She laments the changes—doesn't want Pacific Grove "to become like all the other tourist towns."

And the older man behind the counter nods and gently replies, "Well, but you've got to have *some* progress."

I am so proud of this town for prizing its past, for the fact that here I have discovered, among other delights, a living museum of vintage architecture. And yet, as I learn more and more of the history of the area, and P.G. in particular, I am struck by this one thing: change is *always* happening here. It's not the same as it was fifty years ago. And fifty years ago, it was a lot different than it was fifty years before that. Was there sadness and regret among those who loved The Grove when tent cabins began to make way for tiny wooden cottages?

Only the Stage is Real

And now, as suddenly as it appeared, the gazebo at Lovers Point is gone. Nothing of it remains except for a few bare patches in the grass where it stood, looking so solid for such a short time. Maybe the *Big Little Lies* gazebo is the perfect metaphor. A gentle reminder: here today, gone tomorrow.

It's no longer there, and when it was, it wasn't real anyway. Just an imaginary playset, a painted backdrop lowered over a stage. Only the stage is real, enduring. The rocks remain, the pounding surf.

But we'll see that imaginary café again when the new season of *Big Little Lies* is aired. On the screen will be images of something that is no longer there—was never really there to begin with. At Lovers Point, the mists will roll in from the sea, closing over the scene like the heavy velvet draperies of an old theater. But the mists will part again, to reveal the stage set with different props and new characters; new stories will be written and enacted, and shy, modest Pacific Grove will, I have no doubt, continue to be an inspiration for future generations of writers, poets, artists, and the creators of hit TV shows.

Seminar at Asilomar: Hospitality in Paradise

It's long been one of my romantic notions, to participate in a seminar at Asilomar Conference Grounds. I'm finally getting my chance! My publisher, Patricia Hamilton, has asked me to check out this promotional/hospitality thing going on there to see what might be of interest for her *Life in Pacific Grove* books and other projects.

Having worked several years as a guest service agent in hotels on the Monterey Bay, my favorite part of the job was meeting people from around the world, near and far, and sharing my love of the area and everything it has to offer. So I was eager to gather with a bunch of local hospitality professionals and see what *My Monterey* had in store for us.

Even before my interior design school days in college, I was fascinated by the architect Julia Morgan and I wanted to experience the historic conference grounds she designed for the YWCA in the early 20th century. I had visited her San Simeon creation—the fantastical Hearst's Castle—from the time I was a child, but I knew the rustic architectural style of Morgan's Asilomar retreat was closer to my heart. I imagined being embraced by Asilomar's windswept beauty and weathered old stone and timber lodges, set in the pine woods and dunes overlooking the ocean on the rocky shore of the Monterey Peninsula—and how any experience of learning would be enhanced, just because it was taking place *there*.

They say you should write what you know, but as a romantic suspense novelist you get to use your imagination to write what you can only imagine. In my first book, *On the Edge of the Woods*, I gave my architect-heroine a seminar at Asilomar because *I* wanted to attend a seminar at Asilomar. (And never mind what I had her doing after the seminar, in the dunes with her dashing love interest. After all, it *was* a romance novel.)

So here I am, years later, actually *at* Asilomar, attending a seminar in one of Morgan's original buildings, the rustic, glorious Chapel.

We are gathered in this lofty, sweet-smelling space with a fire going in the stone fireplace, while outside the waves are rolling into the shore beyond the dunes; the sky through the branches of the pines and cedars is so blue it's like the color of paint freshly squeezed from the tube. And to think, all this is here in modest, unassuming Pacific Grove.

The presenters waste little time, and short talks are interspersed with videos on subjects ranging from hospitality tips (Smile! Don't roll your eyes when dealing with guests!) to the history of the region. We're treated to a video travelogue with lots of cool drone footage of the Monterey Peninsula, and there's a clip of a frustrated Seinfeld going off on a willfully unhelpful car rental agent. The point is, I guess, that with so many visitors to the area, we all have an opportunity to influence the quality of their experience here.

This program is sponsored by *My Monterey*, a training program from the Monterey County Hospitality Association for Monterey County's guest contact employees. So they're not going to dwell on the charms of Pacific Grove, or any of the other cities of the Peninsula in particular. Besides, the seminar isn't designed to provide in-depth information on area attractions, but given the length and scope of what they're covering, they do a good job of touching on the historical high points of the area, the surprising range of activities available and places to visit.

And then, near the end of the seminar, the presenters get into why we should *care* about bringing in tourism, and how those of us who live here can keep our quality of life while encouraging people to visit, to stay longer—and to come back.

It's this last piece that interests me most, because I already get why we "need" tourists, and how they help sustain aspects of the lifestyle we residents enjoy. I also understand the frustration of those who resent tour buses, increased traffic and parking problems, and the drawbacks of short-term rentals on the local lifestyle.

So I appreciate the program for mentioning this tension between seemingly opposite interests. Lively conversation follows, and the idea of guest education is offered up—the importance of letting our visitors know the nuances of local etiquette. How we can make sure this gets done through official channels, yes, but maybe more importantly, through our personal actions in everyday encounters. One woman shares a story of standing in line at a grocery store and getting into a conversation with a visitor who expressed outrage when charged for a bag. She was able to explain, in a kind and friendly way, why the store was charging for the bag. As residents of a coastal community we have the responsibility and opportunity to share with others who may not know the damage those plastic bags are doing to our oceans and how they harm the animals that live in them. In that moment, feelings of ill-will were transformed into an understanding that might have positive repercussions for the wider world beyond Monterey Bay.

This conversation about a conversation is one I hear echoed often, in the local papers, in coffee houses downtown, and over the dinner table as friends share a bottle of wine, excitement and ideas about bringing the world's attention to Pacific Grove as a blossoming writer's retreat.

Should we encourage them to come—or keep this place a secret as long as we can?

It is with this feeling of push and pull that I reach out to the world, to say hey, look—Pacific Grove is here! Nestled behind the dunes in the Monterey cypress and pine groves, or high on the hill above the ocean, with exotic beaches, unique and crucial wildlife habitat, verdant golf courses, a charming Victorian village with boutique shopping and fine dining.… all this, surrounded by everything else the Monterey Peninsula has to offer.

And here's another secret. While a seminar is a worthwhile and wonderful way to experience Asilomar, it is by no means necessary for the enjoyment of the conference grounds. Asilomar is a California state park, open to all. A short walk up from the beach through the dunes and there you are at the Phoebe Hearst Social Hall. Push open one of the big doors and find yourself in a cavernous Arts and Crafts lodge of mellow redwood paneling like a grand mountain hotel, with comfy seating around a great stone fireplace, and the air sweet with the scent of wood smoke. You'll find a couple of pool tables, a gift shop, and a little café where you can get snacks, coffee, beer and wine.

Take your glass outside and have a chair on the veranda—it's been recently redone, restoring the original Julia Morgan design—and watch the sun set through the trees. Relax. Breathe in the scent of the wind from the ocean. Be amazed. Be grateful. You've found yourself in a magical seaside retreat unlike any other.

And don't forget to recycle that bottle.

Asilomar Conference Center sandy trail to the beach at the tip of the Monterey Peninsula. Photo Peter Mounteer.

Pacific Grove and Steinbeck's Romance Novel

Diane Tyrrel

John Steinbeck – Romance Writer

When you think of John Steinbeck, romance writer probably isn't the first image that comes to mind. But one of my favorite romantic novels is actually a book by Steinbeck. And it became even dearer to me when I found out that so many of its scenes are set here in Pacific Grove, my adopted hometown. The iconic character "Doc" of *Cannery Row* has returned from the war, and in *Sweet Thursday*, he falls for a hooker with—yes—a heart of gold.

Shortly after I moved to Pacific Grove I read something in a promotional brochure saying it had been named the "Most Romantic City in the US." Now, that's quite a claim. After all, in California alone we have Mendocino Village, Catalina Island, and Yosemite Valley. And what about San Francisco? Santa Barbara? Joshua Tree? Julian?

The point is, no matter your definition of romantic, if you're looking for a romantic getaway, in the Golden State we've got you covered.

But when I checked into it, I learned the title of "Most Romantic City" is disputed, though perhaps with less serious consequences than the title "Surf City," which spawned a nasty trademark litigation between Santa Cruz and Huntington Beach, to the point where they were calling each other less picturesque names.

Pacific Grove *is* charming. Beautiful. Mystical. No denying it. But "Most Romantic City in America?" Hyperbole, of course. A promotional slogan.

That's all.

Or … *is it?*

Some strange—and arguably romantic— things have happened here. I met my husband here, for example. On our first date, we took a walk along the shore near the dunes where, coincidentally, Doc and Suzy go after dinner on *their* first date in *Sweet Thursday*.

Sweet Thursday is perhaps one of John Steinbeck's least famous or esteemed books, likely because of its satisfying narrative arc, which resembles nothing more than a traditional romance novel.

Searching for the Literary Romance Novel

It is easy to find a romance novel. There is no shortage of them. And it is not difficult to find a novel that is written well. The world is blessed with more well-written books than I personally will ever have time to read. "Well-written" may be impossible to define, but for our purposes here let's just say that with good writing, the writing itself is part of the pleasure—though I must point out that "good writing" doesn't mean a book will be any good, and a book with less-than-stellar prose can be a success on many levels.

But a book that is both well-written *and* fits the requirements of the romance genre—that is truly an elusive thing. It's not easy to find a book like, for example, Jane Austen's *Pride and Prejudice*. A book you can read again and again and enjoy the subtle humor and turn of phrase. A book that challenges you a little in interpreting the author's slyest meanings, and at the same time, a book that fulfills the romance novel's promise in a satisfying manner. Yes, frustrations do challenge the modern reader—Austen doesn't allow us to actually witness the moment Mr. Darcy takes Elizabeth in his arms for the first time. But some would argue that it's this very off-stage, chaste quality of the exposition that gives it so much romantic charge.

After *Pride and Prejudice*, (which is over two hundred years old) not even Jane Austen matches herself in the name of romance, with the possible exception of *Emma*. Certainly there are episodes in the greats, romantic storylines—like Dorothea and Will's in *Middlemarch*. And the narrative arc of Levin and his bride Kitty in Tolstoy's *Anna Karenina* fits the bill, at least, until their engagement. Continuing their saga into married life takes the story out of the romance genre and into something else entirely. A romance novel is always a love story, but a love story is not always a romance.

When I decided to write my own version of a romance novel, I began by reading piles of books in that genre to figure out the formula. Some romance writers would bristle at the idea of a formula, but hey, I didn't invent it. I did my homework, and (in the days before the internet) that meant writing to request the guidelines from New York publishers that actually spelled out their expectations. Different lines had different requirements, but I learned early on that a love story and a happy ending—or at the very least, a *satisfying* ending—were crucial components of the genre.

When I started, writers were beginning to experiment with more diverse variations on the theme, but the basic elements were understood: polarized characters move from an antagonistic relationship through mounting tension (generally sexual in nature) which climaxes in a denouement of emotional surrender (yes, emotional—a physical union may be explicit or implied, but it is not necessarily of primary importance). Furthermore, in a true romance novel, the relationship itself is the main storyline of the book. There may be a lot of other stuff going on, mysteries and murders and whatnot, but it's *the relationship* that the book is really about.

So as I read dozens, if not hundreds, of paperback novels from all the top romance lines, I realized the stereotype of the romance novel was accurate. My chosen genre was rife with clichés, cardboard characters, and implausible plotlines. And yet the readers seemed to love them. This was liberating.

So what if there just aren't that many great books that truly fit into the romance novel genre? Maybe it's just that the deeper truth of a relationship like Kitty and Levin's is much richer than the story of how two people meet and fall in love. But it's also, I think, because of a stigma against romance novels. Many people will not read a book if they are told it's a romance. Guys especially, but women too. *Romance? Nah, no thanks. Got any murder mysteries?*

What serious writer wants to start with *that* strike against them?

Is that why many "real writers" won't go there, even if they deign to write within the constraints of other genres like mystery, horror and sci-fi, where cardboard characters and clichés abound.

In Steinbeck's *Sweet Thursday*, we get both. A romance novel. And a book in which the writing is part of the pleasure. He gives us conflict, humor, and a satisfying (no, not just satisfying, but—spoiler alert—*happy*) ending. And the romance isn't an episode out of some larger, sweeping, *serious* epic. No, *Sweet Thursday* is one of the few books by a major talent that fulfills the promise of the pulp fiction romance without trying to be much else. No big social commentary, no cynical reminder that most romantic unions, even those born of fiction, do come to an end. Just a fun, simple story with a zany cast of characters. And, like the best of the genre, the book is set in a very particular *place*. The place shapes the characters even as the characters season the place and make it what it is.

Discovering Sweet Thursday

I had never even heard of *Sweet Thursday* until a few years ago, when I fished the battered paperback out of an overflowing bin of used books at the Goodwill Bargain Barn in Santa Cruz. The book was first published in 1954, but the cover art was typical of paperback fiction in the 70s, when this particular edition was printed. A stylized, sketchy drawing of a lost-looking young woman, a battered suitcase in her hands, a glaring sun setting over the canneries. The first edition book jacket shows a much different scene: brightly colored, a bird's-eye view of Cannery Row in a bygone era—and it looks a lot more fun. Both illustrations capture something of the book.

I wasn't a natural-born Steinbeck fan. In school I got the usual force-feeding of some of his *important* works, like *The Grapes of Wrath* and *The Pearl,* and revisited them again when my kids had to read them. Later, a friend and avid fan encouraged me to give Steinbeck another try, to read *Travels With Charley*, which he loved. He pressed on me a stack of additional Steinbeck paperbacks. Already a professional writer by then, I found much to admire in Steinbeck's prose—his deft way with language, humor, irony, and his vivid depictions of place, whether he was describing the Oklahoma Dust Bowl or the San Joaquin Valley. One book that intrigued me, and stayed with me long after I finished it, was *The Wayward Bus*. It had a sort of peculiar strangeness, which is something the curmudgeonly literary critic Harold Bloom contends is always present in great writing.

But it was not until I found *Sweet Thursday* that I fell in love with a Steinbeck novel.

And after I moved here to Pacific Grove, I discovered a new kinship with the book, as I found myself wandering along the beach near the lighthouse where Suzy walked when she was wrestling with her feelings for Doc, or watching the waves break over the rocks of the Great Tide Pool, where Doc went to collect specimens when he was trying to get Suzy out of his thoughts. Like these flawed characters, I too was learning—or re-learning—how to gracefully accept romantic love in my life after going without for a long time.

Though Steinbeck got into hot water in his own hometown for being too much of a social justice warrior, with the hindsight of another era, he's also criticized for his less than politically correct portrayals, including his "misogynistic and unrealistic depiction of women." But I would argue that the author was tough on *all* his characters, as well as fanciful in their depictions. His sensibility was both dark and cartoonish—which is why Thomas Hart Benton was the perfect illustrator for his work. And though Suzy passes judgment on her own profession, the author never does. When I started writing romance, certain publishing guidelines advised that, although it wasn't essential that the heroine be a virgin when she meets her hero, she shouldn't sleep with anyone else once she meets him. For an old white guy writing in the early 50s, Steinbeck was all right.

Pulp Fiction: Suspense, Passion and a Happy Ending

I was introduced to the romance novel, in particular its Gothic interpretations, at an early age when my mother read one aloud in the car on a long family vacation trip. I was enthralled by the suspenseful atmosphere of the book as much as the romance—and the seemingly supernatural occurrences that turned out to have perfectly rational, if deadly sinister, explanations.

My earliest literary influences, after Dr. Seuss and Mary O'Hara, were the pulp paperbacks my mother would include in the stacks of books she brought home from the library every week. There were books for children, but Young Adult fiction wasn't really a thing back then. I poked at the novels my mother had lying around, like *The Adventurers* by Harold Robbins and Jacqueline Susann's *The Valley of the Dolls*, looking for the erotic, adult-themed passages, but other than that, they didn't wake up for me. Instead I devoured the chaste gothic romances, like Victoria Holt's *Mistress of Mellyn* and *Kirkland Revels*. Mary Stewart's prose was dreamier, but Victoria Holt had a knack for relationships.

A book with a suspenseful plotline, a passionate love affair, and a happy ending—set in a beautiful, mysterious place, preferably by the sea, in an old house ... that to me was the perfect formula.

In my early teens, pulp romance gave way to pulp sci-fi, like Arthur C. Clarke's *Childhood's End* and Frank Herbert's *Dune*, the brick-like tome I carried around school for weeks. And thus my less-than-highbrow literary taste was well in place long before high school, where in the early 70s, we spent more time in English classes discussing books like *Journey to Ixtlan: The Lessons of Don Juan* and *Go Ask Alice* than classics like *Hamlet* or *The Old Man and the Sea*. In college I learned to disdain the stilted prose of the run-of-the-mill bestseller, particularly the romance novel. Having discovered "the great books," I turned my back on Victoria Holt, thinking *that* kind of thing was behind me. After all, I had Jane Austen now.

But when I began to write seriously myself, I found to my consternation that what I produced inevitably harkened back not to the canon of great literature, but the pulp fiction—not of my teen years, but my *pre*-teen years.

Years later I re-read *The Mistress of Mellyn* and forgave myself for loving it. The prose was clunky, but it was straightforward and unadorned. Victoria Holt's simple, spare descriptions made the Cornish countryside come alive for me once again, as did her cast of characters. Maybe they were stereotypes or clichés, but they were so endearing you didn't mind. The creepy story woven throughout somehow made the romance less insipid. And Victoria Holt didn't have to worry about sex scenes, because as far as I know, she didn't write any.

Steinbeck, being Steinbeck, is not going to give us page upon page of sexual technique like you might find in a bestselling romance novel today. He doesn't shy away from it, or ignore the issue, but neither does he exploit the sexual tension in *Sweet Thursday*. The author does, however, unabashedly proclaim his protagonist's loneliness, and then generously offers hope of a remedy. At the end of the book Doc and Suzy ride off together, and the happily-ever-after is rendered both humorous and metaphorically apt with Suzy in the driver's seat of the jolting jalopy she doesn't yet know how to drive, stick shift in hand.

Even Steinbeck Came Home to Pacific Grove

Pacific Grove is both setting and character in *Sweet Thursday*, and though we—that is, generations of readers—think of Monterey when considering the Cannery Row locus of the stories, Steinbeck sets scenes in P.G. for both comic relief as well as pathos. The peculiar history of Pacific Grove lends itself to the wacky side trips taken by the author in his "Hooptedoodle" chapters, whereas the rugged rocky coastline provides the illustrative landscape for other scenes in which his characters wander the world with their lonely hearts on their sleeves, looking for love.

So is Pacific Grove really the most romantic city in America?

Actually, the idea of a city being *romantic* is a strange notion in itself, don't you think? What matters is what happens to us when we encounter a place, and that can be many things besides romantic, no matter the reputation of the town. The truth is, I don't much like the word *romance*, except possibly in the archaic, Arthurian sense of the word. And as for the modern romance novel, I seldom read them—*Sweet Thursday* came as a surprise. It's been years since I wrote a romance novel or even worked on one with a client. A *love story*, however, is woven into almost any compelling writing. Or any compelling life. If you spend enough time anywhere, you will fall in love.

You May Fall in Love With the Place Itself

And yet, the more I think about it, it does seem that Pacific Grove might have something special when it comes to romance—and by "romance" I mean the Arthurian-magic kind of romance more than bodice-ripping passion. If there is anything to this idea of certain places on the planet holding some particularly potent power, like Sedona or Glastonbury, I'm beginning to believe Pacific Grove might be one of them. Maybe that's because the land resonates with what it's absorbed, year after year—all the vibes of all the love poured over the place by those who have been smitten with it.

For Steinbeck, it was at least a strong affection. "I like Pacific Grove very much," he said in a 1948 interview with a student reporter he'd invited to his house on 11th Street, a modest cottage built by his father. Steinbeck was in the process of fixing up the place, doing some improvements and repairs, because he had been away for awhile. It's telling that in those days after the war, when the famous author could have gone anywhere in the world, he chose to return to the small cottage where he lived—and wrote—when he was unknown and penniless.

John Steinbeck came home to Pacific Grove.

Cedar Street Times: The Editor is IN
Diane Tyrrel

In the first few months of getting to know my new hometown, Pacific Grove, I eagerly grabbed a *Cedar Street Times* from the newsstand each week. A year and a half later, I still do. The free weekly newspaper has proved to be a reflection of P.G. itself: small-town, local, and full of fun and humor.

It was the humor that I noticed first and most of all. In an era when journalism and the free press is up against a lot of obstacles (but when isn't it?) The *Cedar Street Times* is a singular publication, by turns focusing on serious issues affecting the community and wryly commenting on everything—from neighborhood squabbles about short term rentals and cell towers, to the school sports teams and theater productions.

The publisher offers a lot of space to non-profits, too. But along with the basic informational articles and profiles on local newsmakers, letters, commentary, and opinion, there's always this undertone of fun.

I sometimes wonder what the editorial meetings at the *Cedar Street Times* are like. My image of putting a paper together likely arises from TV, and movies like *All the President's Men,* in which reporters Woodward and Bernstein argue with editor Ben Bradlee about what news is fit to print. Does editor and publisher Marge Ann Jameson listen to her writers' pitches with a jaundiced ear, exhorting them to find more sources, more corroboration? Does she caution Wanda Sue Parrott to stay objective when writing her impassioned column about the homeless? Does she ask Sally Baho if she's personally tasted all the food and tested all the recipes in her *Postcards from the Kitchen* column? Does she require Bill Cohen to provide more than one source when he answers the question "What does God say about …" in his column each week? And what about that Webster Slate? When the publisher allows him to disparage Toyotas as ugly, week after week, does she fear a backlash?

Established September 5, 2008, *Cedar Street Times* was adjudicated a newspaper of general circulation for Monterey County on July 16, 2010. Though conceived as an online publication, Marge Ann Jameson, the publisher who nabbed a 2017 Salute to Small Business Award for "Best Woman-owned Business," determined that it would be easier to encourage readers to check out the online version if there was a print version of the paper available. The idea was that citizens of all communities need a fair and unbiased source of local news, and P.G. is no different.

So Marge Ann set out to create a newspaper by, for, and about the citizens of the City of Pacific Grove with the most comprehensive scope available, "with no agenda other than the fact." The newspaper is said to refuse to publish letters that "do not have a basis in truth."

4th of July Barbecue, Caledonia Park, 2018. Photos Peter Mounteer

The paper reports on city council meetings and committee meetings, and keeps readers in the loop regarding the latest happenings, whether it's about controversial local issues, or celebrations like The Feast of Lanterns, Fourth of July, and The Good Old Days. The stories in this paper are focused on Pacific Grove: P.G. politics, local celebrations, and the people who make Pacific Grove unique.

The *Cedar Street Times* caters to active people who want to be involved in the community, people of all ages with varied interests. Along with political and social topics, the paper spotlights happenings around town and offers plenty of ways to participate and plug in. Much of the newspaper is devoted to upcoming events and reviews of local theater, books, and art. If the editorial standards of the paper sometimes come across as more homespun than the likes of the *New York Times* or the *Wall Street Journal*, it may be due to the same whim that allows for submissions by regular folks, young authors and photographers, as well as those of more seasoned and established writers. In the *Cedar Street Times* it's the voice of the local conversation that matters. The voices don't always sing in harmony, but civil discourse is encouraged, and there's usually a sort of civility even in disagreement.

You'll find regular columnists in your weekly *Cedar Street Times*, which are rotated to present different ideas in each issue and encourage a diverse readership. It's these regular "faces" I've come to recognize that keep me coming back each week for more. There's something amazing about reading a column in the paper and then chatting with its author in a local shop a few days later. When you read Jane Roland's writing in *Animal Tales/Other Random Thoughts*, you get her passion for the community and her energy shines through her words. It's just the same when you meet her in person.

Everyone in the world will pass by her door someday ….

That's how I think about Patricia Hamilton's office in the Giles building on Lighthouse Avenue. Hers is the *Keepers of the Culture* column, with local author and editor Joyce Krieg, in which you'll find curated stories of Pacific Grove and the many people who are touched by this place. Behind the Keepers of the Culture column is an actual tireless force keeping culture here in Pacific Grove.

There are so many other voices in the *Cedar Street Times*, like Diana Guerrero's *Ask Ark Lady*, and Elayne Azevedo who occasionally contributes in-depth articles about P.G., not to mention the Letters to the Editor department, my favorite part of any periodical. The paper publishes images too, of course, such as Joan Skillman and Keith Larson's colorful images and cartoons, and work by local photographers. Scanning the masthead I see attributions for many other contributors, advertising personnel, distribution—and Staff Magician. That may explain a few things.

Cedar Street Times is a free pick-up newspaper available Fridays at locations throughout Pacific Grove and the Monterey Peninsula. Email subscribers receive their edition on Thursday evenings. The paper is distributed at senior living establishments, schools, hotels, restaurants, and newsstands, with distribution points in Pebble Beach, Carmel, Seaside, Monterey, and of course—Pacific Grove. You can even come by the newspaper office at 306 Grand Ave. to pick up your paper.

Press deadline is Wednesday, noon.

High School Breakers Homecoming Game 2018. Photos Peter Mounteer

Steinbeck, Pacific Grove, and Me
David A. Laws

During a summer break from college in the early 1960s, I worked in a London warehouse for a Royal Air Force maintenance unit. Apparently, few aircraft were in distress and business was slow, so I had plenty of time to read. I came across a worn paperback. A semi-clothed maiden on the cover promised the pleasures of a "bodice ripper." Not my usual choice of reading material, but having swept the aisles for the day and with little else to occupy me, I dug into it.

I recall a couple of mildly erotic scenes in *To a God Unknown* but it was the bold writing style and imagination behind the storytelling that captivated me. I had never heard of the author, John Steinbeck, but by the end of the summer I had read every copy of his work I could find. Images of "light gay mountains full of sun and loveliness" and hot dry days in the Valley of Nuestra Señora were particularly resonant in that cold, damp English summer. I vowed that one day I would visit California, bask in the sunshine and see Steinbeck Country for myself.

On graduating with a degree in physics, I found employment in the new business of semiconductor electronics and secured a job with Fairchild Semiconductor in Mountain View. I explored Steinbeck Country soon after I arrived. I walked the hallowed length of a half-deserted Cannery Row, viewed Steinbeck sites in Salinas Valley and the Monterey Peninsula, and hiked trails in the Big Sur setting of "Flight." But otherwise, I deserted Steinbeck for the siren call of silicon as my planned two-year sojourn in California stretched to 50 years and beyond.

As a hobby I wrote occasional articles for the travel sections of the *San Francisco Chronicle*, the *San Jose Mercury News*, and other publications. While researching a story on Steinbeck Country in the early 2000s, I returned to the area and delved into Steinbeck-related places in more detail and I especially enjoyed Pacific Grove. That piece grew into an illustrated guidebook, *Steinbeck Country: Exploring the Settings for the Stories* that later morphed into a website, an iPhone app, and, more recently, a series of online itineraries for bindutrips.com.

After retiring from Silicon Valley, I continued to write. My travels up and down the West Coast confirmed that Pacific Grove was unique. Here I could live in a beautiful ocean-front community where drivers stop to let pedestrians cross the road, shoppers hold a door open for you, and within easy walking distance of an excellent library, hardware store, bakery, and more, all together with a selection of fine restaurants. With my wife Jean, I moved here permanently several years ago and today I continue to give talks based on my Steinbeck material to community groups, book clubs, and classes at the OLLI school on the CSUMB campus. However, the irony that I should choose to live in one of California's least sunny spots is only compounded by my joining the collective chorus for increased rainfall.

Steinbeck: The Untold Stories
by Steve Hauk
Illustrated by C. Kline

Review by Stephen Cooper

Reflecting on "the soul of artists and writers," nineteenth-century philosopher Friedrich Nietzsche observed that art "performs the task of preserving, even touching up extinct, faded areas; when it accomplishes this task it weaves a band around various eras, and causes their spirits to return." Well over one hundred years later, this razor-sharp rumination has lost none of its acumen, and it adeptly describes the stimulating experience awaiting readers of Steve Hauk's ingenious new book, *Steinbeck: The Untold Stories*.

Accompanied by memorable and imaginative illustrations by artist C. Kline, Hauk, an award-winning writer, playwright, and art dealer, has masterfully fused real historical events with fiction to birth sixteen short stories about the characters and complexities in the life of one of America's greatest writers, Nobel Prize winner John Steinbeck.

A former journalist with an easy and engaging storytelling air, Hauk has long indulged his deep-seated appreciation for Steinbeck's literature, and he even lives in the same Pacific Grove, California, house once owned by Steinbeck's closest friend and collaborator, marine biologist Edward Ricketts. In addition to his considerable authorial output, Hauk owns an art gallery in Pacific Grove whose mission statement provides considerable insight into both Hauk and his "untold" Steinbeck stories: "A vibrant artistic community does not function in a vacuum—its artists generally engage with the community and other artists, writers, poets, photographers, and scientists to create a more meaningful society and culture."

Indeed, it is hard to discern a diference between the spirit of creative collaboration inherent in the guiding principle of Hauk Fine Arts and that which developed in the early 1930s on Cannery Row among Steinbeck, Ricketts, and a rotating circle of friends and acquaintances who shared their artistic and intellectual sensibilities. Steinbeck drew much of his inspiration from this creative hotspot while writing his most popular fiction.

Describing its enlightened, electric vibe in her book *A Journey into Steinbeck's California*, Susan Shillinglaw writes, "Rickett's lab was New Monterey's salon, a tiny Bohemian enclave of artists, writers, and musicians who were invited for parties and dinners or simply dropped by in the evenings to see what was happening. 'There were great parties at the laboratory,' Steinbeck recalled, 'some of which went on for days.'" Stressing the influence these low-key, habitual get-togethers had on Steinbeck and his fiction, Shillinglaw observes, "They discussed any and all subjects. . . . If Pacific Grove was Steinbeck's home and writerly retreat, the lab in New Monterey was where ideas were forged. In the little laboratory by the sea, John Steinbeck's mind moved outward. . . . What happened at the lab was the kind of relaxation and friendship that Steinbeck assigns to the paisanos in *Tortilla Flat* or Mack and the boys in *Cannery Row*."

Writing about the "collective mind," Nietzsche concluded, "a good writer possesses not only his own mind but also the mind of his friends." As if channeling the cerebral connection that existed in Ricketts's and Steinbeck's circle, he exhorted, "The most fortunate instance in the development of an art is when several geniuses reciprocally keep each other in check; in this kind of a struggle, weaker and gentler natures are generally also allowed air and light." Similarly, crime fiction writer Lawrence Block opines in his book *Writing the Novel from Plot to Print*, "Many of the characters with whom we people our fiction are drawn from life, and how could it be otherwise? One way or another, all our writing comes from experience, and it is experience of our fellow human beings that enables us to create characters that look and act and sound like human beings."

Granting rare access into Steinbeck's "collective mind" by drawing on chance meetings, conversations, and formal interviews conducted over decades—as well as through correspondence and artifacts that he has collected—Steve Hauk's imaginative stories offer stirring profiles of Steinbeck's friends and contemporaries, who, in turn, allow admirers of John Steinbeck a new window onto his influences, his times, and more broadly, the burden and ecstasy of his genius.

Resisting hagiography, Hauk's stories do not always present a flattering portrait of the artist, a fact the famously self-loathing Steinbeck might have appreciated. For example, in the "The Elevator," Hauk painfully dramatizes the dependent but dysfunctional relationship between Steinbeck and his first wife, Carol. Invited to a party just as his writing career is finally beginning to pay dividends after the acceptance of his second novel, *Tortilla Flat*, for publication, Carol drinks to inebriation as she watches Steinbeck charm an attractive, younger woman—a literature student from Berkeley "who wanted to know about John's book." In another story, "The Application," germinating from Steinbeck's application for a gun permit following several jarring threats he had received, we learn that "his first wife Carol had also wanted children and he'd told her repeatedly it was 'either babies or books.'"

"It's fiction but it's based on a lot of things that happened" Hauk told a reporter for the *Monterey Herald*. Hauk noted "that the stories reflect the pressure Steinbeck felt from those who didn't appreciate what he was writing and his political views and sympathy for the plight of migrant workers." Most of Hauk's stories are about the people who knew Steinbeck personally, such as Ed Ricketts and several of Steinbeck's childhood friends and schoolmates, with whom he stayed in touch despite increasing fame. And then there are glorious yarns about the young artists, actresses, and writers with whom Steinbeck rubbed shoulders, from whom he drew inspiration, and who in turn drew inspiration from him. A few of the stories in Hauk's collection, however—and arguably his best—concern people who had little to no contact with John Steinbeck at all, and yet, like so many people worldwide, were deeply moved, even forever changed, by his books.

Take the gut-wrenchingly beautiful story "On Stolen Time" about a terminally ill man named Paul. By indulging his passion for book collecting, and especially first-edition books by John Steinbeck, Paul is able to beat back death, if only temporarily: "Paul thinks of himself as a saver of words, not a writer or a critic, but the kind of person . . . literature needs." Paul (and Steve Hauk) understand what Nietzsche concluded was "the real immortality, that of movement." Specfically, "what once has moved others is like an insect in amber, enclosed and immortalized in the general intertwining of all that exists."

The son of John Steinbeck's longtime friend and editor, the late Pascal Covici, Jr., a writer and scholar, maintains that "the sense that some sort of 'awareness' has taken place is precisely what Steinbeck's best work—perhaps what most good writing—leaves with a reader." Hauk's *Steinbeck: The Untold Stories* achieves this empathic standard and enters the world of artistic endeavor with the power to move and captivate readers for all time.

••••

About the Author: Stephen Cooper is a former D.C. public defender who worked as an assistant federal public defender in Alabama between 2012 and 2015. He has contributed to numerous magazines and newspapers in the United States and overseas. He writes full-time and lives in Woodland Hills, California. Follow him on Twitter at @SteveCooperEsq *Note: "Steinbeck: The Untold Stories by Steve Hauk (review)" was first published in the Steinbeck Review, Vol. 15 No. 1, 2018, pp. 76-79. Copyright © 2018 The Pennsylvania State University. This article is used by permission of the Pennsylvania State University Press.

Pure Magic Joy
Joy Ann Fischer

Pacific Grove in all its scenic glory,
Underneath the mighty oaks and cypress trees.
Remembering the years here at the coast and our life story,
Engulfed in P.G.'s nature with hummingbird visits and buzzing bees.

Monarch Sanctuary strolls, milkweed planted, butterflies welcome,
Asilomar beach walks, gazebo over look, those come and gone.
Glimpses of Big Sur and Point Pinos lighthouse tours, guiding to and from,
It still seems like a dream come true, but it's where we belong.
Calming breezes, constant ocean waves, foggy misty mornings a new,

Jaunts downtown, Pavel's Bakery treats, a cup of Java, and a book or two.
Outstanding food with sunset views, just for me and you.
Yes, this is the life, P.G. is pure magic joy, and our Blue Heaven's view!

PALMS: PUNKS OF THE TREE WORLD
Evelyn Kahan

Driving on a gray morning
Without the saturation of the sun
The variety of trees
On my forested road
Stood out to be noticed
Without the distraction of color.
Among them two tall palms.
What are they doing here with the pines, redwood
And oak?
Palms, tall, with that ridiculous hairdo.
Lanky, they're taller than most others,
Not even making shade.
The Monterey pine just below them, shorter but
Seeming wiser with age, not intimidated,
Stands in its exuberance,
Limbs thrust out in a dance with the breeze.
I drive on,
Smug in my noticing this balance of nature.

2018

Sitting stately on the beach
The rocks offer their constancy,
Their solidness.
They are quite done
With falling apart.
In the midst of mine,
I turn to them for solace.

They have calmly come to rest
The sea may rage against them
Their breath slowed after a lifetime
Of rough and tumble.
They let the green, cold water wash over them;
Cleaner, brighter for the experience.

Is it the blue of the water that finally calms me?
Is it the regularity?
The calm, then crash?
Is it knowing that even when I sleep it will go on?
That even as he leaves me there is a steadiness.

Patience
Susie Joyce

The Egret knows patience.

Holding fast with clever toes
Spread as wide as saucers,
She positions on a bobbing raft
Of kelp forest canopy,
To wait for opportunity.

Shock of snowy white
All stretch and sharpness,
Even in the push of wind and wave
She maintains tranquility
Standing in measured stillness.

Silver flash below
Triggers shift to crouch.
Cocking bowstring body,
Arrow of beak plunges
in a surprise ambush.

If the fish escapes,
As often it will,
The stealthy demands of this work
Require that she relocates.
Survival demands cunning.

Angel wings arch and reach,
Elevate and deliver
The lithesome huntress
To a fresh outlook,

Where the wait resumes.

POETRY IN THE GROVE – LITTLE HOUSE IN JEWELL PARK

Poetry in the Grove Ending July 7, 2018*
Frank Pierce

Our Poetry in the grove here has had such wisdom great that even
Comes on the days even when it's cold and gray,
To meet our need for change, so vast and wide with impact deep,
To help us all in our City to add a vision on the land we love.
Our need of poems so different and shared in the twilight dim,
Provides motive so great with how to get our hearts aware,
Because of Poetry closure and future sharing is now unknown,
The quest is now for a future change to be.

Where poetry sharing again may come, somewhere to present be,
Great and clear.
So with all your help a future we dare to see the return of poetry near
Somewhere here with words so clear that Poetry is now here.

* Frank delivered this poem on the last day of Susie's leadership. Patrick Flanigan stepped in that day to ensure the continuation of Pacific Grove's Poetry in the Grove.

On a Paper Bag
Patrick Flanigan

A paper bag can be a good place to write a poem,
especially one that is brief
and as ephemeral as a breath, life affirming but not essential.

Anyone can survive with one less breath, one less poem

But this bag may take pleasure in these words
that show that someone knew it was here
and honored it with a poem

Even a humble one
not meant for publication.

Patience

Some things cannot be rushed--- the appearance of a shooting star, the opening of a flower,
the growth of a child, a marriage that lasts.

I do not know how these things happen--- where that blaze of fire in the sky started, what compelled that plant to bloom,
what turned that tiny baby into a woman, why you stayed with me all these years.

I do know that these things cannot be rushed.
They happen at their own pace and are seen only by those patient enough to wait
and lucky enough to be there

Poetry in the Grove is a monthly gathering of people familiar with poetry or just wanting to learn something about it. At each meeting the group selects a poet whose work will be shared the next month.

* In July 2018, Poetry in the Grove was going to end because Susie Joyce, its leader for the past 5 years, was leaving the area. We were sorry to see Susie go and that the gathering of poetry enthusiasts might end.

Meetings date back to 2003 when Cathy Gable, Marge Ann Jameson, Karin Locke, Susie Joyce, and Barbara Mossberg got together to promote an interest in poetry.

Fortunately, Poetry in the Grove will continue to meet—with a new leader—the first Saturday of every month, from 3:00 to 5:00 p.m., in the Little House in Jewell Park, adjacent to the Pacific Grove Public Library at Central and Grand Avenues.

Everyone is welcome. There is no admission fee. All that is required is an interest in poetry and respect of fellow attendees.

We hope to see you there!
—Patrick W. Flanigan

Patrick W. Flanigan: A physician and the author of three books of poetry: *Surviving the Storm, Milk* and *When Sunflowers Speak*. The last title is also available in a DVD version. He is also the author of a folio of nine poems entitled *Freestanding Verse*. Recently he authored a novel called **A Father's Smile.** He was born in Indiana, raised in Ohio, and moved to California in 1973. He says the natural beauty of the Central Coast has inspired much of his poetry, while living in Steinbeck country has influenced his prose. Patrick was a presenter at the first annual Carmel Authors and Ideas Festival in 2007.

THE SCREENWRITERS FORUM

The Art Of The Spec Script
Wolf Bukowski

FADE IN…
THE SCENE: The La Crema cafe in Pacific Grove:

Here, in one of its warren-like maze of rooms, sits a small group of determined screenwriters huddled around a table hunched over their laptops in serious concentration, dialogue, and criticism of the … SPEC SCRIPT!

The discussions are intense. The exchange is a mixture of amusement and serious debate. Several hours pass. The cups are empty; each writer has had their say, and another session of the SCREENWRITERS FORUM concludes. And perhaps one writer may be ever so much closer to a completed script or towards a possible option, a sale, or … File 13.

◎ ◎ ◎

But determined as ever, they will ardently return again with their revisions, rewrites, and readings, to seek that Holy Grail: "the Spec Script"— written on the "speculation" that it will be optioned and eventually purchased by a producer, a studio, or just to find freelance work within the film business. For non-commissioned or unknown screenwriters the spec script can be an opportune way to prove their storytelling ability.

The catchwords are "speculation" and "open market." The odds of a spec script being produced or optioned in the open market are not as good as being given a writing assignment which may offer more opportunity for a career in the film industry.

So our diligent little group of writers is not writing a screenplay for a director, actor, or producer, but first, for the "reader." It may be for a professional story analyst, an agent, but more than likely it would be for a stranger who has the first official read. And who more than likely is an over-worked, underpaid intern, whose in box is full and who knows very well how to use the "delete" function.

◎ ◎ ◎

Thousands of scripts are registered with WGA (Writer's Guild Assoc.) each year; and that's not counting those who have their scripts copyright registered or those who simply do nothing.

Producers get about 10,000 scripts a year, and only about 150 get released. Roughly 60 spec screenplays get sold every year out of a quarter million screenplays in various filmmaking enterprises.

It's not surprising that with computer technology and the extensiveness of the world wide web, a greater number of people are wondering about developing their "great" idea for a movie.

Any script sold to the studios or production companies, invariably is met by its gatekeepers, i.e. the readers (script analysts, etc.) The initial fate of any spec script rests in their hands.

The mastery of formatting and spec writing is a necessary step to creating a readable and marketable script. It is one of the very first things an experienced script analyst looks for, besides clarity, readability, originality etcetera.

All screenplays are stories in pictures, but they must be stylistically in a very fixed, unforgiving screenplay format— especially the spec script.

The first script by an unrepresented writer has to be a spec script and not a shooting script, which is written for the shoot; it is quite different, filled with technical production information, (e.g. camera directions, etc.) and is commissioned (paid for by the studio or producer).

The screenplay format is rather uniquely reductionist, as opposed to the freer open style of narrative prose. Everything: story, characterization, dialogue, even sounds are reduced to what the reader MUST literally visualize. Every word, thought, visual must be written in the present active voice. The scene depicted must happen "right now in front of the reader," even in a flashback scene.

The spec script should say as much as possible with as few words as possible—a mere 100 pages (or less), succinct paragraphs, dialogue, and description. Imagine "translating" a 400 plus page novel into a spec script. But it's been done.

On top of all that it has to be a fast paced masterpiece of compelling storytelling, displaying extraordinary control of the craft. And if that's not enough, it has to be upbeat, entertaining and chock full of unforgettable characters, depicted through dramatic visual action. Each scene focusing on a clear visual conflict.

One day the writer may finish the script. Then what's to be done with it? Start another? No time for that. Before it can be submitted anywhere, there's more work to be done: there's the Log Line, Pitch, Query Letter, Table Reads… and hopefully, someone, somewhere who is willing to read the darn thing.

And indeed, there will be someone … the fellow writers of the Screenwriters Forum, who will actually read and critique each other's screenplay, providing the supportive "first read" each one needs, in an environment of creative process.

It is often said that writing is a solitary activity. However, it need not be. In the support group, one is not alone in this endeavor. Honest positive criticism is an absolute necessity for any writer as it is for any creative endeavor.

⊙ ⊙ ⊙

Thus far, this fledgling group of four writers, has been developing several scripts as well as script ideas from concept to completion. The authors' writing styles and goals differ distinctly from each other.

Mike Latta, for instance, is an ex-Marine, former advertising agency art director, writer, creative director and published magazine and newspaper writer. He is a self-published author of three previous novels and a couple of short stories. Mike, a life-long sailor, lives aboard a traditional sailing cutter, the *Narwhal*, in the Monterey Marina where he is presently working on novel number four and a feature length screenplay.

Mike's screenplay, *Dirt Circles*, which he started writing with the group, is a semi-biographical story based on the events of his colorful life. Originally he started the script years ago, gave up, being frustrated by the rigorous script formatting requirements. Since he started with the group, he is well on his way to completing a spec script.

⊙ ⊙ ⊙

And then there is **Mary J. Fry**, whose love for the written word progressed as she grew up, reading voraciously and writing stories. She wrote poetry and has been published often in literary magazines as she pursued a degree in English literature. Her upcoming novel and also screenplay is *Denim & da Vinci*. Her travels in New Mexico and Italy were also her inspiration for her illustrated book of prose, *Adobe Doorways*, which won the coveted Pegasus award.

Another screenplay, *Cold War*, is a drama depicting an event that occurs in the 60s during the height of the Cold War at the most volatile border point in Europe, involving a maverick revengeful Russian officer and American soldiers, with a remarkable human love affair in the midst of all this.

Mary's main focus for the past many years has been screenwriting. While in Los Angeles, she was able to hone her scriptwriting craft working with a well known director and screenwriting coaches.

Since working with the Screenwriters Forum, she has found that it has afforded an even greater learning experience beyond the script writing craft into how to pitch and promote the project and strategies for success once a screenplay is completed.

Working with the Forum, her current spec script is *Squatters*, a screenplay that fulfills one of the group's goals of creating scripts with low-budget requirements and making it also possible for local production or for any independent filmmaker.

⊙ ⊙ ⊙

A recent arrival to the Forum is **Danielle Mallett**. She is an American young-adult novelist, spoken word poet, and healing advocate, who is a functional movement coach. She is best known for her first book, *Take Me Away With You*, a novel set in Las Vegas, NV, that is centered around a young girl searching for meaningful connections. The heroine gets swept away by all the distractions of the city: boys, sex, drugs, and the tyranny of body image. Danielle's writing focuses on topics of self-reliance, learning, and the mysteries of life.

Her second book, *Get Well With Danielle*, will be published in 2018. It is a guide book for young adults and anyone looking to navigate the healing arts world. If that's not enough, she's working on a five part mystery series.

When she isn't writing, self-publishing or performing poetry, Danielle engages people by having them write and share their stories. She gets kids, young adults, and anyone struggling to tap into their creativity to write and create their own stories.

Her initial project with the Forum currently is an adaptation of her published novel, *Take Me Away With You*. Although this is her first attempt at writing a screenplay, she is assisted by the group members, either individually or together in adapting the story into the screenplay format.

⊙ ⊙ ⊙

The Screenwriters Forum was started in April 2018 by **Wolf Bukowski,** a 32-year Pacific Grove resident. During that time, he commuted between Pacific Grove and Los Angeles, where he worked in the television industry, involved in a multitude of creative tasks.

As television director, producer, editor, and writer, he has been involved in countless projects, live broadcast, talk shows and documentaries in studios or on location. He has received three Emmy awards and various other awards for his work.

Theatrical plays and screenwriting have always been his real interests. In Los Angeles, he was a long time member of the New Playwrights Foundation writers group, which generated original stage and screenplay material. During this time, Wolf enjoyed reading countless screenplays. In the 90s, the group operated a theatre in Hollywood that produced their own original plays. One of them was Wolf's, *Headgames, Tales from the Id*, which he is now adapting into a shooting script for a video production.

Currently, one of his projects is a screenplay entitled, *Spirits in the Mist*, a tale which takes place in Pacific Grove in the 1940s. It deals with witchcraft and human passion and a young refugee child who has a special gift that malevolent forces desire.

One of the reasons Wolf started Screenwriters Forum, other than to experience the incredible creative adrenaline it releases, was developing his own material as well as reading and assisting other writers' works. Here each writer can learn a lot more about their own writing and the work of other fellow members in a supportive imaginative environment… A two way bonus!

◎ ◎ ◎

The Screenwriters Forum, a supportive group environment, considers the Spec Script, script format, the pitch, the log line, the Query Letter, Novels into screenplays and visa versa, and Table Reads— Just for fun or a good laugh, or a nice cup of coffee.

Flash Fiction
Jeffrey Whitmore

Back in 1990, I entered a short-story contest sponsored by the San Luis Obispo weekly newspaper *New Times*. The stories had to be 55 words or less. Mine was 53 words, not counting the title. First prize was to be a bottle of wine.

I didn't win it. Nor did any of the 46 other people whose stories were selected for publication.

When the stories were published, an introduction stated: "Our only real change this year was our decision not to award first, second, and third prizes, opting instead to designate all that appear in print as winners. Somehow we feel better about it that way."

I didn't feel any better about it. But I didn't feel any worse, either. It had been fun, and there hadn't been an entry fee—although I did have to fork over a hefty 25 cents for postage when I sent the story to *New Times*.

The annual contest is in its 31st year, and dozens of such contests are now held around the world. Some have an upper limit of 1,500 words, charge entry fees, and offer large cash prizes. The *Monterey County Weekly*'s annual contest has an upper limit of 101 words, has no entry fee, and awards a first prize of $101.

In 1991 I gave *New Times* publisher Steve Moss permission to include my story in a book of stories taken from several of his contests. His *World's Shortest Stories* was published by New Times Press in 1995 and later reprinted by Running Press.

Then weird things began to happen.

My story began to show up in printed and other media, and also in various adaptations: *Glamour* magazine, the British tabloid *Globe* (positioned next to "Secret behind Cindy Crawford's nude *Playboy* spread"), the *Irish Times*, readings on National Public Radio, several independent films, a tango performance by a Canadian dance troupe, a five-minute opera by composer Wes Flinn, *The Writer's Block: 786 ideas to jump start your imagination*, Jason Rekulak's witty 3"x3"x3" book, H. Porter Abbot's book *The Cambridge Introduction to Narrative*, David Galef's book *Brevity: A Flash Fiction Handbook*, Cristiana Pugliese's online literary study "The Reader as Co-Author: Reading and Writing 'Bedtime Story,'" and, following Steve Moss's death, it appeared in his *Los Angeles Times* obituary.

Now, 28 years after its first appearance, here it is in this book.

Bedtime Story

"Careful, honey, it's loaded," he said, re-entering the bedroom.

Her back rested against the headboard. "This for your wife?"

"No. Too chancy. I'm hiring a professional."

"How about me?"

He smirked. "Cute. But who'd be dumb enough to hire a lady hit man?"

She wet her lips, sighting along the barrel. "Your wife."

Monarch Pub, left, and Farmers Market, right. Page 157 Pacific Grove Golf Links and Lighthouse. Photos Peter Mounteer.

CENTRAL COAST WRITERS — *Nancy Swing*

Pacific Grove is known as an idyllic writers' retreat, and Central Coast Writers makes a heartfelt contribution to that appellation. CCW is one of the largest and most dynamic chapters of the California Writers Club, which grew out of the literary tradition of the East Bay in the early 1900s that included Jack London. 170 members write in all genres—memoir and mystery, fantasy and sci fi, poetry, screenplays and more. The club hosts monthly meetings at Point Pinos Grill, with speakers on writing topics (meetings are free and open to the public), as well as periodic workshops. CCW also encourages young writers through members who help judge submissions to the national Scholastic Art & Writing Awards. In addition, CCW conducts its own annual short story contest for high school juniors and seniors in Monterey County. Central Coast Writers shares a long history with Pacific Grove, a history of mutual support and growth.

The winner of the 2018 Central Coast Short Story Contest, Elias DeLeon (right), with Brooks Leffler, whose photo was used as the prompt for young contestants to write their entries. Elias was awarded $300 for his story, "Rememory."

CCW President Laurie Sheehan and *Scribbles* Newsletter editor Lana Bryan leading members in the 4th of July Parade. That's Laurie driving her modified 1992 Miata Italia, while Lana waves to the crowd. Laurie's genre is mystery, and Lana writes creative nonfiction.

Members meet monthly at Pacific Grove's Pinos Grill for food, fellowship and speakers on topics that include plotting, characterization, editing, research, finding an agent or a commercial publisher, marketing, self-publishing, ebooks, audiobooks and more. CCW welcomes the public to these meetings. For information on the current month's topic, see centralcoastwriters.org. Photo by Gary Parker.

Every year in April, CCW members march in Pacific Grove's Good Old Days Parade. Their signs always get a big crowd response. Left to right: Alana Myles (children's fiction and non-fiction), Nancy Swing (mystery) Joyce Krieg (mystery), Leslie Patiño (novel), Dennis Hamilton (poetry, nonfiction) Russell Sunshine (travel memoir) and Ned Huston (science fiction).

CCW members gathering to march in Monterey's 4th of July Parade. Costumes combine literary references with the parade's patriotic theme. Left to right: Dorothy Vriend (poetry, short story and memoir), Sarah Pruitt (historical fiction), Alana Myles (children's fiction and non-fiction), Patricia Hamilton (memoir, essay, non-fiction; Park Place Publications), Russell Sunshine (travel memoir), and Nancy Swing (mystery).

CCW gives a prize to the member marching in the most creative costume. In P.G.'s 2018 Good Old Days Parade, Dennis Hamilton won for channeling Edgar Allen Poe and his raven. Dennis co-chairs CCW's local high school writing contest with Ned Huston.

Dick Guthrie ready to march with his CCW sign. A soldier since he was seventeen, Dick is finishing his memoir, *Gone to Soldiers, Every One*, honoring the B Company men he commanded in Vietnam, 1967-68.

Kyle Elizabeth Wood (historical nonfiction) and Carol Marquart (plays) sporting costumes that combine literary references with the Good Old Days theme.

Harriet Lynn won the 4th of July costume prize as Julia Ward Howe. Harriet not only writes plays, nonfiction articles and children's stories, she's also a professional producer, director, dancer and actor.

Early morning search for that perfect cuppa. Photos Peter Mounteer.

SECTION FOUR

CONNECTIONS AROUND TOWN

Farmers Market 2009. Photo of Zack and Grace McCoy by Patricia Hamilton.

"Everyone's Harvest Farmers Market provides a catalyst and a spark to keep the heartbeat of Pacific Grove strong."
— Maureen Mason, Everyone's Harvest

FIVE P.G. DOWNTOWN WOMEN IN BUSINESS – REBECCA RIDDELL

Giving Back to the Community

My name is Rebecca and I love Pacific Grove. I'm a lifelong resident and a Pacific Grove entrepreneur. My partner and I have published Discover Pacific Grove for the past twenty-odd years. Discover offers me an opportunity to get to know our local business owners, their staff, and even their families. What I've found is that a good number of Pacific Grove's successful entrepreneurs happen to be women. Let's meet a few of them.

I know Pacific Grove has always been a haven for strong women. Even in its founding in the Methodist Retreat days, we know Pacific Grove was, at the very least, tolerant of women expressing themselves through their work, their words, and their lifestyles. Before the turn of the last century, Pacific Grove could boast (even though boasting was frowned upon) female lighthouse keepers, female architects, female realtors, and even a female mayor. Women with female partners were also quietly tolerated in the religious retreat.

Today, our downtown businesses have a disproportionate number of female entrepreneurs. These women have proven successful in their business endeavors and make time to give back to our community. I have selected a few that I'd like to believe share a number of similar traits with me and love Pacific Grove (almost) as much as I do.

Photo Peter Mounteer:

Marita Johnson:
'A Guardian or Mother Figure'

I met Marita when she purchased a small boutique on Forest Avenue. I was a regular customer of the boutique and was pleased to see she would be keeping it open. From the start, Marita had a strong presence. She exuded warmth and professionalism and welcomed me with a firm handshake, a wide smile, and a strong accent. I wondered what she was doing in this little boutique on a side street of this small town. As time went by we got to know each other. I learned Marita was "a simple farm girl" from Germany who came to America with her new husband, who was stationed at Ft. Ord.

I would say Marita is a guardian or mother figure—gentle, yet firm in her convictions. She is not the type of person to get in your face, yet she will stand strong for her cause and win through sheer conviction. She believes her strength of endurance comes from her childhood on the farm, along with many of her unique characteristics. The farm is where Marita learned the value of hard work, the value of a helping hand, and the value of honesty—what she considers her three most valuable traits. On the farm, where many of life's necessities were scarce, hard work, trust, and compassion for your neighbor were vital components of survival. Coming to America as a young bride of 21 promised her a different kind of life. Here she could nurture her new family as well as her desire to help others by working in the medical field. Marita had yet to master the English language, but this didn't hold her back and she did just as she set out to do. Marita waited until her child was an adult before she started over once again. She studied to become a realtor while working in the medical industry and passed the exam on her very first attempt. Yet Marita took nothing for granted. She worked seven days a week and had a reputation of working every holiday. She earned a good living and made many new friends.

Marita, like 70 percent of America women, isn't a size 6 or even a size 12, and she often found it difficult to dress for success. When she found a size-worthy boutique in Pacific Grove she became a loyal customer. Marita received word the shop was closing and immediately contacted the owner suggesting she purchase it from her. She found herself overnight the proud owner of a boutique and a fulltime realtor. Never having worked in retail before, she drew on her instincts of what she would like to see in a retail boutique. Even today, Marita shakes her head with surprise at the spontaneity of that moment in 2004. It was difficult, to say the least, to learn yet another new trade while knee deep in the success of her last. Yet, Marita showed no fear and after just two years in the business, moved her boutique to a larger location on Lighthouse Avenue and expanded her lines to include so much more of everything! This relocation moved her spirit as well and she decided it was time to follow this new passion fulltime.

Meanwhile, Marita's Boutique had become the "poster girl" for how to do business in Pacific Grove, as it is one of the highest grossing independent retailers in the city. However, it is the relationships she has built that really makes Marita's store special. Her boutique is a place women go to be catered to, to be listened to, and always to be told the truth. Her long-time staff echo her values in hard work, honesty and compassion, to the point that they, too, (with Marita's blessing) would not recommend a purchase they believed wasn't a good fit. When I walk into Marita's I need only announce the intent—be it a gift or an outfit for a special occasion—and her staff is whirling through racks of ready-to-wear and accessories with suggestions that always are just what I'm looking for. Marita's caters to everyone —all ages, all sizes, all price ranges, and so many different styles—all squeezed into her charming boutique. I've heard there are women who schedule their vacations around seasonal shopping at Marita's. Some people go to the spa or to a bar, others go to Marita's ... it's an escape, an experience, a feel-good kinda thing. Marita always says, "Treat your customers how you want to be treated."

Marita's way of doing business quickly earned the respect and friendship of her neighbors. One of those neighbors, the Orlando family, has been a part of Pacific

Grove for as long as I can remember and they, too, just loved Marita. In fact, they loved her so much that when it came time for the Orlandos to retire, they asked Marita to take over their beloved Orlando's Shoe Store in exchange for a small fee and the promise that she would leave Mr. Orlando's hat on the nail in the back room, where it has hung for nearly 80 years. Another spontaneous deal was struck and Marita's Shoes was born. A few years later, Marita heard cries from the residents about the lack of a men's store. So she opened a men's store with brands like Pendleton, Tommy Bahama and more. Marita's boutiques weathered the economic downturn of 2008, when so many of her fellow entrepreneurs had no choice but to throw in the towel.

Even today, when so many of our country's main streets are failing, Marita has some of the most successful retail businesses in the city—three stores, side by side—in historic buildings in the heart of Pacific Grove. It is not without trials and some tribulation, yet Marita's motto is, "You can never predict what is going to happen. If it feels right, just go with it. Once you have it you just make it work," confirms Marita, "Believe in yourself, believe in others, and in God."

Marita's emulates what we would hope Pacific Grove is all about—genuine, warm-hearted people with your best interests in mind.

Tessuti Zoo storefront. Photo Peter Mounteer.

Emily Owens: 'Boundless Creativity and Entrepreneurial Spirit.'

Even though it was some twenty years ago, I'll never forget the moment when I was struck by a window display in a little shop on Forest Avenue. Back in that day, Pacific Grove was home to the assortment of retailers you'd expect to find in a little Victorian town—sportswear, hardware, the five & dime, and such. Yet from that day on, it seemed Pacific Grove would never be the same. In the window I found a scene out of a whimsical dream, with life-sized, stuffed creatures in magnificent patterns and colors, sitting on lavishly painted and upholstered furniture, having tea. In fact, I dreamt of the display that evening. Needless to say, I felt it necessary to find out more about this tea party and its creator.

That's how I met Emily Owens. I learned Emily was an artist from L.A. who happened upon Pacific Grove in 1980, when taking a wrong turn on her way to Monterey, where her husband had just landed a writing job. To this day, she's not sure how she ended up on the Holman Highway, yet by the time she reached our historic downtown, she knew Pacific Grove was going to be her new home. Her arrival brought a refreshing change to the retail doldrums with her boundless creativity and entrepreneurial spirit.

Emily was already an established artist upon her arrival, with her one-of-a-kind art quilt pieces used as backdrops for television productions. Yet it was her daughter's first birthday party that launched her current career. She created her very first stuffed art pieces as special decorations and party favors for the children. Jolly clowns with large, pointy hats, strung as a garland during the party, were given to each child as they left. The clowns were such a hit with the children and parents alike that she began creating many different creatures for her friends and family to enjoy, then began selling them to a few retailers. When a Marshall Field's buyer saw the pieces, her new art project really took off. By the mid-90s, Emily was creating in the living room of her Pacific Grove home hundreds of whimsical creatures for seven Marshall Field's locations as well as the Art Institute of Chicago's catalog. It was time to find a studio.

Emily moved the production to a second floor space on Forest Avenue, just above her current location. The first thing she did was create an eye-catching window display. People would often wander up the stairs to find out what on earth was going on up there. That's how Emily met Mary. Mary, an artist herself, was so intrigued with Emily's work she convinced Emily they should become

partners. Emily would create art, dolls, and clothing while Mary made jewelry and painted furniture and Mary's husband took care of the books. Soon the pair moved downstairs, to 171 Forest Avenue, and Tessuti Zoo was born—"Tessuti" being Italian for "fabric," and "Zoo," well, you'll just have to see for yourself….

Together, Emily and Mary became active in the community, supporting local causes and participating in local events. They spent evenings, birthdays and holidays together. Meanwhile, their store gained notoriety throughout the county and beyond, becoming a tourist attraction of sorts, with many coming to Pacific Grove just to find Tessuti Zoo.

Then came 2010. That was the year Emily and her husband were both diagnosed with different types of cancer. This was also the year that her partner and friend, Mary, told her she was retiring and moving away in a few short months to be with family. It was the year Emily's strength was tested and her dreams were clearly defined. Few knew of Emily's illness nor that of her husband, and Mary departed with love and hugs. Emily had already made her decision. She wasn't about to let this cancer overtake her family and she would continue to run the business as she had all along. Yet, Emily would need her friends more than ever before. That's where Marita Johnson came in. Emily had met Marita when she opened her boutique years before and they always kept in touch with an occasional luncheon or shopping visit. When Marita learned of the situation Emily found herself in, she reached out with a helping hand, working into the night teaching Emily her accounting techniques. Meanwhile, the two became dear friends with Marita making it a point to check in with Emily regularly. Even today, they can often be found together at Fandango conversing, laughing, and sharing the Grand Marnier soufflé. Luckily, both Emily and her husband overcame their illnesses and have grown stronger with each day.

Emily went on to take Tessuti Zoo to the next level. The tiny shop is overflowing with colorful creativity, capable of sparking every sense of your being. One must spend a good 45 minutes, taking a full 180 degree view with each new step, if you are to truly experience it. There's a one-of-a-kind treasure to be found in every nook and cranny—hand-made jewelry, apparel and home decor; as well as a magical children's section with plenty of books, toys, and hand-made apparel. Watching Emily create her magic in the back room, piled floor to ceiling with bolts of colorful cotton fabrics, is like sneaking into Santa's workshop. This is where she finds time to think of fun new things to do for her community.

Even today, some 20-plus years later, Emily continues to make delightful contributions to her community. Those who enjoy seeing the colorful lanterns and butterflies in the trees when they drive down Lighthouse Avenue during the Feast of Lanterns or butterfly season can thank Emily and Tessuti Zoo. It was Emily who took it upon herself to encourage city beautification and won approval to have Lighthouse Avenue decorated with colorful lanterns and giant monarch butterflies in the trees overhead.

Photo Peter Mounteer.

Adrianne Jonson: 'A Living, Breathing Miracle'

When I walked by Artisana Gallery for the first time nearly 10 years ago, I was shocked to smell incense and see Tibetan flags flying on a building across from City Hall. Pacific Grove was changing. I walked in to introduce myself and found a quiet, polite young lady behind the counter making jewelry from precious stones. The shop was definitely a surprise for the senses, with the bright colors, mesmerizing music and the smell of incense. I learned it was a gallery specializing in local, handmade art in many media—jewelry, pottery, paintings, sculpture, and more. Of course, I was curious about who had thought to bring this unique store to Pacific Grove. I learned I was talking to the owner, Adrianne Jonson. She and her partner, Sandy Hamm, were the masterminds of Artisana Gallery. While Sandy worked fulltime in management with Peet's Coffee, Adrianne held down the entrepreneurial fort, as was the plan from the beginning.

Adrianne's story begins in San Diego, where she was raised. She says it was a brutal place back then and an incident when she was 17 years old gave her the final sign it was time to leave. She and a friend were surrounded by five men while in a phone booth and literally had to push their way through the attackers' legs and run straight into the busy street to escape. Then and there she knew it was time to leave. She begged her high school sweetheart to ask his family if they could spend six months in their remote cabin in the woods of Mariposa. It was a go, and off they went into the wilds. There was no running hot water and the bathroom facilities consisted of a bathhouse up over the hill a-ways. But they were comfortable and safe. Six months turned into seven years and the couple married. Just about at that one-year mark, Adrianne's soon-to-be father-in-law offered them his business, a gem and minerals store. Adrianne had worked in retail before and knew just what to do; the store became successful. Over the years, the couple had gained some dear friends with whom they spent a great deal of time. These friends were two gay women that Adrianne and her husband both adored. Yet, after a number of years, their friends ended their partnership and one of the women left the area. A few months later, Adrianne's life changed dramatically.

In 2004, Adrianne woke up one morning and could not see. Her husband was at work, so she called her dear friend, Sandy (the friend who stayed), to take her to the hospital. The results were dumbfounding. Adrianne had Multiple Sclerosis. While she was able to get her symptoms under control with medications, the disease

took its toll on her marriage. Thankfully Sandy stayed steadfast by her side. It was not long after the diagnosis that Adrianne and Sandy knew they were meant for each other. Adrianne finalized her divorce and the couple arrived on the Monterey Peninsula by the end of that year.

Sandy would continue her management position with the local Peet's Coffee and Adrianne would do what she does best—open a retail store. Yet, this would be something different, something unique. Her vision was of a store filled with the works of local artists, including her own work with gemstones and photography. First, Lee Trotter offered her a space on Forest Avenue, which was most definitely a destination location with little foot traffic. Then the economy went to hell in a hand basket and many businesses were going through rough times, with a good number just throwing in the towel. During this time, Mrs. Trotter offered to lower the rent, yet Adrianne just wasn't sure the reduced rent would be enough to justify keeping the business open. Talking with Sandy about the needs of the artists they were working with and the benefits to their new community, they decided to wait just 30 more days before making the decision to close. It was at the end of this small window of time that the owner of Carried Away Boutique was offered a new location and came into Artisana Gallery to ask if Adrianne wanted her old space on Lighthouse Avenue. The location was in the center of downtown, with twice the display space at a very reasonable rent. The only catch was that Adrianne had to make a decision almost immediately. The very same day, she met the property owner and a deal was made with a handshake.

Adrianne and Sandy were overwhelmed in so many ways! They had just made a deal to move their business within days to a location that needed renovating from a clothing boutique to a full scale gallery. It was time to call in the troops! Thankfully, the women had already made a number of good friends with contacts in the construction industry and the work began immediately. Walls were removed and wall coverings changed, and new display materials moved in over a matter of a week and a half.

The new and improved Artisana Gallery opened in 2013 at 612 Lighthouse Avenue in all its glory two weeks after the decision was made. It has been tremendously successful ever since.

Today, Artisana Gallery collectively showcases some 45 unique artists and artisans, including their own works in photography and jewelry design. Items for sale include pottery, metal arts, paintings, Big Sur jade sculpture, incense, candles, statuary, scarves, wind chimes, and more.

Almost immediately upon arrival Adrianne joined the Chamber of Commerce and offered bold and refreshing concepts for invigorating our business districts. Soon she held a position on its Board of Directors. More than eight years ago, Adrianne came up with the concept of First Friday, encouraging downtown businesses to stay open into the evening hours and celebrate the community with special offers, entertainment and complimentary refreshments on the first Friday of each month. As most things in this sleepy little town, it took a while to take off. Today, it is one of the city's most popular regular attractions, drawing families, locals, and visitors to explore our delightful shops, galleries and restaurants from 6:00 to 9:00 p.m. monthly— just look for the green flags!

Adrianne also joined the board of the Pacific Grove Art Center, and works hard to keep this important organization afloat during difficult financial times. She has also been instrumental in keeping Artists in Chautauqua alive as an annual event that helps support the Heritage Society of Pacific Grove. These are just a few of her contributions to our community in just a decade—all of this while fighting a chronic, typically progressive disease involving damage to the nerve cells in the brain and spinal cord, with symptoms that include impairment of speech and of muscular coordination, blurred vision, and severe fatigue. I have found her to be a living, breathing miracle. I am honored to know her and can't wait to see what she comes up with next!

I hope that those reading this story have an opportunity to meet these genuine, impressive women in person. They will greet you with open arms and offer you a unique perspective on what Pacific Grove is all about. It's about the people and a sincere commitment to our uniquely beautiful community.

Sharing Pacific Grove Stories with the Family

Community Book I Launch Party at Chautauqua Hall, 2017.
Patricia Hamilton and her family.
Left: Jack McCoy, son-in-law;
Zack McCoy, grandson; Patricia;
Grace McCoy, granddaughter;
Melanie McCoy, daughter.

Photo compliments of Pacific Grove Photographer Donna Kiernan.

Patricia Hamilton: 'Shaman of Memories'

When I think of Patricia Hamilton, I think of the poem by J. R.R. Tolkien, "All That is Gold Does Not Glitter." I met Patricia at a chamber mixer some twenty years ago. She was the polite one with the bright smile. You'd assume she was shy until she was curious; then the questions would pour out, one after another, in a soft yet determined voice. I learned she was a writer working on a travel book. It was clear even then that travel was her best friend and DNA her driving force. Patricia had followed her family's roots here, to Pacific Grove, proving that ...

"Not all who wander are lost ...."

Patricia was born in Cedarville, California, smack dab in the middle of a large family. Her mother died when she was just 15 and her father nearly killed her in a farming accident. Early on, she knew she'd need to fend for herself. When Patricia wasn't helping on the farm, she spent much of her time reading and wandering through the open spaces, alone or with three younger brothers in tow. It was this upbringing that gave Patricia a love of books, strength in solitude—and leadership qualities.

Yet, she was always inquisitive, eager to learn about people and their interests. In fact, it was in high school journalism that Patricia had her first series of personal interviews published in the school paper, turning one simple question into a bi-monthly column for which she won rave reviews. Could this desire have continued burning inside her for more than thirty years?

"Deep roots are not reached by the frost ...."

Right after high school, Patricia's sister sent her a Greyhound bus ticket to return to California. Without hesitation, the young woman packed a suitcase and jumped on the bus. It wasn't long after her arrival she met her first husband and they were blessed with a beautiful daughter. Her second marriage gave her more opportunities for personal growth (and maybe that was sheer stubbornness—you'll have to ask her), and her third, independence and a career in publishing. Each time, Patricia demanded her equal place in the marriage and after exhaustive efforts to reconcile, decided it was just "time to move on."

"From the ashes, a fire shall be woken ...."

Having visited Pacific Grove during childhood, in 1990 Patricia moved here to care for her Aunt Charlotte, who lived in her grandfather's house at 562 Park Place. Here she

learned about her ancestors in Pacific Grove. Patricia wanted to learn more about her family and herself and began researching family trees, digging deeper and deeper, until she reached her own DNA—her maternal Haplo group V—during the Ice Age in the Basque Country. In the U.S. she began reaching out to long-lost family members and recorded their stories, finding a deep connection to them and then to others, then published a family book.

"A light from the shadows shall spring ....

Patricia learned she came from a long line of adventurers. In fact, she holds an unheard-of count of twenty-three DNA matches with those brave enough to be the first to set foot in the New World. No doubt this is where she gets her explorer gene. She learned her great-great-grandfather was a Methodist minister who was called from St. Paul, Minnesota to the seaside retreat of Pacific Grove in 1890. The Gale descendants also loved Pacific Grove, started businesses, invested in Pacific Grove real estate, and made it their final resting place.

Her first trip to Europe was to the University of Lancaster, England, through the Study Abroad Program at UCSC. After receiving her BA in Philosophy from UCSC she taught English in Spain.

"Renewed shall be the blade that was broken ...."

When her first grandchild came, upon holding him in her arms, she knew her wandering days would be set aside until he could travel with her. No matter. Patricia's life calling had materialized. She found that she was meant to be a story-teller—a collector, an historian, a preservationist of sorts. Park Place Publications, in addition to other works, collects and publishes our stories for future generations to treasure. This book is just one example of her efforts.

Her business launched in 1991, when Patricia's venture published *America's Best Indoor Plants & Plant People*, with personal stories and photos of individual contributors' prize plants and care instructions from all over the U.S.A. From the very start, Patricia was collecting personal stories. The first book to be released under the Park Place Publications imprint was *Tell Me More Ancestor Stories*, featuring family stories by Diana J. Dennett, a ninth generation resident of Monterey who traces her ancestors back to the DeAnza expedition and beyond.

Over the years, Patricia has helped local authors "birth" their own books—more than 200, in many different genres. She wrote and produced a series of travel guides, culminating in 2007 with *California Healthy*, the first ever in-room green guide for Marriott Hotels.

In 2010, she began making annual winter visits to Alamos, Sonora, Mexico, resulting in a book of stories of the 80 expat women who shape the international colony there. *Our Stories of Alamos* was published as a benefit for Los Amigos de Educacion—once again proving the power of sharing our stories.

Patricia's mission to collect stories shifted into high gear in 2016, when she offered free memoir writing classes through the sponsorship of the P.G. Public Library. She says, "After the September and October classes of writing and sharing P.G. stories, I knew a book had to be published for the community." The result was the release some 12 months later of book one of *Life in Pacific Grove*, containing over 400 local stories.

The book you are now reading is the second book in the *Life in Pacific Grove* series, with an emphasis on deeper community connections through essays by local writers that reflect their involvement and love for Pacific Grove. "Can you imagine what an enlightened society we would have today if we had been regularly recording every person's story?" Patricia says. "Today's living is tomorrow's history. Our stories are a grounding and a guidebook for future generations. And don't dare trust others to tell your story—you never know what they might say!"

Her plans through 2019 include creating how-to books for other communities to embark on similar projects to collect and share local stories with the goal of preserving their cultures, enriching their own lives and those of generations to come, both in print and digitally on-line.

Patricia's vision is to promote Pacific Grove as the writers' haven it is. I think she is single-handedly succeeding. Three new books under the Park Place Publications/Pacific Grove Books imprints—including *Life in Pacific Grove: Deeper Connections*—will be launched at this year's Indie Authors Day, an American Library Association event. One is a reprint of Bill Minor's 1974 Pacific Grove book of poetry, prose and artwork, another a detective novel set in Pacific Grove by P.G. author Jeffrey Whitmore.

It seems Patricia has just begun. This shaman of memories plans to launch two national series of community memoir books: Stories of America and Stories of Mexico. She hopes her efforts "will show how peoples of differing cultures can and do live peaceably together, bridging the cultures of Americans and Mexicans."

"The old that is strong does not wither …."

Somehow, she's talked me into contributing to her efforts and I've found it enjoyable. It's given me a chance to better know the woman I will spend eternity with. You see, Patricia's great-great-grandparents, The Reverends Sylvanus and Jane Gale and two of their children—and, eventually, herself—are buried in the heart of the old Methodist section of El Carmelo Cemetery, just down the path from my great-grandfather Will Wright. Right there amidst Pacific Grove's beginnings—and right next to Patricia—my husband and I will rest for eternity.

"The crownless again shall be king …"

Grace McCoy in El Carmelo Cemetery. Photo Patricia Hamilton.

Pacific Grove Takes PRIDE in Our Schools

Rebecca Riddell

Back in the early 1990s, I had a young son in the Pacific Grove Unified School District. I became curious about a Pacific Grove non-profit organization that was helping fund classroom educational programs and decided I'd show up at one of their board meetings unannounced. I assume that didn't happen too often, judging by the look on the faces of many sitting around classroom tables in small chairs at Robert H. Down Elementary School. Yet they welcomed me and asked me to introduce myself and to sit and listen. They were an interesting bunch of people from all walks of life and occupations. Some had children in the district; some just cared about our community's children. All, including Jay Cobb, Linda Pagnella, Linda Jones, Doug Stickler and Bill McElyea, were warm and welcoming.

During the hour and a half I spent in the room, I came to realize this was a very unique organization. The official name is an acronym, P.G. PRIDE, which stands for Public Response in Dollars to Education. I learned the group had been funding education enrichment since 1982 and that a full 98 percent of donations go directly to funding education enrichment activities and programs for all seven schools within P.G.USD. They read off requests coming directly from teachers asking for money for musical instruments, athletics, school field trips, technology, science equipment, stage productions, art tools and facility improvements. The discussions were short as the need was great and the group approved nearly every request before them. I was astonished. I had to be a part of it and asked if they needed any additional volunteers. I was enlisted immediately and was proud to serve this worthy cause.

This is where I met Richard Stillwell, a P.G. PRIDE founder and community leader who owned and operated Pacific Grove Hardware. Today, I count Richard as part of my family and he continues to serve this organization as an Honorary Board Member 36 years after its founding.

'The Place to See Everyone and Be Seen'

One of my biggest jobs was working on the annual Great Taste of P.G., the organization's largest fundraiser and an extremely popular community event featuring the culinary delights of the Monterey Peninsula's finest restaurants, elegant vintages from local wineries, unique local brews, and an exciting silent auction. This is the place to see everyone and be seen if you are at all active in your community. Hundreds and hundreds of locals file into the Spanish Bay ballroom in Pebble Beach each year for this Great Taste of Pacific Grove—an ideal name for an event which is still going strong in the same location nearly thirty years later.

Then there's the Walk with PRIDE held in the fall. This is when I would grab the kid and walk on the P.G. Recreation Trail from Lovers Point to the Aquarium with pledge sheets from our neighbors and friends. Joining us we would always find P.G.USD students and their parents, as well as coaches, teachers, and other community members. They'd walk, run, or bicycle as many times as they wished. This fundraiser is unique in that you may select where your pledge money will go, whether it be the classroom or a specific school program, team, project or activity.

I was also lucky enough to be on board when P.G. PRIDE was recruiting and coordinating over 600 volunteers to help with the 100th U.S. Open, held in Pebble Beach. It was a thrill to experience the excitement of this world-renowned event and provide customer service in the retail shops. In return, P.G. PRIDE received $100,000! Now, nearly twenty years later, P.G. PRIDE is preparing for the 119th U.S. Open and recruiting volunteers. I'm considering joining them once again.

Saluting a New Generation of Volunteers

Over the past 35 years, the organization has raised over $1.2 million dollars for our schools with little to no overhead. It's pretty remarkable to watch first-hand the dedication, sincerity, and hard work that goes into this completely volunteer organization. I am filled with PRIDE to have spent so many years on this board and proud to see the new generation of volunteers who have followed suit.

Today, the organization is headed by an old classmate of mine, Valerie (Fisher) Tingley. Valerie was a student in the P.G.USD and has raised two daughters here, also attending P.G. schools. She has been on the P.G. PRIDE board for over 10 years, serving as the chair for the last four years. The board currently has 14 members, and continues to be made up of alumni, parents, teachers, and community members who share the passion of an enriched educational experience for our students. Many board members also serve the schools and community through PTA, recreational and athletic programs, service clubs ... 'serial volunteers,' if you will. It is always a high-energy group made up of people who demonstrate a great balance of skills, vision, and connections to get things done.

Valerie says, "I am honored to work with this core group of movers and shakers. Their love of community, passion, and abilities has been a continuing theme since the beginning of this organization. Although the specific requests for grants have certainly changed over the last 30-plus years, the need will continue in our public schools. And I hope that as long as there is a need, there will be a community willing to give and participate with P.G. PRIDE to help meet those needs."

I must concur.

KAT, DAVID & MAC – RUSSELL SUNSHINE

A P.G. Story With Wings

Russell Sunshine

The first screech pierces the air above the Grove Market's barrel roof. A second gull hopping on a Fandango chimney relays the alarm. A third triangulates the perceived threat from the dance studio down the Sixteenth Street slope. Far below in the municipal parking lot, Kat remains calm and confident, not deigning to acknowledge the agitated chorus. The only motion is the flapping sentinel wings reflected in her gleaming eye. Without a flinch, her menacing presence is inflicting the desired disruption.

A Featherweight Flying Machine

Kat is a Harris's hawk, a splendid creature who doesn't reveal her full beauty at first glance. When she's at rest, like this morning, you notice a dominant dark-chocolate tone covering her head, neck, chest, wings and back. Against this background, her first mark of distinction is a butter-yellow ring encircling each eye. That same yellow saturates her long, obviously powerful legs and huge clutching claws. Next you spot russet red, decorating scalloped epaulettes from her shoulders halfway down broad wings, as well as curiously delicate feathered ankle puffs. During takeoff or when airborne, she would expose a rich creamy-white belly and rump, as well as a magnificent fanning tail, with alternating horizontal bands of cream and ebony.

In the parking lot, Kat balances without strain on her partner's extended left forearm. Like all other raptors, Harris's hawks are surprisingly lightweight. (A massive Golden Eagle might look like a 20-pound hulk but tip the scales at a mere five pounds.) Despite Kat's 23-inch length and 46-inch wingspan, she weighs only two pounds. "Featherweight" is an apt description for a hollow-boned flying machine capable of breathtaking aerobatics.

David stands as calm and motionless as his hawk, surrounded by panicked gulls. His appearance is more muted than his partner's. His olive-green uniform and matching cap sport logos from his company, Green Fields Falconry. Attached to his chest are the tools of his trade: hawk hoods and a whistle, a leash, swivels and clamps. A black leather gauntlet reaching to David's elbow doubles as landing pad and perching platform. Over his right shoulder, he's hitched a weathered canvas carryall containing all he and Kat will need for this morning's patrol—trail snacks for her, spare parts for her tethers, bottled water and raptor-photo business cards for him.

David Lindenthal-Cox is one of only a relative handful of Master Falconers in all of California. How did this mild-mannered Pagrovian ascend to the top echelon of an ancient guild? Like many an epic quest, this one began at a kitchen table.

It All Started in Third Grade

In 2009, David and his wife Jan were struggling to energize their drifting eldest child. Fourteen-year-old Mackenzie, Mac for short, seemed equally immune to the attractions of schoolwork or sports, surf or skateboards.

David sat down with his son for an awkward heart-to-heart.

"Mac, tell me what turns you on. Tell me your dream. Your mother and I want to help you go for it."

Mac held back for three long beats. "I want to be a falconer."

Images of Sherwood Forest and Hogwarts flashed across David's mental screen. "A what?"

"A falconer."

"Ooookay. But where's this coming from?"

"Third grade."

Mac committed to taking the plunge. "A falconer visited my class at Forest Grove. When I was eight. She carried a huge Golden Eagle on a leather glove. It was awesome."

The teen's tense jaw began to relax. "I didn't want to show my excitement in case the other kids made fun of me. But I made myself a promise. Someday, that would be me."

Mac later told his dad that the school visit inspiration had been reinforced by reading and rereading two iconic books. *My Side of the Mountain* followed a runaway boy as he bonded in the forest with a magical Peregrine Falcon. *Wesley the Owl* celebrated the real-life relationship forged by Cal Tech biologist Stacey O'Brien with an injured Barn Owl.

David had gotten more than he'd bargained for. But he was moved by his son's secret passion. Even though they hadn't a clue where this might lead, he and Jan promised to help Mac get started.

For Christmas, the parents thrilled their son with a copy of the California Hawking Club's *Apprentice Study Guide*. When Mac grew intimidated by this manual's technical vocabulary, David said "Let's look at this together." After three pages came the father's second surprise. "The hook was in my mouth," he recalls. Two pilgrims would embark on this falconry quest.

Becoming a licensed falconer in California is not for the impulsive or impatient. It's a long slog with multiple challenges to hurdle. Of 300 enthusiasts who start the process each year, only 30 stay the course. In 2018, there are only 700 active falconers in the state out of a population approaching 40 million.

California falconry is regulated and managed by the State Department of Fish & Wildlife (F&W). Headquartered in Sacramento, F&W maintains a Northern Regional Office in Fresno and a Peninsula Field Office at Ryan Ranch. The department administers falconry candidates' annual written entry test and awards Apprentice Licenses to the successful test-takers. General Licenses follow after successful completion of a two-year apprenticeship. Masters' Licenses are granted after five more years of demonstrated steady practice.

Actual supervision of apprentices' progress is conducted by one-on-one sponsors. These General and Master Falconers are independent volunteers, but they submit written progress reports to the department that are prerequisites for apprentices to advance. A sponsor guides his or her apprentice in constructing a mews (hawk house) to required specifications and in procuring and mastering required falconry equipment. An apprentice is also required to successfully trap, train and re-release a wild red-tailed hawk or kestrel, one per year, during the two-year apprenticeship.[1]

The California Hawking Club (CHC) has no official role in managing falconry in the state. But the club is actively involved in an unofficial, supporting capacity. CHC experts testify on pending regulations. Club publications inform the public about the sport and assist candidates to prepare for the F&W Entry Exam. The club also helps apprentices attract qualified sponsors, advocates best practices, and hosts periodic meetings and competitions.

David and Mac attacked this credentialing marathon as a tandem team. Prepping for and passing the threshold test at Ryan Ranch took them eight intermittent months of effort. After several false starts securing an accessible and compatible sponsor, apprenticeship consumed another demanding two years, including steady practice trapping, training and re-releasing wild birds. Perfecting their falconry skills until they qualified for Master Falconer status added five years to that calendar. The pair's licenses were only admission tickets. David describes falconry, with deep pleasure, as "life-long learning."

Most of that learning has been hands-on and experiential, refining David and Mac's communication with wary, independent birds of prey. But much of the curriculum has also been historical and cultural, absorbing the accumulated wisdom of an ancient international fellowship.

Falconry is one of the world's oldest sports. Even its definition springs from the past: the taking of wild quarry in its natural state and habitat by means of a trained raptor. The earliest references date from Mesopotamia in 2000 BCE.

David, Kat, Mackenzie and Mora. Photo Maggie Lindenthal-Cox, Green Fields Falconry.

Hunting with raptors was apparently introduced into Europe by Central Asian Huns invading the collapsing Roman Empire in the 4th and 5th centuries CE. A major boost came in the mid-13th century when a German king imported and had translated an Arab how-to falconry manual. During the Middle Ages, falconry captured the fancy of courtiers from Europe through Arabia and Persia to the Mongol Empire, Korea and Japan. European enthusiasm peaked in the 17th century, soon overtaken by hunting with firearms. Falconry is currently enjoying its greatest resurgence in 300 years in the US and UK, spurred largely by successful captive breeding and micro-telemetry. Hawks, falcons and, less commonly, eagles and owls are the raptors normally flown in America.

Even in hang-loose California, falconry is sustained by a hierarchical order of devotees, with apprentices reporting to masters, patiently working their way through initiation. The similarity to medieval tradesmen's guilds is no accident. The sidebar offers a brief taste of falconry's exotic and evocative vocabulary, with strong linguistic roots stretching back 700 or more years but still very much in modern usage. Say these marvelous words below out loud. Several have French or Anglo-Saxon origins, but "yarak" stems from "readiness" in ancient Persian.

Although the California Hawking Club is a relaxed association of widely dispersed and independent members, its leaders clearly consider themselves stewards of a venerable tradition. Far more important for novices than learning antique verbs is absorbing a principled Code of Conduct. Listen to the values implicit in these excerpts from new members' orientation[3]:

- *Falconry is a one-on-one relationship based on trust.*

- *Trained raptors remain wild and are capable of returning to the wild at any time they are flown. They often do.*

- *Birds of prey are trained entirely by reward and the bird's natural response to food is the key. No punishment is ever used, nor is it effective. While dogs will respond to the tone of a voice and horses to the touch of the reins, raptors have no desire to please their human companions.*

- *Wise falconers come to realize that they don't train the birds to hunt. Hawks and falcons are, by nature, successful hunters …. Hawks chase, capture and kill their prey with no training from their human companions. The training in falconry involves having the hawk learn to accept the human as an aid to more successful hunting and to a more dependable food supply.*

TALKING THE TALK[2]

FALCONRY TERM	MEANING
bate	To beat the wings in agitation when leashed and attempting to fly from a perch.
bowse	To drink.
cast	To regurgitate the indigestible pieces of a meal.
creance	A long cord attached to a hawk's leash to prevent escape during training.
eyass	A downy baby raptor, especially one taken from the nest for initial training.
feak	Rubbing the beak against a surface to clean it; the sign of a contented bird.
footy	Grabbing aggressively at the falconer.
haggard	A wild bird in adult plumage.
imping	Repairing and splicing a damaged feather.
jess	Leather strips that pass through the anklets so the falconer can hold the bird and attach the leash.
rangle	Small smooth stones ingested by a bird to help clean out its crop.
snite	To sneeze.
stoop	To dive or swoop down on a quarry.
yarak	A raptor's state of complete focus on the hunt.

- *A skilled, experienced falconer encourages the bird to develop its skills and to improve with each flight. Time, patience and persistence are necessary in order for the falconer to be a good hunting partner to the bird. The reward is the emotional satisfaction of being close to a wild creature as it successfully follows its instincts. The falcon or hawk allows the falconer to be close to the flight, the chase, the capture of the prey. The raptors can travel when they choose, but they choose to stay. Walking the edge of freedom and flight can be a beautiful experience.*

This is the respectful path the P.G. father and son dedicated themselves to following. If the discipline's bedrock restraint resonates with Zen, it may be no coincidence. Much of falconry's ethos was honed in the East.

There's a New 'Kat' in Town

Harris's hawks are among the most prized and popular raptors in American falconry. Keenly intelligent and a quick study, the breed consistently demonstrates hunting enthusiasm and stamina. It achieves its greatest hunting potential when given as much freedom as possible. These hawks are unusually sociable, getting along with other birds and even famously hunting cooperatively in pairs or packs. They are equally appreciated for their relaxed disposition with humans, accepting them as hunting partners rather than rivals.

Their native habitats include a northern range in Mexico, Arizona and Texas, and a southern range in Chile, Peru and Ecuador. They favor dry desert domains. Known since at least the early 1800s, they were painted by John James Audubon and named for his patron, Edward Harris. Diminishing in the wild, they've been successfully bred in captivity since the 1960s.

Prior to acquiring Kat, David had worked with Kit, another Harris's hawk. Although seriously hampered by the loss of an eye, Kit had pluck and persistence and David had been hugely impressed. Father and son were eager to replicate this encouraging debut.

David and Jan purchased Kat as a present for Mac in 2012. Their source was a federally licensed Tennessee breeder. The bird was a 14-week-old, fully grown chick, completely untrained, with no prior human interaction (and thus, implicitly, no prior bad habits.) She was shipped to San Jose International Airport where David and Mac picked her up. David was distressed to discover that the chick arrived underweight, potentially susceptible to disease. But his attitude promptly changed as he and Mac got to work.

First came "manning," getting Kat used to human contact, demonstrating that her falconers presented no threat. David and Mac would take turns sitting quietly

Photo Maggie Lindenthal-Cox, Green Fields Falconry

with the chick for hours, periodically offering tasty tidbits. When Kat started "talking" on Day 3, this was an unwelcome sign she was feeling hunger. So they brought her weight up by slightly increasing her intake.

Falconers name their birds to facilitate initial training. The name is an attention-getter, repeatedly called by the falconer, accompanied by a blown whistle, to train the bird to fly to the gauntlet. David and Mac used a creance, a long cord attached to Kat's leash, to let her practice flying free to the gauntlet. Next David got her attention with a shushing noise, pointing at tidbits dropped to the ground to begin associating the ground with food and game in preparation for hunting. He'd then call her back up to the glove. Repeat, repeat, until novelty became normal.

The most crucial training before flying free was to wed the bird to the lure. A simple sliced tennis ball attached to a seven-foot rope, the lure's irresistible appeal stemmed from the generous meal packed inside. The bird was rewarded with access to this feast whenever the lure was whirled above the falconer's head. This association became so automatic that later in the field, merely lifting the lure from the falconer's field pack and beginning its circular sweep sufficed to bring the hawk winging back without hesitation from any distance or terrain. This crude mechanical summons could prove an invaluable back-up if the falconer lost sight of the bird or its transmitter were malfunctioning.

As a refinement on preparations for hunting, Kat also learned to fly to the T-perch. David constructed this prop from extendable aluminum tubes, topped by a horizontal bar wrapped in thick industrial carpeting. In the field, Kat would sit on this elevated stand, eight feet above David's head, to survey the surrounding terrain.

The sequenced training program proceeded at a rapid pace. Fieldwork began by teaching Kat to be comfortable hopping into and traveling inside her personal transport box in the rear of the van, made attractive by more tidbits to create this positive association. In the field, she was free-flying by Day 10. As training on collaborative hunting began, the hawk was invited to mount the T-perch and David carried it above his head. Kat watched as David's dogs and assistants flushed wild game. Following her natural instincts, Kat chased the first game spooked by the crew. Almost immediately, she was successful. To David's delight, only 14 days had elapsed since the hawk's arrival in California.

During Kat's early years in the mews, David and Mac shared raptor-rearing duties. David's family role as a stay-at-home dad gave him time and proximity to help care for multiple birds. He also carried principal parenting responsibilities while Jan commuted to her Bay-Area executive position.

More recently, as the couple's three children matured and began pursuing higher education away from P.G., David's daily parenting schedule began to lighten up. He increasingly contemplated returning to work. What better solution than working with birds? With Jan's encouragement and support, he founded Green Fields Falconry. The new firm was well-placed to compete when Pacific Grove's government invited gull-abatement bids.

Those Swooping and Pooping Invaders

Like many shoreline communities, Pacific Grove has a gull-invasion problem that only seems to get worse. Western Gulls from the adjacent Monterey Bay have increasingly been attracted to two magnets in P.G.'s downtown business district: an abundance of tasty garbage generated by restaurants, markets and littering tourists; and a compact collection of horizontal rooftops on commercial buildings, ideal for easy nest construction.

Within limits, gulls are a natural and handsome component of the local habitat. Beyond those limits, they become a serious public nuisance. Anyone victimized by a stinky, sticky, slippery projectile of gull poop on their head or car window doesn't need to be convinced of this unpleasantness. More threatening is a dive-bombing attack by an aggressive nesting gull. Scavenging dumpsters and spreading garbage cause additional threats to public health. For years, a loud chorus of complaints has been raised by downtown merchants and innkeepers, residents and tourists, united in urging City Hall to do something about these "obnoxious invaders."

Milas Smith, Environmental Programs Manager in the Department of Public Works, is P.G.'s point man on gull abatement. He's acutely aware of the whole list of gull misdemeanors. But his candidate for worst offense is somewhat surprising. "Most people don't realize it, but downtown gulls' greatest harm is polluting bay water quality." The Central Business District is almost entirely paved and sloping. Few unpaved plots remain to absorb bird waste. Contiguous streets and parking lots combine to form an uninterrupted, impenetrable surface. When periodic rains sluice those streets, all that accumulated gull poop flushes

into storm drains that empty into bay shallows. The acidic wastes are like concentrated pesticides, endangering and exterminating sensitive marine life. That impact is exacerbated when the gulls feed on human garbage instead of their normal shoreline diet, altering the biochemistry of their waste. From the municipal government's perspective, the gulls per se are not the problem; it's their unnatural urban behavior. Screeching squawks are annoying but tolerable. Stained car hoods are nasty but washable. Destroying a fragile ecosystem is another order of magnitude of disruption. P.G. feels compelled to defend itself.

From the outset, City Hall's gull-deterrence strategy has been deliberately non-violent and non-toxic. The endgame was not to totally defeat or drive away all occupying gulls. The more modest objective was to raise the ante, sufficiently disrupting the gulls so that most would elect to nest closer to their traditional shoreline sites, retreating from their downtown encroachment.

The authorities got started by requiring downtown restauranteurs and merchants to adopt gull-proof garbage containers. Anti-littering public education and enforcement were other early, economical and uncontroversial interventions. But the bottom line didn't change; the gulls hadn't gotten the memo. To the contrary, their numbers swelled as marine currents brought an abundance of fish and squid into shallows a few short blocks from downtown. Fat gulls were producing more offspring.

At this juncture, P.G. benefited from the experience and insights of a new city manager, Ben Harvey. In his previous posting in the harbor town of Avalon on Catalina Island, Mr. Harvey had presided over a successful but different gull-abatement strategy—using falconers and their raptor partners to disrupt and discourage nesting gulls. Relying on a natural antipathy between predators and prey, hawk patrols in Avalon deterred gulls from nesting without killing them. Parallel initiatives have been utilized nationwide at airports and landfills, and in Central California's vineyards and berry farms.

Pacific Grove launched its falconer program in 2014. After a brief hiatus necessitated by budgetary constraints, the City Council re-endorsed this approach in 2017, this time committing to a sustained five-year hawk-patrol campaign. Bids were invited for the two-month, April-May, gull-nesting season. A contract was awarded to Green Fields Falconry and David and Kat were ready to strut their stuff.

Two Cops on the Beat

The partners start their walking rounds at 7:00 a.m. With breaks for snacks and David's lunch, he frequently puts in 10-hour days. To spare the bird comparable fatigue, he swaps out Kat with other raptors from the mews. Patrolling continues seven days a week during April and May. There's no contractual requirement for such long hours. David is following a schedule established by his predecessor from the campaign's 2014 phase and now expected by the city. After an initial 21-day solo stretch, the father is delighted when his son returns from a semester abroad to help spell him on the beat.

David keeps Kat hoodless on patrol until she grows tired and begins flapping. Then he slips the hood on to calm and reassure her. She seems to prefer standing more than walking, misinterpreting forward movement as an invitation to fly.

Towards the end of his two-month engagement, David breaks the routine by patrolling in the morning, reserving afternoons for another of his required tasks: dismantling rooftop gull nests. Western Gulls like to nest in clusters. Lighthouse Cinema sometimes hosts eight nests in a row. The gulls aren't great architects, but they're opportunistic, determined builders. They cobble together their nests from any locally available materials they can scavenge. Pine needles, surprisingly, are a favorite component. Plastic bags are seldom neglected. The gulls work overnight, incredibly quickly. After Mac cleared one roof by 6:00 p.m., David found a new, complete nest in the exact same spot at 8:00 a.m. the following morning. Local gulls nest from April through June. The last of these months is mostly off-limits for dismantling, since federal law prohibits disturbing any nest once eggs have been laid. So April and May are the core months for the falconers' interventions.

David and Kat vary their patrol routes so their target gulls never get comfortable with a detected pattern. The objective is to keep the gulls constantly rattled and on-edge, alarmed by the presence of a natural enemy. David and Mac reinforce this impression by tethering plastic raptor kites above downtown rooftops. But the wily gulls quickly distinguish store-bought replicas from the real thing.

Some gull-abatement falconers escalate their campaigns by freeing and flying their raptors downtown. By directly harassing the nesting gulls, their hawks can definitely make the environment less hospitable. But David has taken a deliberate decision to keep Kat and his other patrolling raptors on their leashes. He doesn't want to initiate or provoke unnecessary violence, risking a reversal of public support for the city's program. Hawks could get injured pursuing gulls under cars. Motorists wouldn't tolerate feathered bodies crashing onto their hoods. And pursued gulls could gang up in defensive posses, making for serious aerial combat. Disrupt and deter: that's his low-key approach. And it works. Dramatically. Within seconds of her arrival, Kat on-the-glove alarms an entire neighborhood of settling gulls.

Following Kat and David along the street creates a vertical awareness of downtown dynamics. Gulls are everywhere, on every building in every block, occupying an elevated stratum above mostly preoccupied pedestrians.

Photo Maggie Lindenthal-Cox, Green Fields Falconry

The winged upper-story squatters audibly notice, resent and resist the patrolling pair. When the raptor is on David's arm, the partners are regularly dive-bombed by defensive gulls. The most aggressive pull out of their dives with webbed feet extended in a menacing threat display. Even when the falconer walks without his bird, the gulls have come to associate him with the enemy, retreating over rooflines to take refuge out of sight.

People too come to notice the cops on their beat. Kids almost always take the lead.

One wide-eyed lad is rushed past the pair by an impatient, distracted chaperone. "I like your hawk," the off-balance boy manages to blurt. "It's one of my favorite things."

Kat is obviously the major drawing card. But David's gentle charisma also exerts subtle magnetism. He dissuades would-be touchers and calms anxious parents by softly declaring, "Her name is Kat." The families who linger get a mini-seminar on raptors and falconry. David has given this talk a hundred times. His gift is to make each family believe it's the first. The encounters range from poignant to hilarious, but they always raise sidewalk energy.

A sleepy two-year-old in a pram ignores his kneeling mother. "Look, Tommy! Look at the bird. The big bird. See him flap his wings."

And to David, "Him? Her?"

Then again to her son, "Look at her. Isn't she beautiful?"

After the disappointed mother stands up, apologizes for her disinterested toddler and backs his pram away, Tommy suddenly finds his focus and takes in Kat with a radiant, ear-to-ear smile. Still silent, he extends his yellow miniature backhoe as an offering to his new feathered friend.

Seven-year-old Tessa steps into the pair's path as they turn down 17th Street. "I want a selfie with Kat to post on my Facebook page."

"No problem, Tessa." David recognizes the zeal of a future media producer.

But not with you." Still in second grade, she's ruthless about casting.

"I'm afraid I come with the bird."

"I want Big John instead."

"The Bank of America security guard? I think his employer doesn't allow him to pose for photos in uniform."

Tessa crosses her arms. "But I'll get more Likes!"

On another ambulatory morning, David's taking a coffee break while Kat rests in the van. A curly-haired 50-something man with a much younger female companion interrupts the falconer's curbside latte.

"You remember me. I told you my San Jose girlfriend was coming to town, and I wanted her to meet your hawk."

David smiles politely, wiping foam from his upper lip.

"Well, here she is!" the thwarted boyfriend persists. "Where's your bird? You didn't warn me about no-shows!"

Two British tourists look up from their guidebook, admiring Kat on her gauntlet. Their spontaneous dialogue echoes Gilbert and Sullivan patter.

"You have gulls. We had a carpet of pigeons in Trafalgar Square."

"Nowhere to step. Without slipping."

"But not anymore. Not anymore. We mustered the 6:00 a.m. falconers."

"Bye-bye, pigeons!"

An appreciative Pebble Beach matron stops her husband to shake David's hand. "Thank you, thank you, for what you're doing with the gulls. They covered the roof of our summer place. The skylight was solid white. With … can I say it, Herman?" Then plunging ahead at her husband's nod, "With bird crap!"

Of course, this being Pacific Grove, not everyone shares the proponents' enthusiasm for the city's gull-abatement campaign. One take-no-prisoners critic screeches up in her BMW as David is gathering his kit for the morning's rounds.

"When are you leaving?"

"Right now, ma'am, as soon as I get Kat out of her box."

"Not leaving your van! I mean leaving Pacific Grove!"

"Well, I live here. My family has no plans to move." And trying to keep things civil, "If you mean when does our abatement work wind up, it's on May 27, unless the city extends our contract."

"Well, it can't come too soon!"

"Why do you feel that way?"

"Because you're scaring the gulls away."

"Yes, that's the point."

"But it's not fair. They've a perfect right to live here too!"

"Ma'am, the city feels the gulls are causing public-health and water-quality problems. Discouraging them with raptors is natural pest control."

Speeding away, but not before spitting the last word: "There's nothing natural about you or your bird!"

Mac too encounters occasional hostility, this one of the male persuasion. "You're such a joke! Five minutes after you pass by, the gulls will be back. They're way smarter than you are."

"We don't want to exterminate them. Only persuade them to return to more natural nesting sites closer to shore."

"Good luck with that! No French fries at the shore!"

"Yep. But the new dumpsters are gull-proof. That'll help keep the fries off the pavement. But thanks for speaking up."

Sour grapes notwithstanding, the falconers receive overwhelmingly positive public support. David says that encouragement and the wide eyes of children heal the patrollers' fatigue during 10-hour days.

Soaring in Her Native Element

At dawn in the mews, Kat followed her uncanny pattern, somehow figuring out it was a free-flying day. When David dallied, attending to the other birds, she hopped off her perch, picked up the ring on her travelling tether, and dropped it onto his shoe. As soon as he opened the van's back door, she jumped from his gauntlet into her travelling box.

Now at their destination, David slides the T-perch out of the parked van, extending and locking the hollow pole's nesting segments. The wind is gusting as he eases the hawk out of her box. Conditions aren't improved by a furious crow hovering just above the van, possibly defending a nest. The crow launches an unceasing barrage of protests, soon reinforced by a series of aerial feints and sallies.

Kat is nervous on David's arm, uncharacteristically resisting the hood that he slips over her head to reduce her anxiety. With his right hand, he fits the tiny transmitter onto the back panel of the monofilament harness that encircles her torso.

David relishes these quiet outings. Frequent flying is essential for Kat's health and conditioning. But he too breathes deeper in open spaces. He never loses concentration, swapping out field jesses for transport jesses, then double-checking the leads between Kat's anklets and his glove. Free-flying is the order of the day, but only when safely away from hikers, bikers and dog-walkers. He hoists the light pole and off they go.

This narrow coastal strip is a rich eco-niche hiding in plain sight. Motorists racing by on the freeway glimpse only beige flats. But on foot, the flats dip and swirl, densely covered with knee-high brush. In early summer, the wildflowers are spectacular. California poppies spread electric orange carpets. Indian paintbrush adds a vertical contrasting crimson. Pale yellow lupine climbs six feet tall. Up close, boring dunes become sheer hundred-foot hills, too soft to climb but sculptural in their pristine slopes.

Once David and Kat arrive out in the fields, the irritated crow departs and off comes the hawk's hood. Her first sorties are tentative, as if testing her wings and the winds. The hawk cruises on short hops, alighting on bushes and canvassing the terrain. David summons her back to the perch with shrill whistles and loud barks: "Whoa, Kat! Whoa!" After a while, she seems to visibly relax, enjoying the freedom and the uplifting currents.

The route and rhythm of this procession reveal an unconventional dynamic. This is not man hunting game with a shotgun and a hound. This is hawk hunting game with a supporting human ground crew. Kat is obviously taking the lead. She looks back. She welcomes the beaters and the elevating perch. But this is her show. (Mac later comments with amusement that this hierarchy mirrors a natural pecking order. When Harris's hawks hunt in packs, the subordinate juveniles are relegated to flushing game by flying through and just over brush, while the dominant adults stay elevated to pounce on rousted prey.)

No game yet, despite paths beaten by David's guests. An occasional rabbit is momentarily sighted but Kat shows no interest. And then she's gone, out of sight around the curve of the largest seashore dune.

David is unconcerned. He knows his hawk is out for a romp. She'll come back when good and ready. Modern technology keeps the partners in touch. Kat's transmitter signals a satellite that relays data to David's receiver. The small box forwards digital information to his iPhone. A sharp multicolored grid on the phone's screen pinpoints Kat's stationary location on the far side of the sandy hill.

Soon she reappears on the ridgeline, checking out her team. Now fully engaged, she embarks on a series of patrolling sweeps, eyeing any movements that betray sand-hugging prey.

Kat flying above brush. Photo Maggie Lindenthal-Cox, Green Fields Falconry.

a teeter-totter, tipping back and forth with a shifting center of gravity. It's a private, uninhibited soak. Then up onto an elevated perch for preening, broad wings stretched and suspended to dry the tips.

Flying Ahead to the Future

Two years into its five-year gull abatement program, Pacific Grove is well-satisfied with interim progress. Quantitative success is difficult to confirm, but the city is assiduously tracking the decline in gull misbehavior complaints. For the municipal government, David and Kat's downtown patrols are high-profile and low-cost—good PR and frugal fiscal management. The authorities have noted pedestrians' evident enthusiasm for sidewalk encounters and seminars. Likewise, the voiced appreciation of merchants and residents for David and Mac's vigorous nest clearances.

When she's ready to strike, the closure is swift and sure. From a bush-top launching pad, the hawk rockets silently, skimming dense brush. One hundred lateral feet, two gliding seconds, and the predator nails her target.

By the time David reaches the spot, Kat is already pecking at the rabbit carcass. The falconer squats and twists the rabbit's neck to make doubly sure it doesn't suffer. After initially mantling, with broad wings extended, to defend her prey against his intrusion, the hawk accepts his assistance. David allows his partner to eat her fill satisfying her natural instincts. "Let it lie" is the falconers' protocol, so David lures Kat away from her kill, leaving the prey's remains to nourish wild scavengers.

Some falconers relish the hunt so much that they keep their hawks in the field for multiple kills. David prefers one-and-done, keeping Kat fit and in form without turning soaring into slaughter.

The walk back seems much shorter. The blossoms look brighter. The hawk has exercised in her natural element. At the van, Kat hops into her box with a contented "Nunnhh." On a branch above, even the territorial crow is half-subdued.

Home in the mews, David rinses his hawk with a fine spray, like a gentle rain shower. The moisture sluices dust and grime off of Kat's whole body, from cap to claws.

She seems to like the cleansing and makes no move to shift to the dry corner of her pen. But her eye is on her bathtub, inviting, shimmering and three inches deep. One scoot and she's perched on the rim. Another unhesitating leap and she's immersed to the waist. Almost awkwardly, Kat begins a rhythmic rocking. First she dips her head. Then back onto her fan-spread tail. Again, and again, like

David and Freda, his Red-tailed Hawk, on the job in the streets of Pacific Grove. Photo Patricia Hamilton.

This is not a campaign that will be won in a single annual cycle. It's better understood as a war of attrition. Gulls are stubborn, savvy and territorial. The oldest birds are probably too set in their ways to be persuaded not to nest downtown. But younger generations should gradually get the point: roosts closer to shore are less of a hassle, with no nest disrupters and no fearsome hawks. The relocated gulls' health should also rebound, as they revert to a more normal diet.

David is expanding Green Fields Falconry. As the small enterprise gains momentum, the whole family is getting involved. Mac shares abatement duties with his dad. Elder daughter Maggie handles photography and social media. Wife Jan contributes business-management acumen and moral support. Vegetarian younger daughter Caroline is not thrilled by the half-freezer filled with frozen mice, but she's proud of her father and brother for their falconry expertise.

The mews is also growing. See current roster below.

Another Aplomado may be added to the team to help respond to Watsonville farmers' appeals for raptors to keep starlings and robins from stealing their ripening berries. Free-flying raptors can always get injured or lost on the job. Backups are prudent to honor Green Fields's contractual commitments to clients.

Classroom visits are another logical sideline. Mac is proof-perfect that a raptor on the arm can be a life-changing encounter for primary schoolers with imagination.

Looking ahead, Mac is preparing for a career as a Game Warden with California's State Department of Fish & Wildlife. He's aware of the arc linking his prospective employer to the agency that hosted a nervous teenager's Ryan Ranch entry exam a decade ago.

David would never pretend that gull abatement is what sustains his passion for falconry. Abatement engagements perform a public service and help pay the bills. And he genuinely enjoys pedestrian contact, especially with irrepressible kids. But the chief source of his joy is daily

Photo Nancy Swing.

interaction with intelligent creatures from other species. This non-verbal, intimate communication has never lost its appeal. David's partner Kat is now six years of age. Barring her serious injury or chronic infection, they can look forward to spending another 20 years together.

The mild Master answers the unasked question. His voice is soft but resolute. "I will always be a falconer."

Russell Sunshine is the author of FAR & AWAY: True Tales from an International Life.

ENDNOTES:

1 These are the only two species California authorities permit apprentices to trap and train, so as not to deplete wild raptor populations. Red-tails and kestrels are plentiful, responsive to training and able to readily readjust to the wild.

2 With thanks principally to www.themodernapprentice.com.

3 CHC, *Apprentice Study Guide* (2009)

KAT'S MEWS MATES

WHO'S WHO	WHAT'S WHAT
KIT (aka "The Kid"), the other Harris's Hawk in the mews	Recently returned from breeding service, he's readjusting to home.
FREDA, a Red-tailed Hawk	On loan from David's sponsor, Leo, to help with P.G. abatement duties.
MORA, an Aplomado Falcon	An effective abatement patroller, Mora imprinted on David and considers herself a member of his family. She lives in the house, sleeping directly above the dogs' beds.
RAU, a tiercel (male Peregrine Falcon)	Also backstops on downtown duty.

MEET SANDY, THE WHALE – ELAYNE AZEVEDO

P.G.'s Cetacean Celebrity

Children laughing and sliding down a life-size whale sculpture…families and friends gathering for pictures… visitors learning about gray whale migration … these are familiar sights and sounds in the heart of Pacific Grove.

Whether a resident, tourist, or museum visitor, you must have noticed "Sandy the Gray Whale" gracing the steps outside the Pacific Grove Museum of Natural History, or simply "the Museum" as we locals refer to it.

As a newcomer in 2011, I was delighted to accept a short-term position at the Museum. It was easy to see the educational asset of the whale sculpture, but I was fascinated listening to the visitors' comments and stories. Locals proudly said, "You know, I own a share of that whale." Parents reminisced about the whale's early days on Forest Avenue. People asked about a twin in Santa Cruz.

One weekend I met alumni from Cal State Hayward (now Cal State East Bay) who told tales of the whale traveling coast-to-coast as part of "save the whales" campaigns. I politely smiled as I peered through the window at the four ton concrete sculpture. And, one of my favorites, "I heard that whale flew over the San Francisco Bay!" Listening to these stories sparked my curiosity. I knew little of its history and wanted to learn more about this big, beautiful sculpture—a quiet celebrity and centerpiece of inspiration.

The Artist: An Early Encounter with a Whale

Larry Foster was born in 1934 in Sacramento. His great-grandfather arrived in California on a whaling ship and Larry's dad took him to see his first whale when he was in kindergarten. It was a 66-foot fin whale stretched out on an open railway car. The deflated, dead body of the second largest living animal on Earth left a deep impression.

Larry's artistic skills and interest developed through the years. In 1960, he received his M.A. degree in Fine Art and a teaching credential from Cal State Sacramento. He had the great fortune to be taught by renowned artist Wayne Thiebaud, who was a great inspiration. After graduation, Larry taught high school art. Then, in the mid-60s he moved to the San Francisco Bay Area and connected with artist friends. Through the years he was a faculty member at Cal State Hayward, Laney College and

the California College of the Arts in Oakland. While continuing his own art, he launched into learning the craft and skills of stained glass, refining techniques for making lamps, doors, and windows. Life was full. Still, he carried a deep passion and interest in whales. His first whale art was a stained glass piece. It was nine feet of curved pieces and took a year to build. This illuminated blue whale beauty still shines in a boutique in Oakland.

The Pursuit of a Perfect Model

After designing a whale tail sculpture, Larry began to think about a new, larger project. "Maybe I can do it bigger, even bigger—a whole whale!" While Larry's artistic skills and ambition were strong, his endeavor was complicated. Where would he find a model to use for his subject?

Today we are exposed to bountiful whale images of majestic beauty and awe, stunning photographs and amazing videos. Ecotourism, whale watching tours, sophisticated underwater cameras and technology provide live views. It wasn't so in the mid-1960s as Larry entered unchartered waters. He began looking for photographs, illustrations, artwork, and even text descriptions in books for clues to reveal what a real, living whale looked like. He questioned the accuracy of the few images he could find. His pursuit exposed blimps, the bloated carcasses of beached whales, and images from the whaling industry of flensed and dismembered bodies. There were mythological beasts, cartoons and fictionalized demons in book illustrations. And, repetition was rampant with cookie cutter *Moby Dick* whales everywhere.

Larry's curiosity took him on a lifelong quest as he pushed that childhood image of a flat, lifeless whale carcass to the back of his mind. He set out on a voyage to research and show the world what a "real" whale looked like. "General Whale," a nonprofit organization, was cre-

The beginning of Larry Foster's dream of creating a life-size whale sculpture, as Sandy is fabricated in his East Oakland studio in the early 1970s. Photo courtesy Larry Foster.

ated to promote public interest in whales, dolphins and porpoises. His goal—"to see the traditional whale depicted as the graceful, intelligent and peaceful animal it is, an animal that lives on the sea surface, not one that is a denizen of the deep."

As a faculty member he had access to the UC Berkeley library, where he laboriously searched unindexed periodicals. His pioneering work continued as he poured through published and unpublished manuscripts with astute observation for details. He spent hours analyzing compositions and measurements in *The Norwegian Whaling Gazette* with sharp pencil point-by-point proficiency.

To access authentic resources, Larry started making connections with scientists and museum curators, such as our Museum's Director Emeritus, Vern Yadon. He sent letters and made phone calls to biologists and cetacean experts. (Cetacean is the marine mammal group that includes whales, dolphins and porpoises.) He introduced himself to Dr. James Mead, associate curator of marine mammals at the Smithsonian Institution, who offered him a deal he couldn't resist. In exchange for helping catalog a large collection of rare photos, Larry could have copies of whatever he wanted. He spent long hours in the basement of the Smithsonian going through files. The mutual benefit of this artist-scientist relationship proved pivotal in accessing current and accurate images. Another invaluable resource was Dr. Ted Walker, a leading authority on California gray whales (*Eschrichtius robustus*) at Scripps Institution of Oceanography at UC San Diego. Larry went to meet him, was invited to stay and gained a wealth of photos and transparencies of California gray whales. Eureka! He was thrilled to finally have realistic images of his subject to go forward with creating an image of a whole, life-size whale.

'Everywhere You Walked, It Was Sandy!'

In 1971, with no contract and no commission, driven only by desire, Larry went to work creating a life-size ferro-cement gray whale sculpture. Obviously, the creation of a 40-foot sculpture would require a large space. Larry rented a warehouse in East Oakland as a studio and assembled a team. He fabricated this massive work of art in his spare time, selling illustrations to buy supplies of steel and concrete.

First, he created a model using molded casting plaster. He applied a ratio of one-inch-to-one foot, then took the 40-inch model and made eight transverse sections (imagine a loaf of bread with very thick slices). An opaque projector transposed the model to a life-size 40-foot form. Next, an iron framed armature was constructed and interlaced with five layers of chicken wire. A creamy concrete slushed in a mortar mixer. Larry and his team worked from the inside and the outside, using trowels and wooden blocks to push the concrete into the mesh network. Wiring thousands of individual wire ties proved to be a long, tedious and difficult job. Mesh-tying parties ended with lots of bloody fingers. Larry chuckled, "No sane person would ever do it twice."

He had never actually seen ferro-cement techniques applied, only read about the process in a book. The fer-

Headed to Southern California in 1974 "fluke first" as Larry guides Sandy's tail. She is well designed for travel with only a 3/4" concrete shell, a hollow core and is divided into eight sections. Photo courtesy Larry Foster.

Sandy in the snow! This photograph was taken at Indiana University in Bloomington during the five day public conference, "The National Whale Symposium," Photo courtesy Larry Foster.

ro-cement process is usually used for boat-building, so Larry figured it should work to build a whale. Through the fabrication process, bags of cement ended up being kicked around and the floor of the warehouse filled up with sand. Larry exclaimed, "Everywhere you walked, it was Sandy!"

The project took three years, thousands of hours and a dedicated team to complete, but the leader of General Whale was pleased with the result. In 1974, Larry rolled up the five-foot door of his studio as his hard effort materialized with his dream. There she was—a life-size, realistic sculpture of a gray whale.

On the Road for Educational Outreach

The Baxter Art Gallery at the California Institute of Technology in Pasadena had heard the big news and contacted Larry about its upcoming whale exposition. The exhibition would coincide with the gray whales' winter migration. So in November 1974, Sandy headed south for the exhibit "Caltech Revisited." This was her debut. Rather than a red carpet, this 8,000 pound sculpture's arrival was heralded with the help of a truck, forklift and crane. Whale enthusiasts viewed her close-up during their discussions, while Baja-bound gray whales passed the edge of Southern California.

Boston's Museum of Science called and wanted to know if the whale could be part of their April 1975 symposium, "In Celebration of the Living Whale." Scott McVay, chairman of Environmental Defense Fund's Committee on Whales moderated the event. Exhibits included historical collections, contemporary drawings and a "forty-foot long life-size model." Later in 1975, Sandy was on the move to the National Whale Symposium at Indiana University in Bloomington. This five-day public conference focused on "the preservation of the threatened and endangered whales and the public policy initiatives undertaken as part of this effort." The multi-disciplinary gathering brought together biologists, environmentalists, musicians and other scholars from diverse backgrounds in the public, private, nonprofit sectors, as well as impassioned individual citizens. There were lectures, panel discussions, graphics and, surprisingly, a huge whale sculpture in the snow! It was, after all, November in Indiana.

The following year General Whale made a presentation at The Museum of Arts and Sciences in Macon, Georgia. Larry's graphics from the Smithsonian Institution and the National Geographic Society were displayed, and this time Sandy was exhibited in a climate closer to California's.

And now a drumroll for an aptly titled event, "California Celebrates the Whale," hosted in November 1976 by Governor Edmund G. (Jerry) Brown Jr. An estimated 5,000 to 10,000 people, a third of them children, attended the day-long event at the state's capital, which included exhibits, entertainment and lectures at the Sacramento Civic Auditorium. "If you want to save something you have to celebrate it," Governor Brown said. Speakers and entertainers included researchers Roger Payne and John Lilly; poet Gary Snyder; singer Joni Mitchell; and the Paul Winter Consort. Thirty-seven environmental and conservation groups participated. Sandy's educational outreach also included visits to the Santa Barbara Museum of Art, The Franklin Institute in Philadelphia and the New England Aquarium in Boston.

Meanwhile, here on the Monterey Bay three entrepreneurs were anticipating society's future needs and developing events they called New Earth Expositions with a motto of "living lightly on the Earth." People attended to learn about feeling good, saving water, saving electricity, saving the world, and yes—saving whales. Energy, ecology and personal growth; the expos were part education and part festival. General Whale participated in the San Francisco, Santa Cruz and San Diego expos.

General Whale kept busy co-presenting at conferences, exhibits and festivals. Larry pursued new material as he refined his knowledge of external cetacean anatomy and expanded distinctions in pigmentation. Seventy of his water color paintings were published in *The Sierra Club Handbook of Whales and Dolphins* (1983). He illustrated the Smithsonian Institution's 1984 publication, *The World's Whales: The Complete Illustrated Guide,* and received commissioned requests and contracts for scientific illustrations, posters, charts and paintings which are found in museums, institutions, books, manuscripts and magazines. Some of you may be familiar with his posters, common at schools, comparing the shapes and sizes of whales. He captured the essence of dozens of species in shape, proportion and color, a major contribution to the growing conservation movement. His images elevated the public's awareness for the first time about marine mammals as living, breathing animals.

"If you want to know what whales look like, talk to Larry Foster. Larry Foster has turned whale illustration into a science. The depictions that he has done are the most anatomically accurate I have ever seen. No other artist in history has done so much as Foster to show what a group of previously little-known animals actually do look like."

Dr. James G. Mead, curator emeritus, *the Smithsonian Institution.*

Putting It in Perspective, Then and Now

Most Pagrovians could easily identify the mammal with the longest migration and name our state's official marine mammal. The answers remind us of extinct populations and the decline and recovery of our local California gray whale. It's hard to imagine that not so very long ago, our beaches were covered with bleaching bones of dead whales. Pacific Grove is surrounded by remnants of the whaling industry. To our south across the Carmel River is Whaler's Cove at Point Lobos State Natural Reserve. In neighboring Monterey is the Old Whaling Station adobe with its rose garden and panoramic view of the bay. Just up the coast, a whaling station and rendering plant operated in Moss Landing.

Whale hunting policies changed in 1946 after the signing of the International Convention for the Regulation of Whaling, and a moratorium on commercial whaling was enacted in 1986. The declining whale populations and the concerns of scientists and the public on the impact of human activities prompted the Marine Mammal Protection Act of 1972. The Monterey Bay National Marine Sanctuary was established in 1992 by the National Oceanic and Atmospheric Administration under the authority of the National Marine Sanctuaries Act.

Today we can stand at one of our many whale-watching lookouts at Asilomar, Point Pinos, or Lovers Point and enjoy the vitality of marine wildlife. Our peninsula affords a wealth of resources, people, places and organizations with vast knowledge and sophisticated technology. While we appreciate what we have and don't often take it for granted, it is hard to imagine what it was like in the 1960s when Larry began his quest.

Now let's get back to our story and find out how that big whale arrived in our community.

Community Spirit Gives Sandy a Permanent Home

Sandy arrived in Pacific Grove as a temporary loan to coincide with the 1981 gray whale winter migration. The Museum was interested in updating its displays. Paul Finnegan, the assistant director at the time, had worked at the Smithsonian Institution in the mid-1970s, met Larry there and remembered the life-size whale sculpture. Paul had the idea of renting it for the Museum's exhibit. He discussed the plan with Museum Director Vern Yadon. Messages were traded and soon a 40-foot whale on a flatbed truck rolled through town. Children came running!

The new sculpture was placed on Forest Avenue facing Lovers Point and the bay. Within a year after its arrival, attendance inside the museum had increased and outside

Sandy arrives in Pacific Grove as a temporary exhibit for gray whale winter migration season in 1981. She is greeted by Vern Yadon, curator and director of the Pacific Grove Museum of Natural History. A local lumber company supplied a driver and fork lift at no cost. Photo courtesy *Monterey Herald.*

children climbed on the whale as families snapped photographs. Paul Finnegan noticed how it breathed life into the museum. Obviously Sandy was a hit. The Museum inquired about permission to copy it or even buy it outright. A dialogue opened. Larry was facing health challenges at the time, was finding it difficult to find a permanent place to store the large sculpture, and was open to selling Sandy. The parties agreed to an offer of $24,000 with a timeline of one year.

At this same time, the Museum had embarked on an expansion campaign for a new wing. Vern had already talked to several people who cautioned that two fundraising campaigns at the same time was not a good idea. Competition came in the form of other institutions where the whale had been exhibited that also wanted to purchase the sculpture. Larry preferred keeping Sandy on the Monterey Peninsula, feeling it was a perfect location where whales could be easily seen during migration.

Soon after Larry made his offer, good fortune and fate came into play. Coastal biologist David Shonman was walking by the museum and saw Vern. After hearing about the offer to sell Sandy to the museum, David went to see his friend Milos Radakovich, a former colleague at

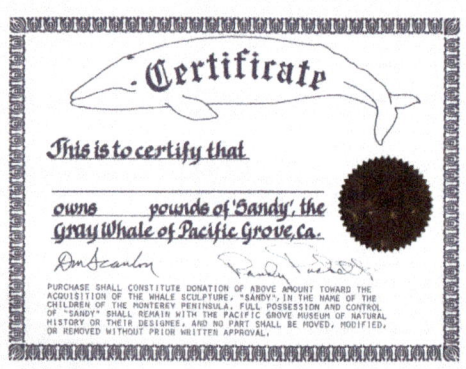

Moss Landing Marine Laboratories and a member of the Monterey Bay Chapter of the American Cetacean Society (ACS). David said, "Sandy is so popular, I bet we could raise the money in the community." Milos had recently heard of a school that raised money for their football field by selling "square feet" of turf for $10. He knew that Sandy weighed approximately four tons, or 8,000 pounds. "Hmmm, an 8,000 pound sculpture for $24,000 … people could 'buy' portions of Sandy for $3 a pound. That could work!" He created an official certificate with illustration and embossed seal.

Volunteers had access to copiers, graphics and office support. Randy Puckett, an artist and current president of the local chapter of ACS, thought the museum's plan to acquire the ferro-cement sculpture was a tremendous idea, and that they should become involved in helping the acquisition happen. The Whale Fund drive officially

Whale Day! Milos Radakovich and David Shonman lead the Whale Fund campaign. Tables were set up at the Museum as volunteers sold certificate shares of Sandy for $3 a pound on March 13, 1982.

opened at the January 6, 1982, Pacific Grove City Council meeting with Mayor Florus Williams and other council members being the first to buy shares at $3 a pound.

By February of that year, nearly $4,700 worth of Sandy had been purchased. The ACS shared progress in their newsletter *Soundings*, "At this writing, 'Sandy', the gray whale in front of the Pacific Grove Museum of Natural History, is well on her way to becoming a permanent fixture! Please hold the applause … We have a long way yet to go and we need people to help us contact schools, local businesses and clubs, and to distribute posters and sell certificates at upcoming community events such as Good Old Days."

Nearly $7,000 had been raised by March 3rd of 1982. Volunteers set up tables and sold certificates at the Museum, and at Grove Market and other prominent local gathering places.

Visitors would stop and ask, "What's going on here?" People joked about what part of the whale they were buying. The community stepped up in multiple ways. A local fireman made a sign, "Help Save our Whale—$3 a pound," that is still in the Museum's basement today. Options emerged for those wanting to "buy big" with the formation of 10-pound and 20-pound clubs whose members received special framed certificates. Fun escalated on March 13 with "Whale Day," a community drive that had all the elements of a festive party—music, cookies, balloons and juggling! Sandy even participated as the object of a tire toss game for the children.

The call for help was even heard across the waters. The Marine Environmental Research vessel *Varua* had been researching gray whales in Hawaii. When the ship docked in Monterey, the crew responded to the whale sculpture's cause. They didn't have extra funds, but Captain Russell Nilsson offered to take groups of 20-to-25 people on all-day whale watching trips, keeping only the expense of fuel and donating all the other proceeds to the cause.

News media provided publicity. "If Sandy the whale were a real estate parcel, 'she' would have 'sold' signs from midriff to tail flukes," the *Pacific Grove-Pebble Beach Tribune*, reported on April 28, 1982, under the headline, "Whale sale no fluke." Donations rolled in from ACS, the Sierra Club, California Heritage Guides, schools and many other groups. The Kiwanis raised money from a pancake breakfast. Children decorated their classroom windows with "Save Sandy." One dedicated first-grader paid a quarter per week on an installment plan towards a Sandy share.

A whale thermometer painted on an outside wall of the Museum helped supporters track progress. Buttons added a visible source of income and people proudly wore their "Sandy Pacific Grove," and "I Love Sandy" buttons.

Slogans appeared on posters and signs. When fear drifted in that the purchase couldn't be pulled together, a new button was designed showing Sandy being hauled-off on a truck with a big slash through the image! This appealed to the fans who feared losing their beloved whale. David Shonman recalls, "I think it was an early example of what is now called crowdfunding. We didn't have to convince people in the community to help … they were excited to step up and help—their enthusiasm was contagious."

Visitors would come to the museum; their kids would be playing on the whale and the parents would end up buying a pound of the whale for their child. Shares were sold to people who gave them as gifts to friends and relatives living elsewhere, even a grandfather in London! It turned out to be great fun, and years later people were still asking where they could get a certificate.

Dr. Donald Scanlon, chairman of the Pacific Grove Museum of Natural History Association, wrote a letter to the ACS in June, "… the board is very pleased with the progress being made. We are confident that with your help the sculpture will be purchased within the time period." The team went all out during Fourth of July week with Whale Days. Paul Finnegan shared the details in an article titled "The Fund Raiser" that appeared in *History News* in January of 1984. The City Council passed a resolution and posters appeared everywhere asking for help. Merchants decorated their store windows in nautical themes. A balloon race featured Flo, a 28-foot hot air balloon shaped like a humpback whale. The P.G. Art Center sponsored a whale drawing contest for children. Local businesses contributed commissions and gave a percentage of their profits in those four days. Some of the many businesses, including Mum's Place, Holman's, P.G. Cleaners, Coast Hardware and McDonald's advertised a "whale of a sale." John's Drive-In on Forest Avenue collected money in a whale fund jar. Businesses that made donations included *Monterey Peninsula Herald*, Bratty Real Estate, Crocker Bank, Digital Research, Cafe Balthazar and Maxwell's Barber Shop. Whale-themed raffle prizes included whale watching trips from Steve Webster, Randy's Fishing Trips and Sam's Fishing Fleet. Other prizes included weathervanes, sun-catchers, the CD "Songs of the Humpback Whale," whale books, bandanas and even a "whale-of-a-soak" from a hot tub rental business.

After a productive few months, the January 1983 deadline seemed uncomfortably close. Vern Yadon recalls, "We needed about $8,000 more, so I contacted my fellow members of the Carmel Art Association and talked it over with them. They are a good crowd of people and all of them were willing to give a painting towards an auction." The plan received great response. Local artists including nationally known cartoonist Gus Arriola, Don Teague from the National Academy and Keith Lindberg, along with many other artists, donated paintings and sculptures. Randy Puckett contributed a whale and calf sculpture. An August wine tasting party and art auction extravaganza held at the P.G. Community Center was a huge success.

Finally, the time came when Milos Radakovich was able to announce: "Sandy, the 8,000-pound concrete whale now reclining in front of the Pacific Grove Natural History Museum, has been assured a permanent home on the Monterey Peninsula, in keeping with the wishes of its creator, artist Larry Foster of Alameda. The community's fund drive for $24,000 went over the top by $4,000 Friday evening when 200 people bid a total of $7,486 for artworks donated by 60 artists. This last event is an example of the kind of community support this campaign has enjoyed from the outset, and I feel extremely proud to have been a part of it."

Sandy had been purchased and it was time for a big celebration! Invitations for a September party were sent

Larry Foster's visit and the Whale Fund reunion on January 27, 2018: The group that led the way in making Pacific Grove Sandy's forever home, standing left to right: Randy Puckett, David Shonman, Milos Radakovich, Vern Yadon, Larry Foster and Paul Finnegan. At front, Sandy's fans celebrate her birthday and enjoy Science Saturday's "Amazing Migration" activities. Photo courtesy Elayne Azevedo.

to over 1,200 donors. Confetti the Clown handed out balloons and the event featured music, food and big smiles. Three hundred cheering children were surrounded by a supportive community and a dedicated team. The campaign had ended after eight months, raising over $31,000 from donors in 20 states and with most of the money coming from upwards of 1,200 individual donations. After the Museum's expansion, money from the auction was used for a concrete pad and the sculpture's relocation. A dedication plaque was prominently placed as Sandy took center stage on Central Avenue.

Celebrating P.G.'s 'Centerpiece of Inspiration'

January celebrates the return of gray whales to the Monterey Bay with Whalefest Monterey at Old Fisherman's Wharf and Custom House Plaza. The Museum's "Science Saturday" traditionally has a migration theme and is also the day children of all ages gather and sing "Happy Birthday" to Sandy. In 2018 a reunion of artists, scientists, community leaders and residents gathered in the Museum's bird exhibit gallery to greet a special guest. People came to honor Sandy's artist and creator, Larry Foster. Former Museum staff and members of the Monterey Bay Chapter of the American Cetacean Society, who helped in the 1982 campaign, were present.

Larry spoke about his background and described how he created Sandy. With his humor and warmth he answered questions, including the inevitable, "How did Sandy get her name?" Singing, birthday cake, cheering children and photographs helped make Sandy's 44th birthday an extra-special day. Larry, his wife Mary, and dog Jack traveled from their home in Fort Bragg, where Larry is working on his biography. They were all given a typical Pacific Grove "Last Hometown" warm welcome.

After the event, some guests enjoyed a scenic walk on the Recreation Trail to catch the activities at Whalefest Monterey. Others ventured out onto the bay on whale watching tours. It was a day to celebrate the success of an artist's curiosity and perseverance, and a community's creative support for a common cause, as well as a day, weekend and season to recognize how far we have progressed with marine mammal knowledge and protection.

Sandy is a treasure in the heart of Pacific Grove and a centerpiece of inspiration. Her travels have stopped, but her endearing popularity remains and her story continues.

Meet the 'Other Sandys'

SANTA CRUZ MUSEUM OF NATURAL HISTORY

Across our bay is another California gray whale sculpture that is often confused with our Sandy. This beautiful exhibit rests under cypress trees in Tyrrell Park at the entrance of the Santa Cruz Museum of Natural History.

Designed by Larry, fabricated by Al Hipkins, this whale was dedicated nearly the same time as Sandy in October 1982. Their sign reads, "She was commissioned by the Museum Association as an educational tool, and to stimulate interest in conservation issues. She is constructed of a wood frame covered with strips of lathe and a layer of cement." This whale was commissioned after over $7,000 was raised through a combination of City Museum Association and Arts Council funds, as well as community donations and proceeds from a campaign of whale inspired local talks, special exhibits, puppets shows, walk-a-thons and more. Local companies like Big Creek Lumber and Lone Star Cement donated materials for the original construction. In 1999 she was repaired by local stone and masonry craftsman Kemper York. Eight years ago additional concrete was added to lengthen the sculpture's life span.

Museum staffers say she is an iconic piece of their history and many local Santa Cruzans affectionately refer to their museum as the Whaling Museum.

LAWRENCE HALL OF SCIENCE, UC BERKELEY

Pheena is a 50-foot fiberglass whale located on a plaza at UC Berkeley's Lawrence Hall of Science (LHS). She is an exact replica of an adolescent fin whale—the second largest whale in the world. She was designed by Larry with support from the World Wildlife Fund. Can you imagine a finback whale flying over San Francisco Bay while suspended from a helicopter? That's what happened to Pheena as she left her construction site at Fort Mason, detoured and landed on the Marina Green to greet fans, and then went on to her permanent home at LHS in 1975.

Like Sandy, Pheena was involved with educational outreach. Both whales were Bay Area celebrities and spent time at the California Academy of Sciences and the San Francisco Zoo. Between engagements they could be seen resting at Fremont's beautiful Lake Elizabeth and in Alameda.

Recently, this well-loved whale needed some repairs. Word was sent out to her fans and money was raised for the restoration. She took a winding truck ride through the Berkeley hills to Richmond's Bay Marine Boatworks for a structural and cosmetic makeover. In October 2017 at "Bay Day at the Hall," Larry was honored and a dedication plaque was installed on the plaza.

Three Foster whale sculptures found homes near two major California bays, each serving as an educational ambassador and providing enjoyment for whale enthusiasts past, present and future. And we now know there is nothing concrete in that rumor about Sandy flying over the San Francisco Bay; Pheena is the flying whale!

An excerpt from the Editor's note, *Pacific Grove Pebble Beach Tribune,* **August 18, 1982:**

It seemed leviathan in nature when it was suggested last January that funds be raised to keep Sandy the gray whale in Pacific Grove. But, true to the best qualities of a community, the residents of P.G. banded together like so many whales in a pod and gave Sandy a permanent home on the grounds of the Natural History Museum. So congratulations P.G! We've got ourselves a permanent reminder that through a common effort we can take on the most Leviathan of projects, even though the ne'er-do-whales said it could never be done."

~~~

"It is a joy to share Sandy the Gray Whale's story with the community that embraced her and rallied together to give her a permanent home. A big thank you to Larry and Mary Foster, Paul Finnegan, Milos Radakovich, David Shonman and Vern Yadon for their generous time, stories, jokes and the many resources they contributed in sharing Sandy's story. Also, much appreciation to the staff at the Museum and the P.G. Library, Marge Jameson and *Cedar Street Times,* friend Ethelyne and many more who have witnessed my obsession with this special cetacean we know as Sandy." ~ Elayne Azevedo

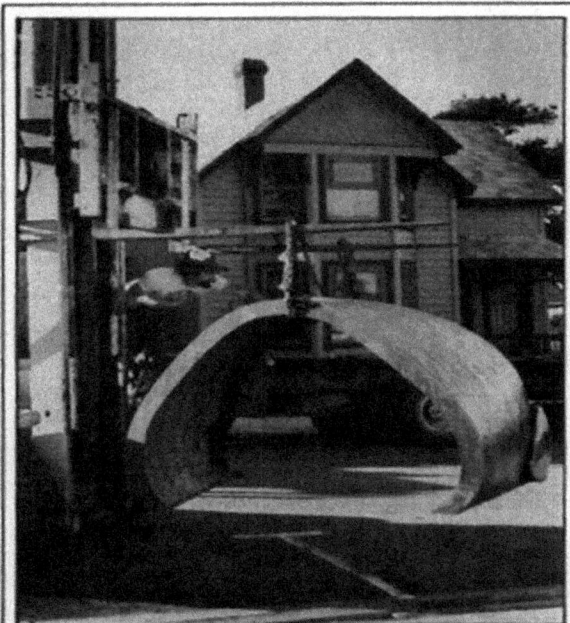

IN CELEBRATION OF THE CETACEAN

PACIFIC GROVE—It's "Gray Whale Month" on the Monterey Peninsula, according to the Monterey Bay chapter of the Cetacean Society, and the Pacific Grove Museum of Natural History is celebrating the occasion by displaying a life-sized 40-foot replica of the lovable creature. Fashioned in concrete by Larry Foster, director of General Whale, a conservation-oriented organization in Alameda, the modular 5-ton sculpture has been hauled, assembled, and exhibited throughout the United States. It will be at the museum until the end of February, to coincide with the annual winter migration of the California gray whale from the Arctic to Baja California.

The Pacific Grove Museum of Natural History
Transition from City-Managed to Non-Profit-Managed: 2007–2010

Photo Pat Hathaway Collection.

This year the Pacific Grove Museum of Natural History celebrates its 135th birthday. Local scientists and teachers established the Museum in 1883 as part of the Chautauqua Literary and Science Center's summer program. It served as a place to keep and display objects of natural history. A small octagonal building provided by the Pacific Improvement Company (part of Southern Pacific Railroad) in what is now Jewell Park was the Museum's first home. In 1900 the Pacific Grove Museum Association was formed to manage the Museum, which had moved to its present location. By 1917 it had grown into a local attraction, and the City of Pacific Grove elected to take ownership of the Museum. The City's charter established a Museum Board to manage the Museum, in collaboration with the Association.

Over time, the Museum Board became advisory to the City Council and the City Manager hired employees to care for the Museum with the assistance of the Association. The arrangement worked well for nearly 90 years, and the Museum has been a centerpiece of our community, educating generations of students, adults, and visitors with exhibits and special programs. The Museum became one of the first in the nation to be accredited American Association of Museums in 1974.

However, as conflicting demands competed for the City's financial resources, less and less went to support the Museum. By 2007, the future of the Museum was in turmoil. The Museum Director had announced his plans to retire, and there was concern about whether he would be replaced. The stories below provide three perspectives on the transition that followed: the Museum, still owned by the City, moved from being city-managed back to being managed by a Board of dedicated volunteers. This public-private partnership supports the vibrant museum we have today.

Perspective from the City's Museum Board
John Pearse*

Natural history museums have always been part of my life. I haunted the Smithsonian's Natural History Museum in Washington while in elementary school, built trails and fed animals at the Arizona Sonora Desert Museum while in high school, and interned at Chicago's Field Museum while in college. I joined the board of the Santa Cruz Museum Association while on the faculty of the University of California, Santa Cruz, and served as a trustee and president of the California Academy of Sciences after retiring from UCSC.

So it was only natural for me to hang around the Pacific Grove Museum of Natural History when Vicki and I returned to Pacific Grove in 2003. Invited to join the City's Museum Board in 2007, I enthusiastically agreed, although aware that the Museum was entering a crisis.

Like most small cities around the country, Pacific Grove was in financial trouble. Merely maintaining infrastructure was challenging, not to mention a natural history museum whose origins went back to the 19th century. The Museum Association, a volunteer group of local enthusiasts, provided additional funding and critical assistance. But the small staff could barely care for the collections or the permanent exhibits, even with the assistance of those dedicated volunteers. Harking back to its origins, the Museum, working with Esther Trosow, had produced a stunning exhibit in 2005 with public lectures on "The Chautauqua Years". But just two years later the curator, Paul Finnegan, saw the problem all too clearly. He recommended that the museum not even try to be reaccredited by the American Association of Museums before he retired. What to do? The Museum was verging on closing.

One member of the City's Museum Board, Geva Arcanin, gathered a group of local scientists to discuss alternatives (see Geva Arcanin's story). The Monterey Bay Aquarium was approached for help. And did the Aquarium ever do so! They helped find funds to keep the Museum open, and members of their staff provided crucial assistance. As in the Museum's early days, local scientists helped put together new exhibits and programs (see David Greenfield's story).

With all that going on, the City Manager, Jim Colangelo, appointed a no-nonsense interim director, Bob Synder, who formed a group of interested volunteers to consider alternative options for some sort of transition to a sustainable arrangement. They settled on a public-private partnership, similar to that of the California Academy of Sciences where the city owns the building and collections and a non-profit, private organization operates the Museum. Problem solved!! Or was it?

As could be expected in contentious little Pacific Grove, all hell broke loose. There were even demonstrations in front of the Museum decrying the "corporate" take-over of the Museum. The City's Museum Board meetings were filled with outraged residents complaining about losing "their" museum to "outsiders" (even though most members on the non-profit organization were residents of P.G.). Closing the Museum was a better option, they said!

Happily, cooler heads prevailed: an operating agreement between the City and the Museum Foundation of Pacific Grove was signed in June 2009, and a new director with business experience, Lori Mannel, was appointed. She promptly hired outstanding supporting staff who worked diligently with volunteers to rebuild the Museum. It was successfully reaccredited. The collections and exhibits are now properly cared for and protected, constantly being upgraded and improved, and multiple programs for people of all ages developed and enjoyed. Butterflies, wildflowers, quilts, nature illustrations, lectures, tidepool monitoring, children's activities, adult-only entertainment – all in no longer sleepy Pacific Grove. What a terrific transformation and lively leap into the 21st century!

*John Pearse has been a member of the City's Museum Board since 2007, and chair since 2011. In addition, he is a member of the Museum's Science Advisory Committee.

Scientists and the Pacific Grove Museum of Natural History

David W. Greenfield*

I was born and raised in Pacific Grove in the 1940s, and I lived here up until I was 10 years old and my family moved first to Corral de Tierra and then later to Carmel Valley. During those early years in Pacific Grove, my mother often took me to visit the beach and tide pools as well as to the Pacific Grove Museum. At that time, the Museum had large dioramas depicting life under the sea, with algae, many invertebrates, and taxidermied fishes; these, along with other things in the museum such as birds, mammals, and rocks, fascinated me. There is no question that these experiences influenced my decision to become a marine biologist.

Three of the Advocates for the Museum: John Pearse, Geva Arcanin and David Greenfield.

Later, while living in Carmel Valley, I attended Monterey High School (at that time Carmel Valley was in the Monterey School District). It was there that I met two fellow students who became not only my friends but also my skin- and SCUBA-diving buddies; this, in turn, brought me back to Pacific Grove where the three of us dove for the once-abundant abalones. All three of us attended MPC after graduation, and there we met Bill Hyler who, at that time, not only taught Zoology at MPC but also ran a small aquarium and gift shop on the wharf. He hired us to collect sea urchins from his boat off the Pacific Grove coast; because no sea otters were in the area at that time, the sea floor was still carpeted with urchins. After we cleaned the urchins, he would sell the tests (or skeletons) in his gift shop. These experiences further intensified my interest in marine biology.

Following a B.A. in Zoology from Humboldt State University, a Ph.D. from the University of Washington, and a long career of university teaching, I finally retired from the University of Hawaii Zoology Department and returned home to Pacific Grove. Here, I once again connected with the Museum—first as a member and, later, joining the Board of the Museum Association in 2007. It was during this time that Geva Arcanin conceived of the idea of inviting a group of local scientists to help the Museum with ideas and exhibits. At the time the Museum had a very small staff to develop exhibits and programs, and much of the work at the Museum was done by volunteers from the Association, so help was certainly needed. That initial meeting of six scientists at Geva's home grew into a group of 14.

As part of this group of scientists, I was involved in the development of two major exhibits. The first exhibit was for the celebration of Charles Darwin's 200th birthday in 2009, which was being recognized at various museums and institutions around the world. For this exhibit, six of us local scientists designed and constructed a series of displays in the Museum's Yadon Gallery: Greg Cailliet, Moss Landing Marine Laboratory; Steve Clark, Pacific Grove High School; Andres Durstenfeld, Monterey Peninsula College; Dave Greenfield, California Academy of Sciences; Steve Palumbi, Hopkins Marine Station; and John Pearse, University of California, Santa Cruz. The displays presented extensive information on Darwin himself as well as on the voyage of the Beagle, the Galápagos Islands and its animals, classic mechanisms and examples of natural selection, and current thinking on the mechanisms of evolution. The exhibit was accompanied by a lecture at Chautauqua Hall by Steve Palumbi and a birthday cake for Darwin's birthday at the Museum; several related lectures at the Museum followed in subsequent months.

The second exhibit stemmed from the first. Because of the success of the Darwin Exhibit, the following year Greg Cailliet and I, both being ichthyologists, decided to organize a large exhibit on fishes called *The World of Fishes*. Through lectures and displays we presented basic information on the diversity and biology of fishes from around the world, creating posters and filling the museum cases with skeletons and specimens—including the taxidermied fish specimens from the diorama that I had seen in my youth, which we found in storage in the basement. We also borrowed from the California Academy of Sciences a full-size model of a coelacanth, the ancient fish called a "living fossil," and put it on display. As mentioned, Greg and I also presented lectures to enhance the displays: Greg's lecture was entitled "Fish Habitats 'R' Us: Assemblages in Monterey Bay", and mine was entitled "Chasing Fishes Around the World", as it presented a brief overview of my fish-collecting experiences on several continents.

One particularly exciting aspect of this exhibit was how other organizations from around Monterey Bay and elsewhere came together to create and organize the exhibit's displays. There were displays in the cases from MBARI, National Marine Fisheries Service, Moss Landing Marine Laboratories, Monterey Bay National Marine Sanctuary, Hopkins Marine Station, University of California at Santa Cruz, Pepperdine University, Reef Check, and PISCO. Concurrently, in the Yadon Gallery, there was an exhibit of underwater photographs of local marine fishes taken by Daniel W. Gotshall of the California Department of Fish and Game.

Over the years this group of scientists has continued to provide assistance as needed to the Museum Board with ideas for exhibits and their displays, but its most crucial role was to step up during the Museum's time of need and transition to help it carry on its important programs.

◉ ◉ ◉

David Greenfield was a member of the Board of Directors of the Museum Association from 2007 to 2010 when it was absorbed by the Foundation of the Pacific Grove Museum of Natural History. In addition, he is a member of the Museum's Science Advisory Committee.

Pacific Grove Museum of Natural History: Getting it Back on Track (2007-2010)
Geva Arcanin*

I became interested in the Pacific Grove Museum of Natural History in 1997, when a friend recommended that I apply for a position on the Museum Association's Board of Directors. I served 1997-2001, including the last two years as Board President. The Museum's budget was always tight, even then.

But in 2007, a newspaper article stunned me: it said that the Museum was in trouble due to City budget cuts and would not be seeking reaccreditation by the American Association of Museums (AAM), a process required every ten years. I thought, "Once accreditation is lost, it is very difficult to ever get it back, especially in times of dwindling dollars." The Museum was badly off track.

As I dug deeper into the history, I learned that ours was one of the first museums in the nation to be accredited, in 1974. The Museum Director, now Curator Emeritus, Vern Yadon, was on that first commission establishing the standards for accreditation across the nation– a matter of pride for Pacific Grove!

At that time, three entities were involved in the operation of the Museum.

1) The City of Pacific Grove, which had acquired the Museum with a special election in 1917 and had operated it continuously ever since. The Museum was first established by scientists and other private citizens at the second Chautauqua Assembly in 1883.

2) The Museum Board, chartered by the City, with five members appointed by the Mayor. The role of the Board had changed from the early days of overseeing all Museum operations and finances to later becoming advisory to the City Council.

3) The Museum Association, a 501c3 corporation, which included a community-based membership, raised funds, and worked closely with the Museum staff to support a variety of activities.

I had moved to Pacific Grove in 1990 with a Masters degree in Management and a background in licensing and accreditation, although in a different field (health care), and I had been a Certified Quality Auditor by the American Society for Quality, in Quality Management Systems.

So in February 2007, I volunteered to facilitate the preparation of the self-study materials for accreditation. I was subsequently appointed to the City's Museum Board. Although the City Manager said that the City wanted to maintain accreditation, the process was slow going.

Many interested parties from the Museum Association and Museum Board tried to think of solutions to the budgetary crisis, including developing and offering the City a revised staffing plan. Even this was difficult when the 2007-2008 budget was slashed 52%.

In May 2007, the AAM sent a letter suggesting an option to voluntarily withdraw from accreditation. This was not acceptable to the City Manager. As the months went by in later 2007, a feeling grew among the staff, the Association, and the Museum Board that accreditation was out of the picture and later, that the City should close the Museum and hire a part-time Curator to care for the collection. The then current Museum Director planned retirement in December 2007 and the Assistant Director was to be laid off in January 2008.

I was asked to continue to pursue reaccreditation and look into what needed to be done. I learned that the previous accreditation in 1996 had been in question and was allowed to go forward only after a phone call by a member of the Museum Board. I called the AAM Accreditation Coordinator, to try to clarify the risks and benefits of seeking re-accreditation.

The Coordinator expressed concerns that the Museum would be unable to fulfill its mission, that it was being "hurt by the parent [the City]," and that "the governing authority is not helping the Museum," referring to the budget cuts. This would result in one of two outcomes: (1) "Tabling" if the problems looked solvable in one year, or (2) "Denial." At the time, there was no remedy for the lack of funding.

After a lengthy discussion, the AAM Coordinator acknowledged another option: to continue seeking re-accreditation. Some museums had used accreditation as a rallying point to focus on rebuilding community trust and financial resources. This gave us a way forward to pursue reaccreditation. If we decided to proceed, she would understand that another extension of time might be required. The AAM offered help and resources; their goal was to get us accredited!

The Coordinator suggested that the required, new strategic plan could emerge from the use of the reaccreditation self-study materials, review of the previous strategic plan, and special consideration of budgetary and organizational restraints. This process would fulfill one of the AAM criteria for accredited museums.

Finally, as a result of this conversation with the AAM, I had a way to proceed. I understood that compiling these materials was building a base for whatever came next for the Museum, whether accredited or not. At least, a new Museum Director would then have organized materials in the nine areas of the reaccreditation self-study. These comprised nine questionnaires, about a hundred pages, and a large binder of 56 demonstration documents of multiple pages each. The completed materials weighed 18 lbs! A very large package was sent to AAM in February 2008 and this was only the beginning!

The Way Forward

In reviewing the files, I had been reading about the Museum's origins and history with the early scientist supporters of the Museum. I was feeling discouraged until this new "Aha!" moment. I suddenly grasped that what the Museum needed now were scientist supporters, like in the early days, when they had created and sustained the Museum.

I talked to a few Pacific Grove scientists I knew and invited them over for an informal meeting about the Museum: Dave Powell, retired Monterey Bay Aquarium exhibit designer; Dr. Dave Greenfield, Professor Emeritus, University of Hawaii; and Dr. George Matsumoto, Education, MBARI. They brought Dr. Bob Lea, retired Fish and Game, and Dr. Margaret Bradbury, retired Ichthyologist, San Francisco State University.

We met at my house and gathered around the dining room table in late September 2007. I chronicled the Museum's problems and I asked them whether I should keep going with the reaccreditation. All responded, "Yes," with one cautious person saying, "Well, maybe not." The consensus, however, was that reaccreditation was important for future grant requests, relationships with other institutions, and opportunities for loans and traveling exhibits, as well as assurance to the public that the collections were well protected and maintained.

That first meeting with five scientists in 2007 turned into many more meetings with more scientists into 2007 and 2008, with the scientists providing ideas and support, developing exhibits, and more. One scientist applied to the City's Museum Board and was accepted; one applied to the Museum Association Board and was accepted; he also presented a 2009 Exhibit Plan in 2008, during a time of staff transition. The scientists planned and executed the Museum's Special Exhibits in 2008-2009 (see David Greenfield's story). Ultimately, a group of fourteen agreed to be called "Scientist Friends of the Museum," a step that was critical to the reaccreditation process.

At the first scientist meeting in 2007, Dave Powell spoke up and offered to talk to Julie Packard. Afterwards, he sent me a draft letter to review before sending to her. I responded, "Oh, you have described so many problems!" I didn't want to discourage her with the 52% budget cut, staff leaving, the City not having replacement staff, not knowing what would be happening with the collection, the exhibits, etc. Dave said that she should know all of the challenges the Museum faced, and we agreed to send the letter!

Dave then set up a meeting with Julie in early October 2007. There were four of us attending: Scientists Dave Powell and Dave Greenfield, Association Board President Fran Horvath, and myself, a member of the Museum Board. I remember feeling like dancing in the parking lot after the meeting! Julie Packard had offered to help us, with guidance from her senior staff. She subsequently set up a conference call for me with the Packard Foundation to discuss the Museum's needs. She had given us many ideas to address many problems, but the best was the feeling that we were not alone.

After talking with the Packard Foundation, I followed up with the City Manager regarding the need for an interim museum manager. On December 4, 2007, the City Manager submitted a written request to the Packard Foundation for an Organizational Effectiveness grant for "$50,000 to provide funding for a new position, Interim Museum Manager." The grant was awarded!

Also in 2007, after discussing the Museum with a friend, her family donated $5,000, to be used for science education for children meeting the State Science Standards. The money was used to buy the children's microscopes that are still in use 10 years later!

During 2007, I continued to work on the reaccreditation process daily and for many hours, meeting or talking with many different people involved with the Museum, the City, the community, the AAM, developed strategies, compiled documents, wrote responses to the interminable questionnaires, and involved many individuals in the process. The AAM provided another extension of their deadline for completion. They could see that we were acting in good faith!

One day in January 2008, I entered the Museum to work on the reaccreditation, expecting no one to be in the building. The last employee had been laid off earlier in the month. There were young people in the Museum from the Aquarium's Guest Relations staff. What a great surprise! Their supervisor was training them as docents for the Museum. They worked two shifts, one in the morning and another in the afternoon, for about six months, in order to keep the Museum open – and they were good at that job: lively, greeting visitors, explaining the exhibits, and collecting visitor data.

In February 2008, the City hired an Interim Museum Manager, Bob Snyder, with the $50,000 Packard Foundation grant. Bob was a retired Superintendent of some very large school districts across the country and also an Aquarium volunteer.

At the same time, I had completed the reaccreditation documents. They were signed by Bob Snyder, then by Mayor Dan Cort, and were mailed to AAM, by the deadline on February 22, 2008 (an 18 pound package). Jim Covel and J.R. Rouse were instrumental in the final compilation, duplication, and labeling to specifications of the materials – a hectic last two days! As stated earlier, this was only the beginning. AAM reviewers scrutinized all documents and came back in April with concerns in several areas, including fiscal stability. They requested a response by July 1. This was another beginning of back and forth with the accrediting organization, the American Association of Museums, and their concern for the Museum's fiscal stability.

Interim Museum Manager Snyder and I shared some office space upstairs in the Museum. One day I suggested the idea of a transition team to help advise with the operations and plan for the Museum. He asked if I had any idea of who should be on it, besides himself. I suggested two from the Museum Association Board, two from the City Museum Board, and I gave him the resume of an interested student in the Museum Studies class at CSUMB. Bob liked the idea and filled out the team with another scientist, the Aquarium's Guest Relations Supervisor, and the Assistant City Manager.

The eight members on the Transition Team met every Wednesday morning for two hours starting in March 2008 throughout 2009, and into 2010. This team developed the strategic plan and business plan, including a rolling two-year budget that was crucial for the on-going operations, as well as satisfying the many reaccreditation requirements, including governance and fiscal stability, a continuing AAM concern.

In March 2009, as a part of the planning process, volunteer consultant Steve Dennis conducted 28 community interviews and held a community involvement day with teams brainstorming Museum ideas. He wrote a report describing future scenarios for the Museum, based on these activities. The Transition Team used these ideas in their planning for the future.

The Transition Team worked hard to develop a workable plan for the Museum and a feasible budget, producing a pivotal document written by Judd Perry in May, 2008, "Summary of Transition Team Strategic Planning for Pacific Grove Museum of Natural History: Attachment A, Mission Statement and Strategic Goals; Attachment B, Proposed Museum Budget - 2008/09 and 2009/10."

Two main changes were proposed:

1) The impact area of the Mission Statement was expanded beyond Monterey County to include the Central Coast, with the thought of a larger population base calling the Museum their home.

2) A new non-profit foundation, with the Museum as its sole reason for being, formed to raise funds and to work with the City to operate the Museum for the City.

When the Transition Team was ready, in early May, I wrote a letter to the Packard Foundation from the Interim Museum Manager and myself, describing the formation of the Transition Team, the Team's accomplishments, and the need for the City to hire a permanent Museum Manager, since the Interim was to leave in early August. At that time, unless hiring took place, there would be no Museum staff, only volunteers.

The letter to the Packard Foundation included the "Summary of Transition Team Strategic Planning," new Mission and Goals, Museum Draft Transition Budget 2008/2009 version 2.6, and Museum Draft Strategic/Business Plan.

June 2008 was a critical time with the great accomplishments of many people.

1) The City Council approved the new statement of Museum Mission, Vision, and Goals as well as the concept of a new foundation to work with the City in operating the Museum.

2) The Packard Foundation met in June and approved the Transition Team's request for $230,703 for fiscal year 2008/2009, supported by personnel, planning, and budget documents. The grant letter added further, "In 2009, we are also willing to consider a request of approximately $235,000 for fiscal year 2009/2010."

This set the table for the many needed changes.

1) Interim Museum Manager Bob Snyder left in August, having provided an important liaison between the City, the Museum Board, the Association, and the Transition Team.

2) With increased funds, the City now appointed a committee of community members to interview candidates and to hire a new City employee, Museum Manager Lori Mannel.

3) The Transition Team continued to work with the new Museum Manager to develop extensive work plans, with task due-dates to satisfy reaccreditation requirements and to implement the strategic/business plan.

4) Simultaneously, the Transition Team developed the construct of a new non-profit, public benefit corporation to negotiate with the City to operate and to fundraise for the Museum.

Changes in each of these areas in 2007-2010, involved the community in supporting the Museum: the scientists, the Packard Foundation, the Monterey Bay Aquarium staff, new money, new staff, the Transition Team, the consultant's community-involved planning, an earlier committee's new staffing plan and the City Council, with the Museum Board and the Museum Association, along with the work of many individuals. <u>The reaccreditation progress guided this complicated process that required new development in so many areas. It required building a new organizational structure and the means for on-going support.</u>

This was not the end, but yet another beginning!

◎ ◎ ◎

*Geva Arcanin was a member of the Board of Directors of the Museum Association from 1997 to 2001, serving as President from 1999-2001, a member of the City's Museum Board from 2007-2009, and the Foundation's Board of Directors from 2009 to 2017. In addition, she is a member of the Museum's Science Advisory Committee.

◎ ◎ ◎

Special thanks to Vicki Pearse for going through all of the text and carefully editing it.

"Frontier Chautauqua" book
Betty Lou Young

In Support of the P.G. Museum of Natural History

August 15. 2007 email to: Geva Arcanin

In response to your e-mail message, I would be very pleased to give you permission to use the Pacific Grove chapter in my "Frontier Chautauqua" book in any way that would help the planning committee of the Pacific Grove Natural History Museum and I wish you well in your endeavor.

In researching and writing my book (a twenty-year project), I have paid many visits to the museum and have appreciated its fine research facilities and its helpful staff. I have also appreciated the fact that the spirit of Chautauqua still lingers over Pacific Grove—on its quiet streets lined with Victorian homes and cottages, and in the museum, where wide-ranging topics of educational interest are so well presented.

Pacific Grove was unusual from the beginning. It was the first independent Chautauqua in the West—by many years. Founded in 1879, it was built on the site of an earlier Methodist camp meeting—another unique feature—the only one on the Pacific Coast to emulate the Eastern

Chautauquas in this manner. Its first summer program was also dignified by the presence of Dr. John Vincent, who founded the first Chautauqua assembly on Lake Chautauqua in New York in 1874.

The first full session was remarkable in that the founders were all top-flight educators—the presidents and most honored professors from the Bay Area colleges—Berkeley, Mills, San Jose, University of the Pacific, and later, Stanford. No other Chautauqua assembly the country over can make this claim. Many continued on to give regular courses each summer, taking advantage of the unexplored natural environment to study botany, geology, marine life, and, especially, conchology. The eminent professor, Dr. Keep, who taught conchology laid the foundation for the great collection of shells that still resides at the museum, and interest in the natural sciences was a magnet that drew an avid following. The natural science museum for which the groundwork was laid then remains a community treasure.

The founders of Pacific Grove didn't stop there. As the oldest established assembly on the West Coast, it sent its most inspiring leaders out to found other Chautauquas in key locations where interest had been shown. Thus, Pacific Grove sponsored assemblies at Hot Springs on Lake Tahoe, along the Sacramento River at Shasta Retreat, down south in Long Beach, and at several sites in Oregon—notably Ashland, Gearhart, and Gladstone—providing organizational expertise and sharing talent for their classes and programs.

Chautauqua was responsible for another Pacific Grove tradition—the Feast of Lanterns, in 1905, but its heyday was almost past by 1913, when Asilomar offered competing and more attractive facilities for cultural and educational events. The last tent-style Chautauqua was held in Pacific Grove in 1929.

I sincerely hope that you can keep your wonderful museum alive and well. —Betty Lou Young

Chautauqua Hall, corner of Central Avenue and 16th Street, photo by Patricia Hamilton 2011.

Oak lichen moss in the forest. Photo Wolf Bukowski.

DREAMS OF PACIFIC GROVE – WILLIAM NEISH

The first play I ever saw was *Treasure Island*, when I was seven. It was put on by the Drama Department of Boston University. My parents had just divorced and my brother, sister and I were staying with our mother's family in Brookline, following a stay with our father's family in Colorado. Before that we'd been in Nahant, Annapolis, East Greenwich, Coronado, and Monterey, where I was born.

I remember being fascinated by this stage set. The curtain rose, and suddenly we were in a big Colonial tavern, with a worn wooden bar and what looked to be an actual stone fireplace. There was supposed to be a storm outside, conveyed by whistling sound effects and a real branch tapping against a real window, far upstage. I was captivated by the fact that someone (or a group of people, as it was a rather elaborate environment) would take the time to put this set together . . . that they would actually choose all these things to create a unified whole.

It suddenly struck me that things in an ordinary household were chosen, too, just like these things onstage had been. I guess I'd never been in a furniture or paint store, and just thought a house had always been the way it was, forever.

I pretty much became a homebody from that point on, and stayed that way when we moved back to the Peninsula a year later. The outside was wild and unpredictable (traffic! birds!) but inside, things were arranged for you. A house wasn't full of things that had just blown in by the wind, stopping when they met a wall. No, here were chairs from my mother's childhood back east, or curtains she had made herself after selecting a fabric, or books we'd all pulled from a long row at the Three Rings Book Shop on Fisherman's Wharf. It's not that these were expensive things, but they made me think of people . . . specific people reaching out specific hands to make or choose something. It was as if the hands of the first owner or craftsman and the hands of the present met when the chair or the curtain or whatever was touched. And I liked that. It was a little like time traveling.

I might have liked working on houses as a career, but I was put off by the fact that even the world of interiors was so vast . . . made up of stones and plaster and wood, tiles, porcelain, metal and fabric. Then you had electric wires and drains and all kinds of mysterious gizmos that hid in the walls, all interconnecting in scientific ways that become confounding and overwhelming, even deadly if mishandled! But I love standing in a space that's been engineered by choices, that's been edited by finance (like everything in life is) and dictated by a specific personality's taste . . . there's something about it that's very emotionally revealing. When you're looking at a person's room, you're looking at the person.

After the curtain came down on *Treasure Island* and we left the Boston area, my mother took us to the place she'd been happiest during her ever-mobile, military marriage; the Monterey Peninsula. I was lucky she picked Pacific Grove for us, because I immediately loved everything about it. Its small size (easy to navigate with a child's brain), its sense of unruffled tradition, the green all around. I even loved the fog, which gave a sense of privacy and mystery.

But best of all I loved its houses and buildings, with their long histories.

When I was asked what section of *Life in Pacific Grove: Book 2* I would like to write, I immediately thought of the old local interiors I'd known. Perhaps my chapter could be called *Our Buildings, Ourselves*. It could be about places from childhood I still love visiting now that I'm back almost half a century later. Because even though things never felt completely stable again after the divorce, the sense of protection these places gave in my childhood is still vivid to me. The memories of them are so strong that no matter where I've lived since (Boston again, New York, Los Angeles), they've always returned to me in my sleep.

I would sometimes dream I was back in Miss Coons' class at Lighthouse School, or backstage inside the Wharf Theater where I began acting, with its quiet, grey carpeted floors, smooth plaster walls, and small balconies.

But mostly I dream about my childhood house on Bentley Street. Sometimes I will be playing with my sister in front of the fireplace, but most often what I dream is that the present owner is away, and I have snuck inside to look around. Once I had a nightmare that the place had been gutted, and inside the still-standing walls was just a dark pit in the earth. The whole inside of the house had simply disappeared, and I looked in through the door as I cried and cried.

Happily, though, in real life that house is still there. And the inside looks just as nice as it always did. I know because once when I was circling the block, thinking about buildings from my past, the owners, who were outside gardening, spotted me and invited me inside.

Welcome to my childhood.

219 Bentley Street

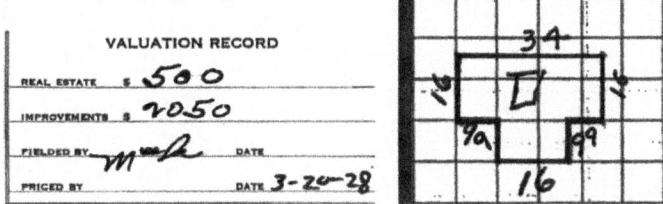

1928 construction permit from City Hall.

My parents bought our house in 1973, following their divorce. Invested in being "ladylike," my mother somewhat recklessly waived alimony. She did want a safe place to bring us up in, however, so in their final act as a couple my parents looked at two small houses in Pacific Grove. They picked the first one.

Bentley Street is just two blocks long, a hill that starts at Lighthouse Avenue and climbs to George Washington Park. Watching house hunter shows today, I guess we had incredible luck. We just walked in, our mom liked it, and the next day they signed the papers. A big plus was that in addition to the adjacent park, Lighthouse Elementary School was just a block away. It wasn't really by the beach and it wasn't really downtown, but both were clearly visible from the roof if you climbed up there (something we were not allowed to do.)

There was a front yard, a back yard, a detached garage, and along the side a small wilderness hung with Spanish Moss. We children thought this belonged to the city. Maybe my mother actually knew it was ours, yet needed a good excuse to keep us from building a tree house out there. They didn't have tree houses in Boston, and besides which, someone would probably get gouged by a rusty nail.

The records said our house was built in 1928 at a cost of $2,050 for a D.S. McDaniel, and the neighborhood was originally a subdivision called Pacific Grove Acres. (Not everyone knows P.G. is broken into 17 distinct areas with official names.) This particular corner lot had been vacant all through the Victorian era, hence the little wilderness along the side facing Heacock Avenue. Subsequent owners added a second, some would say unsightly, story . . . but when we lived there it was a bungalow, which is a floorplan that has all the living spaces on the ground floor. (If your bedrooms are in the attic, the structure's classified a bungaloid.)

I like a one-story home, myself, because you can usually hear who's in the house with you. Once I was visiting a friend deep in the country and we came back to her big farmhouse at midnight after seeing a scary movie. Even though we went through the place room by room, floor by floor, there was no guarantee someone else wasn't moving through the house too, cleverly and quietly keeping an equidistance from us using the back staircase. *Never again!*

The floorplan of the Bentley Street house (shown to the left) was four rooms surrounding a centrally placed fireplace. This is maybe the oldest, most cost-efficient way to include a fireplace in a building, because the warmth from the firebox and chimney help heat all the surrounding rooms even without multiple openings, mantlepieces etc. (When you put a fireplace on a side wall, half the heat goes outside.) Thankfully, someone had added *one* furnace grate in the main room over the years, and that's what really heated the place; it was only 688 square feet.

The fireplace was usually for company, anyway, and when we built a fire we'd throw orange peels on it to make a nice scent. There was also a powder you could pour on top of the logs that supposedly changed the flames into different colors. Sadly, like with Sea Monkeys, there wasn't as much to look at when you actually used this powder as was advertised.

The nicest thing about that house was the communal feeling of how the rooms radiated off from the living room, just like the heat did. We traded bedrooms over the years as our tastes changed, but we were always the same distance from each other, with the living room and the fireplace squarely in the middle. It gave a feeling of constancy. And just like our cats, we were in and out of each other's rooms all the time, anyway. For instance, my mother didn't like the big, long bedroom on the south side of the house, but its huge closet was always hers. When my sister and I shared that room when we were little, she'd wake us up when she came in to pick out her clothes for the day.

In high school I did eventually branch out by claiming the breakfast nook off the kitchen for my room. (It was a small enclosed porch that everyone else found too cold.) That room didn't have a closet because it was all windows, but I seemed to only wear polo shirts, jeans and sweaters by then, which could all go in dresser drawers.

I think the reoccurring dreams I have of revisiting that house are about the uncertainty of life. Unfortunately, having moved so many times even before Bentley Street, I have a lingering fear of where I will rest my head. And will the same place be there tomorrow?

If I had a child, I would tell them it's more important to *have* a head rather than the same old place to rest it . . . but still, both are important..

1025 Lighthouse Avenue – Lighthouse Elementary School

Many days, the fact that Lighthouse Elementary School was just a block from our new house didn't stop us from being tardy. Our whole Bentley Street household had a very lax sense of time. My working single mom was not only busy but a bit flighty. In addition she was very beautiful, which for better or worse teaches you the world will wait.

Like Forest Grove Elementary and the high school, Lighthouse was a series of separate buildings that could be accessed by sheltered, exterior walkways. (This is a layout that's suited to warmer climates. You don't see it much on the east coast.) The main structure, which flanks Lighthouse Avenue, was done in 1948 by Carmel architect Robert Stanton, who also designed the Monterey County Court House. The five smaller outlying buildings were added later.

Jennifer Bradley, David Neubert, Luke Coletti, Michelle Darragh, Linda Harris, Lisa Benevides, Carie Miller, Stephanie Butzlaff, Larky Reese, Gerard Issvoran, Deborah Gonsalves (who I still call Debbie) and I were all in the same grade at Lighthouse and whenever I see them around town I feel this bittersweet rush of affection. They go back to just about my earliest memories! And I have never met a girl who was prettier than our classmate Kim Blackwell. She had heavy, dark blonde hair and the blackest eyelashes and brows I'd ever seen. (There were five Blackwell daughters in total, all stunning. Their mom, the envy of the PTA, looked like she was one of them.)

In fourth grade Kim and I founded the short-lived Treasure Chest Players and our searing portrayals of Hansel and Gretel enraptured the entire kindergarten class for one glorious hour. We were instant legends. It's true some would say Stephanie was also quite memorable as the wicked witch, but I maintain it was really *our* show.

Stephanie's star would continue to rise when in the sixth grade she so brilliantly played Annie Sullivan in *The Helen Keller Story,* which we wrote ourselves. But the surprise breakout sensation was Michelle, who brought down the house as Mrs. Keller, screaming herself awake from a nightmare about her little girl's dark future. (Sadly, I must report that Lisa was *not* well-behaved backstage, refusing to pipe down when I, as harried director, fruitlessly tried to call the cast to order. I have since forgiven her.)

Jon Organ and I started SCSC (the Secret Creepers Spy Club) in fifth grade, and David later became a member. We thought kids would make great spies, yet to our dismay we found there wasn't too much suspicious activity to spy on in our quiet seaside hamlet. Jon's parents then abruptly divorced and his mom surprised us by even more abruptly partnering with a lady, so it seems we weren't naturally very intuitive to begin with. Neither of us would make it to the Pentagon.

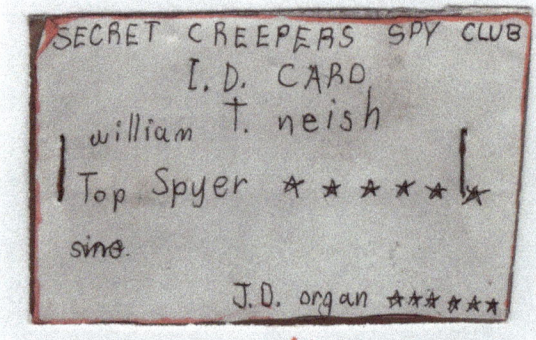

I still call that campus "Lighthouse School" even though it closed in 1979 and is now known as the Adult Education Center. With less foot traffic there these days, and a community garden added, there are now deer in residence.

I visit the deer once in a while. And for many years I've had dreams about the school.

In my dreams I am in Mrs. Slater's second grade classroom. It's within an old, barn-red rectangular building cut into several long rooms that are filled with high windows. This is the room where I started school in Pacific Grove, and where I auditioned for my first talent show. (I sang *Edelweiss,* a capella.) Mrs. Slater was the teacher who suggested I take her friend Marcia Hovick's weekend acting classes, which later led to roles in New York and Los Angeles.

In the dream it is evening, and there is some kind of arts festival going on. I am grown up, and have walked, uninvited, into some sort of gallery opening in Mrs. Slater's room. There are short, experimental films being shown on the walls, but what I look at are the linoleum floor, the low bookshelves, the peaked roof with rafters overhead. I feel celebratory, in wonder to be back in this place I've been locked out of with the passing of time.

I look out the windows and see the side lawn where Debbie and I and all the rest played red rover. I was usually picked last, but in the dream I am happy, remembering a place I gathered with children I will go through years and years of experiences with, until graduation sends us all to different towns in 1983.

More vivid than the room's physical details is the feeling of excitement that I am *back*. It is almost like Dorothy waking up at the end of *The Wizard of Oz* and embracing the world she once took for granted as wonderful. I don't know that things really *were* so wonderful at that time, but it does somehow connect to me in a deep enough way to always be in my dreams.

226 Willow Street

My mother's best friend was another single mom/school teacher named Mary Lent, whose daughter was best friends with my little sister. They lived on the second floor of a large Victorian in the neighborhood next to us which was founded in 1887 and called the Second Addition.

At the corner of Willow and Short Street, you went up an outside staircase that entered straight into the Lents' kitchen. Like the rest of the house, inside and out, it was all white, with some touches of stained glass.

This large apartment has always stayed with me as quintessentially Pacific Grove, circa the Bicentennial. It was classical and very clean but also a touch Bohemian.

Several styles overlapped in Mary's house. First, there was the twisting, jogging Victorian architecture itself, which had a pitched ceiling full of dormer windows that created softly shadowed nooks and crannies. The walls had rows of all kinds of books and plants. Older pieces of family furniture were mixed with mid-century things, like a Danish modern coffee table that Mary had probably bought as a bride. There may or may not have been a Native American blanket draped over the back of the couch, but there was a definite handcrafted element in the colorful pieces of Mary's hand weaving that were around, and her bright, unframed canvases. (She sold purses and paintings at craft fairs on the weekends.) There was a large, intimidating loom of blond wood that stood by one window. We weren't allowed to play with it.

The Lent apartment looked like a place you wouldn't openly smoke pot in, but that you wouldn't necessarily be thrown *out of* for smoking pot in, either. It was artistic yet restrained. The fact that it was old yet new was epitomized by the freestanding metal fireplace in the living room, unapologetically bright orange. (This lurid monarch butterfly color and beige are basically used interchangeably in our town.)

Mary moved when the house was sold several years later and my mother considered buying it. She ultimately felt it was too big, completely forgetting that Mary and her kids could have stayed upstairs and we could have just taken over the first floor. Today, Mary and my mom would have bought the house together, but people were less creative about real estate deals back then.

When the Realtor showed us the whole house, there was an odd feature about the downstairs that still crops up in my dreams. In one bedroom, you entered a closet and then within, off to the side, there was another door that led to a small, enclosed room. The children of the family that was moving out had used it as a fort. I have no idea why a house would be built like that. It's a little eerie. Unless you were the killer in *The Amityville Horror*, why would you need a small, windowless room, so hidden away?

Sometimes in my dreams, there is a room off a closet no one knows about. At first I'm pleased to discover an extra room in my new house, but then I become uneasy as I realize there's no other way out of that secluded space. It would be an ideal meeting spot for the Secret Creepers Spy Club, should we ever regroup . . . but what's frightening is someone could corner you in such a space and no one would know how to get in to help you. They'd just hear a muffled tussle and squeaking within the walls and think you were a mouse.

My ideal house would *not* include a spooky, isolated, secret room. It's just too mysterious and would attract ghosts. But I have asked local architect Rick Steres to do a plan of this particular one from my nightmares, so you may build one if you so desire. Keep in mind it would never meet any building code (the hallways especially are too narrow) and you'd have to clandestinely create it without permits.

Just please don't invite me to your housewarming. *I won't attend!*

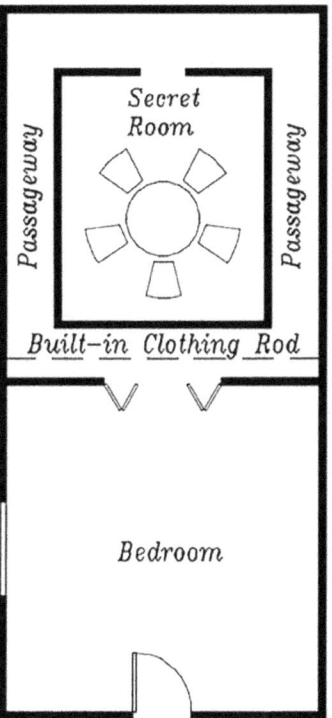

835 Forest Avenue - Junior High School

In my day, what's now Pacific Grove Middle School was called the Junior High, and it just had grades 7 and 8. From 1911 to 1961 this same building was the high school, though it had to be almost completely rebuilt following a fire in 1946. Before all that, the high school had been the upper floor of a Victorian on Pine Avenue that stood where Robert Down Elementary School is now. Prior to 1888, classes were taught in a back room at Chautauqua Hall.

That's a very convoluted history for a small town where little seems to change! *Won't somebody think of the children?!*

But back to me. I loved being in junior high in 1978. The building was just the right size and felt like a real facility, what with it being two stories tall and all. This was the big time . . . with ovens to burn things in during Home Ec, many different teachers, and school dances! You really did feel grown up there, away from all those babyish grade schoolers you'd left in the dust. We'd traded in our cubby-holes for lockers. *Gee, Your Hair Smells Terrific* was in the air, *Grease* was on the screen, and after seeing Brooke Shields in *Pretty Baby* I was convinced we'd been separated at birth. She was a high fashion model playing a child prostitute from *Belle Époque* New Orleans. Clearly we were soul sisters.

A number of us had been tested and deemed "gifted" in grade school, and we were still grouped together for science and history classes in junior high. We therefore spent the whole second half of the day together. We dissected fetal pigs side by side and it was very bonding.

It seems everyone now scrambles to call their child gifted, but back then it was more of a drain on a household. Parents were like, "Oh, great . . . my child tested as 'gifted'? I suppose now I have to buy them a *chemistry set!*"

I revisited the middle school recently with a tour guide, and was struck by how low the book shelves in the library were. We might have felt grown up in 1978, but it looks like we were really still very small! The building itself is still fantastic though, with sky-lit high ceilings in the hallways. Here and there are bits of vintage cabinetry from the 1940s. It has a very serene feeling and I love it.

My favorite class was chorus, taught by Mr. Dill in a room over the wood shop. This was a snug space (now used for storage) where we would plaintively bleat *You Light Up My Life* and Olivia Newton John's *Sam*. During the holidays we would sing Christmas carols, plus one Chanukah song for good measure, at Holman's Department Store. We also did a production of *Tom Sawyer*, which is the one play I've ever done that I have no memory of . . . aside from the fact that I wore a beige sweater as Huckleberry Finn. Desiree Maysonave played Becky Thatcher.

The dreams I have about junior high are of singing as a group in chorus. I never did learn how to actually read music, but I loved the team effort of dividing into parts to create harmonies. Truthfully, they had to make allowances for me because I could only remember the melody, and so was put with the sopranos.

But even if the others were doing the heavy lifting, I liked being part of a unified whole where we were all at least trying to create something nice.

Pacific Grove Junior High / Middle School Auditorium.

◉ ◉ ◉

302 Park Street

Naming houses goes back to when they were large enough to take on a significant personality, or when they were so out-of-the-way they lacked an address. (Monticello, Thornfield Hall, Bleak House, etc.)

My childhood friend Sara Moore's house had several addresses, being two old Victorian buildings joined together. And it certainly didn't lack personality. Looking back, it could have been called *Some Point*.

At some point, the two old houses were merged, flanking most of a block on Laurel.

At some point, Sara's elderly father had died. He was the science fiction writer Ward Moore and chose the house because he wanted something within walking distance of the post office and the library.

At some point, Dan, an old family friend, moved into the best upstairs room and was rarely seen again. Dan was a periodic binge drinker who lapsed into a lisp under the influence. We'd hear him warbling over the house intercom, installed back when Ward was sick, weakly and eerily calling for Sara's mom, Raylyn. (*"Waywin, Waywin..."*)

At some point, I basically moved into Sara's house, and at some point, Raylyn decided Sara and I were mature enough to come and go as we pleased while she typed manuscripts and graded papers in her office off the kitchen. A teacher at Monterey Peninsula College, she published a biography about L. Frank Baum and several novels.

Left to our own devices, Sara and I rather quickly became teenage alcoholics. To our credit, we did get sober years later. We were both from fairly lax households headed by school teachers, were in advanced English classes, and had absent fathers; Sara's was dead, mine overseas. Sara skipped two grades in grammar school, which she later thought was a disastrous course of action she wouldn't recommend to anyone. It made her the very youngest in her class by a wide margin.

Sara had freckles, enormous blue eyes, and streaming red gold hair. Looking back, she's the only person I could ever get a good night's sleep beside. We curled up like kittens together, no secrets between us, and dreamed of moving to Hollywood. I never had to "come out" as gay to Sara, just as I never had to come out to my own sister. I truly loved Sara Moore, which isn't something I say easily.

Her house on Laurel was cool, dim and shadowy, with high ceilings and not much furniture. The bare wood floors felt wonderfully chilly under your feet and there were unexpected stairs here and there that lead up and down through the rambling place. Her own room was painted purple, and we would listen to David Bowie and Queen records in there. She also had a deep closet that ran far into the crooked house. (At one time long ago it might have been a hallway.) Many things had been stored there by various family members and forgotten over the years. We never got to the back of it.

She had eight brothers and sisters, all older, from her parents' five marriages, and those siblings occasionally passed through town. There was an out-of-tune piano in the living room where whoever was home would gather to sing folk tunes and Tom Lehrer songs.

> *The cutest boy I ever saw*
> *Was sippin' cider through a straw*
> *The cutest boy I ever saw*
> *Was sippin' cider through a straw*

Sara said she had never pictured herself as an older person. And she indeed died young, as she always thought she would. One November, working as a counselor at the Beacon House, she simply fell down dead like a character in a fairy tale.

But in my dreams about her it is always summer, which is when we had the most time together. There was an old pink rose bush with tiny buds by the front porch, and the petals are everywhere in the dream. We're lying on the roof of her house with our friends Kaylyn and Nora, reading each other quizzes from old, furled issues of *Seventeen* magazine. Or we're playing cards on the porch, or making iced coffee in the kitchen, or singing around the piano.

> *In the velvet darkness of the blackest night*
> *Burning bright, there's a guiding star*
> *No matter what or who you are*

There are never any adults around in the dream; it's just us in the summer sunlight in a crazy old house I call *Some Point*, where we can smoke cigarettes if we want to.

Get the Look:
The Pacific Grove Maiden Aunts Brigade

I think of Pacific Grove as being like *Brigadoon*, limpid and magical. It's sedate, a tiny old town awakened from a hundred-year sleep. And we cherish our dowdiness! How *jarring* it is when someone buys a house here and adds a massive, highfalutin second story and guest wing . . . or tarts up the place with an overkill of very bright colors. That's a painted lady, San Francisco style. At heart, we're more a collection of maiden aunts.

Pacific Grove has its own particular look; muted, filtered through the mist and fog that regularly rolls through town. And let's face it; the light and overall vibe here has never been bright and sunny, as a rule. Our old buildings reflect that. Historically, they've usually been cream, tan, gray or white . . . colors found in stone that integrate with the natural landscape. With these soft neutrals you can stake your individuality by picking any color for the trim.

If you suffer from seasonal depression and simply *must* veer from this admittedly limited palette for your building, it's yellow that's most often chosen . . . but a creamy yellow rather than canary or Peking. If you crave a blue house, it's best to go with a shade from our cold, silvery ocean. Think *overcast,* and avoid shrieking sky blues and turquoise. Red should be barn red, with a brown undertone. And unless it's dark green trim for a white house, the best green for P.G. is a dusky eucalyptus shade with some gray in it. (Our local rock is the softly mottled *granodiorite* with quartz speckled through it, after all.)

The adventurous will shock us with anything above and beyond these softly weathered tones. And any deer delicately picking their way past a house done in bright, bursting Southwestern or Palm Beach colors will become disoriented.

Now, if you're not thoroughly cowed and browbeaten, let's enter the P.G. house itself.

For the interior, the time-honored look is Educated Easy. The Grove began as a summer community, and summer houses are more relaxed than those used year-round. So ideally there should be a slightly unfinished look here and there, as if you merrily abandoned your curtain project to go dig up shells on the beach or buy artichokes at the Farmers Market. A perfectly done room is too showy for we humble cliff dwellers. At least one uncompleted project should always be in view. (Plus an abalone shell, for guests who smoke to use as an ashtray.)

Plain white curtains tell the world you're focused on hard work rather than tending finery. Checks are acceptable. Lace is for brothels. If you absolutely *insist* on bright or patterned curtains, please at least line them in plain cloth so the whole street isn't exposed to your jazzy audacity.

In decorating your classic P.G. house, imagine you have an invisible maiden aunt living with you . . . one like me who regularly gasps *"Egads!"* The Maiden Aunts Brigade takes down pictures we feel are "too fast," though exceptions are sometimes made for nude figure studies by local artists. Lemon and lime colored tile hurt our eyes, and even stripes must be minimized. We need a chaise by the window to sink onto, with a good reading lamp and bookcase of Dickens within arm's reach. We certainly cannot master newfangled light dimmers, and mottos stenciled onto the wall confuse us. We can only sleep to the quiet sounds of an old house settling and its single-paned windows rattling softly in warped frames. Spotting a Jaguar automobile makes us think we've awakened on the Continent, or at Clint Eastwood's fancy schmancy Mission Ranch in Carmel.

Upholstery must be pet friendly, as our inner maiden aunt is cold and wants to snuggle with a fur baby. Or four. If a piece becomes worn out, it's best to throw a chenille bedspread over it. (This can go in the wash.) If you do make the shockingly exorbitant gesture of reupholstering something, using the duller, wrong side of the fabric can help it look immediately at home. For above all, our inner maiden aunt detests anything new.

For her sake, keep things simple, soft and orderly. And then when you're an old local auntie yourself, you'll still feel right at home in your old, seashore home . . . with its rotary dial phone still on the kitchen wall.

PRESCRIPTIONS · FILMS · STATIONERY
LIGHTHOUSE PHARMACY
LIGHTHOUSE AVENUE
PACIFIC GROVE, CALIFORNIA
—We Give S & H Green Stamps—

Carmel Hardware
PAINTS · KITCHEN EQUIPMENT
SPORTING GOODS
Phone 7-6049
P. O. Box 1625
Dolores St. Carmel-by-the-Sea, Calif.

WILDER & JONES, INC.
MECHANICAL CONTRACTORS
PHONE 5-5993
1525 Fremont St. Seaside, Calif.

Lover's Point Inn
17th and Ocean View
Pacific Grove, California

Hour Shoe Store
MAKE HOUR SHOE STORE YOUR SHOE STORE
566 Lighthouse Avenue
Pacific Grove, California

Bible Book Store
BIBLES & RELIGIOUS BOOKS
GREETING CARDS · RECORDS
STATIONERY
SUNDAY SCHOOL SUPPLIES
136 Bonifacio Place, Monterey, Calif.

China Importing Co.
WHOLESALE & RETAIL
Silks, Linens and Art Goods
The House of Quality
Phone 5-6601
464 Alvarado Street Monterey, Calif.

SPROUSE-REITZ
5-10-15 CENT STORE

588 and 590 Lighthouse Avenue
Pacific Grove, California

Bay Radio Service
RADIO AND TELEVISION
SALES AND SERVICE
PHONE 5-5689
Forest Avenue
Pacific Grove, California

Millers Shoe Store
Expert Repairing
NEW SHOES AND BOOTS
618 Lighthouse Ave. Monterey, Calif.

FARMERS INSURANCE GROUP
DALE WARD & SON
PHONE 5-5113
243 Del Monte Monterey, Calif.

RED O'DONNELL
Angel Food Do-Nut Shop
PHONE 2-4004
433 Alvarado, Monterey, California

Thomas H. French
GLASS & MIRRORS
131 Lighthouse Ave. Monterey, Calif.

RADIO · PARTS   REFRIGERATORS · RANGES
GRANTS HOME SUPPLIES
PHONE 5-6031
213 Forest Avenue   Pacific Grove, California

Billie Dahl's Dress Shop
LADIES' APPAREL AT
POPULAR PRICES
PHONE 5-5393
604 Lighthouse Avenue

GOOD LUCK SENIORS
Midway Drug Store
PHONE 5-6325
601 Lighthouse Ave. Monterey, Calif.

Compliments of
RASMUSSEN & MOODY
SPORTING GOODS · MODEL SHOP
490 Alvarado Phone 2-4088

Monterey Auto Sales
S. BURWELL, Proprietor
199 Lighthouse Ave. Monterey, Calif.

MEADOW GOLD DAIRY
PHONE 5-6429
800 Lighthouse Avenue Monterey, Calif.

Tyler's Union Gas Station
LIGHTHOUSE AVENUE
PACIFIC GROVE, CALIFORNIA

— 1955 High School Yearbook Ads and Campus Photos —

Best Wishes to Class of "55"
SCHACKER'S FABRIC STORE
211 Forest Avenue
Pacific Grove, California

Best Wishes Graduates
Pacific Grove Realty

CONGRATULATIONS AND BEST WISHES
TO THE GRADUATING CLASS OF "55"

Holman's
PACIFIC GROVE
PACIFIC GROVE, CALIFORNIA
HOLMAN'S COMPLETE ONE-STOP SHOPPING

"YOU HAVE TRIED THE BEST
Alicia's Ice Cream Shop
NOW SERVE THE BEST"
Forest Avenue
Pacific Grove, California

Congratulations Class of "55"
Grove Creamery
Pacific Grove, California

Pacific Grove CAMERA EXCHANGE
THE PENINSULA'S MOST
COMPLETE CAMERA SHOP

549 LIGHTHOUSE AVENUE

CONGRATULATIONS SENIORS
ART ZELLES
LADIES APPAREL
ARTHUR & HAZELLE RATHAUS
Monterey, California

CENTRAL GROCERY AND MEAT MARKET
COMPLETE ONE-STOP MARKET
FREE DELIVERY
Phone 2-5829 635 Lighthouse.

PENINSULA AUTO PARTS
PHONES 5-5107 & 5-5108
336 Washington Street
Monterey, California

PAR 45
MINIATURE GOLF
SNACK BAR
PING-PONG COURT
150 Central Ave. Pacific Grove

THE OLIVERS'
MISSION ART AND CURIO SHOP
SINCE 1896
Art Materials · Picture Framing
Phone 5-4557
120 Alvarado St., Monterey

Best wishes to Graduating Class of "55"
RANDY'S TOTS TO TEENS
Pacific Grove, California

HARVEY'S LUNCH
HOME COOKED MEALS
205 Forest Ave.
Pacific Grove, California

RUGS · BLANKETS · DRAPES
Highland Cleaners
DELIVERY · SERVICE
HOUSE OF QUALITY
PHONE 5-3223
1027 Pine Avenue (off Fremont), Seaside, Calif.

ORDWAY PHARMACY
WATSON AND DOW
PHONE 5-3348
398 Alvarado Street
Monterey, California

CONGRATULATIONS
PELICAN BARBER SHOP
Forest Avenue
Pacific Grove, California

Top Hat Market
PACIFIC GROVE'S
COMPLETE FOOD MARKET
FREE DELIVERY
Lighthouse Avenue
Pacific Grove, California

Modern Pacific Grove Women at Back Porch Fabrics, Central and Grand Avenues, reinventing and practicing the traditional look of all things quilted. Owner Gail Abeloe (second from left), operates a full-featured quilt store with a very full schedule of classes. The classroom also serves as a Quilt Gallery, usually featuring talented local artists, and occasionally quilters with a national reputation. www.backporchfabrics.com. Photo Peter Mounteer.

For historical purposes only; we do not endorse any candidate.

2018 Mayoral Candidate
Dionne Ybarra, 20-year P.G. Resident

Reporter James Herrera, *The Monterey Herald 7/31/18**

Seeking to bring diversity to the face of the city council, an emphasis on more green initiatives and policies that foster affordability for renters and buyers, Dionne Ybarra has announced her candidacy for mayor of Pacific Grove.

"I'm running because I'm a long-time resident who's been working the last year with county political figures, and it's time to use my experience to give back to the community," said Ybarra. "I feel I bring a new face of diversity to anything the council has done before and new experience."

Currently the mayor and six of the seven city council members are men.

The candidate said her Mexican-American heritage represents one of many diverse groups that have come to live in P.G. from all over the world bringing different cultures, languages, and perspectives.

"I hope to initiate that step forward and by doing so, others will be encouraged to do so," said Ybarra.

The candidate said she feels as a mother of five children ranging in age from 27- to 3-years-old, it affords her a current perspective. Ybarra said she wants her city to be an affordable, welcoming place for her kids to be able to come back to after college to live and work.

Ybarra, a P.G. resident for 20 years, emphasizes her qualifications as an environmental candidate who has founded an environmental nonprofit, works for the Nature Conservancy, and hopes to bring sustainable development goals to the table.

"I think the value of our stewardship needs to be higher," said Ybarra.

The candidate is for taking a look at rent control—"I'm not far off from supporting it" —and for stronger controls on short-term rentals. Ybarra believes that the challenges STRs bring to the community can be solved without the threat of losing the small town feel in P.G.

She is against installing a cell tower next to Pacific Grove High School,

The candidate also wants to be a leader who restores relationships among neighbors.

"You lose your choices when you don't have a voice, or the representation isn't representing you," said Ybarra.

*—used with permission of the Monterey Herald

2018 Mayoral Candidate
Rudy Fischer, Council Member

The most valuable asset I bring to the job of mayor is eight successful years on the City Council. During those years I spent a lot of time listening to the citizens of the city and looking in-depth at our problems. I have a deep understanding of what our residents want; and fixing up our infrastructure and parks, protecting our coastal areas, and keeping our neighborhoods safe and quiet will all be high priorities for me.

Just as I do now, I will be out in our neighborhoods talking to people and looking at the issues to figure out what works best for everyone. I also intend to continue to spend time with city leaders in other local communities to address our common issues of water, housing, crime, recreational opportunities, and maintaining a robust regional economy. We are all part of one area and I think it important that we all talk and work together to look out for our residents.

Too often people look at our cities only as places to live. They should also be places where we celebrate the accomplishments of our students, our sports teams, and our volunteers. I also want us to build a city that is financially viable for years to come. This involves looking for new revenue; but also includes working with our local businesses to allow them to grow and expand. Pacific Grove has some great opportunities to both add revenue to the city and to make it a better place for all of us to live in. Let's seize those opportunities together!

My experience over the last eight years makes me extremely qualified to now lead the city as mayor. I have learned how the city works. But I have also learned how we can work in partnership with community organizations, other public agencies, and private individuals to provide services and develop solutions to issues. I have proven that I am thoughtful, creative, and pragmatic in coming up with solutions to problems in collaboration with others. You want that in a mayor—and in your council members.

2018 Mayoral Candidate
Bill Peake, Council Member

Shirley and I moved our family from the SF Bay Area to the Central Valley in 1990. Hanford had low home prices, so we could afford a down payment on a house in Pacific Grove. In our opinion, P.G. has it all: beautiful coast, a small quaint town and lots of trees. Not to mention a beach and tide pools which our two young boys enjoyed.

Starting with Tim and Cleo McCoy, folks were very nice to us. The McCoys sold us the house and lived next door. We enjoyed visiting with them: Tim would have on hand Hershey's chocolate bars for the boys and we took pleasure in visiting with Cleo, who was bedridden. Perhaps it was because Shirley's mom used a wheelchair that made this connection special.

Over time, we became aware how much the community cares about the town and each other. It is astonishing. Not everyone agrees, but overwhelmingly we share respectful differences of opinion. We have a phrase on our block "living in paradise" perpetuated by our neighbor, Chubb. It's a good reminder to see the bright side of things.

Retirement allowed me to give back to the community. It didn't take long before I was a lighthouse volunteer, on the Recreation Board and later the Heritage Society Board. It's easy to make new friends volunteering and I also discovered the satisfaction of helping out through local government.

I also found a larger challenge being on City Council. It's a humbling experience. There is much to learn as to how the City operates and how the community thinks.

Being a patient, respectful listener and transparent with your thoughts goes a long way to building trust. These attributes should carry over to local government. I've read that folks place much higher trust in their local government than state or federal governments. As Council members, we should be available and earning that trust every day.

Much of local government is providing those services we all normally expect: good roads, storm drains, sewers, parks, police, fire, library, etc. But besides these, we need to be proactive stewards of our wonderful coast and its wildlife. And, we need to face challenges such as city finances, the local economy and housing for those who work in P.G.. Having a caring, open and respectful local government will go a long way to helping us meet these challenges successfully.

Affordable Housing

A Desirable Yet Elusive Goal
Councilmember Ken Cuneo

Wherever you look in California the words "affordable housing" are tossed around like bonbons, particularly by politicians. It has become the Holy Grail, with everyone having his or her view on how this chimera of a goal could be achieved.

Statewide data indicate that there 2.2 million individuals needing affordable housing, while there are only 640,000 units available as affordable housing. Well over one million are thus cut off from this type of housing. Of the 30 most expensive housing markets in the nation, 21 of them are in California. So the challenge both statewide and locally is very high.

Now I, too, proffer some thoughts, mindful of the thousands already on paper. Affordable housing is a flexible target, meaning that what is considered affordable in Billings, Montana, is certainly not affordable on coastal California. Thus there is an almost unbreakable rule that states that available financial assets must match the cost of living of a locality. Break this rule and there will be the continued stress of having to move from place to place for shelter. I have personally helped to move several individuals from one residence to a cheaper place. Often the best solution, although not widely agreed upon, would be to move to another city or state. If you cannot make it on the Monterey Peninsula, maybe a move to Redding or Ukiah would ease your burden.

So what can we do? Well, first accept that an affordable housing program may reach some, but not all who require it. The tried and failed practice of packing the poor and indigent into high-rise towers cannot be used today. In Pacific Grove, the Vista Point apartments were built using some federal funding. It houses hundreds of senior citizens in an affordable housing situation in studios up to two bedrooms. Since it sits directly across from the Sally Griffin Active Living Center and the Recreation Trail, it works well for those lucky enough to get in. Now, since it was built with federal funding, these apartments must be made available to anybody from any state in the Union. Consequently, not all residents in Pacific Grove can get in. The waiting list is extremely long and unfortunately some on that list will pass before their number ever comes up.

Rather modest progress can be made by integrating some affordable housing individuals with other individuals who pay market rate. This could be done by constructing mixed use buildings that would include small businesses on the first floor and housing, some of it affordable most of it market rate. A twist on this mixed use style could be to add a third floor dormitory. This would consist of single rooms with closet space, a desk, and a small refrigerator. Meals would be taken in a communal dining room, while bathrooms and showers, communal style, would be at both ends of the floor. This was how most of us were housed in college; it is not a new idea, rather a return to the old idea of a dorm or a boarding house. Rent would be very low and the residences would cater to the poorest who would otherwise have no shelter whatsoever. This would remove some of the homeless from our streets, provide them with shelter and give them an address needed for any type of employment. Other options could include the building of tiny homes of up to 300 square feet. These minimal sized homes are cheap to build.

Pacific Grove has taken a small step forward by adding a housing goal belatedly to its annual goals. This simply means that the council is thinking about doing something. It does not mean that at this stage something is being done. Because of its precarious finances compared to other neighboring cities, Pacific Grove out of necessity has had to spend on other priorities.

For funding, P.G. could set aside a yearly sum of $150,000 that would be used only to build or restore a property or even to purchase a property. This could be augmented from both private funding and the 26 or so state and federal programs out there. It would be appropriate to have someone on staff who could write a series of grant applications to tap into these programs.

Having enough funding on hand from all sources is needed to lure a developer into a commitment to build affordable housing. The developer needs to see profits emerging from any project; no profit, no construction.

There are over 1,000 second homes that are vacant in P.G. If the city could convince some of these property owners to long term rent out their homes, this could add housing stock to the inventory. Two or more individuals could pool assets to pay rent.

As there is no single path to achieve affordable housing, individual cities have been extremely creative in coming up with their own unique plans that cherry pick from the best ideas out there. P.G. should review these plans and adopt the best processes from these.

In summation, P.G. has recognized this as a goal. Next is to draw up a housing plan that includes targeted actions.

There are many who seek the Holy Grail.

Making a Good City Even Better

We at Life in Pacific Grove *asked one of the members of our City Council, Rudy Fischer, to write about some of the major and minor accomplishments that have affected our city over the past six years—and to provide some of the back story on how those changes came about, as well as their likely long-term impact on the community.*

Doing Away with Those 'Smoke-filled Rooms'

The Pacific Grove City Council is guided on a continuing basis by the Ralph M. Brown Act. Passed in by the state legislature in 1953, it guarantees the public's right to attend and participate in meetings of local legislative bodies. The intent was to do away with the "smoke-filled rooms" where decisions were made without the public having any input or representation. It requires that everything the council does as a body regarding city business be done in front of the public.

Because Pacific Grove has a seven member council, that means if three members are privately discussing a city issue and a fourth council member joins in, all talk on the topic must stop. That doesn't mean council members can't all be together at a party or event—they just can't discuss city business. Now, that has created some very interesting situations. When more than three council members are in a car going to an event, there is not much they can talk about. As a result they have had riveting conversations about such things as bridge building, plumbing, the weather, their houses, sports and sometimes about the council members who are not in the car (technically, that's not city business).

Many people don't realize that the City Council really only has one employee, the City Manager. All of the other city employees work for the City Manager, who has professional experience in actually running a city on a day-to-day basis.

A council member's most important role is to attend city council meetings, know the issues that have been presented, discuss them, and vote on the direction the city should take on an issue. Their statutory responsibility is almost entirely limited to acting as a body, and they actually. have little to no statutory authority as individuals. That is why the council as a body manages the City Manager—not individual members. The council is the liaison between the voters and the city staff.

City staff and the city attorney are much more familiar with the laws and regulations a city must abide by than the members of the council. So when you tell your favorite city council person "you need to fix this or that," that's not what a council member is able to do. They listen to the residents, but also get professional input from the city staff and then make general policy decisions. City staff then implements those decisions and actually makes things work.

Saving the Lovers Point Children's Pool

A good city council finds some way to get things done for their city's residents if at all possible. In June of 2013, Pacific Grove opened the new Stillwell Children's Pool at Lovers Point. Because of the deterioration of the 42 year old pool, the council had decided the year before that it needed to be replaced or removed. It had deteriorated to the point it was no longer safe for kids and, because of stringent environmental restrictions on building near the beach, repairs seemed too expensive to just about everyone—and the city just did not have the money to do that at that time. As a result, the City Manager recommended that we do away with the pool.

But at the following council meeting a fairly large group of parents, grandparents and children set up beach chairs outside of City Hall and asked the council to save the pool. They also addressed the council with that request (sometimes with very emotional language). After much debate the council finally agreed to allow it to be rebuilt at its current location, but only if those who wanted to save this icon of Pacific Grove could raise the $250,000 estimated cost to tear out the old pool and build a new one.

And with that, the residents really got to work. Don Mothershead had wrappers made for cans in which to collect change at major events like Good Old Days. The Masons provided a spaghetti dinner and Charlie Higuera of Grove Market offered a tri-tip dinner, both with the funds going to the effort. Many other organizations and individuals also donated to "Save the Pool." Some of the major members of the "Save the Pool" organization were Wendy Giles, Steve Thomas, Petula Lee, Bill Peake and Jordan Gasperson.

The City Manager and members of the council also called a few people they thought might be able to make large donations to help get the effort started, even offering them the naming rights to the pool in exchange for a significant contribution. "Mr. Pacific Grove"—Richard Stillwell—stepped in and gave the city a check for $100,000. Then City Manager Tom Frutchey asked him not to give it to the city outright, but to make it in the form of a matching contribution for other donations up to that amount.

The campaign exceeded the $250,000 goal by a long shot. In fact, it raised over $280,000; which meant that even after the actual $220,000 cost of the pool's construction was paid, the city had almost $60,000 left over for pool equipment and an endowment fund for future maintenance and repairs.

In 2017 over 400 children were registered for swim lessons and over 2,000 children swam during the recreation time. One of the results of the recent Recreational Opportunities Survey was that the Children's Pool is one of the three most popular recreation programs in the city.

The Stillwell Children's pool today.

Meet Some of Our 'Super Volunteers'

Our country is blessed by volunteerism in general. According to the Corporation for National and Community Services' 2016 report, 63 million Americans gave almost 8 billion volunteer hours to some organization or other in that year alone.

Pacific Grove has more than its share of volunteers. Countless volunteers work at the Point Pinos Lighthouse, the Heritage Society, the Monterey Bay Aquarium, and many other landmarks. They serve on the city's boards and commissions, and work with education groups like Monterey Reads. Through I-HELP, hundreds of people in our area help out at the more than 30 churches that provide shelter, meals, and some comfort to the homeless.

Volunteers renovated the Little House in Jewell Park at little cost to the city, and care for the plants in the median strips downtown. They can be found helping at CHOMP, delivering food to shut-ins through Meals on Wheels, or picking up trash at the beach or around the city. In short, they can be found everywhere.

Pacific Grove also has a host of "super volunteers" like Marabee Boone, who was Citizen of the Year in 2016, and Larry Esquivel, Volunteer of the Year in 2016. Marabee was a member of the Feast of Lanterns Board of Directors for years, keeping a beloved community tradition alive. Feast of Lanterns is great for the development of poise and professionalism among the city's young men and women, and brings the community together for several weeks every year.

Larry has been a reserve Police Officer for almost 30 years, and seemed to be a fixture at every event in the city. He and Ken Rolle, Steve Gorman and Mark Young kept showing up for duty and helping out at city events. Many Pagrovians were sad when the reserve program was eliminated as part of a police department reorganization once the department was fully staffed.

And there are people like Victoria Carns who, with her husband, former general Michael Carns, shows up for events and is always present at the Fun in the Park event during the Christmas holiday season. Victoria has been a volunteer ambassador for the Chamber of Commerce for over 20 years. And she is not the only volunteer to help Moe Ammar run one of the most active chambers on the Monterey Peninsula. If you go into the chamber office any day of the week, you will see Diane Garrison, or Marlyn Andreas, or Dee Boyer or Michelle Niesses, or Margaret Stewart (Volunteer of the year in 2018) or many others just giving of their time to help the chamber. And who can forget Nadine Annand, who volunteered for 57 years until her death at age 99?

The really remarkable things is that people don't just volunteer for big events or organizations. Pacific Grove also has neighborhoods where residents go out and pull weeds in the park across from their house; where individuals or a couple of friends walk around picking up trash along the streets of their neighborhoods, around the schools, on the outside fence of the golf course, or even along the Recreation Trail. There is no formal program for this community spirit; people just do it!

The point is, if you see refuse lying around in your neighborhood, you can call Public Works—though it won't be high on their priority list. You can also grouse about it. Or, grab a bag, call a neighbor to help, and clean the neighborhood yourself. Your neighborhood will be better for it, you will feel better, and your neighbors will appreciate what you are doing.

City Events Bring People Together

Pacific Grove residents and visitors have a variety of annual events to look forward to: Good Old Days, the Feast of Lanterns, the Butterfly Days, and the Fourth of July and Christmas celebrations at Caledonia Park. Then there are the Car Week events: The Little Car Show, the Worldwide Auctioneers Pacific Grove Auction, the P.G. Rotary Concours Auto Rally.

City events serve to bring the community together and allow strangers to become friends in a comfortable setting. The fact that people come from other cities to participate—and leave money in our stores and restaurants—doesn't hurt either.

Pacific Grove wouldn't be Pacific Grove without the monarch butterflies, the Butterfly Parade, Good Old Days, and certainly not without Feast of Lanterns. Every year members of the city council get introduced to the

Royal Court—a welcome break from all the serious business of running a city. Every year the council gets to meet a group of young people who take on a role representing the city, making presentations around the city and elsewhere, developing poise, professionalism, and their public speaking abilities.

The Saga of Brokaw Hall

Brokaw Hall, located in the middle of the Monarch Sanctuary, was a lightning rod issue around 2011. This building had been built in 1914 and used for a time as housing for instructors at the former Del Monte Military Academy in the 1920s. It was then used as shelter for a forestry work camp in the 1930s.

The city came into possession of the building through the acquisition of the Monarch Sanctuary through the Butterfly Bond in the 1990s. By then, the building was being used as a rental duplex. The owner announced plans to build condos or apartments on the land that provided a winter home for the monarch butterflies. In response to that, a group was formed to figure out a way to buy the property. They were able to put a bond issue on the ballot, and passage of this bond made it possible for the city to purchase the property.

But what to do with the now-empty building sitting near the butterfly clustering sites? It had been added on the city's Historic Resources Inventory list, but because of its remote location and a lack of funding at the time, the building had not been maintained. The city was in dire financial straits from 2007 to about 2012. For some time the city had been cutting back on staff and other expenses significantly; dropping from 238 employees in 2007 to only 130 in 2011.

Unfortunately, an empty building will quickly deteriorate and become difficult to rehabilitate—and Brokaw Hall was no exception. By the time members of the council and city staff went in to look at it in late 2011, they had to wear hard hats and breathing masks for their own safety. Cobwebs and mold abounded, and the inside looked decidedly fragile.

Some members of the community wanted us to save Brokaw Hall, but it was now a hazard. The council did respond to the requests to save it, though, and asked for estimates to fix it up or replace it. The cost was staggering. Part of that was because it would have to be made ADA compliant. This would have required a complete overhaul of the building and a redesign of the entire sanctuary.

A city has to make good decisions about where to spend limited resources, and at the time P.G. had very limited resources. One of those decisions was whether to save a building that no one would use or increase the city library's operating hours. The council made the latter decision because the library staff and open hours had already been dramatically reduced. The situation at the library was reaching a critical point.

The upshot of the demolition of Brokaw Hall, though, was that the city was able to clean up the path in the sanctuary, which created a more expansive Monarch Sanctuary in which residents were able to now put in nectar plant beds for the butterflies that visit us each year. The city was also able to build an ADA compliant path through the sanctuary, with rope barriers to keep people from trampling the underbrush and the butterflies. The bond, by the way, was paid off in 2017.

Some of the nectar beds in the Monarch Sanctuary.

The Pump House

Another similarly contentious issue faced the council in 2014 and 2015, when the city had to make a decision about an old, abandoned pump station owned by Cal-Am. Some of the senior officials from California American Water approached the city to let us know that they had no use for the building, but they didn't know what to do with it. It sat in the middle of a five-way intersection and had been run into by at least one car, visibly damaging the structural integrity of the building. Cal-Am was justifiably concerned about liability if another motorist ran into the building and was hurt.

The building itself was small, only about 860 square feet in size, and was located at the center of a roundabout at the intersection of Sinex Avenue, Eardley Avenue and 9th Street. It had been built in the 1930s as an unreinforced masonry building, and Cal-Am had inherited the building in 2008, when they took over the old Monterey County Water Works company.

Though it had been operated as a "Valve House" by the old company, by 2013 all of the pump equipment had been modernized and placed behind the fences at Cal-Am's David Avenue Reservoir site. Cal-Am was no longer using it. In other words, it was old, abandoned, of no practical use, and was becoming derelict. The landscaping around the building was still attractive, but the building itself had deteriorated—some due to neglect, but much due simply to the age of the building and the fact that it had been hit by a car.

Again several residents came forward and wanted to save the building because they felt it was a significant historic building. The city did investigate; conducting a thorough, 42-page study before issuing a Pump House Historic Demolition Permit. Now, such a study is not that simple a task. Staff had to look at all angles and aspects of the building: its history, how it affected the local environment, its aesthetics, biological resources, if it contained hazardous materials, etc.

Even after the Demolition Permit was issued, some people still wanted to save it. They suggested moving it somewhere else and fixing it up. But then what? The council continued to look at uses for the building and could find nothing practical.

The council did consider having the city's Public Works Department use the building as a place to store equipment and supplies. But the employees who would have to park in the middle of an intersection to load and unload these supplies were more than a little concerned about the risk of working in the middle of an intersection. In addition, part of the study that staff conducted also pointed out that it would cost hundreds of thousands of dollars to restore the building to a structurally sound state. On top of that, the residents who actually lived in that area wanted a park-like traffic circle instead.

After a lot of debate and study, the decision was made to knock down the building and turn the property into a park with some metal art pieces and a sign in the middle to commemorate the site of the old pump house. Several residents in that neighborhood have told the council that they appreciate the new park and that it has made traffic in that area much safer.

Picture of the Park in the intersection.

A Happy Ending at Lovers Point

But not all encounters with historic buildings end in them being knocked down and replaced. The Beach House restaurant at Lovers Point is an example of a historic resource that continues to prosper and thrive.

The history of this building traces back to 1902, when the city bought the property then known as Pacific Grove Beach from the Pacific Improvement Company. Sometime after that a man by the name of William S. Smith "strolled among the flowers, the sea scents, the slight fog, the boulders … rubbing his eyes and thinking how best to use the property."

Mr. Smith had previously built a small building in which the modest people of the time could change from their street clothes into swimming duds. They could then go down to the small cove below the building and splash in the water. Even though the building was only considered a shack, many people used it and it became quite a successful venture, earning him the nickname "Bathhouse" Smith.

It became so popular, in fact, that Bathhouse Smith decided that the cove was too small. So he leased several mules and hauled some dynamite to the cove, setting it into strategic places. Then, according to the *Cedar Street Times*, in the "early hours of a crystalline morning" he set off an explosion and "expanded" the cove.

Later, he built a Japanese teahouse, planted a bunch of flowers and shrubs, and hired the Sugano family to run the operation. They were to "brew savory teas to serve with sweetened biscuits."

In 1948 the tea garden and bath house were torn down and replaced by another building, which became Slats restaurant in the 1960s and 70s. A complete remodel then turned this into The Old Bath House restaurant, which operated until 2005 when it, too, closed.

Mark Farina painting of the Beach House restaurant, presented to the city by developer Robert Enea.

Council member Rudy Fischer recalls, "Around 2011 I remember going through the old building with Jim Becklenberg, our Director of Finance at the time. We were at an event at Lovers Point and he told me he had the keys and asked if I wanted to see the inside. I jumped at the chance and had one of the eeriest experiences of my life. I told my wife later that it felt like walking through the Titanic. The shelves at the back of the bar still had all of the bottles on them, and there were still drink glasses on the bar, their contents evaporated long ago. Many of the tables were still set with silverware and napkins still folded into peaks, though now covered with a great deal of dust. The kitchen still had pots, pans, and baking sheets sitting as if just waiting to be used."

But the building had sat empty for more than six years and it took two restauranteurs and a developer with courage and vision to take it on as a project. Over a long period of time, the city worked out a lease and they went to work fixing it up by expanding the building and making it ADA compliant. They also reversed the bar so patrons can now look out on the bay, and added an outdoor patio that is protected from the wind and covered with solar panels, which provide the restaurant with a good part of the electricity it uses.

As part of the project, the developers also put in showers for the Children's Pool and public restrooms on the ground floor. This allowed the city to remove the old restrooms that had been in the park, getting rid of an eyesore and enhancing the beauty of the open expanse of parkland.

The restaurant now has a small area below available for breakfast or lunch. The owners worked with the Coastal Commission for two years to obtain approval to use it as a coffee shop in the morning, finally agreeing not to open until 9:00 .m., when the park starts to come alive anyway. This café is now open for people visiting the beach or going for a walk or bike ride along the Rec Trail.

One can only imagine if Julia Platt were alive today, she would go there every morning, check her email, and enjoy a coffee while looking out at the bay she helped to save.

Helping to Solve Our Water Problems

One of the responsibilities of being a member of the city council is to serve as P.G.'s representative on one regional organization or other, which gives an opportunity to do things that benefit all of Monterey County. These include organizations such as Fort Ord Reuse Authority (FORA), the Association of Monterey Bay Area Governments (AMBAG), the Transportation Agency for Monterey County (TAMC), and others.

One such organization is Monterey One Water (M1W), dedicated to helping solve the water needs in our area. Our whole region faced multiple problems that threatened the Monterey Peninsula's water supply. The state had issued an order telling Cal-Am to reduce the amount of water it takes from the Carmel River by about two-thirds. At the same time, the water drawn from the Seaside aquifer is set to decline by more than half. The state also experienced a five year drought from 2012 to 2017. All of these things created an obvious problem to be solved.

The group realized that a great deal of already-treated water from the wastewater plant was allowed to flow to the ocean. Cleaning that water further, along with other sources of water, could provide a good portion of the water the Peninsula needs. It would require a significant amount of money to do that, but then state funds became available. M1W put together plans and applied for the loan funds, eventually receiving an $88 million 1% loan from the state—as well as $25 million in grants.

Many factors came together to make this happen. The Marina Coast Water District, the City of Salinas, the Monterey County Water Resources Agency, and the Fort Ord Reuse Authority all pledged support for the project. The California Public Utilities Commission also approved a three-way water purchase agreement whereby M1W sells the water to the Water District which, in turn, sells it to Cal-Am. This was regional cooperation at its best.

A lot of people said M1W couldn't or shouldn't do this project, but it turns out that it will eventually produce between one-third and one-half of the water the Peninsula needs. Moreover, it will be produced in an environmentally beneficial way.

The Pure Water Monterey Groundwater Replenishment Project is designed to produce 3,500 acre feet per year (afy) of highly purified water. This is then sent to an injection well and put into the ground to replenish the Seaside Groundwater Basin. This allows Cal-Am to reduce the water it takes from the river by that amount, also reducing the amount of water that needs to be treated by desalination.

The overall project also allows for a "drought reserve" of 1,000 acre feet, which will involve putting an extra 200 acre feet per year into the aquifer until that 1.000 AF goal is reached. That will then remain there to be drawn out in dry years if needed. All of the work will allow M1W to produce water by June of 2019.

It is important to note that the agency is not doing this by itself, but is working with close partners: the Monterey Peninsula Water Management District (MPWMD) and the Marina Coast Water District (MCWD), as well as state agencies and Cal-Am—the eventual recipient and distributor of the water to Monterey Peninsula water customers. This did not just happen; but is the result of a lot of negotiation with water partners and the eventual customer, Cal-Am.

Almost as soon as the funding came through, several groups asked if the size of the water project could be expanded. After looking at this, a plan was put together and, if the desal plant does not get up and running in time,

Pure Water Monterey will be able to expand and provide more water.

Listening to the Public: Parking Lots and Memorial Benches

The council and city staff had been looking to change the hours that people could park in the city-owned parking lot behind Lighthouse Cinemas. The city wanted to leave some of the parking as open 24 hours a day, but also planned to convert more spaces into two and three hour parking.

What was happening at the parking lot is that many of the people who work at the stores and restaurants downtown during the day park there and walk to work. Then, when they go home, other people come in to park for the evening shifts at the restaurants, B-and-Bs and hotels. The council wasn't aware of this and was just thinking about restaurant and movie theater patron parking until one nearby resident, Dixie Layne, informed us about the rhythm of activity. Hearing from a citizen who knew the full story allowed the council to develop a much better policy that accommodated the needs of everyone.

A few years ago the city decided to clean up the list of memorial benches. This program allows people to lease a bench for $250 and inscribe the names of people they wish to memorialize, and the city maintains it for five years. If the lease isn't renewed after five years, the name is dropped from the bench.

This process usually works well, but once in a while, a name falls through the cracks. Such was the case with Sally Griffin. Sally had founded the local Meals on Wheels program, and the Sally Griffin Active Living Center on Jewell Avenue is named after her. She had a passion and concern for senior citizens and raised almost a million dollars toward building the center; which provides meals for seniors and those who are homebound. The organization has a host of volunteers who put meals together and deliver them to people from Marina in the north to Carmel Highlands in the south and Carmel Valley to the east. Many homebound seniors depend on Meals on Wheels for nutrition and socialization.

Sally had also been fairly prominent in the P.G. community and was the first female member of the Kiwanis Club, a social services organization which has a mission of "improve the lives of children and their communities." So the council contacted the Kiwanis Club so that they could save her bench for at least another five years.

A recent survey found that the ratings for the Pacific Grove city council are 50% "favorable and somewhat favorable" versus 31% "unfavorable." These favorable rankings are higher than those for governments of many other cities.

Most of what the council does is setting policy, and people generally don't see the direct impact of that on their lives. What they do see is how the city operates—if the roads are in good shape, whether the streetlights work, and if the city if kept clean and safe. The city of P.G. is rolling out some major initiatives that are going to do even more—fixing up parts of Fountain, and 14th. streets, and repairing Pine Avenue and rebuilding Congress Avenue from David Avenue to Sunset Drive. The city will also slurry seal miles of road surfaces in the next several years and will be fixing up the coastal areas and the parks.

Making Changes for Today's Needs

Often there were good reasons why something was done a certain way years before. It met a need at the time. But sometimes conditions and circumstances change and things have to be managed differently.

Examples of what the council has accomplished:

—**Protecting Wildlife**: Although the city long had a plan in place to protect nursing harbor seals, there was neither ordinance nor a plan for protecting these local animals. The council finally put that ordinance into place in November of 2013 and instituted penalties for people who interfere with protected wildlife, especially during the pupping season. Through our own liberal interpretation of California Coastal Commission rules, the city was able to use fencing along the Rec Trail to provide a high level of protection to the harbor seals at this vulnerable time. The city had put in an application with the Coastal Commission, but was unwilling to wait for a decision and so the fence was erected despite the lack of approval. The Coastal Commission later said "good job" and approved the permit.

—**Improving Business**: After many years of restrictions on expanding the cities hotels, motels, and bed and breakfast inns, the citizens of Pacific Grove passed Measure U to allow those places to update and expand their properties. Several of them have since added more rooms and fixed up their properties.

—**Municipal Code**: Through the work of the Planning Commission, the city greatly streamlined the permit approval process in Pacific Grove, wrote common sense language around secondary units and windows, updated building fire codes for downtown, changed parking limit times in most areas of downtown, and updated the business license ordinance.

After a lot of work on the part of both the City Council and the Planning Commission, a new downtown sign ordinance was approved at the end of 2013. This includes graphics that make it easier to understand and use the city's policy; it streamlines the process and provides for "over the counter" review and approval. Right now the ordinance applies to just downtown Pacific Grove, but eventually streamlined sign ordinances will be enacted for the Forest Hill, Central Avenue and American Tin Cannery areas.

—Tree Ordinance: After many years of a very controversial and divisive tree ordinance that required a two-for-one replacement in the case of tree removal and punitive measures if it wasn't done correctly, the council pushed through a policy that lets people control their own yards and doesn't punish people for liking trees. This policy calls for a one-for-one replacement of trees removed (though you are free to add more if you wish), took out the criminal clauses, and brought penalties in line with the Municipal Code. This is a much more "people friendly" policy which allows residents much more discretion on what they do with their own yards.

As part of this effort, the city hired consultants to look at P.G.'s 26,000 trees and the health of our urban forest. This study found that the Asilomar Dunes is the largest plantable area in the city, and George Washington Park is the nexus (center) of our urban forests. The city is now looking at putting in place a continuous planting program that would plant a certain number of trees each year so that the city will always have some young trees as well as older ones.

—Infrastructure: In order to meet environmental compliance requirements, in the last few years the city has replaced ten or more miles of sewer and storm drain lines; with more to come in future years. As part of this effort, the city also rebuilt many of its pump stations, giving P.G. a more solid infrastructure that should last for many years. While not sexy, what goes on underneath the streets of the city is very important, and the council has committed to making necessary improvements. Much of this work will also keep pollution from running into the bay, protecting the wildlife there.

Included in this project was a major sewer and storm drain replacement project around Sinex Avenue, Gibson Avenue, 14th Street and Junipero Avenue. The infrastructure was very old, some parts dating to 1911. There were collapsing pipes, as well as potential cross contamination from the sewer lines to the storm drain lines. Since these latter run down to Greenwood Park and the ocean, this had serious repercussion in keeping pollutants out of the ocean and in maintaining clean water for swimmers at Lovers Point.

This was a huge undertaking and was paid from several sources, both Pacific Grove budgeted funds and state grants. The city also expanded two dry weather diversion storm drain outfalls near the Hopkins Marine Station and at the Monterey Bay Aquarium, part of which is in the Pacific Grove city limits.

Recently several state agencies issued orders on how cities need to handle stormwater that goes into the ocean. These new orders have created major headaches for cities throughout California, but because Pacific Grove started working on these issues ten years ago, installing five capture and diversion (CDS) units from the aquarium to Lovers Point, our city is way ahead of most others in meeting these requirements. The CDS units create a trash and pollution barrier, and much of the stormwater heading to the ocean is captured, treated, and diverted to the Monterey One Water pollution control plant in Marina.

—Sidewalks: The "High Hats and Parasols" column of the March 2011 edition of the *Cedar Street Times* quoted from a 1911 newspaper: "In 1911 Pacific Grove enjoyed few paved roads, fewer paved sidewalks. The laxness of the town council prompted private citizens to take up the cause." Over 100 years later, and with external funding now available to add to our own, the city is making a concerted effort to rectify this situation. Over the next several years the city will fill in the gaps in the sidewalk network on the main streets of Pacific Grove.

Walking has become more and more recognized as a basic form of transportation, and something that contributes to improved health and fitness for a city's residents. Virtually every trip that a person undertakes, regardless of his or her eventual mode of travel, has a walking component. And walking constitutes a higher percentage of trips taken in dense urban areas: downtowns, around schools and colleges, and in areas where public transit is an important way of getting around.

As part of the "Safe Routes to School" effort, the Public Works department will be spending $60,000 per year for about 10 years to put in ADA-compliant ramps and to add or repair sidewalks where they are needed. Some 1,500 linear feet of sidewalks have already been repaired and 200 ADA-compliant curb ramps at the corners of sidewalks have been installed. The city has also replaced about half of the burned-out street lights in Candy Cane Lane, with more to come.

—Golf Course: After some delays, lights in the Municipal Golf Course parking lot have been installed for safety in the evenings. The city has contracted with CoureCo, a major golf course management company, to manage the city's golf course in a professional manner. Several years ago a new sign was put up at the entrance to the course with the words "All Are Welcome" prominently displayed. Because of the look of the clubhouse, and the location of the links next to the ocean, some people previously thought it was a private club and wouldn't venture in. The course is looking good, still has discount cards for locals, and is operating at a high level of professionalism.

—**The Local Water Project**: In December of 2017 a three-year project was completed to plan, design, construct, and commission our own Local Water Project to convert waste water to non-potable water for use on the golf course. Doing so frees up to 125 acre feet of water for the Carmel River and other uses. Since this water is less expensive than potable water from Cal-Am, it also saves the golf course a great deal of money,

As a result, the city has taken over the Cal-Am meter that feeds the golf course, and two other meters have been eliminated. Those meters provided water to the front nine holes of the golf course and are no longer needed. The greens will still need to be flushed on occasion, but with limited experience with recycled water, it's unclear how often this will need to be done.

—**City expenditures**: The FY 17/18 $23.6 million budget is on-track for the city to maintain a balanced budget. The proposed FY 18/19 budget shows $25 million in expenditures with about $23 million in revenue. This extra $2 million draw down from our General Fund is a one-time event to fund Capital Improvement Projects to start on some much needed infrastructure work.

—**To revitalize downtown** the city has rolled out a Façade Improvement Program to great success. Some of the businesses downtown are already looking better; and the program is being renewed for the coming year. At the same time, a downtown improvement/flower basket program is in place, as well as new trash containers. As part of the general improvements, new and improved newspaper racks are in the works.

(continued on next page)

Making of the Pacific Grove Little Free Carnegie Library
Donald Livermore with Bill Pagano

I was approached by Cathy (Cathleen) Gable, from P.G. Friends of the Library—and Built for Books visionary, creator and program developer—to consider building a Little Free Library book box replica of the original Carnegie Library in P.G., circa 1908. It would be for a silent auction fund raiser for the planned remodeling of the library. I said I'd think about it but did not commit. After receiving an old 1930s record player stand and a bookshelf from the Holman home, I thought about constructing a miniature rendition of the original library, using wood from those items.

I enlisted my neighbor, Bill Pagano, to help with some of the design features. Bill is a detail guy and took on the windows, doors, and roof like a trooper. He did an outstanding job on much of the finish work. Cathy came by a few weeks later to say hello and check out one of our many little free libraries in our neighborhood. She also kind of apologized for putting me on the spot about building one for the Friends of the Library. At that point—and almost complete—I showed her what we had done. She was thrilled to say the least. I had planned to drop it off at the library but she offered to pick it up later for the upcoming 110th library birthday celebration. It is truly one of a kind and a local treasure for whoever wins the bidding.

Don and Bill's beautifully rendered Little Free Carnegie Library will be on display—and filled with books to borrow—outside City Hall, at the entrance to the Youth Center.

Cathy Gable, Little Free Carnegie Library visionary.

The Little Free Carnegie Library made its first appearance at the 110th anniversary party of the Pacific Grove Public Library in 2018. It is now on display at City Hall, near the Youth Center. Above is the cake served at the celebration. Photos Patricia Hamilton.

WHERE CITIZENS MAKE A DIFFERENCE

Elected and appointed officials rely on the citizens of our city to do their part.

10 THINGS YOU CAN DO TO HELP YOUR COMMUNITY

1. Get to know your neighbors. Just introduce yourself or ask them out for coffee. Keep an eye on each other's house when one of you goes on a trip. Pull your neighbors trash can in when it is in the street. Make your neighborhood a more pleasant place.
2. Shop local. Buying at your local stores supports people in your community. You can often find items you won't find at the huge mall, and you may run into a neighbor and rekindle a friendship—or start a new one.
3. Attend council meetings. Attending a meeting or two will give you a different perspective and a great deal of information on what is happening in your community.
4. Become involved in civic events by volunteering to serve on a board or commission. Whether serving on a city board or commission, or just helping out at a city event, you can help make your community a better place to be; and serving on a city body will expose you to issues in-depth and allow you to influence developments in your city.
5. Figure out what your community needs and look into what it would take to put that in place. Then, prepare a talk to give at an event or a city council meeting to see if others are interested in your project. Take on a project and drum up support.
6. Just help out. We have lots of events to raise money—for a cause, to clean up a beach or park, to improve a school. Look for what interests you.
7. Volunteer with an established organization in your community. Whether it is putting together food packages at Meals on Wheels, serving meals to the homeless, helping at the St. Vincent De Paul thrift shop or the American Cancer Society's Discovery Shop, or working at an animal shelter, you can meet potential new friends while helping others.
8. If you see trash or graffiti in your community, pick it up or clean it off. Your neighborhood will be cleaner, you will get some exercise and get to know your neighbors better.
9. Attend community events. You can usually find information about fairs, parades, and special events in the newspaper or online. Even if you just show up to walk around at Good Old Days or another event, you add to the crowd and let others know that this is important and you care.
10. If you are a business person, sponsor a youth team or a scout troop. Local teams are always in need of money for uniforms and equipment. Work with your employees to make a team feel recognized; while at the same time helping their kids be kids.

Most of all—just enjoy living in our little woodsy city by the sea!

Asilomar beach. Photo Wolf Bukowski.

What's That Old Barn Doing Here?
Mimi Sheridan

Anyone familiar with downtown Pacific Grove has probably noticed the old barn on Laurel Avenue, just west of City Hall. Ketcham's Barn sticks out like a sore thumb among the city buildings and neatly-painted houses. How did it get there and, perhaps more importantly, how did it come to still be here in 2018? The answer is vivid testimony to persistence and voluntarism, and dedication to Pacific Grove's history.

The barn's origins are somewhat mysterious, according to extensive research by the Pacific Grove Heritage Society. Mrs. I.A. Hill of Salinas bought the property from the Pacific Improvement Company in 1886 and, in 1890, sold it to J. H. Ketcham. He lived in Monroe County, New York, and evidently never lived in Pacific Grove. The barn was most likely built in 1892 and, soon afterward, in 1893, Ketcham sold the property to Celia Dickinson Smith. Her son, E. Cooke Smith, a prominent banker and realtor, is said to have used it for his horse and buggy. These were only the first in a long chain of owners, as the property changed hands ten more times before it was purchased by the city in 1980.

City ownership made sense because it was surrounded by City Hall and other city properties. But what would the city do with a rather decrepit old barn? Some thought a parking lot was the ideal use, despite the fact that it was listed in the Pacific Grove Historic Inventory.

At this point, the Heritage Society stepped up. Although it had been founded in 1975, the group had no home of its own. Meetings rotated from one member's home to another, and its archives had no permanent place. Under the leadership of President Lila Staples, the Society proposed that it lease the barn for use as an administrative and historic center and, in turn, help the City renovate the building. In June 1980, they signed a 20-year lease.

The Society, with its minimal budget, had taken on a tremendous task: to renovate and maintain the building and to raise the needed funds—estimated at $20,000. Fortunately, the members and the entire Pacific Grove community were equal to the task. Engineers and architects donated plans and expertise. Steve Honegger took on the role of contractor. Numerous people and businesses gave goods or labor, including lumber, plumbing, roofing, painting, electrical and mechanical equipment and even a flagpole. Foundation grants, individual and business donations, and funds from a rummage sale and home tours helped to meet the goal.

Finally, in April 1981, construction began. It was a big

job. The structure had to be reinforced and insulation and sheet rock installed on the interior. There was only one window and door, so more were installed to bring in light. The second story gained a new floor and stairs to replace the ladder. Although it had water and electricity, a bathroom and new lighting were needed.

Work proceeded amazingly quickly. The grand opening was held on October 18, 1981, only 6 months after construction began and 16 months after the lease had been signed. The final cost was $27,381.86 for the renovation plus $6,625,51 for furnishings, display cabinets and a fire alarm system.

However, something was missing. Once the barn was renovated, the vacant lot next door cried out for attention. In 1982, the parcel was added to the lease, and the Society set out once again to plan and raise funds for a major project. Donations of labor, planning and money allowed the park to be completed in 1984 at a cost of nearly $10,000.

Heritage Park is no ordinary place. It is a tranquil retreat with a unique covered wishing well fountain surrounded by terraced beds lush with roses, perennials and shrubs. People often take advantage of the convenient benches to take a break and enjoy the flowers and the fountain.

Having an established location at long last transformed the Pacific Grove Heritage Society. They have significantly expanded their archives and photo collection. The barn is also a place where the people of Pacific Grove can easily come to see for themselves how their city began and how it has grown over time. The Society opens the barn every Saturday afternoon for people to see the exhibits and artifacts and learn about their own homes.

Note: The barn's history was first published in the Fall 2006 edition of The Board and Batten, *the newsletter of the Heritage Society of Pacific Grove. This article is updated with additional information. Special thanks to Don Beals and Steve Honegger for their assistance. Learn more about Pacific Grove history and the Heritage Society at* www.pacificgroveheritage.org.

THE HERITAGE SOCIETY 2017 AWARDS – JEAN ANTON

191 Ocean View Boulevard—bronze award for Remodel Addition 2017

872 Laurel Avenue—bronze award for Preservation 2017

126 16th Street—bronze award for Preservation in 1993 and Certificate of Commendation for Remodel Addition in 2014

701 Congress—bronze award for Remodel Addition 2018

1142 Crest Avenue—bronze award for Remodel Addition

302 Monterey Avenue—bronze award for Remodel Addition 2018

The Farmer's Market: In the Beginning
Vicki B. Pearse

Farmers' markets are something special. I love them. So when John & I moved from Santa Cruz back to P.G. in 2003, we at once started going to the Tuesday market on Alvarado Street, riding our bikes on the Rec Trail, returning loaded with fresh fruits & veggies.

Fast-forward five years to the exciting prospect of a farmers' market in P.G.! Our very own local market. Was this for real? Where would it be? Who would operate it? As a member of Sustainable P.G. (S.P.G.), I became an active advocate.

In 2008, P.G. chose the non-profit Everyone's Harvest (EH) to run their community farmers' market on Lighthouse in the heart of downtown. This opportunity was a turning point for EH, leading to increased collaborations and partnerships around the County. It was also a turning point for P.G., as the market became a popular and important social hub. No longer was downtown P.G. empty and quiet on Monday afternoons. It was a new place, with a lively, festive atmosphere. Perfect, I thought. John and I quickly adopted a new weekly routine.

But people in P.G. love to squabble, and soon there were murmurs about the main street being closed to cars for even those few short hours. A movement emerged to push the market off Lighthouse. Was this for real? Where would it go? Again I was sucked in to represent S.P.G. I loved the market and was determined to see it continue and thrive. There followed a series of four long, excruciating meetings to work out a plan. Representatives of the city, the business community, EH, S.P.G., and the police argued and argued over various proposals. So many pieces had to fit—a central level site, traffic flow, safety, neighbors, and more. I began to despair that I'd lose my wonderful market because we'd never solve the puzzle.

Eventually, we did — *whew!* — and the solution was elegant and unique. In 2010 the Farmers' Market moved off Lighthouse and down to Central Avenue, where it has become the heart of a new center. Flanked by the Museum, the Library, and Jewell Park, it is today more vibrant than ever. Is this for real? Yes! Was my own job done? Well, no. My championing the market revealed my passion, and EH asked me to join their board of directors. So now I enjoy the market every week while also getting to participate in the ongoing development of its programs for education, health, and good eating, along with those of several other EH Farmers' Markets in Marina (the first, started by Iris Peppard as a college project!) and in Salinas.

Is the future of P.G.'s Market secure? We can't take that for granted. It occupies a central location for which there will always be competing pressures and interests. But the Farmers' Market belongs where it is, and I hope that all the members of our community get to continue to enjoy it into the future. —Everyone's Harvest Board Member

The Conviviality of Public Spaces
Maureen Mason

Many towns have a few historic public buildings and a little park, but few experience the vitality and energy created by the year-round Monday Pacific Grove Farmers Market.

Once Everyone's Harvest was relocated opposite the Natural History Museum, P.G. Public Library and Jewell Park, I became a regular Monday afternoon shopper. I've loved the opportunity to interact with the many organic farmers who've introduced me to new vegetables. They offer preparation advice, too, making this an unbeatable combination.

I've come to rely on the quality and freshness of fruits and vegetables available every Monday.

But the most unique part of my P.G. Farmers Market experience comes from the diversity of weekly community interactions: whether it's seeing families with young children playing in the park and picnicking, or volunteers campaigning about voter issues that affect the public, or local non-profits gathering donations, or people bringing their food scraps down to the market for composting, or people new to town engaging for the first time with those who live here—Everyone's Harvest Farmers Market provides a catalyst and a spark to keep the heartbeat of Pacific Grove strong.

At a time of much political polarity in our society, the P.G. Farmers Market also provides our community a safe space to engage with others in civil dialogue. Frankly, people who greet each other while purchasing fresh green vegetables or strawberries are unfailingly congenial to one another in spite of their political differences. Healthy food sited amidst an historic civic core nurtures all Pagrovians.   —Board Member, Everyone's Harvest

Bees pollinating rosemary bushes. Photo LeeAnn Stewart

PACIFIC GROVE FARMERS MARKET – CENTRAL & GRAND AVENUES

Photo John Pearse

Photo John Pearse

Photo Everyone's Harvest

Photo Everyone's Harvest

Photo Everyone's Harvest

ROTARY CLUB OF PACIFIC GROVE – DAVID A. LAWS

Celebrates 70 years of "Service Above Self"

Established in 1948, the Rotary Club of Pacific Grove has served the community for 70 years. From hands-on building projects to funding local youth and library programs, the Club has helped the needy, supported families, and promoted peace, harmony, and fun in our backyard and around the world. Some of the many activities that Rotary members have initiated or contributed to any include:

- Organizing the Rotary Invitational Track Meet at Pacific Grove High School since 1968.
- Managing the annual Good Old Days parade.
- Dramatic readings of the Declaration of Independence on the Fourth of July in Caledonia Park.
- Building the Little House in Jewell Park (and 50 years later rebuilding it to meet ADA standards).
- Restoring the gazebo in Jewell Park.
- Building Washington Park and elementary school playground equipment.
- Funding Sea Otter and Whale statues in Berwick Park, and signage at the Museum of Natural History.
- Donating manpower and funding to convert the auditorium at the Middle School into the Pacific Grove Performing Arts Center as a community show place.

Organizing the track meet

Building the little house.

Completed little house today.

Repainting and restoring the gazebo in Jewell Park.

Museum Signage. Rotary past presidents, Tom Greer and Tracy Perkins, left. Museum Director Jeanette Kihs, right

Performing Arts Center entrance.

The Sea Otter statue by Chris Bell.

- Staffing and funding Rotacare to provide free medical services for the uninsured.
- Preparing regular I-Help dinners for the homeless.
- Distributing dictionaries annually to all Pacific Grove third-grade students.
- Providing scholarships for college and leadership training to high-school seniors.
- These services are supported by distributions from the Pacific Grove Rotary Legacy Fund and grants from the national Rotary Foundation. The Fund is sustained by donations from Club members and two major annual fund-raising activities:
- A Beer and Wine Garden at the Good Old Days arts and crafts street fair.
- The Pacific Grove Rotary Concours Auto Rally, the first and one of the most popular free-to-spectators events during Monterey Car Week.

For more information about the Rotary Club of Pacific Grove, please see the website at www.pgrotary.org or contact the president or membership person listed on the home page.

Rotacare free medical services

I-HELP crew prepares dinner.

Dictionaries for P.G. third graders.

Good Old Days Beer Garden.

Mayor's Proclamation in Honor of the Rotary Club of Pacific Grove's 70th Birthday

WHEREAS, the Rotary Club of Pacific Grove was chartered in 1948 as a service club organization in the spirit of "Service Above Self," inspiring members to provide humanitarian service, encouraging high ethical standards, and promoting good will and peace in the world; and

WHEREAS, the Rotary Club of Pacific Grove has initiated and contributed to numerous community projects and events, such as refurbishing the Pacific Grove Middle School Auditorium into the Pacific Grove Performing Arts Center; the 1952 construction of and later remodeling of the "Little House in Jewell Park" gazebo; participation in the I-HELP program providing dinners for homeless men and women; coordination of the annual Good Old Days parade; and was the driving force behind the formation and management of the on-going weekly Peninsula Rotacare Free Medical Clinic; and

WHEREAS, the Rotary Club of Pacific Grove has supported the youth of our community through sponsorship of the annual PG High School track meet, held continuously since 1968; the annual donation of dictionaries to each 3rd grader in Pacific Grove elementary schools; and providing annual college scholarships to four PGHS seniors; and the proceeds of our Pacific Grove Auto Rally held for the last 23 years during Concours week have gone to numerous youth programs in our city; and

WHEREAS, the Rotary Club of Pacific Grove has brought funding into our community through Rotary District grants, including recent projects such as signage for the pollination garden at the Pacific Grove Natural History Museum and support for necessities for homeless women served by the Gathering for Women; and

WHEREAS, the Rotary Club of Pacific Grove has worked with Rotary Clubs around the world to eradicate polio; has contributed to earthquake and fire relief efforts; and has supported Rotary Youth Exchange programs to help train the leaders of tomorrow to be active builders of a more peaceful world; and

WHEREAS, the Rotary Club of Pacific Grove now celebrates its long history of making positive, lasting change in communities at home and abroad; and

WHEREAS, the city of Pacific Grove recognizes and honors the many Rotary Club service projects benefitting our community over the past 70 years, I recognize the Rotary Club of Pacific Grove for all of their philanthropic endeavors geared toward making our community a better place to live and work; and

Therefore, I, Bill Kampe, Mayor of the City of Pacific Grove, do hereby proclaim June 19, 2018 as Rotary Day in Pacific Grove, and encourage all citizens to join me in extending gratitude and congratulations on behalf of the City to the Rotary Club of Pacific Grove on its birthday.

Bill Kampe
Bill Kampe, Mayor

Pacific Grove Rotarians who generously supported the publishing of this page in the Concours 2018 booklet: Evan Allen, David Dormedy, Jane Durant-Jones, John Goings, Richard Gray, Tom Greer, Lynda Johnson, Bill Kampe, Michael Laredo, Alex Lorca, Tracy Perkins, John Shuman, Ted Voigt.

Pacific Grove Concours Auto Rally
Friday, August 24, 2018

24ᵀᴴ Anniversary Celebration

PHOTO: Early Auto Rally meetings were held at Alan Cohen's Lighthouse Café, (now Holly's). Shown in this photo of the first Auto Rally committee, counterclockwise, Brandy Falconer, Alex Rodriguez, John Sutton, (unidentified), Ray Ching, Jim Watts, Mike McNally, Dana Annereau, Jeanne Byrne, David Dormody, Ray Byrne, Steve Covell, Alan Cohen, John Clark, Judy, John Qualia.

Congratulations and a hearty thank you to all the committee members, volunteers, sponsors and advertisers who have participated over the last 24 years! This charitable event has been an immense joy and could only have been this successful because of you. Thank you all!

The twenty-fourth annual Pacific Grove Concours Auto Rally, which has raised more than $300,000 for youth programs on the Monterey Peninsula, will be held on Friday, August 24, 2018. Each year the event takes place on Friday of the Concours d'Elegance weekend at Pebble Beach and the Rolex Monterey Motorsports Reunion at Laguna Seca.

The Pacific Grove Concours Auto Rally is geared for people who own and drive their own classic and vintage cars. The rally draws 200+ participants and 5,000 spectators line the rally route.

This year's event marks the organizational transition from Pacific Grove Youth Action to Pacific Grove Rotary.

The Pacific Grove Concours Auto Rally was started in 1995 as a fund raiser in support of the Pacific Grove Youth Center and other youth programs. Pacific Grove Rotary joined P.G. Youth Action nine years ago as a 50% partner for the rally organization. P.G. Rotary has provided volunteers and board member support.

Additional information about the rally may be obtained by calling 831-372-3861 or online at www.pgautorally.org. Registration forms may be downloaded from the web site. Hotel and other visitor information are available by contacting the Pacific Grove Chamber of Commerce at 1-800-656-6650.

Pacific Grove Rotary ♦ P.G. Concours Auto Rally P.O. Box 51453, Pacific Grove, CA 93950, 831-372-3861

EXECUTIVE COMMITTEE

John Shuman - Event Chair
Matt Bosworth - Treasurer
Jeanne Byrne – Director
Vic Johnson – Director
Steve Covell – Director
Mike Milliorn – Director
Lindsay Munoz - Director
Executive Assistants – Patti McCarty and Carol Fuessenich

COMMITTEE MEMBERS

Ray Byrne, Scott Emmett, Richard Gray, Arleen Hardenstein, Lynda Johnson, Steve McCulloch, Bruce Obbink, Tracy Perkins, Patrick Ryan, Nate Steen

PERSONAL REMINISCENCES

Then and Now
Judy Wills

As I was growing up, every other summer my family would come to Pacific Grove from New York to visit my maternal grandparents. Struggling to survive in Nebraska during the Depression, grandfather and grandmother made the decision to go west. They packed their five children into the car and headed to California. They settled in the Monterey Peninsula area. My grandfather had many different jobs. One that stands out was his partnership in the Cerney and Vachal grocery store in the Oak Grove area. He would tell us stories about the Cannery Row winos sitting out back drinking the wine, just like in the Steinbeck novels. Grandfather was also the store superintendent of Holman's Department store for many years. I will be forever thankful my grandparents lived here and introduced us to such an idyllic spot.

Every visit here, my sister, my four brothers and I would badger my mom until we got to cross the street and go to the beach. My grandparents lived right across from Hopkins Marine Station Beach, which is closed now for research and harbor seal habitat. But back then it was open to the public. We felt it was our own secluded beach because no one else would be there. We would search for shells and hermit crabs – I especially liked the olive shells because we did not see those on the east coast. The water was very cold, but we did not care; we had to go in – it was summer! We all still love the ocean, and my siblings are drawn to Pacific Grove each Thanksgiving for our annual family reunion. Though these days none of us go swimming, we do go whale watching, kayaking and birding instead.

As a child walking past the small houses in the retreat area, I told myself that one day I would live in P.G. and buy one of those houses. Well, I did manage to get back to P.G., but not to buy one of the retreat houses. Having owned a two-hundred-year-old home in NY made me realize how much work went into the upkeep of older homes. After visiting my parents in California, my husband and I fell in love with Pacific Grove. We decided to move here and it was the best decision of our married life. Now, every day as I walk along the ocean path, I smell the tangy salty ocean breeze and the memories from my childhood come swarming back. It's only half a mile, as well as half a century, to my grandparents' house.

The Mermaid on the Garage
Devora Stark

In every quaint historical Victorian, in every fifties mid-century modern, in every sixties apartment building, in every place where people live in Pacific Grove, there is a story to tell. Wandering through our town I wonder about those stories and how people came to live here, and especially how they chose to paint their houses in such charming combinations.

My house is a two-story nondescript stucco. It does not have much character. No, it *didn't have* much character when it was brand new and I moved in thirty years ago. Walking around my neighborhood, I noticed an adobe house with a lovely painting of a super-sized California poppy curving around the window. That was my inspiration. Murals in general are enriching and entertaining. I wanted one. But I am not an artist, so for many years I asked every artist I knew, and even called the high school to ask if it could be a project for an art class. No luck. I watched as the mural on the recreation trail came to be, thinking that someday a mural might happen at my house.

One serendipitous afternoon in Moss Landing, my friend from Santa Cruz and I encountered an enchanted house. There were shells in the yard and paintings on all the surfaces. There were glass bottles glittering on a tree. "I wish I knew the person who lives here," I sighed.

That very evening my friend called to tell me that there was a full page article in the Santa Cruz Sentinel with pictures of that Moss Landing house, which belonged to an artist, Nancy Russell. To my surprise, I was acquainted with that woman through a mutual friend. This was a sign. The mural was meant to be. When we talked, Nancy was enthusiastic about the idea.

Of course Pacific Grove required an ocean scene. I like to swim, and so as a child I identified with mermaids. Nancy painted a mural with a mermaid on my garage. Small mirrors make the mermaid glitter, and she has brown hair like me.

My house is no longer nondescript. There is a mermaid that greets anyone who passes by. Just like me, she is thankful to live in Pacific Grove.

The House My Father Built
Judy Avila

When I was eight years old, back in our little village in the Azores, Portugal, I remember my father receiving a letter from his brother, John, who lived in California. My uncle asked if he would like to come h elp build a new home in Pacific Grove, where he had just bought a lot. He lived in Richmond at the time and planned to retire in Pacific Grove someday. My uncle would pay all expenses my father incurred with this trip.

My father was a good carpenter, but wages on our island were so low that it was difficult to support a family of seven (a wife and five daughters). After much soul searching and with my mother's support, he decided to make the trip.

The house was built on Jewell Avenue and after fourteen months my father returned back to the Azores. Eight years later, in 1958, I arrived in Pacific Grove to spend some time with Uncle John and his wife, Aunt Mary, to attend school; another great opportunity they offered to me.

So I found myself living in the house my father had built. It meant a lot to see his initials: H. T. R. 1950–1951, engraved on the cement right outside of my bedroom. He had talked about this house and described it many times, but it was so much nicer than I anticipated. I had my own comfortable bedroom and bathroom, with hot water running in the faucet, a light switch instead of a kerosene lamp, and a gas stove and a fridge in the kitchen. Those were all luxuries which I had never had before. I had to pinch myself many times to make sure I was not in a dream. I could not thank my Lord enough for this gift in my life.

As much as I missed my parents and my sisters back home, I loved Pacific Grove and everything about it. I really wanted to remain here. A year and half later I was granted a permanent residency card. Again this was one of the greatest opportunities in my life. Now I could really grow roots in Pacific Grove, and call it home.

A few years later my husband and I were married, and we moved into a home he had purchased. This house was on 15th Street, right behind where the Lighthouse Theater is now. Soon after, we had to sell the house to the city of P. G. for the current parking lot construction, and this time we moved to Pine Avenue across from the fire department to a much nicer home. Four years later we started raising a family and needed a little more space. We moved to Lobos Avenue where we raised our two boys and still live. This has been a wonderful home.

Now our oldest son owns the house my father built, and whenever our extended family gathers together, it is usually there that we all meet. He and his wife remodeled it years ago and landscaped the yard, and they (and my two grandsons) generously welcome us. For me this house holds a lot of memories and I love the idea of our family enjoying it for generations to come.

Monarch Lane and Victorian Paint
Terry Piotrkowski

Our first Pacific Grove mailing address was 1155 Monarch Lane. Nestled in a pine grove was a tiny studio apartment that my husband and I shared with two friends and a mischievous German shepherd. Married all of three weeks, our first paycheck was still five weeks away. My student teaching assignment offered no pay—only college credit.

I still wonder where my husband heard about a very large Victorian on Central Avenue that needed to be painted. Why the owner hired three enthusiastic, energetic, and thoroughly unqualified young men who did not possess a paintbrush between them is still a mystery. Buckets of sage green paint sat on the front stairs. A generous cash advance provided brushes and sandpaper plus enough peanut butter and jelly to feed this optimistic trio (also the pup and me) as they labored to prep and paint. With no ladder available, a rope was slung over surrounding trees to hoist an unsteady painter in the air as the eaves went from white to green. Working from early morning till dusk, the task inched along slow and steady like the tortoise in that legendary race until, finally, that house was done…turned a warm green like the surrounding pines. Those boys fulfilled their verbal contract, returning home with cash enough to last!

Two of these laborers were new teachers and one a teacher's aide…with school starting regular pay would follow. It's been 47 years since that painting job. I pass by the house on Central Avenue often. It is still a deep sage green. I can't help but wonder about that generous stranger who saw three young men who needed a hand and were willing to tackle the job…did he see them dangling from that rope as they applied new paint to wood… did he smile at their method?

This example of kindness was how Pacific Grove welcomed us into the fold. Our two friends (and their pup) moved away but my husband and I stayed, teaching a combined 64 years in P.G. Schools. Like our precious Monarch Butterflies that journey home to Pacific Grove, Monarch Lane was where our journey began…in P.G. where we raised our children and now watch as our grandchildren grow up in *the last hometown*.

Helen and Rick Invite You to a Party!
Helen Ogden

I believe our first party was in 2003. The initial inspiration was one of the openings at the Pacific Grove Art Center. We began with small intimate gatherings prior to the openings, a chance to chat with a few friends over a glass of wine and some nibbles. Nothing fancy, cheese and bread, vegetables and dip, whatever looked good at Trader Joe's. Sometimes guests would contribute something too. When it was time we would all walk over to the PGAC, our de facto community center in P.G., the only place where the community gathers on a regular basis for pure enjoyment. Thus began what Rick and I like to think of as "soirées," though certainly not on the order of those from the days of Gertrude Stein, et al. Oh, to have been a fly on that wall!

The next logical extension of our soirées was an annual Christmas event—the tree trimming party. Both of us being height challenged, we joked that we needed tall people to help us put ornaments at the top of our tall tree. Our guest list, however, does not discriminate against those kindred spirits who also have to shorten their pants and cannot reach the treetop. Having a tree trimming party also gives us an excuse to buy a larger tree, always a real one, which I find so many people give up on once the kids are grown and have fledged.

We have ornaments aplenty, as we have been collecting mementos of our travels for the tree over many years. Not Christmas ornaments, per se, which are available in the ubiquitous "Christmas shops" that one finds around the world. We look for something more personal or emblematic. Some of my most treasured: the black shiny stone Rick picked up in Antarctica, the gold tassel from an abandoned overstuffed chair in a vacant lot in Delft, the small woven basket from Botswana, and the scallop shell we wore for our 500-mile walk on the Camino de Santiago. Some are treasured gifts, like the stuffed stocking trimmed in mink from Rick's grandmother's stole that no family member wanted to wear.

The Christmas party gives me an excuse to make cranberry-nut bread and for Rick to make a large pot of mulled wine, which he always starts with a cup of last year's batch, like a sourdough starter of sorts. It gets ladled it into our many "collectors' item" tacky Christmas mugs, our version of the tacky Christmas sweater. (Recipe: Equal amounts of fruity red wine and unfiltered apple cider, 3 oz., of commercially available mulling spice in a muslin bag or cheesecloth, brown sugar to taste, one whole orange studded with whole cloves. Heat to simmer. Do not boil. Serve hot.)

Houses in PG tend not to be large and it can be difficult to accommodate a crowd. And why is it that no matter how crowded, people always end up in the kitchen? There must be some law named for that phenomenon. In winter, it presents more of a challenge, but even in a typical P.G. summer staying warm keeps people from spreading outdoors.

Our summer tapas party has its origins in my connection with Spain, where I lived until I was seventeen.

Welcome Kaito!
Barbara Kraus
P.G. ESL Teacher

Barbara's son, his wife, and Kaito.

Pacific Grove has a lot of people who look like my grandson, Kaito. He came to P.G. from Japan in April with his parents to begin a new life. Kaito says in Japan almost everyone looks about the same. But here, everyone looks different!

But the most interesting and exciting thing that Kaito discovered is that there are many different languages here, too.

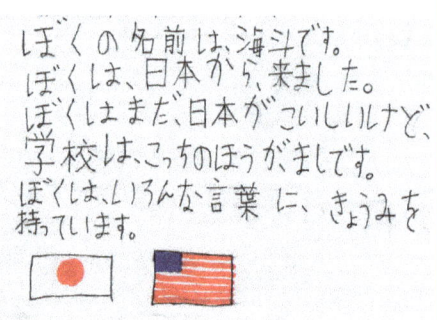
Kaito wrote his story in English and in Japanese, shown below.

In Forest Grove Elementary School there are students who speak French and Spanish and Arabic plus a few who speak Japanese and other languages. When Kaito meets someone, his first question is "What language do you speak?" The sounds of Spanish are particularly comforting to him because their vowels are clear and non-changing just like the vowels in Japanese. Being bilingual isn't enough for him! So he is studying Spanish and other languages on his mother's iPad whenever there is a little extra time in his day. Living in Pacific Grove has opened up a new world for my grandson. It is a world of diversity and acceptance. P.G. is the perfect place for Kaito.

I can't say that at that age I frequented tapas bars, but the tapas culture still took hold of me and evolved into an annual celebration of Spanish food. At first, we served just tapas of various kinds, and sangría of course. Rick's 70th birthday was the catalyst for adding a giant paella, his request, and now a requisite extension. The giant pan requires a giant burner, which requires outdoor cooking, which brings at least some guests outdoors despite the customary summer chill. One of my favorite tapas is 'tortilla española', which has nothing to do with Mexican tortillas. (Recipe: Cook one chopped onion and 3 sliced medium sized potatoes in plenty of olive oil until softened but not mushy. Let potato-onion mix cool. Mix 5-6 eggs with 2-3 tsp. salt in a large bowl. Add cooled potato mix to eggs and pour into preheated non-stick frying pan with enough olive oil to generously cover bottom of pan. Cook over medium to low heat until bottom is lightly browned and egg is beginning to set. Carefully flip tortilla on to a large plate and slide back into frying pan. Cook until lightly browned and egg is cooked through. Use wooden toothpick to test for doneness. It takes some practice to flip it, but it's worth it.)

Truth be told, the paella party is also an excuse to have two of my best and oldest friends, who also lived in Spain, come to visit for that weekend and lend a helping hand.

Our guest list is quite eclectic and, thankfully, always growing. You never know who you might be sitting next to, a scientist we've met over a glass of wine at a local tasting room, a musician we've met at a performance, a Trader Joe's employee with a friendly smile, a local writer, an artist, a teacher, a woodworker, a librarian, a doctor, a lawyer, but alas, no Indian chiefs—yet.

Though it is a lot of work to throw a party, like many things that take effort, the good bits are remembered and the dirty dishes are soon forgotten.

A Walk Back in Time
Ann Dee

As I walk up the steps and into the foyer of this beautiful old two-story house where I live, I am transported into another dimension in time.

Built in the Victorian era, the foyer is still furnished with chairs, side tables, a settee, and an old console radio of that time.

From time to time a cat made of cloth is mysteriously found sitting in a different spot in that foyer.

This house, built in 1915 on Central Avenue in Pacific Grove, CA, received its first residents then, who called it home.

This was in the Rag-Time Band era. Songs like 'Twilight, Twilight', 'Gunga Din', and John Philip Sousa's 'Stars and Stripes Forever' were some of music probably listened-to from this old radio that still sits here today.

It was the second half of World War One, and the Germans had launched a Zeppelin raid on England. Winston Churchill had resigned his post as First Lord Admiralty and rejoined the Army as Battalion Commander. America became allies with Great Britain.

War time songs like 'It's a long way to Tipperary', 'Over There', and 'Til We Meet Again' were reminiscent of everyone's emotional sentiment of that time.

Just a few years previously the first Model T Ford went into production in 1908.

When I take walks around my neighborhood, where most of the houses were built in the late 1800's and early 1900's, I wonder about the history of these old homes, and the people who lived there over a hundred years ago.

In 1915 women's fashions changed for the first time as the hemlines went up to mid calf. The bathing suits were now one piece suits, with arms exposed from the shoulder and legs exposed down to just above the knee.

Men's trousers were worn cuffed at the ankle and creased. A sport coat, vest, and bow tie were popular. Men were very seldom seen without a hat. The Fedora or flat top straw hats were commonly worn.

Little boys wore knicker pants at half calf, with suspenders, and button down shirts. The newsboy cap was popular back then too.

Little girls wore their dresses knee length, with stockings knee high. A popular style was loose at the waist with a sailor style collar. It was popular, too, to wear a big bow in the hair.

The cars, the fashions, and music have all changed, but as people have we changed that much from that time so long ago? I pondered that question.

As I continue my walk towards downtown Pacific Grove, I pass several churches built in the 1800's. I imagine horse drawn carriages, ladies in their long dresses with bustles, ornate hats, and gloves to their elbows. Men are wearing long tail coats with vests, and a top hat or a derby.

With the question of how have we changed still on my mind, I take my regular route down Central Avenue. I stop at the Library, built in 1906, and even in this day of electronic entertainment I am pleased to see the Library with people who are still avid readers of books.

I pass Jewell Park, where a boy is tossing a ball to his dog to fetch. Small groups of people are sitting on blankets with their picnic lunches. A group of people have gathered around the gazebo to listen to a young man who is playing lively tunes on a fiddle.

I take Grand Avenue towards Lighthouse. I am keenly aware and observant of the people, and the old buildings that have housed many varieties of retail businesses since the 1800's.

I routinely stop at the Variety Gift Store to pet Harley the 'Shop Dog.' She's a sweet, tan colored Staffordshire bull terrier with big beautiful brown eyes. I sit and chat with her owner, a very pleasant woman.

I continue on my way and stop at the 620 on the Avenue Gift Store to see Poppy, a tiny little Chihuahua who had been rescued from an abusive situation. She now wears a little pink and gray sweater, and she snuggles into her fuzzy blanket. She is now obviously loved and well taken care of. The proprietor of the shop and Poppy's 'person' knows exactly why I am there as I walk in the door, and she smiles. The kindness reaffirms my belief in human compassion.

I stop at the Imagine Art Supply store from time to time when I need to buy supplies there and to see Jude and Jordana, two cats that are often seen sleeping on the front window shelf. Jude is nearly 14 years old and would prefer that

you speak to her softly, and wait for her to let you know when she is ready for you to pet her. Jordana is three years old and is all over the place. She is often seen on a top shelf that is nearly ten feet high. I always enjoy my conversations with Jude and Jordana's 'person' and owner of the shop.

I pop in and out of all the shops along the way. I have a cup of tea and one of their famous oatmeal and raisin cookies at The Bookworks, or a bowl of soup at Victorian Corner, a smoothie at Juice and Java. I have been to all the shops at one time or another, and while there's not always conversation, there are always smiles and pleasant greetings.

As I listen and observe, my faith is restored that perhaps we are no different from the people that lived here over a hundred years ago, at least not in the things that are important, like kindness and compassion.

When some of my grandchildren came to visit from another state, I took them to the Point Pinos Lighthouse, the oldest continually operating lighthouse on the West Coast. There a small woman in her elder years was our tour guide. She told the history of the lighthouse with such excitement, as if it was the first time she had ever related this story to anyone. My grandchildren listened with great interest.

We then went to the tide pools where we collected sea shells and sea glass, and observed hermit crabs. My great-granddaughter squealed with excitement at her first sighting of a sea urchin. They were all so excited at the sight of harbor seals and sea otters, even spotted a few dolphins.

Fishing boats and sail boats dotted the horizon. We walked the path from Lover's Point to the Kissing Rocks, and took in the beauty of the shoreline. The smell of the ocean breeze, the sound of the waves as they hit the rocks and create huge plumes of white caps. The shrill squawking of the sea gulls added to the magic. Deer are seen often as they are free to roam this place that is also their habitat.

My grandchildren had their picture taken atop the stone whale in front of the Museum of Natural History, and the monarch sculpture, and also at other landmarks of Pacific Grove.

We sat in the gazebo just north of Asilomar Beach and watched a beautiful sunset as geese, pelicans, and other species of birds were silhouetted against a raspberry and orange colored sky.

As I observed their excitement of each experience, I imagined that they were no different from the children of over a century ago.

May we never lose our excitement, nor take for granted all the beautiful things that are so abundant for us to enjoy. Let us never stop showing human kindness and compassion.

Recently I was expecting company and had ordered pizza to be delivered to my door. As the delivery man (who was probably in his early 20s) entered the foyer, he exclaimed with great excitement that it was just like going back in time, like being in an old movie. I loved his expression, and the fact that it had come from someone of a much younger generation, and then I told him, "That is exactly how I feel every time I walk through that door!"

"P.G.BM255"
Tania Panarello

On a recent trip in April to Pacific Grove, my family and I were leisurely strolling from vendor to vendor at the Good Old Days Celebration when a man from a petition booth asked me, "Are you a resident of Pacific Grove?"

I paused, then replied with a wistful, yet hopeful smile, "Not yet."

August 2018 will mark Rick's and my 18th wedding anniversary and eleventh stay at the Martine Inn – our first in over thirteen years, and first in the Family Suite.

Unlike my New Yorker/Floridian-hybrid husband, a Navy transplant who found his way west to balmy San Diego and the brisk Bay Area, I was born and sourdough-bred in the East Bay suburb of Livermore, California—home of the fastest rodeo and historic wine country. Until age ten, I spent lazy, breezy summers fishing off the pier at Seacliff Beach, down the hill from my grandparents' little beach house in Aptos. We'd venture often into Santa Cruz for intense Skeet Ball rounds and ring tosses at the clown's mouth from our mighty steeds, or seek thrills on the Giant Dipper and Logger's Revenge.

When my grandparents began renting out their cozy refuge on Rio Del Mar, my divorced working mom had to find a new vacation escape for my little brother and me. Enter Monterey Bay Aquarium.

MBA (as we call it) opened October 20, 1984. There was no skywalk then, and it was probably about half the size it is now. My grandfather may have instilled my love of the ocean deep within my soul, but the aquarium breathed salt and light into it.

Throughout the years, I would visit Monterey Bay with family, friends, and even Oceanography classmates from Las Positas College, just to have an excuse to escape to the coast.

My husband booked our first stay at the Martine Inn on Valentine's Day weekend in 1999. I had been to Pacific Grove before—and maybe love indeed was in the air—but I fell hard this time for this amazing yet unassuming town, sandwiched between touristy Monterey and artsy Carmel. P.G. was to me what Baby Bear's belongings were to Goldilocks – it was *just right*.

Rick fell in love with P.G., too—and the Martine Inn. We were engaged that first trip together to P.G., and we were married at 255 Ocean View Boulevard on August 5, 2000. Our friends and family had so much fun, they wanted to hold yearly reunions in P.G.!

Three years later (with many day trips and overnights in between), I brought our son, Dominic, then 8 months old, to our first Butterfly Parade. I discovered the event online as something to do while Rick worked his long weekend shifts. Dominic instantly took to the sea air and naturally enjoyed the aquarium (as did younger brother Vincent); we became MBA members soon afterward.

Our boys, now 15 and 13, still look forward to trips to P.G.. No visit—day or overnight—is complete without the traditional stops at MBA, Bubba Gump's, Lover's Point, and a run or drive along the P.G. coastline. The wonderful folks at Casa de Amigos know us and Freddo, our German Shepherd-mix, quite well, as do the local trails; the excellent staff at Peter B's are getting better acquainted with us, too.

Our devotion to P.G. is expressed in our email address (pgbum255@yahoo.com) and our '95 Honda Civic's whale tail license plate, P.G.BM255 (**Pa**cific **G**rove **BuM 255**), to honor the significance of the Martine Inn in our lives. Vincent has promised us that, someday, when he is a rich and famous actor/director/producer/screenwriter (after a distinguished career in the Navy, of course), he will buy us our dream home in P.G..

And yes, someday we do hope to retire in P.G.—if we could just stop spending so much money there! Thank you, P.G., for all you have given us.

New Artist in the Community
Richard Jenson

I first visited Big Sur in 1979, and moved to the Monterey Peninsula in 1988. Being a native Denverite, I discovered the California lifestyle similar to the relaxed pace and temperament of Colorado. My personal sense of ecological and political awareness meshed easily with the Central Coast outlook and focus. Having one of the world's best aquariums and the stunning Big Sur coastline were added bonuses. I call the Monterey Peninsula our home now. Neither one of us wish to live away from the ocean again. The Rockies are wonderful, but the Pacific Ocean is majestic and limitless.

I taught primary special education in the Monterey and Carmel school districts. And much to my surprise after my retirement, I became an abstract acrylic painter. I was introduced to acrylic pouring medium and never looked back. It was a new product and I needed to learn its nuances and applications on my own. My process evolved and has been recognized for its differences to other acrylic techniques. Pouring medium allows me to manipulate colors and movement solely by paint application and gravity. No brushes are involved in what I do. After being poured, I have about 45 minutes to manipulate the paint before it begins setting. Paintings dry completely in 24 hours. The medium allows colors to interact without blending, and it dries to a glossy, durable finish.

In the past, I exhibited at Del Monte Lalla Grill and the Aiyana Spa of Carmel Valley Ranch. In July, I experienced my initial First Friday Pacific Grove opening at the Lauris Wellness Center and Gallery. It is exciting to be welcomed into the artist community of P.G.. I became acquainted with other local artists who were generously positive of my works and curious about my techniques. I anxiously await the next First Friday to continue my dialogue and interactions with this new community. It has reenergized my desire to create new works, and discover new applications.

I lived in Pacific Grove for almost a year, many years ago. My apartment was behind the post office, making it easy to acquaint myself with the variety of businesses and restaurants. I enjoyed my time being a P.G. resident. When our friend, Lauris Austin, approached my partner and I about remodeling her new business space into a wellness center and gallery, we jumped at the opportunity. After several weeks of hard work, we installed my paintings into the new space. This has been a true team effort. Lauris offers a variety of massages, facials, readings and other instructions. My partner, Jaime Rosario, has a successful massage studio, Honu Spot, in downtown Monterey. This is an exceptional opportunity to participate in the growing exposure and diversity of the art presented for First Friday P.G.. I hope to be a contributing member of this expanding community for a long time.

How Two Poets Changed My Life
Rosi Edwards

In the fourth grade when I was ten years old, my teacher read the poem 'Annabel Lee' by Edgar Allen Poe to our class.

It made such an impact because my own history had been chaotic and this poem allowed me to believe that there was love and caring in the world and it could last past our own death.

> It was many and many a year ago
> In a kingdom by the sea
> That a maiden there lived whom you may know
> By the name of Annabel Lee
> And this maiden she lived with no other thought
> Than to love and be loved by me.

> *I* was a child and *she* was a child
> In this kingdom by the sea
> But we loved with a love that was more than love—
> I and my Annabel Lee;
> With a love that the winged seraphs in Heaven
> Coveted her and me.

The poem goes on to tell about her death in "this kingdom by the sea" and his lifelong reaction was to cherish this love they had shared. To my heart and mind this opened the idea that love and caring were possibilities in life. Someday I would find "a kingdom by the sea" and "a love that that was more than love" and lasted after life itself. This childhood fantasy sustained me for years.

Many and many a year ago, I was born in a "kingdom by the sea," the Aland Islands archipelago located in the middle of the Baltic Sea. Our island was the largest of the 6500 islands that composed the archipelago, being twenty-five miles by twenty-five miles. The occupations were farming and seafaring. It is a beautiful place, blue water almost everywhere the eye could see, forests, immense blue skies, roads that were made of red granite. The smell of the sea and the beauty of the island itself are captivating. I will not dwell on winters which were not so wonderful, as we would get the cold and snow and wind from Russia and only five hours of daylight.

My mother emigrated to "the new world" in 1921 when she was seventeen years old and entered the wild and exciting world of New York city in the roaring twenties. She found employment in the mansion of the world's reputedly richest man, John D. Rockefeller.

In 1930 she returned for a visit to Aland, married my father, and left again in 1934. She would not ever consider living in Aland again after the magic of New York city and the comforts she had there: electricity, indoor plumbing, hot water from a spigot, three meals a day, a private room with her own bathroom. This was not to be given up to return to farming, no electricity, no indoor plumbing.

My parents and I came together as a family and we emigrated to the New World. Due to parents who both needed to work, they found a foster home for me and visited when they could on weekends. I was separated from them until I was ten years old when my father moved all of us to an apartment in mid New York city; the richest zip code in the city. Tammany Hall had redrawn district lines, allowing me to attend the best elementary school in the city. Almost seventy years later, it remains the best elementary school in the city. My girlfriend and I were in the redistricted area and we were the only fourth graders who did not have either a chauffeur or a nanny picking them up after school.

I went to college, graduated from college, did the usual 1950s pattern: married, had two sons, (David and

Douglas Snider), and became a housewife. I did not find a "kingdom by the sea and a love that lasted forever" at this stage of my life.

When the children came of school age, I returned to school and five years of night attendance gave me a graduate degree. I found employment and met a co-worker who invited us to cocktails, dinner and an evening of poetry and music. The second miracle of my life was in store. Just as we were leaving, he called out, "Wait, wait, you have to read one more poem." With one foot out of the door and snow falling on my head, I read a poem by Robinson Jeffers, our Carmel poet. The next years I read everything I could find and his poetry was so lyrical and so descriptive of a land I had never imagined to exist, the Monterey Peninsula.

There was nothing else to do except to take my sons and go across our beautiful country to see the fabled land which he described. After that it was impossible to do anything else other than move to the Monterey Peninsula. Here were trees and forests, magnificent huge puffy white clouds, the deep aquamarine and glorious smell of the ocean, clement weather. It was a joy to the senses to arise in the morning and see such beauty.

Moving here again changed my life. A fellow worker wanted to introduce me to one of her mentors. I met her mentor, Father Dwight Edwards, and eight years later we married. I had found "my kingdom by the sea" and "a love that was more than love."

Dwight died on Thanksgiving Day 2016. We had twenty-six years together; it was twenty-six years of a love affair and a marriage.

I am grateful for the good fortune of my life, for good health, for my darling beloved, for being able to live here for fifty-two years and end my days here; for my sons, for my grandchildren; for work that was rewarding and a pleasure to do.

My heart is filled with gratitude.

Fifi's and Us
Cynthia Beach Guthrie

After a lifetime of moving, my husband and I settled on California's Central Coast. Having lived in eight states and nine countries, we've tasted food in hundreds of restaurants. But Fifi's of Pacific Grove found a place in our hearts, starting with the food, but not ending there.

Fifi's is a small eatery located on the corner of a non-descript 50's era strip mall on a heavily traveled road leading into Pacific Grove. Enter and you're in an authentic French bistro with crisp white cloths on the tables, upholstered dining chairs, red velvet curtains at the windows, hanging candelabra with fresh flowers and real candles, paintings and gold leafed mirrors, good music and good wine and good French food. Good service, too. The French onion soup is the best, better than any we tasted during the four years we lived in Paris.

Fifi's French proprietor, Michele, created all this. With her decidedly French style and graciousness and in her enticingly accented English, she greets you at the door. My husband Dick, who attended a French boarding school in his youth, always converses in French with Michele which she appreciates, and he does, too. Fifi's became our go-to favorite local restaurant in a place we now call home.

One event embedded Fifi's and Michele in our hearts forever. Our 40th wedding anniversary occurred only two weeks after we'd celebrated our daughter's wedding in the glorious oak-filled hills of nearby Carmel Valley. Still recovering from that grand event, we decided to have a quiet, low-key anniversary dinner. We made a reservation at Fifi's for us and our son Park, his wife and baby son.

Saturday morning Park telephoned from his home in San Francisco to say they were running late and would come directly to Fifi's to meet us for dinner. We suspected that he might have something up his sleeve as we were a nomadic family who liked to "mark the occasion" whatever it was. Rituals gave us some continuity and stability during our traveling life and we liked creating them.

So when Dick and I parked outside Fifi's and spotted a friend's car, we weren't entirely surprised. And sure enough, when we walked into the restaurant, Michele was mysterious, but beaming as she escorted us to the back alcove filled with balloons and streamers. Exuberant sounds of "Surprise, surprise!" came not only from Park and his young family, but from old friends and Dick's brother and his wife who had driven down from Tahoe. The champagne flowed and we chatted with some of our favorite people in our recently discovered favorite restaurant.

As we were about to sit down, I shrieked, at first in fright, and then in total disbelief and shock, as from under the white-clothed table, up sprang our daughter Laura! The bride!

Laura, Cynthia, Park and Dick Guthrie.

Dick and Cynthia with their first grandchild, Kai.

Just the day before Laura had returned to her home in NYC from her honeymoon in Spain. Then she hopped on a plane to fly all the way across the country to come to her parents' 40th wedding anniversary celebration in California. Her brother wasn't really late leaving his house that morning—he was picking up his sister at the San Francisco airport. We were stunned...and deeply touched.

Fifi's, with Michele's attentive care, has been the scene of many gatherings and good meals and memorable moments in our lives ... but none will ever match our 40th. How could it?

Because Dick and I have always been the ones leaving or arriving during our nomadic wanderings, it never occurred to us that Michele would ever leave! Fifi's and Michele and Calvin have been part of the landscape of our lives here on the Central Coast since we discovered them in 1997. So with mixed feelings, as our 55th anniversary approaches, we thank them as they begin their retirement in Spain, and send them on their way. *Bon Voyage*, friends!

Someday and the Magic Triangle
Jim and Barb Gianelli

Approaching the peninsula by Highway 1 just north of Seaside is like coming out of the ordinary world of black and white and entering the magical world of Technicolor, just like in the *Wizard of Oz*.

We lived in the apartments on Forest Avenue and Ocean View Boulevard with a second floor corner unit. We had panoramic ocean views: Lovers Point from our front balcony and the shimmering lights of Monterey and Seaside from our dining room. Dinner in the dark provided the most stunning view.

Lovers Point is an almost exact replica of where we got married after college, on the grass at La Jolla Cove, a perfect place to begin our married lives. We got our first real adult jobs when we lived here, Barb at CHOMP as an RN, Jim as an attorney at a local franchise law firm. P.G. was a place we celebrated on a daily basis. Walking/jogging along the Ocean View paths, exploring the unique and fun shops up in town, and carrying our two-person raft across the street to the ocean off Lovers Point, often bringing a backpack filled with a feast of bread, cheese and wine. We would tie onto kelp, watching the otters, sea lions and sometimes even porpoises up close while soaking in the changing hues and colors as the sun descended. Barb's first birthday in P.G. was incredible—viewing the Feast of Lanterns from our deck with friends—best view in town! Watching people laughing, dancing and conversing in so many different languages made us feel joyful, at one with and connected to the whole world. We felt that there was no place else we needed or wanted to be. P.G. was the magical place where our precious first son Matthew was conceived. Our Lovers Point apartment was the first "dot" on what we came to call our "magic triangle."

Although we had hoped to nest, progress in our careers and raise our family in P.G., life was busy making other plans. But throughout it all, pursuing our careers and raising our family in the Gold Country foothills, we were always returning and staying connected to our beloved Pacific Grove, bringing our family to cozy places like Lighthouse Suites and Andril Fireplace Cottages. Finally in 2010, we made a very extravagant decision—we leased a home on the corner of Egan and Del Monte for a full year. This vacation home was the second "dot" of our "magic triangle." We were testing the waters. Yes, there was more traffic, more tourists and everything was more expensive, but the magic was still there!

Now it is nearly 40 years since we first lived at Lovers Point as we now enter the next phase of our lives: free, retired and with children and grandchildren living on the coast nearby. We finally own a place in P.G. on Lighthouse and Cedar, the third "dot" of our "magic triangle."

We have made it home to our beloved Pacific Grove, this time for good. "Someday" has finally arrived.

Samira: The Story Of A Special Rescue Dog
Flora Anderson

The François Factor

I was reading the *Monterey County Herald* knowing full well I should have been getting dressed for a friend's memorial service when I heard water babbling onto my kitchen floor. François, my eight-month old black kitten adopted a few months earlier from AFRP, had torn apart the cat drinking fountain. Quickly I blotted the water and got ready to leave.

The following day, I decided to put François to the test and reassembled the fountain, minus the water. Like a flawlessly obedience-trained dog, his eye contact and focus were perfect. Once assembled, it took François less than a minute to dismantle the fountain, including pulling out the filter. I bagged up the fountain for delivery to the AFRP Treasure Shop for resale to a less mechanical cat.

As I left, I looked across the Holman building parking lot and couldn't believe my eyes. An Afghan Hound was being unloaded from the rescue van. I hadn't seen one in decades. From that distance, I could see the bright red streaking job on the dog's coat. I drove closer for a better look.

The dog was a mess. In addition to the red streaks, her coat had extensive matting, with noticeable chunks having been cut out. When I rolled down the window, she stuck her nose inside my vehicle.

At the moment, I had no thought of adopting and I was determined not to fall in love. But there had been rumors of break-ins at my complex, so a guard dog might be useful, and the more I reflected, the more I suspected this dog might not be an easy adoption for AFRP.

So I took her on a preliminary test walk. The evaluator from AFRP told me this dog had "no confidence" and "no idea about being a dog." Her age was estimate at two-and-a-half years. Her rescue name was Marilyn. Fortunately, that one didn't last. Shortly thereafter, it would be changed to Samira, Arabic for "friend."

Getting to Know You

My home was vetted. Problem. Cats! Little macho François hissed and bared his fangs. Samira turned away from him as though this were some kind of joke. Maja, the older, purebred rag doll, took one look at the newcomer from her perch and went back to sleep.

Then there was the agreed-upon AFRP training class. All other dogs were small, Chihuahua mixes and one corgi. Then there was my now-shaven, long-legged "mini horse." We were not the star pupils of that class, but enrolled in another group later in the fall. Progress was made and a relationship developing. The cats turned out to be no problem. François was fascinated and Maja wasted no time and not much effort making clear beyond any shadow of a doubt who was boss.

However, Samira needed exercise. I took her to the SPCA Sunday morning off-leash sessions. She would walk around for a while, then go to sleep under an oak tree. She would also sit and stare into the "detention center" as though she thought it might be the VIP lounge. At the end of one session, she grabbed a treat bag that an owner had left on a bench and somehow got it attached to her nose. Then she took off running, top speed, around the yard. Eating on the run? The trainer couldn't open the gate until Samira could be corralled. We were all laughing. Eventually, Samira deposited the bag precisely where she had found it.

Making the Rounds in P.G.

Laundry days are spent at my friend Loni's Sudz Cyber Laundry in Pacific Grove. The wash cycle is perfect timing to walk Samira from Sudz to the AFRP adoption center on Fountain Avenue and back. During these walks, many people from all parts of the USA and the rest of the world have stopped to ask questions and photograph Samira. I am always proud to explain that she is a rescue dog and to mention AFRP. Many people have shared their own rescue stories.

One time I noticed a woman studying the P.G. tourist map and looking distressed. I asked if I might help. She indicated that she had taken a long, relaxing walk and now couldn't find her car. I suggested that the police might help, but she didn't have a cell phone. No problem. We can use mine. The P.G.PD came quickly and helped her find her car. The following day, I stopped by the Police Department to thank them. That was when I learned about the drug disposal machine located at the front door. Subsequently I have used that machine to dispose of all my outdated medications.

We complete our cycle back to Sudz, passing by the P.G. Post Office. Samira knows exactly where the Sudz treat door is located. It's her goal. Head directly across Lighthouse Avenue and get her treat. The Sudz staff excels with the treats menu and keeps an excellent, varied supply on hand, with special concern that the treats be healthy. Then during the drying cycle, I read and Samira relaxes in her famous Sphinx pose, taking up the maximum space on the floor.

Sudz is pet friendly. One day, a man was coming down the steps with his pet. Samira couldn't wait to greet the new arrival. Surprise! It wasn't another dog. It was his pet pig on a leash. To their credit, both Samira and the pig kept their cool.

Samira Makes a Quantum Leap

Pacchetti Dog Park is Seaside's treasure. The park is two-plus acres, fenced, with a separate small dog area, and is well maintained by a staff of volunteers. Recently I have taken Samira there daily, and it has resulted in a quantum leap forward in both her behavior and our relationship. At first, she would run only around the peripheries of the park and would not socialize with other dogs. Now she runs full speed and interacts with other dogs. She can stop and change direction on a dime. Before, she would never play with a ball. Now she chases balls, grabs them and takes off with them, sometimes to the frustration of the owners. She has also developed a flirtatious and coquettish streak with other dogs. Often she runs with a young Doberman Pinscher and a Vizsla, who are comparable in size to Samira. The other day, she preferred to run with a group of tiny dogs who were more than capable of keeping up with her.

Every day is different depending on the combination of dogs and people. There are different times: morning, mid-morning, the "lunch bunch," afternoon and the after-work group. I have been experimenting with different times and have enjoyed getting to know many people. While the dogs do their thing, the people socialize. I have met residents from all over our area, part-time and seasonal residents, visitors, and military people. The list is endless. Each person and dog has its story. Examples include a newly arrive military family from Korea whose dog was adopted from a dog café, fairly common in Asia and just now catching on in the USA. I hear many rescue dog stories, often from horrendous conditions, and each owner shares strategies for getting the dog on track. Pacchetti Park can also be an excellent place for networking.

Learning Patience, Persistence and Consistency

Samira and I are three years into the relationship. Not only has Samira changed, but so have I. I have had to learn that things will happen in time, and on Samira's terms, not necessarily mine because I want it. Patience, persistence and consistency.

I have observed people's reactions to her. In Pacific Grove people ask to approach her, pet her and then tell me, "Thank you for letting her make my day." I encourage interactions with all kinds of people and ages with careful supervision. My goal is to have Samira pass the tests to become a certified therapy dog. This could allow her to visit facilities. As I write, this is a work in progress. Still, our relationship has come a long way and continues to evolve and improve.

Feast of Lanterns Pet Parade participants. Photo Patricia Hamilton.

Christopher Bell:
The artist behind P.G.'s iconic images.

For Whom the Bell Tolls

Nancy Bell with Stan Countz

As you stroll through America's Last Home Town along the bike path near Lovers Point, you may have passed by Berwick Park. There resides the bronze sculpture called "Life at the Top" by the late, noted marine sculptor Christopher Bell. It depicts a mother and baby otter at play with the Monterey bay as a backdrop. Christopher spent hours scouting out the perfect spot between the trees where it now sits. Christopher and the Pacific Grove Rotary Club presented this bronze sculpture to the city in 1994. It has become a popular local landmark, appearing in countless tourist photos and serving as the backdrop for quite a few weddings in this beautiful park.

Another "Life at the Top" sculpture sits at the Portola Plaza Hotel in downtown Monterey, where the Christopher Bell art gallery was located for many years. He opened his first gallery on Grand Avenue behind the Pacific Grove Museum of Natural History. Many art galleries have been located there, but Christopher's was the first. He later moved his gallery, The Christopher Bell Collection, up across Lighthouse to 213 Grand Avenue before he was invited to open a larger, more prominent gallery at what is today the Portola Plaza Hotel.

The Butterfly Children, Frozen in Time

The other noted Christopher Bell public bronze sculpture in Pacific Grove is "Butterfly Children" in front of the P.G. Post Office. This life-sized statue, purchased by the city in 1996, was created to honor the thousands of local children who have participated in the popular annual Butterfly Parade in October, a celebration of the annual migration of the monarch butterfly to the Pacific Grove area.

On the day of the sculpture's dedication, Janice Hare brought her first grade class from Robert H. Down Elementary School, dressed in their colorful, homemade orange and black monarch butterfly wings. They, along with other members of the community, helped to dedicate this new community landmark.

Sculptor Christopher Bell managed to feature both of his sons in "Butterfly Children." Five-year-old Jordan was the model for the boy, but that's the other son Aaron's turned-out foot! The model for the little girl was Michelle Annereau.

"The Prodigal Son," another of Christopher's public bronze sculptures, is located in the foyer of Wellspring Church (formerly Mayflower Presbyterian) located on Central Avenue in Pacific Grove.

Before he passed away tragically in December of 1997, Chris had created hundreds of limited-edition bronze sculptures and one-of-a-kind fabricated pieces on a variety of themes, from nautical and maritime to covered wagons to miniature mailboxes.

It All Started with a Visit to New England

An avid model-maker as a boy, Chris was drawn to the three-dimensional medium of sculpture. Chris first felt the allure of the sea when he visited New England as a child. After a brief apprenticeship, he set out on his own in 1973. This is when Chris and I met and married. By 1976, his name was becoming known in collector's circles and he was creating commissioned pieces for the annual World Offshore Technology Conferences at Houston's Astrodome, the largest trade show in the world. His work reflects a life-long fascination with the real and imaginary inhabitants of the sea.

His bronze sculptures were featured for many years, starting in 1987, at the Maui Marine Art Expo benefitting the Cousteau Society. His work was shown at the opening of the Cousteau Parc Oceanique in Paris. One of his pieces was also displayed on Cousteau's *Calypso*. Christopher's work has also been included in the prestigious "Mystic 100" and "Mystic International" at Mystic Seaport, Connecticut.

His work appears in collections in Europe, Canada, Australia, Saudi Arabia and Israel. Private collectors of his work have included such well-known public figures as Allen Funt, creator of the *Candid Camera* TV show, evangelist Billy Graham and baseball star Reggie Jackson.

Jordan Bell, one of our two sons, has been a student of his father's art since he was just two years old, when he would sit beside his dad with his arm around him and "help" him create sculptures in the first Grand Avenue gallery. Jordan's five-year-old image can be seen in his father's "Butterfly Children" sculpture on display in front of the Pacific Grove Post Office. The little girl is Michelle Annereau. Some people think the little girl looks like me—I did do modeling for his sculptures during our marriage of nearly 25 years. Christopher included our other son, Aaron, in this statue by turning Jordan's foot out, as it appeared in a favorite family photo of Aaron.

Christopher used to refer to me as his "chief critique artist." With my feedback, he altered many of his creations, including the "Butterfly Children" sculpture. In the clay version, one day he "decapitated" Jordan's head in order to change the direction of his gaze.

Following His Father's Artistic Path

His "butterfly child" days long past, Jordan went on to apprentice with the sculpture and mold-making instructors Peter Parch and Gary Quinonez at Monterey Peninsula College. Currently, he is a *patineur,* applying patinas on the work of world-renowned Monterey sculptor Richard MacDonald.

Jordan's first bronze, "On the Ball," depicts a pelican balancing on a buoy ball and is a reflection of his and his father's love of marine art and the sea. Jordan is an avid surfer and rock collector and when he's not in the studio may be found collecting jade in Big Sur or catching waves along the central coast.

Christopher jokingly referred to himself as "Mr. P.G.," so it's fitting that his sculptures decorate our town. The family will always miss Chris; he said he was "one in a million," and we so agree. His memory lives on in his beautiful bronzes in Pacific Grove, Butterfly Town USA.

Note: Jordan and Christopher Bell's bronze sculptures, including miniatures of several, may be viewed and purchased at www.bellbronze.com. Nancy Bell manages the collection.

Nancy Bell, with sculpture of mother sea otter with her pup, now in Berwick Park.

The Feast of Lantern's 'Princess Diamond'
Nancy Bell with Stan Countz

The wonderful hometown Pet Parade happens every Friday just before the Feast of Lanterns in Pacific Grove. Last year's Pet Parade was graced by our English Staffordshire bull terrier Kayla as Princess Diamond.

Kayla was so very good and patient in keeping on her diamond tiara, princess cape and Feast of Lanterns décor. I think she enjoyed all the attention! She was accompanied by me and my sister Lin Mapstead. Lin wore her traditional kimono.

Years ago we even had our cat, Cubby, in the parade! The large decorated bird cage kept him quiet and safe. Our sons, Aaron and Jordan, also rode their decorated bikes in the Pet Parade. It is not to be missed, so entertaining and hilarious! Go see it.

Maybe Kayla will be in her Santa costume next year!

Pride of Medeira plant. Photo Patricia Hamilton.

The Day Tom Hanks and Hollywood Came to Town
Nancy Bell with Stan Countz

Exciting news came to us in 1989 when my husband, Chris, and I were invited to appear as extras in a movie, *Turner and Hootch,* being filmed in Pacific Grove. Our dear friends, Bob and Judy Williams, had their 1928 Buick touring car in a car show scene that was being staged on the grounds of the Point Pinos Lighthouse. One hundred other classic cars in primo condition and their owners were taking part in this exciting Hollywood film venture.

Chris's job was to shine the hood and mine was to pass by with a silver tray of yummy hors d'oeuvres. Every time they did a retake—and they did them a lot!—we had to do it again. "One retake for every movie theater in America," Chris joked.

One of the three dogs playing Hooch was supposed to pee on the tire of one of the cars. That's a lot of pee! Well, at least he knew the "lift the leg" trick. The other two Hooch dogs knew other tricks. I think one of them must have known the drooling trick, as that was so memorable in the movie!

I hadn't received the message to wear light summer clothes, so I scored by being sent to the "starlet trailer" to change into a seersucker suit and nylon stockings. Closest I've ever gotten to a starlet—Mare Winningham, who played veterinarian Dr. Emily Carson in the movie.

We also had lunch and dinner on the set—all 100-plus of us. Delicious!

Tom Hanks, of course, was there … fascinating to watch! I had the chance to meet and shake hands with

him as my friend, Dori Post, went to college with him up in the East Bay.

Chris and our sons, Aaron and Jordan, were on their way to school one day when they passed Tom Hanks in the crosswalk. Tom said to Jordan, "You're not going to put that straw in your ear, are you?" So they also met and shook hands.

Tom was very friendly and personable while he was here in P.G. for the filming. We met a set worker who sent us an autographed picture of Tom, which is on our shelf.

After all that filming and paying $100 to each owner of those 100 classic automobiles, they had "the noive" to cut the entire scene from the movie! How dare they cut our one moment of fame!

Miss Nattress

We have all had that one teacher that made a difference in our life. Joan Nattress was my PE teacher at Walter Colton Junior High in 1966. She was best known as the long time (more than 30 years) Pacific Grove Adult School exercise teacher at the Sally Griffin Center for Living. How rare to have a teacher who taught you in junior high, and then to teach you even more than you thought possible—after you retire! Her classes were peppered with exercise and wonderful music was lots of advice. But don't worry, Joan, none of your students will quote you! Miss Nattress left us suddenly at 83 years old. She will be missed by many in Pacific Grove and beyond.

— Linda Pagnella

Photos by Patricia Hamilton.

Annette Corcoran: 'A Unique and Beautiful Talent' by Nancy Jacobs

Annette Corcoran is a nationally known ceramic and porcelain artist. She graduated from El Segundo High School and won an academic scholarship to the University of California at Berkeley where she received a B. A. degree. She continued her education in art and ceramics at Long Beach State University and Saddleback College of Marin. She married and had three children, all the while working in ceramics. Her husband has been very supportive. Annette's ceramic and porcelain works show a unique and beautiful talent as she understands beauty in form.

Annette loves every aspect of the ceramics process. She said, "I love working with the clay, I love the glazing and I love the firing." In essence she loves the whole process, including designing beautiful and unique pieces. In 1987, Annette Corcoran authored the book *Birds and Teapots*, published by Dorothy Weiss Gallery.

1984 brought the aquarium to Monterey and Pacific Grove; 1985 brought Annette Corcoran, as her husband wanted to live near the water and was attracted to our beautiful coastline. The grand opening of the Monterey Bay Aquarium brought 30,000 people to Cannery Row. The city of Pacific Grove was represented by Mayor Florus Williams.

Times were changing on the Monterey Peninsula as the aquarium brought nationwide publicity, and tourist gridlock. Still things were not much different in Pacific Grove. An artist-supporting café that both beginning and established artists frequented received criticism and eventually closed. The place where artists, writers and musicians gathered was no more.

If people enjoy the Pacific Grove shoreline they have a small group of people to thank and that includes Annette Corcoran along with Bud Nunn, Flo Schaefer, Lee Willoughby and others who fought to preserve Rocky Shores. Annette recalls that "politics in Pacific Grove got ugly, really ugly and very nasty." Some of the people involved moved as a result. Bud Nunn, a retired Naval Postgraduate School professor, had lived in Pacific Grove for approximately eighteen years when he and his wife packed up and left for the Gold Country. When Bud died they scattered his ashes at Rocky Shores.

The turn of the century brought much sadness and depression, first with 9/11, then in 2008, the economic meltdown and recession. The 1990s were an interlude of happiness, success and hope that we may never see again. Other initiatives that were important in preserving Pacific Grove as a residential community were Preserving Open Spaces and the Motel Initiative, keeping motels in character with the residentail aspect of town. However, as with all things in Pacific Grove, only time will tell. In the meanwhile we still have Annette Corcoran designing those gorgeous teapots and other ceramics and porcelain! And if anyone is interested in visiting the Moulin Rouge on screen, there are two movies with that title, one filmed in 1952 and the other in 2001.

Washington Park
Robin Aeschliman
May 2017

This morning I walked by a young pine I'd propped up during one of last winter's furious and luscious storms, let its prickly needles brush my cheek, muss my hair ... and hoped no one would come along and break its tickling arms.

In 1948, Mayor LaPorte and his posse of City Fathers determined Washington Park should be a trailer park. I honor the extraordinary effort of City Mothers Anne Fisher (her husband director of Hopkins; she an accomplished woman in her own right), Anita Church, and Bertha Strong. Together, they successfully petitioned for an initiative. The election preserved Washington Park—the last wild wood in the city's historic core—and determined its future.

"Wash" Park preserve, an unsculpted gift of place unique to Pacific Grove and the Peninsula, is my neighborhood best friend. In its wild woods, I've walked an abundance of dogs and children. And played hide-and-seek with both. We've tossed pine cones to a succession of golden retrievers, chased dragons, and played king-of-the-fallen-tree with generations of our brood. With a measure of success, I've taught the inquisitive little ones to recognize sticky monkey, miner's lettuce, wild mint, wild cucumber, blackberries, rattlesnake grass, wild iris, monarchs ... and, to steer clear of the two "P" words, poop and poison oak.

I grew up in the forested hills of Old Monterey. The forest that embraced our home was my playground. My little childhood legs took me up hill and down in search of wild iris and fairy lantern bouquets for Mom. In December, with my dad, we'd find the perfect Christmas Tree. Pine.

My coming of age was lockstep with *The Bulldoze Period*. Mountains were sculpted into terraces, forests flattened, historic town centers razed. The world around me, and beyond, was a palette for "progress." Wild iris and fairy lanterns and romps in the woods disappeared.

In 1972, because we could not afford Monterey or Carmel Valley (ponder that, dear reader), my husband and I bought a house in Pacific Grove—a fixer with good bones. From the street it oozed "home"—inside, oh dear. It came with a bonus—the 20 acre wild woods of Washington Park a block away. We did not intend to remain in the neighborhood forever. It appears, though, we have. The woods anchor us and provide our children and grandchildren with, to a small degree, the same happiness of a long ago childhood neighborhood just over-the-hill in Monterey. Mine. Throughout the intervening years, 45 now, over-wintering monarchs disappeared; the clumps of wild iris have gone missing. I've found just one little fairy lantern. The woods, though, endure ... and so do we.

In the 1980s when our youngest was a toddler, my husband crafted a portable swing—a board with a rope strung through the hole in the middle. Dad and son walks took them and the swing to the perfect branch. Ryan, and sometimes his buddies, had a little swing in the dappled shadow of the boughs of an oak.

Long ago, and for a few years, leprechauns appeared on St. Patrick's Day. Really. Gathered at the base of a big-daddy pine near the Laurel Street path teeny green-hatted ceramic figures picnicked amongst the clover ... and warmed hearts, big and little.

Wash Park's whispering wind, its tall pines silhouetted against the intense sunset brilliance of a gold-leaf sky, romps with our dog—or kids, or both, the hammer of woodpeckers and chatter of squirrels, the indecipherable conversations of a variety of chirpers ... roly-poly bugs scurrying from dirty little hands ... beloved memories.

Walks in Washington Park bring peace, sort my day ... it is more than a neighbor; it is my muse, my North Star.

Robin's son, grandson, and great-granddaughters.

Grove Market Celebrates 50 Years and Next Generation

The Higuera Family with Katie Shain

It is rare these days to enjoy celebrating the success of a real, live 'family' grocery market. Grove Market in Pacific Grove on Forest Avenue is celebrating 50 years in continuous business, serving the peninsula and beyond.

Grove Market is consistently filled with the choicest cut meats, the finest deli selections and the absolute freshest produce and dairy options available. All the congratulations go to Charlie Higuera and his devoted family.

Higuera is a local living legend at this point, and the reasons are limitless. Native American, Higuera was born in New Monterey and grew up in Pacific Grove. From Robert Down to P.G. High, Higuera participated in all the sports from football to track and received his first job from the Davis's at Forest Hill Market, currently the home of Trader Joe's. "Bob and Lynn Davis's were like family," said Higuera. "Bob treated me like I was his son."

After returning from a tour in Korea with the Marines, Higuera was welcomed home to a position waiting for him at Forest Hill Market. Those were the days of prohibition in Pacific Grove, but just up the hill it was considered a "different world."

Mastering the art and skill of butchery, requires the prowess of knowing and understanding the anatomy of how to dissect primal cuts of meat into appropriate section cuts, which in Higuera's case, was handed down by generation. Initially from his uncle to his brother Clarence, Higurea said, "I had an idea. I always liked the idea of being an entrepreneur."

The inspiration that induced Higuera's "idea" to come to life came from his notice of the quonset hut on Forest Avenue, owned by the Giles family, which had not found a use. "I think I can make a go of this," thought Higuera one day. He forged ahead, gathered up a quorum, made an offer, which procured the current location celebrating its 50 years as a landmark. To this day that original agreement holds the same bond.

Granddaughter Kristy Mason has picked up the mantle on the art of butchery and is known to show up at the market any time between 1a.m. and 4 a.m. depending on the day's activities, needs and demands. Devotion to Mason's grandfather is paralleled only by her brother, Johnny Mason, who handles all of the day to day produce requirements, which is no small task, (they purchase entire fields of asparagus).

Besides maintaining the market, and raising a family, Higuera has always been a highly valued community member. For over ten years straight, Higuera has sponsored his old alma mater's "Shoe Dance." Higuera has been a member of the volunteer fire fighter department and sat on the board of the recreation center, plus the many donations he makes to the community at large are immeasurable.

Everyday you'll find Higuera's family continuing their pride of ownership in offering, delivering and catering the best foods under the expert supervision of daughter Kate. Higuera is very proud of his family and all of their efforts, as well as the additional 27 employees that it takes to keep Grove Market running smoothly.

Thanks for the memories, congratulations, and here's to many years to come for Grove Market!

For his 85th birthday this year, Grove Market owner, Charlie Higuera, received a special gift from his two sons and two daughters—a 1932 General Electric refrigerator, custom converted to a portable smoker by Matt Wilson. Where the electric motor used to be lies a charcoal burner, and above are eight racks, which can hold 12 split chicken breasts each. Racks can be removed to hold larger food. The smoker was used during the Concours Auto Rally to prepare dinners for the exhibitors. Family members, left to right, George and Kate Matuz, Kristy Mason, Charlie Higuers.

Photo Wolf Bukowski.

Dawn patrol. Photo Peter Mounteer.

SECTION FIVE

ADVENTURES ON MONTEREY BAY

Lovers Point Park. Photo Peter Mounteer

"You just go out to enjoy it, and if you catch a fish, that's a bonus.
Just go for the excitement of being out there.
People live their whole lives and never get to do that."

– Ken Rockefeller, Monterey Bay sports fisherman

Commercial fishermen on Monterey Bay off Berwick Park.. Photo Patricia Hamilton.

Dropping a Line into the Waters of Monterey Bay
Ken Rockefeller with Patricia Hamilton

Forty some years ago, sport fishing first became part of my life with a piece of bamboo, a string and a hook on the end of it. We did something we called pole poking. At low tide you could stick your pole in a hole and pull up fish right from the rocks. You'd be surprised what you could catch at low tide. Then we turned it into a competition, to see who would cast the farthest out into the water. You'd think the bigger fish would be in the deeper water, but that's not always the case. Underneath the rock you're sitting on could be the biggest fish. You just never know. Then there came a point where we noticed the boats out in the bay and we realized we could never cast that far, and we figured those people in the boats must be catching a lot more fish. So we evolved into fishing from boats. But it all started with a group of young boys out on the rocks, off Berwick Park, seeing how far we could cast. Throughout life, we always wanted to get out on the water.

I still remember the first time I went out on the bay in a boat. I felt just total excitement because you have no idea what danger lurks underneath in that deep canyon. When you have a great whale come up beside you and breathe out and spout and then humpbacks breaching right next to you, it's like, "Wow, what an experience!"

I knew a person whose life was actually taken by a shark. It's not just the sea life that's dangerous, but the sea itself. With a rogue wave, when you see it from the shore it may not look that scary, but once you get out into the power of that wave and the surge, you understand the power of the sea. You may be out there in a boat and you feel like you have everything under control. And then one wrong move could put everything into jeopardy. So you have that sense of excitement out there.

When you're sport fishing, you get to see the commercial fishing industry at work, because Monterey Bay has a fairly large fishing industry. It is highly regulated now, both sport fishing and commercial, not like when we used to just go down to the beach to fish. We literally went right down the street and threw a line, or we'd launch the boat off Lovers Point or any place where we could get the boat down to the water's edge.

Now the only place you can launch a boat are the Coast Guard pier and by the Monterey harbormaster's office. You launch from there and then you come back to the local waters by Pacific Grove because rockfish and ling cod like to be near the rocky ledges going down into the canyon.

'Like Hoping and Wishing'

When you're fishing, it's like you're hoping and wishing. If you're diving, then you're hunting. I've done both. It's a whole different experience than being on top of the water throwing down a line. When you're on top, you can only imagine what's going on below the surface, what bait to use and the play of the lure. What usually works is squid, anything that is indigenous to the area, something the fish normally would feed on. Squid seems to be the number one thing to use round here, squid and anchovies. Local grocers will have frozen squid.

It used to be that every store around here had a fishing department, but now you're not going to find that except at stores like Outdoor World or Big Five. Back then, if you opened a store, you had a fishing section, permits included. Now to get a fishing license you have to go Outdoor World or Big Five, or go to the Department of Fish and

Game up at Ryan Ranch. You can get a one-day permit at Fisherman's Wharf because they have the commercial party boats. These are businesses that take people out to fish, but they have to make sure everyone is licensed and they don't go over their quota of the day.

Each type of fish has a limit as to how many you are allowed to catch and keep on any given day. Some have a moratorium or are only "catch and release" because they're endangered. Others have a season, or a size requirement, such as 24 inches long for ling cod. The regulations can get very complicated. A seagoing rainbow trout is a completely different fish when it comes back, but it's still a rainbow trout under the regulations.

If you have a run-in with Fish and Game, it is best to be polite and get things solved instead of trying to be insubordinate. There's always something they can get you for, always a loophole. But if you play by the book, and you're in the license and it's an honest mistake, you'll usually be okay.

For example, when you catch salmon in the ocean you would have to clip a fin and if you didn't clip the fin you can get in trouble. Now this year is different when it comes to clipping the fin. So make sure that you read your regulations and rules and stay up to date. You can get them online or ask for the little booklet of regulations when you get your license.

If you look at a map of Monterey Bay, you'll see much of it is restricted when it comes to fishing because of the sanctuary protections. You can no longer walk down to the beach and throw a pole in. There is one place between Lovers Point and Point Pinos, a pull-out with around eight parking spots, and that's the only place where you can throw a line out. On a boat, you have to stay out of those restricted areas. If you go floating into Hopkins, you're going to get a fine because it's restricted. The restricted areas are marked off by buoys, and you don't want to go past the buoy. Stay so many feet away from any wildlife and don't disturb them. Use common sense out there and you won't get into trouble. I don't know what the consequences would be if you fished in the waters off of Hopkins Marine Station, but I'm sure it would be severe. Thousands of dollars probably, and they'd confiscate your boat.

The Importance of Playing by the Book

Once you break the law, Fish and Game has a lot of power, more power than your local police because their jurisdiction is the State of California, and they carry guns. They're out in boats and a lot of them stay in trucks on shore with field glasses, especially since we have abalone on our shores and a lot of abalone poachers. They also sit down at Fishermans Wharf watching the two boat docks. It's easy for them to ask to see what's inside your cooler, and you have to show them. When you get your license, you sign a statement saying that anyone from Fish and Game has the right to search your belongings. And as long as you're playing by the book, you have nothing to worry about. And if everybody plays by the book, we'll have plenty of fish for future generations.

We didn't have a crab season a couple of years ago because of a parasite. There are certain shellfish or crustaceans that aren't edible or good for human consumption at certain times of the year, because of bacteria or something in the water that's not good for it. So I think it was the iodine inside the crab at the time that made them close the season. So they had all these crab fishermen who are depending on getting the crab that year for their income and they weren't able to do it.

I just had my first crab pot this year. I haven't dropped it yet, but everybody tells me that when you come up to your crab pot, it's going to be empty because the guy who came before you already emptied it for you. Well, that's not right—it's just plain wrong. But it was easy. When you pull up a crab trap, you only get to keep around half. They have to be a certain size, and they cannot be female. Any that don't meet the criteria get thrown back. How do you tell if it's a female? There's a certain pattern on the

belly and it's wider. The pots they sell now, it's more or less a cage with string on it. The string gets eaten away and deteriorates after being in the water so long. If you don't have the string and you pull up your pot and Fish and Game is there, they're going to fine you and maybe take your cage. When you drop your cage, you have to have a leaded rope so it doesn't float and get into a boat's propeller. You have buoy to mark where you dropped it. When you come back, you either pull up 250 feet of rope up to your boat by hand or you get a pot-puller, which is a motorized wheel. You get crab pots the same place you get fishing equipment, Big Five and Outdoor World. Or you go online. There is a tackle place over in Sand City above an auto repair shop, and in Salinas there's a store called the Tackle Box, but the selection is limited.

Fishing in the winter months is very dependent on the conditions. If it's rough you're not going to find anybody out there. We used to see a lot of nighttime fishing in the wintertime. You would see the whole bay lit up, these huge lights radiating off in the fog of these huge lights, trying to bring the squid to the surface. They would be fishing for squid using a purse net, which is a big net that comes off the large ship with a small boat to hold it in one area. When it reaches a full circle, they cinch the net and bring everything up in the net.

'A Bay Within the Bay'

In the night time you can hear crystal clear everything that's being said on the boats. It was the weirdest thing. During the daytime, they're all trying to figure out where the prime spots will be. They just know from years of fishing and from the winds and currents. Whoever gets out there first gets the prime spots. From Lovers Point to Hopkins is like a bay within the bay. You can have white caps out in the bay but it will be calm here. The squid like it here because they don't have to fight the current.

It doesn't seem to me as if there is as much kelp as there used to be. The winter waves break it away and it can grow a foot in a day. I can always remember the smell of rotting seaweed and I haven't really noticed that lately. The winter waves would rip it out and then the waves push it up onto the shore, where it would deteriorate on the shore.

If you see a party boat coming back from the sea towards the harbor, you'll see usually about 15 seagulls flying around following the boat, wanting handouts. And that's because the crew cleaning the fish take the guts and toss them overboard. Okay, that's where the seagulls go. They're on top of that one.

The boats fishing in Monterey Bay come from all over, not just our area. You'll see names all the way from Alaska to Newport Beach. It just depends on where they can make the most money. I'm sure most of the fishermen out there now are fishing for more than one thing. Those crab guys, the year the season didn't open, they must have had a secondary fish. When they bring up their nets, it's going to have other things than just the fish they're searching for. If they're fishing for squid, they can only keep squid. Everything else they have to throw back. That's part of the deal in being able to fish with that net. They used to dredge in Monterey Bay, take big chains and scoop up from the bottom and come up in the nets and everything would be in it. They were just destroying the bay, and that wasn't all that long ago.

Now we have cruise ships coming in, bringing the world to Monterey Bay. Only certain lines have been approved. Any type of fishing boat can come in as long as you obey the rules and regulations. They'll put a stop to it if you don't. They're very strict in this area. We used to have naval vessels out there all the time, minesweepers and the like. I'm not sure why we haven't seen many lately. Used to be, they'd pick you up and let you tour the ship. They'd stop here because of the Naval Postgraduate School.

'One of the Scariest Experiences I've Had on a Boat'

My brother-in-law had a 26-foot Cobalt, an inboard motor boat. We were all going to go out fishing with about eight guests. We're off Point Pinos and the motor stops. And here I am with eight people on the boat and it's not my boat. The swell is increasing to about 12 feet and that means the face of the wave is getting closer to 20 feet. So it's a pretty rough day and I'm sitting dead in the water. What happened is we lost one of the belts to the motor. I know you should bring extra belts with you, but that didn't happen with me. I just remember going down to the bottom of the swell and my stomach just going up through my neck, going "oh my god." Because all I see is water around me. And then reality hits you real quick. There's no fishing here. We're not here to fish anymore; we're here to survive. Am I going to drop the anchor and try to swim in? What am I going to do? You have to be prepared when you're out on a boat, especially if you bring passengers, because their life is in your hands. And I literally thought about dropping anchor and swimming in. I could have called the Coast Guard, but I didn't know how to work the radio at the time. That's one of the scariest experiences I've ever had on a boat. My guests were scared too because they saw me on top of the boat, jumping up and down and waving. They figured out pretty quick we were in trouble.

God blessed me with somebody coming by in another boat. They threw a line and towed us all the way into the Coast Guard pier. It must have been a 50- or 60-foot yacht. This guy comes out of a back door; it looks just like a back door to a house this thing is so big, and he says, "Hey, you guys need a tow?" And I say, "Yes, sir!" I never saw the guy again, but I can only imagine what's going through his mind. He sees these kids out there in their early 20s at the most, just frantic. So if I'm ever out in the water and I see another boater in distress, I'm always going to go help them. It's the rule of the water, if someone's in distress, you help them.

I recently picked up a 15-foot Valco, which is an aluminum boat. I bought it "as is" and my nephew and I were going to fix it up. It is seaworthy and is totally legal and licensed and has life preservers on it. So we're ready. But the motor that came with it is a two-stroke motor. Two-stroke motors and four-stroke motors are two different beasts. A two-stroke motor is very powerful and gets you around, but it runs on a mixture of gas and oil, not eco-friendly. A lot of people don't sell them anymore. Right now the Monterey Bay doesn't have any problem with having a two-stroke motor in it, but a lot of lakes in California won't let you get within 50 feet of that lake. It took me awhile to rebuild it, then went out and made a voyage, just powerhouse. But I knew something could fail, so needed a backup plan, not just one but a couple if you can. I got an electric motor and I got oars. It wasn't all that long until the two-stroke went out so I put the electric motor on it. Lo and behold if it didn't fall apart on the way in either. So now I'm with my oars. I looked at the electric motor and the prop was just spinning circles around the water. I have two motors and neither of them work. Great.

I pull the oars out now. I'm off of Cannery Row and you may think Cannery Row and Fisherman's Wharf, it's not that far. Well, try rowing it sometime. You have the wind blowing in one direction and it's not towards the harbor; it's blowing you towards the middle of the bay. And they have the swells to deal with and usually when anything like this is happening, it's not a sunny, beautiful, calm day. It's usually rough. The clouds are coming in and the winds are howling. And that's what it was like when this happened. But, I made it. And when I got to land I was very grateful. But that's one of the reasons I like being out on the bay—"Wow, this is exciting and challenging."

'Fish Out the Sardines— We Need to Feed the Troops'

Back in the day, we had the sardine industry. I've heard that early on, experts were warning that we would fish all the sardines out of the bay, but someone, possibly Roosevelt himself, said, "Fish out the sardines—we need to feed our troops." Now they've made a comeback. But it's not worth it to have an industry for sardines these days because tourism is much more profitable. And a little cleaner too. The sardines are back, but I just throw them back.

We have a salmon season which starts in April. The salmon come into the bay and then continue north. When the salmon come back, it's like a surfer with waves—everyone's out there fishing. Stay away from weekends. On the weekends, you have everyone from inland coming to the shores to go fishing and it just becomes crazy out there. You have people who have never been out to sea before, like a guy trying to back a trailer down a launch who has never done it before, and it takes an hour or more. And then when they get into the water, they can't figure out how to start the motor and they're blocking the dock. Meanwhile, I know what I'm doing. My boat runs, and I just want to get out there.

The Legend of the Lucky Lure

There's a lot of preparation involved in getting your boat ready to get out to sea, getting the right rig for the fish you're trying to catch. And you always find yourself thinking, it would have been so much better if only we'd done something differently. The last time we went out, I thought we'd brought everything but we didn't bring any squid! Both of us thought the other was bringing it. We thought we'd catch live squid, but nothing's happening. So we gave up on that and used artificial lures. I had a real special one for ling cod, my lucky lure. The time before this, I lost it. The lure was stuck on the bottom and the guy I was fishing with wanted to leave. It was his boat, and he was telling me, "It's just a lure," and I'm saying, "You don't understand, dude, it's my lucky lure!" But he wanted to go in, so I had to cut my line and I lost my lucky lure. So this last time we were out, I was the only one to catch anything. I used a halibut rig and brought up a red vermillion, which is the Pacific coast version of the red snapper.

There are so many different species of fish out in Monterey Bay, and each has its own set of regulations. The challenge is telling them apart, so you know whether you're allowed to keep it. The party boats have pictures of all the different fish. Right now, there's a moratorium on rock cod. In my teens and 20s, I never would have dreamed we wouldn't be allowed to fish for rock fish, because there were so many of them. But it became overfished, and then you have certain individuals who think everything belongs to them and they'll take it all. You just can't do that. So they finally put in a rule, no rock fish. That just broke my heart. And then they put in rule that you can't fish from the beaches or the rocks. Now you've got to be out on a boat. There are reefs out in the deeper waters where you can fish for the rock fish.

A friend of mine bought a 26-foot Osprey. He had to have everything perfect, so there was two years of preparation. We finally took it out this year to Moss Landing and back. We ended up off of Point Pinos and that's where I threw in my lucky lure and caught two ling cod within 15 minutes and he didn't catch anything. He didn't understand about my lucky lure at the time, but later on he went to the store, but he couldn't find anything just like it. I spent hours searching online, but couldn't find it. He found something close, so we dropped those in and nothing. Not a nibble. See? That was the lucky lure.

There are so many things you can drop down there, and that's the difference between hunting and fishing. There's no guesswork when you're down there on a dive. I've caught ling cod both ways. I've been down there with something called a Hawaiian sling, which is a pole with a rubber band on it. You put the piece of rubber around your hand and when you release the tension, it lets the pole lunge forward. The pole has a prong on the end. You get to go down and pick which fish you want, instead of just taking the one that bites. You can use a spear gun, but they often malfunction.

'Like Being Robbed at Gunpoint'

One time we were free-diving down by Highlands Inn. Visibility must have been 200 feet, crystal clear—just incredible. We were picking up oysters and scallops and eating them at the surface and thinking this was pretty cool. There were beautiful schools of ling cod. When you get ling cod over 24 inches, they're mad at you and they don't want to come with you. I've already got a couple of rock cod and a ling cod on my stringer, and I figure one more and I'll have enough. Next thing I know, I'm bent in half; my head is hitting my feet, and I'm being plowed through the water. All I could think of, this is a great white about to sink its teeth. But it was just a sea lion taking my stringer and it plowed me through the water and it totally exhausted me. It's the last time I went out, by the way. I was spent after that. It took me for a ride; it must have been at least 20 miles an hour and it bent my head down to my feet. I can't believe I didn't see it coming. It was a big lesson for me; don't just focus on one thing when you're down there. Always know what's around you. I barely made it to the beach. I was in shock, more or less. I had no fish; I'd just been hit and my mind was spent. I thought I was done, that those teeth would be sinking into me. But no, it was just a sea lion. It was one of those beaches where I had to climb a cliff to get back to the truck and I couldn't get up the cliff. I laid on the beach, crying, a grown man. I just wanted to go home and get into dry clothes and I'll go to the store and buy a piece of fish. I don't care. Everything was perfect that day until I got robbed. It felt like being robbed at gunpoint. But, it was his before me. I was out of my environment.

If you've ever seen the front of a ling cod, they've got these two front fangs. This guy that I'd caught with my sling was at my neck's edge and he's squirming and I could just picture him getting my ear or something. All of your adrenalin is pumping. But since I got caught by that sea lion, I haven't gone out hunting anymore. I'll stick to the top of the water and throw a line in. I have friends who go out in kayaks, but I've seen too many YouTube videos of these kayaks being rocked by the great whites and I say, "No, thank you." The bigger the boat the better.

'If You Catch a Fish, That's a Bonus'

You just go out to enjoy it, and if you catch a fish, that's a bonus. Just go for the excitement of being out there. People live their whole lives and never get to do that. I live right on the edge of the map and I go out on this beautiful, pristine water and it's been preserved. There's such a difference. I've been out on water that's completely brown. It'd be a beautiful day and the water wouldn't reflect blue. Just brown because it's polluted. I've seen this down south and up north in San Francisco. Our Monterey Bay is blue and pristine and beautiful.

The first thing you do when you're out on the water is find landmarks so you can situate yourself. You can't just

Chris Bell's Sea Otter Bronze in Berwick Park by the Recreation Trail along the bay, Photo Peter Mounteer.

Scenic bench looking east to Lovers Point Park, by the Recreation Trail along the bay, Photo Peter Mounteer.

drop a line anywhere, because a certain fish is down there and he's not going to be eating anything except squid. Everything eats squid. If you're trying to catch halibut, you're going to have better luck fishing with a different rig than you'd use for salmon. Mooching is what you do off a party boat, which is just dropping a line in with an anchovy at the end of it and crossing your fingers. Then there are the downriggers; that's when you're trolling for it and you have these large flashers that are about 100 yards behind your boat, and the line from your fishing pole is connected to a hook and a weight that will take you down to the depth that you want to be. So if you hear that the fish are running at 80 feet, you'd have a little bit more weight on your line to take you down to 80 feet. You need to know your depth and keep yourself in this area.

I use different poles for different types of fishing. On the beach, I use a surf casting rod, which is longer and casts further. When I'm fishing for halibut I use a stiffer pole without a lot of play on it. Salmon, a shorter pole with a little bit of play on it. That's salt water. Freshwater, you'd use a smaller pole with lot of play because the slightest nibble you want to play the hook. On the water, anything is going to swallow your hook. You don't need to worry about setting the bait in the ocean. You need to reel it in as fast as you can, because otherwise a sea lion is going to take it off the hook. If there's something on your line, get it in or you lose it. Freshwater, you need to finesse it. In the ocean, get it in or you're not going to eat!

Years ago, the fishermen were able to carry shotguns and carry sticks of dynamite and explode them near the sea lions. Now they don't let you do that, and I don't think you should. But if you're fishing for a living, you have a different view of things. I'm a sport fisherman. I go out whenever I can, but it seems that the older I get, the less

Surfers at sunset on Asilomar Beach. Photo Wolf Bukowski.

time I have for it. As a kid, I was out there every day, and every weekend out on a boat. It just doesn't seem like there's enough time in the day anymore.

You need to look at the water before you go out. Are there any whitecaps? What are the swells like? Is there a storm coming in? If you notice, right before the storm there's always a lull, like glass. It's a great time to go out. But if something goes wrong and you're stuck on there and the storm comes in, then it's a different story. You can check for storms online, or go to the harbormaster's office and they have the week's forecast posted.

The China Connection

Interesting thing about squid. They stuff it full of ice right there on the commercial wharf. It gets sent up to Watsonville, so I've been told, and they package it to send it to China, and then they send it back. And your Monterey Bay salmon, if it's frozen, I can guarantee you it's been somewhere else before it comes back to Monterey. They don't pack it here.

At the commercial wharf, the distributors are like the middlemen between the commercial fishing boats and the restaurants. If I want to get a big piece of fish, something I know is fresh, I'll go to the place at the end of the wharf. It's become more well-known. Fifteen years ago, you'd have to knock on the door and talk to the fisherman who'd been on the water all day and see what he'd got. Now it's out of a deli case.

'If It Smells Like Fish, It's Not Fresh'

I like to cook fish with the least amount of stuff on it if it's fresh. If it smells like fish, it's not fresh, that's the rule. Seafood is just so clean-tasting, especially if it's fresh, from the same day. If you eat it all the time, you're going to start getting bored with the same preparation. So you start fixing it a different way. My favorite is probably an egg wash with a little panko bread crumbs, and sauté or fried with a little butter. Salmon, put it on the barbecue or blacken it. If you catch a salmon, you've got more than one dinner and a few lunches. Poached with hollandaise sauce is always quite tasty. Barbecued with any kind of topping. Blackened in a Caesar salad. Ling cod, panko it. Or just take herbs, put it down with the butter and sauté it. If you like tomato sauce, use that. If it's fresh, you can't go wrong. Living so close to the Salad Bowl of the World, so many things grow fresh around here, and then with the fresh seafood, we have the best of land and sea.

Free Diving for Abalone

We used to dive for abalone. Across the bay is where we'd get the big red abalone. You can't do abalone in Monterey Bay anymore unless you free dive, and you have a limit. If you're south of Yankee Point, you can use tanks. You'd usually find abalone around 20 feet down, and the water looks very different when you're in it compared to being up on shore. We call them vaults, little hidden treasures, where the abalone flourish. You usually paddle out and use an inner tube as a marker and you dive. If you don't have good visibility, it's all fill. You can't see your hand. So you dive deeper and if you find one, you've got to get it off the rock. You have to get your iron underneath it, get it off the rock, get control of it, get it to your body, and get up to the surface. The first time I went out, I found a 13 inch helmet, a real monster, and I wrestled it to my chest. I come barreling to the surface, out of breath, and popped out in the middle of a wave. The wave pummeled me. My mask's gone, my weight's gone, I've got one flipper on, and I had a rip in my suit. And I had my abalone! I just remember scraping myself up on a rock, taking off the top of my wetsuit, and I'm still 200 yards off shore. But I'd gotten my abalone and nothing is going to stop me!

But that's what makes it so exciting. When you start your dive, you follow a piece of seaweed. You climb that piece of seaweed down like a rope. You're putting your hands down and here comes a monkey-face eel. They're ugly, and they like to hide in little hidey-holes where you put your hands. But you've got to do it if you're going to get an abalone, because they're not sitting there under a neon sign saying, "Come over here, dude. I'm right here!" You look in a place that doesn't get a lot of surge, where they're not getting beaten by the waves all the time.

Once you let go of that seaweed, you may come up in a totally different place and your bearings are nowhere in sight. The current will just pull you before you even know it. One breath will take you 200 feet away. You learn a whole new respect for the water. Sitting in a boat, you doze off and next thing you know, you've lost your bearings. That's why you always do those second checks on your boat, make sure everything is working. Because if you're stuck in the middle of the bay and have to oar your way in, no thank you. I'd be shooting a flare gun.

It's not for everyone. I see guys spending $30,000 one year on all the gear and then selling it the next year for $10,000. They'd had enough. They say the two happiest days of boat-owner's life are the day he buys it and the day he sells it. There's constant maintenance and constant preparation, and it seems like you always forget something. It really takes a different type of person to love it.

◉◉◉

PERSONAL REMINISCENCES

Kayaking on the Monterey Bay
LeeAnn Stewart

I have only been kayaking out on the Monterey Bay a dozen times or so, since moving to Pacific Grove full-time seven months ago. When I'm kayaking on the bay, my mind is transported to another world, uprooted from the servitude of land. A feeling of tranquility washes over me and, at the same time, my senses are sharpened and focused. Sights, smells, and sounds are all around me: golden kelp floating in the deep blue water, kelp crabs and small mollusks, jelly fish and swirling silver sardines, the Cannery Row noontime whistle, splashing of the waves against my kayak, the soft sound of a seabird flying overhead and the gentle sea breeze on my face and blowing through my hair.

From my bedroom window, by looking through small open spaces between four houses, I can see a patchwork of the Monterey Bay. I see enough to let me know what the conditions are on the water. When I see whitecaps, I think to myself, "It's way too choppy." But when I see that the water is calm, my heart leaps and I can think of nothing else but putting on my white ball cap and taking my kayak out. I prepare my kayak "Fiona" by setting it on a wheeled trolley and strapping it down tight. Out of the driveway and down my short street, crunching the oak leaves lately fallen from the trees, into the alley filled with the smell of geraniums and mint, and then cautiously, carefully wheeling it out into the slow-moving traffic and across Ocean Boulevard where the scent of salt fills my nostrils and I quicken my pace to the Rec Trail.

I roll down the paved and sand-shouldered trail toward Lovers Point together with the many bicyclists, walkers, runners, children, and dogs. Along the way, I glance out toward the bay, hoping to spot a whale spout or a pod of dolphins or sea lions swimming, or sea otters enjoying their lunch of urchins or crabs. I walk until I reach the overlook of the beach and continue around the backside of the volleyball area and over to the boat ramp that curves around on the far side of Lovers Point Beach. I pass the jumpers and wheel myself down to the bottom of the ramp where I remove the trolley and secure it carefully in the back storage compartment of my kayak. Then I drag my kayak down the soft sloping sand to the water's edge

until my sandals are wet with the infamously cold water. I don my life jacket and wade into the water up to my knees with my kayak. Then ever so gracefully, I get myself seated and glide out onto the water where once again, free from land, I scan the horizon, looking for wildlife in this breathtaking marine sanctuary.

The first time I saw a sea lion while kayaking, it had just surfaced to breathe and I heard a loud exhale about 3 feet away from me. Huge, shiny, and black, it startled me because I wasn't sure what kind of animal was so close to me. I feel comfortable on the bay, but this is open water inhabited by dangerous animals and my self-preservation instincts were on high alert.

Nearby, a group of swimmers, all wearing yellow swim caps, were swimming out to a yellow buoy, just offshore between Berwick Point and Hopkins Marine Station. The huge sea lion looked at the group for a moment, and then, to my horror, it headed straight for them. I felt a dreadful worry come over me and I thought that the swimmers might be in danger. What should I do? Then I saw the sea lion join the swimmers, swimming alongside them and underneath them. The swimmers didn't miss a beat. They just kept on swimming out toward the buoy. I paddled over to meet them, asking them questions and talking to them about their experiences as they rested briefly at the yellow buoy.

The group calls itself The Kelp Krawlers and they meet every Sunday at Lovers Point beach to swim ½ mile out in the bay and back again. There are swimmers of all levels, men and women, who have this one thing in common: they love the Monterey Bay.

I felt an immediate connection with them, either to satisfy a maternal urge to protect them or to one day rub wet-suited elbows with these brave athletes. I admired them for their heartiness and enthusiasm. I decided that in the future, I would join them with my kayak on their Sunday swims whenever my schedule allowed, kayaking ahead of them or behind them, guiding them away from large kelp forests and accompanying the last swimmer back to shore. Will I ever swim with this group in the Monterey Bay? I was told that wearing a wetsuit is a must and I have just purchased my first wetsuit. I do feel there is safety in numbers but I am still hesitant. For now, I am content to kayak on my own and with this group experiencing their swim from the safety of my kayak until I build up enough confidence and courage to join them.

Seagull and Football
LeeAnn Stewart

If I hadn't seen it with my own eyes .....

One sunny afternoon, while walking up the curving boat ramp at Lovers Point beach, I glanced over at the smaller beach that is closest to the tip of the point and I noticed some young boys playing with a small football, about the size of an avocado. As I stopped to watch the boys and their game, one of the boys threw the ball enthusiastically over his friend's head and it landed with a splash into the water. A seagull who had been sitting nearby and apparently watching, swooped down to the water and plucked the small football out of the water with its beak. The boys began to wave their arms and shout at the bird as it began to fly out away from the shore. But then within the span of a minute or two, it turned around and flew back toward the boys. All of the sudden, it dropped the ball, which landed almost into their hands! The boys were thrilled to have their ball back, shrieking and jumping around. It was their lucky day! ~

Before …

Whale Sculpture at Berwick Park
LeeAnn Stewart

It was a dark and stormy night....

In late January 2016, the rain was pouring and the wind was howling throughout the night. We were just settling into our new home on 11th Street and we were getting used to the creaks and groans and the whistling of wind as it passed through our doors and windows. On that night, the wind was so strong that our doors were rattling. In the middle of the night we heard a loud CRACK!, which startled us. But we were too warm and cozy inside to venture out until the following morning.

One of the large trees in Berwick Park was almost completely stripped of its large branches, and all that remained were two very large and shattered tree trunks. It was very sad to look at, but nothing could be done to repair it to its former version of itself.

… after.

Fortunately, some very kind people with vision put their heads together and came up with the idea of the whale sculpture, found funding and approvals and an artist. Nearly two years later, it has become one of the icons of Pacific Grove, where guests and neighbors snap their family photographs daily with the beautiful Monterey Bay in the background.

Whale Welcome
Emily Miller

I grew up tidepooling in Half Moon Bay on weekends with my family. We'd take a short drive over the coastal range from the Peninsula and find ourselves in the world of anemones, sculpins, and urchins. It fostered a love of the natural world that grew into a career as I pursued graduate studies in ecology. I studied anadromous sturgeon in the San Francisco Bay and, like these fish that journey upriver to spawn, I found my mate, Jonathan, inland at U.C. Davis. But like sturgeon that return to the sea, I longed for the coast. Fortunately I was offered a research position at the Monterey Bay Aquarium after I finished my graduate degree.

Jonathan and I decided to take a leap and migrate coastward from the Central Valley at the beginning of 2018. At first sight, we fell in love with an upstairs unit of a majestic old Victorian house overlooking Jewell Park a short walk from Lovers Point. After carrying boxes up and down the stairs we took a break and walked along the coastal trail. As we walked, we saw sea otters in the kelp, bobbing harbor seals, and sun-bathing cormorants. Suddenly, a gray whale's arched back rose from the surface near shore and dove, flipping its fluke into the air, not once but three times. We knew this Pacific Grove wave was welcoming us home.

History of Bathhouse Smith
Rudy Fischer

But not all encounters with historic buildings end in them being knocked down and replaced. Here I am thinking particularly of the Beach House lease and the Holman Building condominium project. The Beach House Restaurant, for instance, had a long history as The Bath House Restaurant before becoming the current fabulous restaurant.

In 1902 Pacific Grove bought the property then known as Pacific Grove Beach from the Pacific Improvement Company. According to an article in the *Cedar Street Times* some years ago, sometime after that a man by the name of William S. Smith "strolled among the flowers, the sea scents, the slight fog, the boulders … rubbing his eyes and thinking how best to use the property."

Now previously Mr. Smith had built a small building

which the modest people of the time could use to change from their regular clothes into swimming duds. They could then go down to the small cove below the building and splash in the water. Even though the building was only considered a shack many people used it and it became quite a successful venture.

It became so popular, in fact, that William Smith decided that the cove was too small. So, according to a *Cedar Street Times* article of ten years ago, he leased several mules and hauled some dynamite to the cove, setting it into strategic places. Then, in the "early hours of a crystalline morning" he set off an explosion and "expanded" the cove.

And he continued to use explosives for some time to reshape Lovers Point into what we now enjoy. In my mind this shows two things; (1) that there was no Planning Commission and no noise ordinance at the time, and (2) the need for both.

In 1904 he added several salt water baths, earning him the nickname "Bathhouse" Smith. About this same time he built a Japanese teahouse, planted flowers and shrubs, and hired the Sugano family to run the operation. They were to "brew savory teas to serve with sweetened biscuits." In 1948 the tea garden was torn down.

According to research by Dixie Lane of the Heritage Society, the building that houses the Beach House Restaurant had served as a bathhouse up until sometime late last century. By the time Robert Enea, Kevin Phillips, and Jim Gilbert started renovating the building, however, the pumps, pipes, and other equipment that had served the baths had long since been removed. Kevin did report that "there were still stairs and ramps going in all kinds of directions" when they built the café and restrooms in the downstairs part of the building.

A Day at The Dunes
Sharon Law Tucker

In 1955, when I wasn't spending my summers with family in Big Sur, I was with my girlfriend and her family spending leisurely afternoons in Pacific Grove picnicking near the sand dunes along Asilomar Beach. The dunes were monoliths ranging from 10 to 25 feet high. We would play hide-and-seek for hours, or try our best to climb as high as we could. As the sand gave way beneath out feet, we would drop to our stomachs and roll down to the bottom, laughing all the way, ending with mouthfuls of sand, only to start all over again.

The dunes stretched out to what is now Spanish Bay. Where the dunes met the forest, the sand was harvested for commercial use. Sand was loaded onto a conveyor belt elevator, then dumped into rail freight cars. As many as eight freight cars would carry the sand along the train tracks to a sand plant in an unincorporated area on the border of Seaside. This area would eventually become known as Sand City. But back in my day, there were just a few shacks, auto repair shops and the sand plant. Not much else of any significance.

One interesting story: When Waikiki Beach on the island of Ohau, Hawaii, was decimated from a hurricane, sand coming from the Pacific Grove sand dunes was shipped from the Sand City sand plant to Hawaii to rebuild the beach.

Today, the once impressive dunes are almost leveled, considered fragile and off-limits to foot traffic. A wooden boardwalk provides walking access from the roadway to Spanish Bay, and the train tracks remain buried underneath the biking trail. But I'll always remember those glorious days of sunshine and picnics, running up and down the giant sand dunes of Pacific Grove.

Asilomar Beach. Photo Peter Mounteer.

A Pagrovian Scrapbook
Edward E. Jarvis

A main branch of my family began its American adventure at Williamsburg, Virginia in 1673, and every few generations, saddled up and moved a little farther west—to North Carolina, Tennessee, Arkansas and Colorado. I was the first to be born in California, almost due east of here, in the San Joaquin Valley. So here I am in Pacific Grove, as far west as you can get without getting wet, having completed the three hundred year westward trek my family began in the new world.

I came to Pacific Grove in 1969 to begin my practice as a doctor of chiropractic. Our town looked a bit different then.

My office until 1973 was on Forest Avenue directly across from City Hall, which at that time also housed the police station and jail. In those days we had four or five policemen who, in their khaki shirts and green wool trousers, looked more like forest rangers and were armed only with their .38 caliber revolvers. They walked their beats, knew who the good guys were as well as the bad. They were mostly in their forties and fifties and were often seen chatting with the locals on a street corner. A couple of times there was a burst of excitement in my waiting room as patients watched with amusement the attempted escape of a "perp" being booked; the mad dash down Forest Avenue with a gaggle of police in tow, à la Keystone Cops!

In those days housing in Pacific Grove was very inexpensive—no one wanted to live in our summer fog—and so our town was the locus of the flower children at the height of its era. Many of my patients were of that community—members of the counter culture—some of whom went outside to cheer on the escapees! On another occasion the animal control officer parked her mobile kennel in front of my office and went across the street into the police station. One of my tie-dyed patients went out and emptied her truck of its contents, two dogs and three kittens, and distributed them among my other waiting patients, who took them home.

Pacific Grove had at that time Holman's Department Store, the hub of downtown, as well as Sprouse Reitz, three mom and pop groceries (Grove Market being the beloved survivor) two pharmacies, and many shops that catered to a vibrant local population.

Lighthouse Elementary School, where my daughter attended kindergarten, was a populous hub of learning, as was David Avenue Elementary School.

Unfortunately, years later, the rise of Silicon Valley and the instant wealth for many also severely raised real estate prices here, and many homes became weekend homes

Scotsman Dr. Ed Jarvis and his bagpipes.

for out of town residents, thus decreasing our permanent population base which supported our local shops and schools. It resulted in a change toward tourism. But still, what a wonderful little town we inhabit.

I am a nature lover and savor the proximity of the wild fauna: deer, fox, raccoons, coyotes, squirrels, and even our occasional resident mountain lion.

I also enjoy the high drama of our shoreline, the border between two entirely different worlds. I often take my bagpipes to a promontory near Rocky Shores and play for whatever is swimming by or flying overhead. On one occasion last year as I played, two humpback whales breached repeatedly just offshore as a pod of dolphins were leaping after a school of fish, pelicans diving among them. All of this directly in front of me!

On another occasion as I played the regimental charge of a Scottish Highland regiment, "Caber Feigh" (the deer's antlers) I heard a repeated clacking sound behind me as I faced the ocean. When I turned I witnessed two stags in the height of testosterone poisoning having a disagreement as to who should be doing the local studding!

Perhaps the magic of our Peninsular niche goes beyond personal experience. When my younger grandson, Ben, was nine I rented a kayak at Lovers Point and we paddled to Cannery Row, then backtracked to Point Pinos. As we neared Lovers Point I saw a bottle floating in the kelp bed. I told Ben that we should gather it up and dispense with it when we got ashore. He excitedly said that maybe there was a message in it. Maybe, I said, smiling at his innocence. But, lo! When we took the bottle aboard there was, indeed, a piece of paper rolled up inside. The bottle was a wine bottle of a small Washington state vineyard. The enclosed note was a heartfelt farewell from a young woman to her fiancé, who had been killed in battle in the Near East. "Should we put it back?" asked Ben. "I think it has reached its destination: Lovers Point." I told him. We decided to set it alight on the point and let the smoke carry its message to its intended recipient.

I love to travel and would even live in a couple of other places for several months, but Pacific Grove as Home is rooted in my soul. Whenever I return from vacation I drive along Ocean View Boulevard and think to myself that if I didn't live here I would crave to do so. Then I put a smile on my face and head to our little street near the concentrated wilds of Washington Park, feeling most blessed among men. After all, how few places offer a quaint, friendly town proximate to wildlife and a dramatic, rugged coastline, all within a short walking distance.

DUET

Last night they came to my dream
and I heard them, their high
alto chorus moving through a singular
melody, calling to me. So today
I go to the strand above wave worn
boulders, watch the breakers roll in
rhythmically sounding their cadence.
I lean the sturdy arms of the drones
against my shoulder, let escape
my life's breath into the bag, press
it against my ribs, the pipe's wail
reaching out to five otters who
now swim close, stretch their torsos,
listen as the music, its hum
and plaint, moves in a slow
dance over the swells inviting
the humpbacks' song rising up
from the depths to a duet of wonder,
of awe, our voices primal, harmonizing,
filling the vacancy between worlds.

Edward Jarvis
3/18

Where Is Mr. Coffee?
Evelyn Kahan

I always enjoyed it when I'd drive around the bend just past the golf course pond and see the bright, colorful umbrella next to the tiny vehicle where Mr. Coffee brewed his delicious coffees. At the edge of the continent he'd sit reading a book between customers. A congenial fellow, he'd put his book down, step to the rear of his trucklet where the coffee gizmo was and make pleasant conversation as the gizmo steamed away and the surf sprayed up from the rocks just yards in front of us.

We'd chat about the book he was reading, his surfing days (in the past now due to his aching, aging back). I'd think of other folk, at the edge of their continents, perhaps lopping off the top of a coconut to drink, or holding a mug of hot chocolate at the edge of their tundra far off. You could meet people from all over the world, touring the west coast, and unite in coffee sipping with them. Sharing the view was special.

I could simply go to one of our many fine coffee establishments in downtown P.G. and also converse with town folk and tourists. That's very good to do; however, it's not the same as standing on the very edge of the Pacific shore, staring out at the salty water with Mr. Coffee and whoever happens by.

He's never been there on a consistent basis, but rather as a nice surprise that causes me to drink my second cup of the day; usually I drink just one.

Seeing that expanse of water and dramatic jutting rocks, the waves rushing toward us, I know how small we are and that we're just visitors on this earth. Seeing the umbrella and the man at the edge of the continent reminded me of Greece, Argentina, New Zealand, and humanity. How a small comfort, a brief conversation, can make for a lovely day, adding to the charm to our lovely Pacific Grove.

No sign of the umbrella nor the man in months now.
Where are you, Mr. Coffee?
Come back.

Note: Mr. Coffee can still be seen today, serving customers in Pacific Grove by the bay.

Jim Willoughby: Prince of Tides
Susan Goldbeck

Prince of Tides is the moniker given to Pacific Grove's own Jim Willoughby in a *Los Angeles Times* article about his leadership in the protection of the sea life at the world renowned tide pools at Point Pinos. These tide pools are off the coast not far from Crespi Pond and the Point Pinos Lighthouse.

Willoughby was raised at the Hopkins Marine Station where his father long worked as supervisor of the building and grounds. Jim's father worked beside such notables as the premier marine biologist Doc Ricketts, who had a laboratory nearby. From the time he was a boy, Willoughby developed a love of the sea and its creatures. He especially loved exploring the magnificent tide pools in front of the marine station which were protected and off limits to public access. This interest in marine life eventually led him to earn a master's degree in natural science and he then spent twenty-five years teaching science in San Jose.

After his retirement, Jim and his wife Lee moved back to Pacific Grove in an area of town not far from the beach and a short walk to the Point Pinos tide pools. They spent a great deal of time at the tide pools on their daily beach walks and soon became alarmed at how much the sea life there had depreciated over the years. The once bountiful Point Pinos tide pools that Jim knew as a boy were no more. Both he and Lee observed the reasons why on a daily basis.

The invertebrates and other sea life at Point Pinos were being loved to death. Loved by tourists who took home sea life to eat or for collections. Loved by scientists and aquarium personnel both local and otherwise who were taking from the area for research, exhibits, and feeding of other sea life.

The Willoughby's soon learned that it was not just the taking which appeared to be all but unregulated or even monitored, but also the indiscriminate trampling of the area by visitors. Fish and Game regulations that did exist were unenforced. There was no real record of what was being taken from Point Pinos or why. Willoughby decided that he would do something about it, and he did. The Coalition to Preserve and Restore Point Pinos Tide Pools was born.

Jim Willoughby and his co-chair, esteemed underwater marine photographer Chuck Davis, also a resident of Pacific Grove, started the Coalition to Preserve and Restore Point Pinos Tide Pools. The group, mostly composed of concerned citizens from Pacific Grove and local divers, worked very hard to get the word out about the problems occurring with the tide pool life in the Pacific Grove Marine Gardens, which borders the entire coast of Pacific Grove.

The response of local residents was immediate and enthusiastic. The reaction of the scientific community was surprisingly less so. It seems the Willoughbys started a bit of a turf war, the scientists taking a rather elitist approach to the issues of what was causing the depredation of Point Pinos tide pools. The leaders of the scientific community, at least some of them, claimed that Willoughby had no scientific proof that humans were causing the undisputed degradation of the area.

Despite the hue and cry of local scientists—after all, Jim Willoughby was just a science teacher—the members of the Coalition kept working, although they were surprised and discouraged by the reaction of these local

Dawn at Hopkins Marine Station. Photo Peter Mounteer.

scientists. It did not take long, however, for the same scientists to admit that they had no proof that the degradation of the tide pools was related to something other than human activity.

In spite of this initial setback, members of the Coalition pushed forward, talking to concerned citizens about the subject of the protection of the Point Pinos tide pools. It was arduous ground-up hard work which culminated in circulating a petition to put a measure on the ballot, an initiative which would create a permanent no-take zone along the Pacific Grove coastline, including the Point Pinos tide pools, excepting only the taking of specimens related to scientific study. The Willoughbys set up tables in front of the P.G. post office, marketplaces, and whenever and wherever they could connect with Pacific Grove residents to collect voter signatures. It worked. Over 1,700 signatures were collected to get the initiative on the ballot, twice the number needed to qualify.

As required, the initiative was placed before the Pacific Grove City Council, which adopted the ordinance, making a public vote on the initiative unnecessary. It became the law in this town. The Point Pinos tide pools were a no-take zone. It was a huge success for the Tidepool Coalition and the Willoughbys.

But it did have what former Mayor Sandy Koffman later described as "an incredible response" from the people of Pacific Grove. It was clear the residents of Pacific Grove wanted their tide pools looked out for, protected, and restored. Most folks thought the Coalition members, led by the Willoughbys, were on the right path. Eventually the efforts of the Tide Pool Coalition caught the attention and then support of environmental conservationists Sea Shepherd's Paul Watson and Jean-Michel Cousteau. Lengthy articles were written in the *Los Angeles Times and San Francisco Chronicle* on the work and efforts of the Tide Pool Coalition and its founder, Jim Willoughby.

Ultimately, the California Marine Life Protection Act (MLPA) was passed in 1999 which required the California Fish and Game Commission to reevaluate all existing marine protected areas and redesign new Marine Protected Areas (MPA's) as a statewide network. The Point Pinos tide pools now lie within fully protected restricted use areas which supplants the city ordinance. Still, the protection and hopefully the preservation of the Point Pinos tide pools that the Prince of Tides, Jim Willoughby (along with other members of the Coalition) achieved still remain. As Mayor Sandy Koffman observed at the time, Jim Willoughby and his Tide Pool Coalition "deserve our thanks and congratulations."

Amazing Monarchs
Betty A. Sproule

For a walk in the winter afternoon sun, my favorite place is the Pacific Grove Butterfly Sanctuary. The butterflies overhead marvel with their ability to lift above the trees, to soar in the air, and to glide on the breeze. They return to their favorite spot, resting on a tree branch where their friends have gathered. All fold wings and become hidden in the beauty of the landscape and the rustle of the leaves.

Amazing how monarchs navigate to find their customary place in Pacific Grove. Each year a new generation of butterflies returns to where their ancestors have been, but the destination is a first for any one individual. Somehow these butterflies know instinctively what took me 60 years to figure out: Pacific Grove is a special and wonderful place to be. We are lucky to join the monarch butterflies in finding a perfect home.

Tidepools at Asilomar Beach. Photos Patricia Hamilton.

A Majestic Sentinel in Greenwood Park
Bonnie Sailer, Artist

Trickling of the creek, chirping of birds, and frenzied barks of two squirrels playing tag lured me into this noticeably cool, fragrant green haven. All forms of nature in their resplendent glory live here. Literally a stone's throw from the immense beauty and roar of the sea, yet in another world of organic glory; an ethereal world of quiet, of moss and water.

My steps softly sank through deep layers of crunching leaves, pastel colored - striped bark, lush oxalis and yesterday's scattered blooms of tangled nasturtium. Setting light was low in the sky and glaring; straining its way through tall strident eucalyptus. Under the bridge - water rapidly coursed over plants and rocks, heightening colors, gurgling; singing a tricking, playful - and echoing tune.

Deer shyly peered through the shadows of a palm. Then, an almost imperceptible overhead shadow brought attention to a fleeting glimpse; softly flapping feathers of white – the lengthy trailing legs of an Egret - in stance to land ever so gracefully into a cushion of eucalyptus.

Then there she was. In astounding glory; the majestic oak. Tall, and standing sentinel. Arms outstretching to filter the kaleidoscope of colored light that was hers; light passing through her limbs. The energy she gave altered me to a state of bliss and awe. She is strength and beauty; she is a life giving tree, the "Majestic Tree of Greenwood Park."

A Majestic Sentinel by Bonnie Sailer, 30"x20" oil on linen.

Harbor seals and a few pups at Hopkins Marine Station protected harbor on the Rec Trail. Photo Patricia Hamilton.

Photo Peter Mounteer.

Old railroad trail. Photo Wolf Bukowski

SECTION SIX

SPIRITS IN MOTION

Sunset on the edge of the continent. Photo Wolf Bukowski.

"We are working toward more stillness …
to be aware of the mind in a clear, quiescent state."

– Buddhist Chant for World Peace

President McKinley visits First United Methodist in Pacific Grove, May 1901. Pat Hathaway Collection.

Pacific Grove Churches
Gary Baley, writer and photographer

Introduction

Since Pacific Grove's history is inextricably linked to religious origins, I proposed to the *Cedar Street Times* newspaper a weekly column that would profile one house of worship every issue. Marge Jameson, the editor, took a chance and thus the *Sanctuary of the Soul* column was born—the source of these articles in this second volume of *Life in Pacific Grove*.

As of this writing, all but three houses of worship that had begun in Pacific Grove have been profiled. The histories of two have largely been lost. The Latter Day Saints (Mormon) church, originally on Pine Street, had moved to Monterey; and the Community Missionary Baptist Church with a mostly Black congregation now worships in that building. I had attended there some twenty years ago when it had a thriving African-American congregation, a charismatic preacher named Rev. Hooks, and a spirited choir that exalted the heart. But now that congregation has dwindled, and the founding stories may be lost forever.

The *Sanctuary of the Soul* has been more to me than just a newspaper column. It has been, and continues to be, a spiritual voyage. After talking with pastors, priests, elders, rabbis, and congregations of diverse faiths, I've learned that all seek peace and reconciliation with one another, albeit with different voices and under different names.

From the small A-Frame Baptist church on Funston Ave. with a single stained-glass cross, to the grand Catholic Saint Angela Merici on Lighthouse Ave. with seventeen huge stained-glass windows, to the Buddhist Dharma in a modest yellow home on Forest Ave, all offer some "sanctuary of the soul" to those who seek. Peace be with you.

The Historic Churches of Pacific Grove articles presented here were first published in Pacific Grove's hometown paper, The Cedar Street Times. *Photo Credits: Historic (black & white) photos are courtesy of the Pacific Grove Library, Pacific Grove Heritage Society, individual church archives, and various public-record sources. Contemporary (color) photos were taken by and are Copyright © 2018 Gary Baley.*

St. Mary's by-the-Sea at Twelfth Street and Central Avenue was built in 1887 and has a remarkable collection of antique stained glass windows—some by Tiffany & Co.

The prominent red Gothic building on Central Avenue at Twelfth Street is Pacific Grove's oldest church, founded by seven women who organized a guild in 1886 to raise money for its construction.

P.G.'s First Church: St. Mary's by-the-Sea

Founded in 1887, the prominent red Gothic church on Central Avenue at Twelfth Street is the oldest church in Pacific Grove, but it is not Methodist as one might expect; it is Episcopalian—Saint Mary's by-the-Sea.

In February 1886 seven women formed the Saint Mary's Guild to raise money for construction of Saint Mary's. Helen Reed, Mrs. J.M. Page, Mrs. F. May, Mrs. E. F. Easterbrook, and Mrs. Hollenbeck were among the early supporters of the Guild. A plot of land was donated by the Pacific Improvement Company (now Del Monte Properties). The building opened on June 19, 1887, and was formally dedicated the following month. Modeled on a church in Bath, England, it measured 32 feet wide, 70 feet long and had a spire of 75 feet. The first rector was Rev. J. Fred Holmes.

The building has since been expanded to twice its current size. It has a remarkable collection of antique stained glass windows. Five pairs along the north wall and five pairs along the south wall are of pointed-arch design. The most prominent window on the east wall above the altar is called The Annunciation and depicts the angel Gabriel announcing to Mary that she will bear the Christ child. This window consists of over 3,000 pieces of glass. Above the west entrance within a pointed redwood arch are ten windows with a center wheel in a lily motif, which represents purity.

The Episcopal faith originated during the American Revolution when patriots in the Anglican Church split from the Church of England. The life and work of the church is centered on racial reconciliation, evangelism, and the environment.

An avid surfer, sailor, painter, scuba diver, guitar player, ship captain, sailing instructor, and 12-year Episcopal minister—all these qualities make up the newest rector at Saint Mary's bytheSea—Father Jeffrey C. Lewis, who hails from Maine. Sandy blond hair, azure eyes, clean shaven, tall, this man might easily be found on the cover of *Gentlemen's Quarterly*—my first thought upon meeting Father Lewis. "There are about 200 here on a typical Sunday, mostly white," he said "but we are a politically diverse group with flaming liberals and Trump supporters sitting side by side." He explained that "our faith leaves room for our honesty—we're all in this together." He elaborated that the church is very socially engaged, supporting the civil rights movements and calling for full equality for gays and lesbians, even blessing same sex marriages.

Jeff said, "I feel like I was called to be here." He was just passing through, surfing down the California coast on vacation, and he learned that Saint Mary's was searching for a new rector. He invited me to attend his institution ceremony, coincidentally on the following day, which I gladly accepted.

At the institution ceremony, the Master of Ceremonies was Rev. R. B. Leslie; Bishop's Chaplain, Rev. James Booth; Wardens, Jim Riedel and Mickey Welsh; Acolytes, Matthew Elliott and Nina Hubrich; Lectors, Hersch Loomis and Ann Pettit; Deacon, Rev. Dr. John Lewis; Litanist, Lisa Bennett; Presenters, Cynthia Guthrie, Don Fennell, and Rosi Edwards; Chalice Bearers, Jim Riedel and Celeste Ventura; Ushers, Kit Franke and Bruce Obbink; Organist, Coral Malpede; Music Director, Jeannie Young; Altar Guild, Kathy Hunter, Emily Griffith, Jane Gamble, Sally

Deykerhoff and Georgia Booth. As the community gathered, they were welcomed with music by Coral Malpede on piano, Jordan Goodwin on fiddle, and Tyler Wiederanders on mandolin. The ceremony was led by the Bishop of the Diocese of El Camino Real, Rt. Rev. Mary Gray Reeves.

At first I thought this would be a solemn affair, but I was surprised at the amount of joviality, laughter, and good humor throughout. There were of course serious readings from the Bible, homilies, singing from the hymnal, and prayers. After the letter of institution was read, Rector Lewis and Bishop Gray-Reeves strolled down the aisle sprinkling holy water on the congregation left and right while giggling and laughing all the way. It was a delightful sight! At the conclusion, the Lord's Prayer was recited and Holy Communion was offered.

• • •

Saint Mary's participates in the local I-HELP program which provides food and shelter to the homeless. Plus every Monday, Wednesday and Friday people in need can get help with food, clothing, bus passes, and emergency money for bills.

Saint Mary's by-the-Sea, 146 Twelfth Street at Central Avenue, Pacific Grove CA 93950, website www.stmarys-bythesea.org, or call 831/373-4441.

The original Methodist church on Lighthouse Avenue between Seventeenth and Eighteenth streets. "…an impressive Gothic structure with a huge auditorium and dining hall, it attracted various conferences and religious groups. Presidents Harrison, McKinley, and Theodore Roosevelt addressed assemblies here as did other notables of the day including Susan B. Anthony, Georgia Harkness, Bishop Pitt, and Maud Booth."

Pacific Grove's present First United Methodist Church at 915 Sunset Drive was dedicated in 1963 and is known as the "butterfly church" because of the abstract butterfly stained glass window.

The Butterfly Church: First United Methodist

Pacific Grove was founded in 1875 when David Jacks donated five acres of land to a group of Methodists from San Francisco who formed the first West Coast Chautauqua retreat here. Chautauqua was an urbane educational movement popular in the late nineteenth and early twentieth centuries throughout America that was seen as a counterpoint to "vulgar" vaudeville. Although founded by Methodists, Chautauqua maintained a principle of non-denominationalism and featured notable speakers on social issues of the day. It might be compared to contemporary TED talks.

Church services were held in an openair amphitheater amid the local oak and pine forest where the Pacific Grove Public Library now stands. In 1877 services were relocated to a cottage where the Centrella Inn is now located. The first Pacific Grove Methodist Church building was dedicated in 1888 on Lighthouse Avenue between Seventeenth and Eighteenth streets. Its first bishop was Dr. Thomas H. Sinex. It was an impressive Gothic structure with a huge auditorium and dining hall, and it attracted various conferences and religious groups. Presidents Harrison, McKinley, and Theodore Roosevelt addressed assemblies here as did other notables of the day including Susan B. Anthony, Georgia Harkness, Bishop Pitt, and Maud Booth.

In 1955 the congregation voted to construct a new church building. Ground was broken in 1962 and the new building was dedicated on Palm Sunday 1963. The old building was demolished, but some of the original stained glass can be found in various homes in the area. The circular wood and glass centerpiece from the south bell tower now hangs in the second floor hallway of Pacific Grove City Hall.

The cavernous First United Methodist Church of Pacific Grove displays an abundance of light and space. The

Sanctuary is a bright white brick structure with external buttresses in subdued red. The interior measures 40 x 128 feet and can seat 350 in 46 pews. It is accentuated by an abstract butterfly stainedglass "Resurrection Window" in the semi-circular apse surrounding the altar. The structure is longitudinally placed north-south on a five acre lot that fronts Sunset Drive at 17-Mile Drive. The entrance faces north. Windows run the full length of the east and west sides of the nave. Portable hearing devices are provided for those who need them, although an electronic audio system saturates the Sanctuary with sound front to back. Sliding doors open to a patio on the east where Friendship Time coffee and snacks are provided after the service. The patio also incorporates the cross, brass bell, and foundation stone from the original 1888 church building.

Reverend Pamela Cummings has ministered at First Methodist for seven years and retired in June after 39 years with the United Methodist Church. She was raised in Redlands, California, and attended Pacific School of Religion in Berkeley. Her congregation numbers about 135 plus numerous visitors, mainly from Defense Language Institute and Naval Postgraduate School. About 20 children attend Sunday school. Pastor Cummings describes the church as racially mixed, but "primarily Anglo" and she speaks out on social issues with an inclusiveness toward minorities, gays, and lesbians, saying, "We're all created by God; our task is to remain loyal to the never-changing God in an ever-changing society."

Since 1988 the Church Mouse Thrift Shop ministry has provided fair priced goods, a Christian presence which promotes charitable giving, and a source of direct financial grants to local nonprofit organizations. The One Starfish Safe Parking and Support Service Program and the City of Pacific Grove have made it possible to provide legal, safe parking for a limited number of homeless women in the church parking lot. The church is also active in the I-HELP program, hosting up to 30 men on the third Wednesday every month with a hot dinner, a place to sleep, a breakfast and a bag lunch for the following day.

• • •

First United Methodist Church of Pacific Grove, 915 Sunset Drive, Pacific Grove CA 93950, call 831/372-5875. Email: office@butterflychurch.org. www.butterflychurch.org.

Choir in the Apse of the First Methodist Church

The original church building at Fourteenth Street and Central Avenue was built in 1893 and soon destroyed by fire. Its replacement was constructed in 1911 with a brick exterior from a Seaside brickworks and twin towers, only one of which remains today. The interior is lit with large stained glass windows along the walls.

For many years, the church at Fourteenth Street and Central Avenue was known as Mayflower Church. In 2018 the Mayflower congregation felt the need to rename the church when the church replant was underway. The church is now known as Wellspring Church.

'Doing Life Together': Wellspring Church (Mayflower Presbyterian Church)

Mayflower Congregational Church was organized in Pacific Grove on November 29, 1891, with a membership of 40. In 1893 its first building was constructed on Main Street (now Central Avenue). In 1909, the church obtained the first pipe organ on the Monterey Peninsula—a donation from Andrew Carnegie. Just a few months later, a fire destroyed the building and the pipe organ. The present structure was built in 1911 with a brick exterior from a Seaside brickworks and twin towers, only one of which remains today. The interior is lit with large stained glass windows along the walls. Facing Central Avenue is the largest—a wide, pointed arch in memoriam of John Henry Goodell which depicts Jesus as shepherd holding a lamb and a staff while walking between two sheep.

From the '40s through the '60s church membership held at about 350. The church withdrew from the Organization of Congregational Churches in 1953 and became a self-supporting, self-governing, non-denominational church, known as Mayflower Church of Pacific Grove. A separate Sunday school annex was constructed in 1970. In 1989, the church body voted to become a part of the Presbyterian Church USA and entered into the process of redevelopment. In 2015 the church became affiliated with the Covenant Order of Evangelical Presbyterians or ECO, a more conservative Presbyterian movement.

The Mayflower congregation felt the need to rename the church when the church replant was underway. The new pastor, Tony Trabak, asked the congregation to jot down ideas for a new name. Over several months of discussion and prayer, they settled on Wellspring Church. Paul Davis, one of the church elders who has been attending this church for 55 years, said, "What I like about the name is that it reinforces our need for Jesus—the living water, the abundant source and wellspring of life."

Pastor Tony Traback is a young, outgoing dynamo of a man with a plan—replant Mayflower. Short, black, curly hair and beard to match, dressed in distressed jeans and a plaid shirt, he could be mistaken for a construction worker—a carpenter perhaps—not that he would object to that simulacrum. Married with two young children, he moved his family here from Washington State where he was pastor of a non-denominational church. Earlier, he ministered at The River Church in San Jose, and before that he served as a Peace Corps volunteer in Kenya.

Tony explained the re-plant as a refocusing of the church to create apprentice communities that are "guided by the Spirit, shaped by the Scriptures and embody the welcome of God." He elaborated, "We want to make leaders who direct communities that launch a Jesus movement in the Monterey Bay area. We shouldn't be just creating Christian bubbles; we need to be a blessing to the nation." Tony uses the acronym ABLE meaning: **A**ttend to the spirit. **B**less someone inside and outside the church every week. **L**earn from the life of Jesus. **E**at with someone outside the church as a way to be present in the community.

The Well is Wellspring's intergenerational gathering of Jesus followers who desire to be "so shaped by the scriptures, saturated in prayer, and transformed in community that we embody the welcome of God," Tony explained. "We meet weekly from four to five-thirty on Sundays at Mayflower." He said that between meetings, they try to "do life together" through play dates, dinners and just hanging out.

There are about 110 members with 10 families under 40 and about 24 children in the congregation. Tony said, "There is some racial diversity, but the congregation reflects the community and is mostly Caucasian." But he added, "My dream is a multiethnic body to benefit all of God's people." He has opened a dialog with the city of Pacific Grove, seeking ways that the church can contribute to the community, and that resulted in several local non-profits utilizing space in the church.

The Mayflower building is 26,464 square feet. "It is huge, historic, and a gift that we want to serve to the community," said Tony. There are three levels: basement, main floor, and upstairs, plus an annex. Over 20 multipurpose rooms and a library are available for meetings or meditation, each room bathed in a soft, warm luminescence from multi-hued pastel, stained glass windows.

The annex has several spacious rooms now available to the community that can be reserved for short or long term use, some carpeted, some concrete, and some with hardwood floors. One room is set up as a clubhouse with a Narnia-like wardrobe entrance. It is complete with a stage, curtains, props, a model castle, and a puppet-show platform. Another room with a concrete floor can be used for art or grimy construction projects. Several other rooms are awaiting some community non-profit use.

• • •

Wellspring participates in the local I-HELP program for the homeless twice a month, and holds dances in the Fellowship Hall, potluck lunches at Caledonia Park, and bonfires at Asilomar beach. Last fall they had horseback riding, boating, and surfing parties. Pastor Tony invites everyone: "If you have kids, come and have fun with us. Neighbors, coworkers and classmates are welcome too."

Wellspring Church, 141 Fourteenth Street at Central Avenue, Pacific Grove, CA 93950. Call 831/373-4705 or email office@wellspringchurchpg.org
website: www.wellspringchurchpg.org.

First Church of God (*Cedar Street Times* 5-11-2018)

The Christian Church at 442 Central Avenue, shortly after its construction in 1896.

The plain white exterior façade, almost frail in appearance, hides some surprises inside.

For the 'Thinking Christian': The Christian Church of Pacific Grove

"A Spiritual Sanctuary for the Thinking Christian" is the invocation on the sign fronting the quaint, white nineteenth century chapel located at 442 Central Avenue—The Christian Church of Pacific Grove (Disciples of Christ). These words have always appealed to me as I drove down Central Avenue many times over the years, so I was eager to learn more about the church, its theology, and its mission.

In the late 1800s a group of women in Pacific Grove started a prayer circle in their homes following the sermons of a Disciples of Christ evangelist. The circle grew to the point where the women sought a permanent structure. For several years they raised money through bake sales and donations, finally securing the $300 needed to construct their church.

In 1896 the sanctuary was complete, and it stands today basically unchanged from then except for the addition of a rectory, office and gift shop. It is a modest church with only 18 pews, but could seat 100 with a squeeze. It has a stable congregation numbering about 90 with about 50 worshiping each Sunday. The plain white exterior façade, almost frail in appearance, hides some surprises inside. Thick, prime California redwood beams form the walls and vaulted ceiling, including two flying buttresses. It is solid and impressive for its size. Three pairs of antique stained glass windows grace the west and east walls. Downstairs at the rear of the sanctuary is a full-immersion baptistry, a choir room, and a community room with full kitchen and an espresso machine. Upstairs is a meditation room, a playroom for toddlers, and a very special bridal room appointed with antique furnishings and large enough for a pizza party as the bride and her entourage prepare for the big event below.

I interviewed Pastor Daniel William Paul in the church's community room where he brewed up a fine latte and offered muffins and cake for our half-hour chat. He explained that after every service he does the same for the congregation—coffee time is when the congregation breaks into small, lively discussion groups around eight intimate circular tables.

Pastor Dan is a big man with a full head of wavy brown hair, a cherub face, and huge hands. Although his congregation has been stable for years, we talked about the decline of religious congregations throughout America in recent years. He opined that people are drifting away from the large, almost commercialized, churches and seeking something deeper and more meaningful at a personal level. Originally from Pittsburg, Pennsylvania, Pastor Dan is the church's 39th pastor and has served here for 19 years. I asked about the invocation on the sign. "You're not going to hear a fire-and-brimstone sermon here," he said. "We want people to think for themselves, to become engaged with the community and nurture their spiritual nature."

Pastor Dan noted that this church is open and accepting of all. "Churches must adapt to the sensibilities of the culture," he said. "Ours is the first mainline church to have a woman as president, Dr. Sharon Watkins, who also chairs the National Council of Churches." He also pointed out that the Christian Church (Disciples of Christ) is the founding denomination for about 20 universities, including Texas Christian University and Chapman University, where Lyndon Johnson and Ronald Reagan, respectively, were members. Another notable member of our church is William Barber II, president of North Carolina' NAACP chapter, who started the 'Moral Mondays' civil-rights protests," Pastor Dan said.

The church participates in the local I-HELP (Interfaith Homeless Emergency Lodging Program) feeding and sheltering the homeless, and in the international Shoebox program, giving toys and necessities to needy Third World kids. The church also maintains a summer camp in Auburn, California, where middle school students from around the state can spend a few weeks camping and hiking. The Blue Theology Mission Station is a ministry of The Christian Church of Pacific Grove where current science in marine biology informs a theology of creation care. Their mission statement is to provide learning and serving experiences in ocean stewardship for youth groups, adult retreats, and clergy renewals.

• • •

The Christian Church (Disciples of Christ) 442 Central Avenue, Pacific Grove CA 93950; website www.pacificgrovechurch.org or call 831/647-8467.

The Center for Spiritual Awakening at 522 Central Avenue strives to provide "ancient wisdom in a modern way."

'Infinite Experience': The Center for Spiritual Awakening

"Ancient Wisdom in a Modern Way", the motto of the Center for Spiritual Awakening, is emblazoned on the interior cornice in the center's lobby at 522 Central Avenue at the corner of Fountain Avenue in Pacific Grove. It is also found, along with the Tai Chi symbol, on almost every piece of collateral material printed or posted online. This motto advances the guiding principles of the center, namely to coalesce the essential truths found in all religions with current scientific knowledge.

The center's building was originally constructed May 8, 1923, by the First Church of Christ Scientist congregation. Later it was renamed the Pacific Coast Church for a time before adopting its present name.

The center's spiritual director for 40 years, Dr. Bill Little, holds a PhD in physics and is grounded in the spiritual traditions of Christianity, Buddhism, Hinduism, Taoism, and Native American teachings. His congregation numbers about 150. "How can I help you?" was his welcome as I stepped into his modest office and took a firm handshake.

I had expected a stuffy academic type, but Bill was pleasantly approachable. Lean and standing about five feet six inches with short graying hair and wire rimmed glasses; his demeanor suggested an athlete rather than a math professor at Monterey Peninsula College. "You find in Buddhism, Christianity, and Hinduism we are meant to be the conduit of a Divine Mind," he explained. "Traditional religions are centered on an enlightened personage such as Buddha, Jesus, Krishna and Mohammed, but the non-traditional approach to religion realizes that same state of enlightenment can exist within every individual. That is the process of spiritual awakening. That's how we awaken from a finite experience into an infinite experience," he said.

I asked him to explain "infinite experience." He said, "Through meditation we can drop through the mind and sense a vast spaciousness. Buddhists call it *the void*, Holmes, *the infinite mind,* and physics *the unified field.* Modern physics is drifting into the metaphysical, the universe is made of mind," he said. "The very act of thinking or observing brings about change. These truths are found in the words of Jesus, 'It is done to you as you believe' and in the passages of Buddhist text, 'what will happen to you is what you think—no more, no less.'"

Dr. Little explained, "We gather to celebrate the truth of who we really are. The individual is cosmic at the core, and by repeatedly exploring this truth from many points of view, we come to accept it fully. The service is designed to provide a long period of uninterrupted spiritual awareness for all present. Music and prayer, as well as digital media, are used to amplify the talk. The overall effect is to quiet the rambling mind and access the deeper sense of *I*," he said.

Following the Sunday program, from 11:45 to 12:30 The Circle Group meets. "We look deeply at the topic of the day and how to integrate it into our own spiritual path. We discuss, without ego, ways in which each person might look at their lessons and what to do with that insight," Dr. Little said. The center conducts a children's program Sundays from 10 to 11:30 am.

The center operates The Mindshop, a bookstore and gift shop with an abundance of metaphysical books and "magical gifts for all." It also provides a tranquil garden setting for quiet reflection, meditation or reading.

The Center for Spiritual Awakening hosts and participates in many community events and parties throughout the year including: concerts, Summer Solstice party at the Hacienda, a Hacienda gala with Bach musicians, Point Lobos discovery walks, multi-media art classes, Christmas candle-lighting program, and a New Year's burning bowl ceremony (meditation to release resentment and worry), to name a few. "We are a vibrant community that welcomes everyone. We explore the intersection of science and spirituality and the common threads of wisdom woven through the world's major religions. On this path we are led to a spiritual awakening," Dr. Little affirmed.

• • •

The Center for Spiritual Awakening, 522 Central Avenue, Pacific Grove CA 93950, website at www.csa-pg.org, call 831/372-1942 or email TheCSA.Info@gmail.com.

Peninsula Baptist Church (*Cedar Street Times* Feb 16, 2018 pg 13)

Peninsula Christian Center traces its roots to the 1920s and the founding of the First Pentecostal Church of Pacific Grove, located at the corner of Pine and Grand avenues.

The building that now houses Peninsula Christian Center was built in 1963 as First Assembly of God. "The church opens its doors during every Pine Street parade, often providing free water and refreshments."

'Spirit-filled': Peninsula Christian Center

In 1908 a group of "spirit-filled" Methodists began meeting in homes and later in the Methodist Church of Pacific Grove on Wednesdays. After outgrowing the borrowed facilities, the group rented a vacant Presbyterian Church building at the corner of Pine and Grand avenues and established the First Pentecostal Church of Pacific Grove. The rent was $4 per month; but in 1922 they purchased the building for $3,000 and incorporated as First Pentecostal Church, affiliated with the Assemblies of God. Their first pastor was Edith Freeberg. In 1924, Rev. Cecil Ellenwood became the first full-time pastor. In 1963, under the leadership of Rev. Dennis Davis, the congregation relocated to a new, larger building which became the First Assembly of God of Pacific Grove at Pine and Fountain Avenues. In 1980 Pastor J. Wilkerson led expansion of the church, which was still affiliated with Assemblies of God, but renamed Peninsula Christian Center of Pacific Grove.

The church contains a sanctuary which can seat 150, a bandstand, two nurseries accommodating 20 children, a teen room attending about 10, a kitchen, an upstairs sound booth, office, ocean-view room, and outside playground. A live band performs in every service with song lyrics displayed on two huge LCD monitors hung above the stage for benefit of the congregation who often sing along with raised arms in praise of God. The church owns three properties in the same block, two houses and a six unit apartment building, one unit of which serves as a parsonage.

The congregation is transgenerational but not as transracial as they would like. Their disappointment is understandable since the Pentecostal movement began in a Los Angeles African-American church, the Azusa Street Revival, in 1906. The services were led by Rev. William J. Seymour, who preached racial reconciliation, and whose services were accompanied with testimonies of miracle healings, laying of hands, and speaking in tongues.

• • •

The PCC supports Al and Friends, a ministry for the needy in Pacific Grove, by supplying food and other necessities every week. The church has also adopted a needy family of eight, furnishing gift cards for food, gasoline and clothing. New Christmas presents are collected by contributions from the congregation so that each needy family member receives 12 presents on Christmas Day. Every month the church visits the Carmel Hills Care Center for support, fellowship and prayer, and a Fall Festival is held each October 31 with a family fun house and a bounce house for kids. The church opens its doors during every Pine Street parade, often providing free water and refreshments.

Peninsula Christian Center, 520 Pine Ave, Pacific Grove CA 93950. Website www.pccpg.org, email info@pccpg.org, call 831/373-0431.

"Often referred to as the 'mother church' by the African-American community, it was the first church on the Monterey Peninsula with a predominantly African-American congregation."

First Baptist Church in its early days at Laurel and Fourth streets. A local socialite, Sarah Bodfish, donated the money to purchase the land for the first church building.

The Mother Church: First Baptist Church of Pacific Grove

In 1638, Roger Williams established the first Baptist church in America at Providence, Rhode Island. The first ordained African-American Baptist was George Lisle (1750-1820), a slave from Georgia who was emancipated prior to the American Revolution.

In 1845 during the lead-up to the Civil War, the issue of slavery split the American Baptists into anti-slavery Northern and pro-slavery Southern Baptist conventions. Even after the war, the two remained as separate denominational entities. The Northern Baptist Convention is now known as American Baptist Churches USA, or ABC.

The history of First Baptist Church of Pacific Grove is sketchy but important as its success gave rise to many other churches for the non-white residents of Monterey County. The story presented here is taken mostly from the excellent compilation of Ibrahim Omer's "First Baptist Church of Pacific Grove History." Often referred to as the "mother church" by the African-American community, it was the first church on the Monterey Peninsula with a predominantly African-American congregation. Rev. Joseph Sutton of Seaside's Friendship Baptist Church said in 1952, "All the Negro Baptist churches on the peninsula sprang from the First Baptist Church of Pacific Grove."

The church was founded in 1907 with Reverend Lewis from San Jose holding services for 60 once a month at El-Bethel Mission, 541 Lighthouse at Fountain. Later Rev. Emmett B. Reed from Spokane, Washington, was recruited as the first fulltime pastor.

Circa 1909, Sarah Bodfish, local white socialite and wife of businessman George Fenwick Bodfish, donated money to purchase land for a permanent church building. It was constructed at Fourth and Laurel Streets with its cornerstone laid by Alvin Lewis. The original address was 229 Fourth Street, later changed to 258 Laurel. Originally the congregation was inter-racial with a philosophy of tolerance and inclusion. However, by the 1930s the congregation was exclusively black, according to Evelyn Smith, wife of former Pastor Wellington Smith, who in 1931 organized the first NAACP chartered branch in Monterey County at the church.

In 1965, under the leadership of Rev. Richard Nance, the old church building was demolished and a new sanctuary was built that could hold 400 worshipers. In 1987 an east wing was added with a choir room, nursery, classrooms, a study, and an office.

Reverend Warren Bryant came to minister at First Baptist Church of Pacific Grove in January 2018. He was raised in Pittsburg and joined the Army at 17. After his tour of duty, he wanted to become a police officer, but at 24 he was called to the ministry. He attended Newburgh Theological Seminary and was ordained at the Prince of Peace Baptist Church in Terre Haute, Indiana. Then he spent eight years in San Jose and about a year and a half attending Community Missionary Baptist Church in Pacific Grove. He and his wife Judy have one grown daughter.

Rev. Bryant is determined to make his church more diverse. "Now there is only one white parishioner in a congregation of 35," he said. "My challenge is to create an atmosphere where the local [white] neighbors feel comfortable visiting our church."

• • •

Pastor Bryant plans an outreach into the local neighborhood by hosting a pancake breakfast in the near future—going door-to-door to distribute invitations. "I don't want this church to be an island," he said. The church's Esther's Circle supports Martha's Kitchen, a Salinas-based charity that provides food to the needy at Dorothy's Place in Salinas.

First Baptist Church of Pacific Grove, 246 Laurel Avenue, Pacific Grove CA 93950. Call 831/373-0741, email blessings@firstbaptistpg.com, http://firstbaptistpg.com/.

The original St. Angela's at Eighth and Central was constructed in 1929. Its altar and interior were designed by liturgical artist Euphemia Charlton Fortune, who in 1928 founded the Monterey Guild. The altar is being used today—the Saint Angela's Blessed Sacrament Chapel. The first mass

at the current St. Angela Merici Church, 146 Eighth Avenue, was held in 1957. Its design incorporated mid-century Swedish modernism-minimalist architecture and was laid out along a north-south axis with the street entrance on the south.

Celebrating 90 Years: Saint Angela Merici

"We are a diverse Roman Catholic community welcoming to all people—a community united by our love of God and commitment to serving and supporting others."

The church's namesake, Angela Merici, was born in the middle of the 15th century in northern Italy. After being orphaned and experiencing the death of her sister, Angela took vows of poverty and promised herself to God. During a pilgrimage to the Holy Land she became blind but resumed her journey. After praying before a crucifix on her return trip, she regained her sight at the same place where she had lost it on the island of Crete. She also had a vision of young women ascending to heaven on a stairway of light and heard a voice saying she would establish an order of maidens as she envisioned. Later, she founded the Ursuline Order in fulfillment of that vision. In 1827 she was canonized.

The Saint Angela Merici parish was instituted on May 31, 1928, under the authority of Bishop MacGinley of the Diocese of Monterey-Fresno. Father Charles Kerfs was its first pastor and served until his death in 1949. Weekday masses were held in a home at 132 Nineteenth Street, and the first Sunday masses were held at the Theosophical Society Hall at 160 Monterey Street in Pacific Grove with about two dozen members. As the congregation quickly outgrew its rented hall, the first church building at Eighth and Central Avenue was constructed in 1929 and seated 180. Its altar and interior were designed by liturgical artist Euphemia Charlton Fortune, who in 1928 founded the Monterey Guild. The altar is being used today—the Saint Angela's Blessed Sacrament Chapel.

Continued growth fostered plans for a new church in 1950 designed by John Taras with room for 400 worshippers. A two-story house nearby, the "Victorian House," was purchased for the convent. Groundbreaking for new church occurred on August 1, 1956. Its design incorporated mid-century Swedish modernism-minimalist architecture and was laid out along a north-south axis with the street entrance on the south. The first mass was celebrated on December 8, 1957. Over the years it had been updated and renovated to seat up to 750. The old church building is now the Central Presbyterian Church with a predominantly Korean congregation.

Dedication of the new church building was delayed until 1964 when the last three of seventeen stained-glass windows by artist Gabriel Loire of Chartres, France, were installed above the entrance—an 18-foot high tryptic titled the Resurrection of Jesus, the Crucifixion of Jesus, and the Ascension of Jesus. These three windows were duplicates—the first set having been lost aboard the Italian SS *Andrea Doria* when it sank in 1956. After installation of the tryptic, Bishop Willinger led dedication ceremonies for the new building.

Seven windows on the east wall show Saint Pius X; Saint Patrick, Our Lady of Fatima, Saint Anthony of Padua, the Virgin with Infant, Saint Joseph and the Child Jesus, and Saint Thérèse of Lisieux. Seven windows on the west wall depict Saint Angela Merici with family, Saint Angela praying before the Assumption of Mary, Saint Angela's vision of ten virgins, the healing of Saint Angela, Saint Angela founding the Ursuline Order, Saint Dominic, and Saint Ignatius of Loyola.

In 2017 the parish celebrated 60 years in the current church building, and on May 31, 2018, it celebrated 90 years as a parish community.

The current pastor, Irish-born Father Seamus O'Brien, is a graying, soft-spoken man in his 60s with a consolatory Irish brogue. He has rectored at Saint Angela Merici since 2013—the tenth pastor of Saint Angela's since its inception 90 years ago. Prior to Saint Angela's, Father O'Brien served as chaplain at Dominican Hospital and, since 2010, pastor at San Agustin Parish in Scotts Valley. He serves a congregation approaching 1,000 members of which typically 750 come to masses on weekends. Father O'Brien feels blessed to be here and hopes everyone in the community, any-faith or no-faith, will visit and experience the wholehearted welcome that awaits.

Over 40 active ministries outreach to the larger community including Saint Vincent de Paul Society, The Catholic Daughters of America, Knights of Columbus, Our Lady of Fatima, and several others.

• • •

Saint Angela's Pre-School offers morning preschool and extended afternoon day care for all children 2 to 5½ years old regardless of faith. I-HELP prepares and serves dinner on the second and fourth Thursdays of the month to 25 homeless men. A food cupboard provides for collection and distribution of food to those in need every Tuesday and Thursday from 1:30 to 2:30 pm and manages a county food bank distribution on the first Monday of the month throughout the year.

Saint Angela Merici, 146 Eighth Street, Pacific Grove, CA 93950. Call 831/655-4160, email stangelachurch@stangelamerici.org, https://stangelamericipacificgrove.org

St. Angela Merici at night

Stillness and Awareness: Manjushri Dharma Center

"Meditation is medicine for the mind," said Khenpo Karten Rinpoche, lama (priest) of Pacific Grove's only Buddhist Dharma Center. He was born in the Himalaya Mountains in 1964 and ordained as novice priest in the Karma Kagyo lineage of Tibetan Buddhism at the age of 12. Khenpo has been in the United States since 2008 and has taught meditation in the modest yellow house at the corner of Forest and Sinex since 2015. Before that he lived and taught in Seaside, Boston, Berkeley, Portland, Hong Kong, Singapore, India and Tibet at various times.

Many Tibetan Buddhists and their spiritual leader, the Dalai Lama, now reside in India due to the Chinese occupation of Tibet. Khenpo travels widely and teaches Shamatha meditation, which aims to quiet the mind by looking inward at three facets of the mind itself: stillness, movement, and awareness. "We are working toward more stillness," he said "… to be aware of the mind in a clear, quiescent state."

During our interview, I discovered a soft-spoken, clean-shaven man in a maroon robe with a short golden jacket and a playful sense of humor, often reaching for his prayer beads and smiling when he needed time to contemplate a question about his religion. "Buddhism does not worship a god," he explained. "Everything is from your mind. Dharma is an unexcelled way to gain control of the mind."

The word "dharma" originates from Sanskrit, meaning to hold or protect. It generally means teachings of Buddha or "cosmic law." Khenpo said that in listening to dharma there should be four reliances: the teaching not the teacher, the meaning not the words, the definitive meaning not the provisional meaning, and the transcendent wisdom not ordinary consciousness.

The center has a Sangha, or membership, of about 100 with roughly 20 attending services on Saturday mornings and Monday evenings. Visiting lamas often come to the center to teach. Recently nine Tibetan monks of Drepung Loseling, India, performed spellbinding, multi-phonic chanting for world peace at the Manjushri Dhar-

"We are working toward more stillness … to be aware of the mind in a clear, quiescent state."

he Manjushri Dharma Center at 724 Forest Avenue features teachings that focus on "finding 'the middle way,' avoiding the extremes of self-indulgence on one hand and self-denial on the other."

ma Center. They also spent 7 days constructing a sand mandala at the Sunset Center in Carmel. When done, they dispersed the sand, gave half to visitors and spread the remainder in the ocean as an offering for world peace.

Buddhists worldwide number nearly 500 million with the vast majority, 481 million, found in Asia. North America is second with 3.9 million, Europe third at 1.3 million. Half of all Buddhists reside in China. They represent only 18 percent of the total Chinese population. Interestingly in Asia, the median age of Buddhists is older than the general population (34 vs 29), whereas in North America the ratio is reversed (33 vs 37).

Three main branches of Buddhism are Mahayana Buddhism prevalent in China, Japan, South Korea and Vietnam; Theravada Buddhism mainly in Thailand, Myanmar, Sri Lanka, Laos and Cambodia; and Vajrayana (Tibetan) Buddhism found in Tibet, Nepal, Bhutan and Mongolia.

Although the religion of Buddhism claims no god, Gautama Buddha, an ascetic who lived in eastern India several centuries BCE, is its central figure. He is reported to have said, "You are your own master." His teachings focus on finding "the middle way," avoiding the extremes of self-indulgence on one hand and self-denial on the other. That focus forms the basis of the religion. Buddha described the middle way as a "Noble Eightfold Path" of right understanding, right thought, right speech, right action, right livelihood, right effort, right mindfulness and right concentration. The goal of Buddhism is to attain Buddhahood, a state of enlightenment often called "Nirvana," a release from the rebirth and suffering of sentient beings.

• • •

Services are held Mondays 6:30 pm to 8:30 pm Amitābha practice and Saturday meditation sessions are 10:00 to 11:00 am. Visitors are welcome.

Manjushri Dharma Center, 724 Forest Ave, Pacific Grove CA 93950: Call 831/917-3969, email khenpokarten@gmail.com, or visit www.khenpokarten.org.

A Diverse Congregation: Seventh Day Adventist

"Rest on the Sabbath. Heed Old Testament dietary codes. Be ready for Jesus to return at any moment." These are some basic tenants of the Seventh Day Adventist church. Bucking the national trend of declining church membership, the SDA is the fastest-growing Christian church in North America, according to *USA Today*. They must be doing something right.

On Pacific Grove's upper Lighthouse Avenue, just on the outskirts of downtown, is the Monterey Peninsula's Seventh-day Adventist Church, founded in 1949. The SDA church takes its name from its observance of the Sabbath on the seventh day of the week, Saturday, and its belief in the Advent—the return of Christ to Earth in the near future.

I arrived early for my interview with Pastor Gary Ford and mistakenly wandered into the church's lower level community room where several of the congregation were busily preparing lunch. A young lady realized I was lost, and then escorted me outside and around the block to the main entrance on Monterey Street. I entered the chapel as Pastor Ford was completing his sermon and was immediately struck by three things: It was packed. It was diverse. It was lively. A church deacon said this was a typical turnout, about 140 people. The mix of cultures and races was remarkable; all were well represented.

After the sermon, the service ended and people began to mingle and chat with one another in animated conversations. I introduced myself to Pastor Ford, a lean middle-aged man about 5'8" in a charcoal suit, pink shirt, and a black-and-white retro tie. Then we proceeded to the community room where a long table was laid out with an inviting array of potluck dishes and a line of eager kids impatiently waiting for the blessing before being served. The food looked like what one might expect at any potluck gathering, but that was not exactly the case. The SDA are a healthy lot—there was no caffeine, no soda, no alcohol, no sugary sweets, and no artificial ingredients. Dessert consisted of fresh fruits of various kinds. The room was full and overflowed to the outside patio. Almost everyone, young and old, looked fit for a marathon.

On the vitality of the congregation, Ford said, "Our church goes back to basics, and our eating habits follow Old Testament dietary codes." A *U.S. News & World Report* article titled "11 Health Habits That Will Help You Live to 100," lists #8 as "Live like a Seventh Day Adventist." The article continues, "Seventh Day Adventists have an average life expectancy about a decade longer than the average American."

The Seventh Day Adventist Church at 375 Lighthouse Avenue is part of "the fastest-growing Christian church in North America, according to *USA Today*."

Over lunch, Pastor Ford scarcely had time to eat as he enthusiastically talked about the church and his ministry. He has ministered here since 2014, having previously served 20 years in southern California as an evangelist after graduating from La Sierra University in Riverside. Upstairs, there are two rooms for the children's school and the pastor's office, which contains a library, a desk cluttered with the signs of an active mind, and in the corner a triplescreen computer used for preparation of PowerPoint presentations for each sermon. Pastor Ford's wife Yvonne is Principal at the Peninsula Adventist School, a K-8 Christian school in Seaside which accepts children from all religious or secular backgrounds.

Ford explained that SDA is a Protestant Christian denomination officially founded in 1863 in Battle Creek, Michigan. It arose out of the Millerite Movement of 1833. Today it has 20 million adherents worldwide. Adventists believe in the Trinity, the infallibility of scripture, and investigative judgment. They do not ascribe to creeds and they are usually apolitical.

Ford volunteered that all SDA ministers are salaried, which eliminates financial pressure and enables the focus on ministry. Excess funds in larger churches go to supporting smaller churches and to Third World missions. Regarding the diversity of the congregation, Ford said that SDA is the most diverse mainstream religion in the nation. Pew Research backs him up, reporting: "Seventh-day Adventists are among the most racially and ethnically diverse American religious groups: 37% are white, 32% are black, 15% are Hispanic, 8% are Asian and 8% are another or mixed race." They also report 45% are Democrat, 35% Republican, and 19% Independent. In the ideological spectrum, 37% are conservative, 31% moderate, and 22% liberal.

SDA has missions in over 200 countries and supports 7,200 schools and over 600 hospitals. Adventists Community Services has agreements with states around the country to provide disaster warehouse services.

Dr. Ben Carson, former presidential candidate and the current United States Secretary of Housing and Urban Development, is perhaps the bestknown Seventh-Day Adventist. Others include former slave Sojourner Truth and Texas Congresswoman Sheila Jackson Lee and California Congressman Raul Ruiz.

• • •

Seventh Day Adventist church, 375 Lighthouse Ave, Pacific Grove CA, call 831/372-7818 or website www.monterey.adventisfaith.org. Peninsula Adventist School, 831 Mescal Street, Seaside CA, call 831/394-5578 or email yford@pas.today, website http://peninsula22.adventistschoolconnect.org/.

Other Pacific Grove Churches

Bethlehem Lutheran, organized in 1914 in Pacific Grove, now at 800 Cass Street, Monterey.

Central Presbyterian Church, organized circa 1959, 325 Central Avenue.

Chabad, organized in 2004, 620 Lighthouse Avenue #100.

Church of Christ, organized in 1943, 176 Central Avenue, Pacific Grove (inactive).

Community Missionary Baptist Church, organized circa 1983, 401 Pine Street.

First Church of God, organized in 1952, 1023 David Avenue.

Forest Hill United Methodist Church, organized in 1954, 551 Gibson Avenue.

Jehovah's Witnesses, organized about 2008, 1100 Sunset Drive.

LDS Church (Mormon), organized in 1938, 401 Pine Street, now at 1 Skyline Drive, Monterey.

Lighthouse Fellowship, organized in 2006, 515 Junipero Avenue.

Peninsula Baptist Church, organized in 1949, 1116 Funston Street.

Saint Anselm's Anglican Church, organized in 2008, 375 Lighthouse Avenue.

About the Author

Gary Baley with Rev. Jeff Lewis at St. Mary's.

My ancestors were Scot-Irish Methodist farmers who emigrated from Ireland to up-country South Carolina just prior to the American Revolution and soon became rebels in the cause of independence. After the war, they followed the westward expansion of the United States to Alabama, Mississippi, Tennessee and Texas.

During the Civil War, they were Methodist abolitionists in Texas. World War II brought my mother and father to Oakland, California, where I was born. In college I majored in physics with a minor in journalism, and during summers I'd come to Pacific Grove to go scuba diving—in the process acquiring an enduring love of the sea and marine life. That sentiment led me to join the U.S. Coast & Geodetic Survey where I served aboard the newly-commissioned USC&GS ship Oceanographer (OSS-01) as ship's photographer on its maiden voyage to South America and then its eight-month Global Scientific Expedition circumnavigating the earth and providing conclusive evidence of continental drift. I am a certified Rescue Diver and hold a BLS certificate. After those stints at sea, I worked in Silicon Valley for various technology companies, including Telcom General, and Hewlett Packard as their first dedicated representative in Monterey County. Later I started an electronic and print publishing business called The Abstract of Monterey County, which I operated for about 15 years in Pacific Grove. During this time, I founded a dance club called Swing Monterey where I met Sawako, my wife-to-be. The club led the performances during the First Night 2000 millennial celebration. My business closed after access to the public records I had depended on was terminated. Then I spent nine years in Japan teaching medical English and editing medical research papers for Japanese scientists and doctors. I returned to Monterey County in 2017 and am now a freelance writer and photographer.

In appreciation for Jo Mora, talented local artist, and also for our neighboring towns on the Monterey Peninsula. This colorful map by Jo Mora is on display at the Pacific Grove Public Library. Photo Peter Mounteer.

P.G., Tai Chi, & Me
Jeffrey Whitmore

"Something Bigger Than Oneself"

I owe my introduction to tai chi to the People's Republic of China and the Pacific Grove Chamber of Commerce.

In the early spring of 2007, I took part in a nine-day tour to China sponsored by the P.G. Chamber in conjunction with the Chinese government. Its purpose was to promote business ties between America and China. About $1,400 covered hotels, meals, tour guides, entertainment, airfare to and from China, and all transportation within it. What a deal!

One cool, hazy morning in Beijing, which was similar to the weather we'd left back in Pacific Grove a few days earlier—although certainly smoggier—we came across twenty or so men and women of all ages who were gathered at the end of a large park. They were engaged in some sort of communal exercise, and they moved in unison, slowly and gracefully. They weren't wearing uniforms or costumes of any kind. Like those in our tour group, they were dressed for the weather.

I asked our guide what they were up to.

"They're doing tai chi," he said. "It's based on a Chinese martial art. It's also a healing art. That's why they practice it here every morning." He pointed to several buildings at the far end of the park. "That's a hospital," he said. He turned back toward the people who were doing tai chi and smiled. "Those people have a popular saying: 'Which end of the park will you choose?'"

I'd seen the Keanu Reeves movie *Tai Chi Man*, and knew tai chi was a martial art, but I never thought it had anything to do with healing. Certainly not by the standards of the villain Reeves portrayed. Seeing it being practiced in Beijing was an interesting curiosity for the moment, but I couldn't envision that one day I'd be practicing it and teaching it at the Sally Griffin Active Living Center in Pacific Grove.

Thanks China!

Thanks P.G. Chamber!

I didn't get involved with tai chi again for another six years. Not the martial art, but the healing art. When I did, I found it mind blowing, life changing, spiritually enlightening, and—well—a lot of fun.

For me, it still is.

In high school, I loved playing sports but hated practice. For one thing, it involved too much running. In an actual game, running made sense—and was fun. In practice, though, it seemed both boring and tiring. It was also a form of punishment. You make one clever adolescent remark too many to the coach and it's, "Okay wise guy, you owe me five laps around the field. Get cracking!"

Later, in Army basic training, running was also punishment. (Then again, everything in basic training was.)

Once back in civilian life, fully realizing that—despite my aversion to it—exercise was a *good* habit, I decided to drop it like a *bad* one. And for the next twenty years I worked diligently at avoiding it.

But in the late summer of 1982, I was tricked into signing up for the Big Sur River Run 10K. I was editing a regional magazine then, and Monterey County Judge Bill Burleigh stopped by my office with promotional material for the race, which he'd founded a year earlier. (He later became a founder of the world-acclaimed Big Sur Marathon.)

For reasons that escape me now, I told him I was thinking of taking up running.

He handed me an application form for the upcoming race.

Caught off guard, I said something like, "Sounds great. But, uh, I just don't have the time to train for it."

He said something like, "No problem. It's not till the end of October. That's plenty of time to get in shape, but registration is closing fast. You can fill it out now. A check, cash, or credit card is fine."

I was cornered. I filled out the form, wrote a check, and tried to remember whether 10 kilometers was more or less than 10 miles. There was no Google then, but with the aid of a dictionary and a calculator I figured out it was 6.2 miles. Small relief. It still seemed beyond the reach of human endurance.

The next day, resigned to my fate—and betrayed by my big mouth—I went to The Runners, a dedicated sporting goods store in New Monterey, and bought a pair of running shoes (sneakers, I thought, only more expensive); some silky underpants-like shorts; and a fancy sleeveless T-shirt.

Discretion being the better part of valor, I waited a few days before trying out my new racing gear. It was a brief trial. Close to a once-around-the-block venture. But day by day I persisted, and before long the block count grew.

What amazed me was how soon I began to enjoy running. Although the first couple of weeks were drudgery, I forced myself to run every day. Within a month, I was looking forward to the training runs. Hmm. Maybe there *was* something to this fad.

I ran the Big Sur River Run that October, and over the years I ran a lot of other 10Ks, a few half-marathons, and in 1989 my *only* marathon. I finished the Avenue of the Giants Marathon—in agony, gasping and wheezing in relief—in 4 hours and 50 minutes.

[**Editors note**: Five years later, Oprah Winfrey ran the Marine Corps Marathon in 4 hours and 29 minutes, beating Mr. Whitmore's time by more than 20 minutes—and she crossed the finish line *smiling*!]

I never claimed to be a speed demon. Richard, a pal from The Wednesday Night Laundry Runners—a group that assembled weekly at the old Mission Linen Laundry across from the P.G. High football field—once analyzed my running problem for me. By that time in his life, Richard had run more than 80 marathons. *Really*. He weighed in the vicinity of 120 pounds, and his legs accounted for about 100 of those pounds. (*Not* really—but he was definitely built to run.)

His analysis was brief. "Your snail-like velocity," he said, "is caused by your legs being shorter than your torso." He shrugged. "I've noticed that you actually look taller when you're sitting down."

Maybe so.

I ran—if only slightly faster than I walked—from my early forties until my early seventies. Except perhaps for the last several miles of my solitary marathon—when I contemplated death, and was close to welcoming it—I truly enjoyed my runs. Eventually, though, I began to feel a burning sensation in my throat when I started a run. It would subside after ten minutes or so, but it worried me. I mentioned it to my doctor at the VA clinic, and he suggested I take a stress test.

Turns out I was stressed.

Further exams revealed arterial blockage. A short while later, a doctor at the VA hospital in Palo Alto put a stent in my chest and told me I should stop running.

About three decades earlier I'd quit smoking and drinking, and I had to admit that dropping those two habits had made me healthier. But I felt that giving up my running habit would do the opposite. Nevertheless, I reluctantly followed the doctor's orders. I added a few more medications to my morning load and traded running for walking.

The problem was, walking didn't give me the satisfaction that running did. I missed the camaraderie of running with friends and missed the runner's high that even a plodder like me felt on a leisurely trot through the Del Monte Forest, along the Pacific Grove shoreline, or through the wilds of Jacks Peak and other scenic local areas.

I needed a new healthy habit.

One Monday morning, after a routine checkup at the old VA clinic on Ft. Ord, I asked at the front desk if there were any exercise programs available through the VA. The clerk said there might be tai chi classes on Tuesdays and Thursdays; he wasn't sure. As my thoughts flashed back to the park in Beijing, the woman in line behind me tapped me on the shoulder. "It's Mondays and Fridays," she said. "Today's class starts in ten minutes. Follow me."

⊙ ⊙ ⊙

The class—about a dozen men and women—met in a small conference room at the rear of the building. Tom Hawkinson, a VA nurse and certified Tai Chi for Arthritis (TCA) instructor, welcomed the newcomers and gave a brief lowdown on the benefits of the program. TCA is the first of the Tai Chi for Health programs that Australian physician and tai chi master Dr. Paul Lam developed in conjunction with other physicians and tai chi experts.

In his teen years, and well into his twenties, Dr. Lam had suffered from severe arthritis. Nothing eased his symptoms. After a friend told him tai chi seemed to benefit some arthritis sufferers, he gave it a try. He enjoyed doing it, and over time his symptoms lessened. They eventually disappeared.

⊙ ⊙ ⊙
Spirituality

"People see spirituality in many different lights. I see it as something bigger than oneself—for example, the desire to contribute to the common good. The positive interaction between people through tai chi principles fosters a stronger community spirit. …Tai Chi for Health is a tool that helps us develop an inner sanctuary of strength and harmony in our overstimulated world and has nothing to do with any religion."

-- Dr. Paul Lam, from *Born Strong: From Surviving the Great Famine to Teaching Tai Chi to Millions*

After TCA was endorsed by the Australian Arthritis Society and the American Arthritis Society, Dr. Lam created a host of other forms, all based on traditional tai chi healing practices. Eventually he founded the Tai Chi for Health Institute. Literally thousands of instructors around the world now teach his programs, including the tai chi instructors at the Sally Griffin Active Living Center.

After a series of gentle warm-up exercises, Tom walked both the newcomers and the regular participants through a few of the movements. One of the first moves he demonstrated was "open and close." It's a breathing exercise designed to foster energy, and it's a component of many Tai Chi for Health exercises. In it you stand with feet apart, elbows down, the hands raised about chin height, and the palms facing each other about a head's width apart. As you breathe in, you separate your hands slowly until they're shoulder width apart. As you exhale, you bring your hands slowly back to the starting position.

Tom said that with practice, when you separated your hands, you might experience a sensation in them similar to the feeling of resistance you feel when you pull joined magnets slowly apart. And then, when you moved your hands closer to together, you might experience the opposite resistance, similar to what you feel when you push together magnets of the same polarity.

He led us through the exercise several times and—wonder of wonders—I felt the sensations he'd described.

I'm a slow learner, and it took time and patience for me to learn the moves of the various forms of Tai Chi for Health I now practice. But then and there, that first jolt of tai chi energy—or "qi" as it's spelled, and "chee" as it's pronounced—made me a believer.

After a year or so I began to study with other trainers, first with Hei Takarabe, a Tai Chi for Health Master Trainer at the Oldemeyer Senior Center in Seaside, and then with Dr. Stephanie Taylor, a Master Trainer from Carmel Valley.

Hei was born in Japan in 1938 and at the age of twenty came to Southern California to attend college. After graduating from UCLA he attended the San Francisco Theological Seminary and became a minister. After serving for 17 years at a church in Sacramento, he was called by El Estero Presbyterian Church in Monterey, where he served until his retirement in 2003.

In 1985 he'd taken up tai chi, learning a Yang-style form from a book. By 2004, his ministerial duties behind him, he sought a teacher who could take him deeper into the practice of tai chi. That year he attended a weeklong Tai Chi for Health workshop at Pacific Grove's Asilomar Conference Grounds conducted by Dr. Paul Lam himself.

At the workshop, he met Dr. Taylor, a physician specializing in women's health care. She'd visited Dr. Lam in the 1990s and was impressed with his ideas about Tai Chi for Health. Although she was well versed in aikido at the time, she was concerned that an injury to her hands could limit her effectiveness as a doctor. "When you practice aikido," she says, "you need to work with a partner. And if the partner is inexperienced, the likelihood of an injury increases."

You don't need a partner to practice tai chi, and she replaced aikido with tai chi.

Hei studied with Dr. Taylor following the workshop, and she became his mentor, colleague, and friend. Now, as a TCH Master Trainer himself, he frequently teams up with her at the TCH classes she teaches at Chautauqua Hall in Pacific Grove. All the current instructors at the

---

◉ ◉ ◉
What's in a Name?

If you've ever seen a group of people practicing tai chi in a park—anywhere in the world—it's likely they were practicing the Beijing Form, or the Peking Form, or the 24 Form, or the Simplified 24 Form, or the Standard Simplified Tai Chi 24 Form, or—as it's called by the Tai Chi for Health Institute—the 24 Forms.

Whew!

Different names, but they all refer to the same set of 24 Yang-style tai chi moves created in 1956 by The People's Republic of China. They wanted a short, standardized, easy-to-learn, enjoyable, and healthy exercise for their citizens, and they directed the National Physical Culture and Sports Commission to develop one. A collection of tai chi experts pared down the traditional Yang Style Taijiquan 108 Long Form, which took from twelve to eighteen minutes to complete, and came up with the 24 Forms, which is usually completed in four to six minutes. It caught on worldwide. It's not hard to learn, and you can squeeze three sets of it into a coffee break. Plus—like all tai chi forms—it's good for you and it's fun.

Both Liana Olson and Linda Goulet teach the 24 Forms at the Sally Griffin Active Living Center in Pacific Grove; Dr. Stephanie Taylor teaches it at Chautauqua Hall in Pacific Grove; Hei Takarabe teaches it at the Oldemeyer Center in Seaside; and Jesse Richards teaches Tai Chi for Beginners, an introduction to the 24 Forms, at Scholze Park in New Monterey.

Sally Griffin Center tai chi instructors Jeff Whitmore and Jesse Richards goof around with some tai chi postures. (photo credit: Chuck Davies)

Sally Griffin Active Living Center have studied with Hei and Dr. Taylor.

After one of Hei's Tai Chi for Arthritis classes, a friend told me someone was teaching a class in Tai Chi for Energy at the Sally Griffin Active Living Center in Pacific Grove. The center's located a few blocks from Lovers Point, a ten-minute walk from my house. I thought it might be worth a try.

It was.

Jesse Richards, the instructor, taught two forms then, Tai Chi for Energy (TCE) and Tai Chi for Diabetes (TCD). They differed from Tai Chi for Arthritis, but under her tutelage I eventually learned both forms. I'd been certified to teach Tai Chi for Arthritis, but was less interested in teaching it than in learning more about the form. But I caught the teaching bug from Jesse. She has a great sense of humor and shows real interest in and respect for her students. Thanks to her example and mentoring, I went on get certified to teach TCE and TCD.

In November 2015, thanks to Jesse's support, I began teaching Tai Chi for Arthritis at the Griffin Center and assisting her with her own classes.

The Tai Chi for Health programs taught at the Griffin Center (and worldwide) are recognized for their health benefits by the Harvard Medical School, among many other supporters. People of all ages can practice them, and the longer they practice them the greater the benefits. The programs consist of gentle exercises that strengthen muscles and ligaments, improve balance, promote cardio-vascular fitness, and help prevent falls. Besides that, they're stress-free and foster a sense of well-being and community spirit in those who take part in them.

Often movies featuring a martial art—whether it's Karate, Kung Fu, Tae Kwon Do, or some other style—will include a sequence in which the star gets his or her early training from a stern elder. Lots of heavy discipline: running up hills, kneeling on rice, boot to the head, bruises, sweat, and finally—whew!—mastery of the art and a smile from the strict task master who was doing all that rough stuff for the trainee's own good.

Today's gym rats—like cinematic martial arts teacher—are inspired by the idea: "No pain, no gain."

The opposite theory applies to Tai Chi for Health exercises. Pain blocks the flow of energy. And—to state the obvious—it hurts.

Tai Chi for Health moves are gentle and smoothly flowing. Participants are encouraged to modify any move that causes the least discomfort. They're taught how to perform it within the limits of their comfort zone and imagine that they're completing the full move. It's not cheating. The full benefits of the exercise can be realized, because imagination itself can physically affect for the better the neural pathways through which energy flows.

Several years ago, I had arthroscopic surgery on my right knee, and it still acts up now and then. Certain tai chi moves can occasionally irritate it, but if I feel the slightest twinge, I simply modify the move and imagine I'm completing it. Because tai chi moves are slow and smooth, it's possible to be aware of such problems and deal with them before they cause trouble.

Among the other benefits of tai chi, there's no need to buy special clothing. People who take part in tai chi competitions or demonstrations tend to wear traditional silk or cotton outfits. But for most tai chi practitioners, almost any, loose, comfortable clothing is fine. I favor sweat pants, loose long-sleeve shirts, and flat-soled shoes. You can buy specialized martial arts shoes, but I usually wear skateboard shoes. They're flat-soled and comfortable, and they're often on sale at your local sporting goods store. (So far, the courteous cashiers have never suggested I'm a bit old for skateboarding.)

Some participants wear regular street clothes to class. We don't encourage it, but so long as their clothing doesn't affect their safety, it's up to them.

The physical benefits of tai chi are terrific. But perhaps equally rewarding are the associations with other tai chi players.

Players?

it because I always felt uncomfortable when I tried to sit cross-legged? (Those damned short legs again!)

But spiritual or not, the deeper I delved into tai chi, the more I sensed something transcendental was happening. Since my very first tai chi class at the VA clinic, I've looked forward to every session—either as instructor or student. At the end of every class, I've always been glad I took part in it. I've experienced such warmth and learned so much from the fellow tai chi players in my classes at the Griffin Center, I feel we aren't just friends, but part of an extended family. Now more and more—when practicing tai chi by myself, with a few friends, or in a large group—I sense the "inner sanctuary of strength and harmony" that Dr. Lam described in his autobiography.

It feels good.

Today—on a welcome, sunny morning in Pacific Grove—I think of a misty morning in a Beijing park some six-thousand miles and eleven years away. In my mind's eye I watch a gathering of people move in a communal ritual that seems to flow as smoothly as a river, a performance that seems more a dance than a martial art. At the far end of that park, I can make out through the haze a cluster of hospital buildings.

And here at home in P.G., as my own tai chi journey continues, I'm grateful I chose the right end of the park.

Indeed. It's a common term used by those engaged in tai chi, because there's so much joy involved in the art. There's a pleasure in the movements themselves, like the pleasure one finds in dancing. And there's also the pleasure of gathering with friends in a communal activity.

There *are* tai chi competitions. You can find them on YouTube, and they're amazing. But Tai Chi for Health is non-competitive. Players—ah, what a nice term!—work at their own pace. There's no end goal in sight. The winning is found in the journey.

I'd never been much interested in meditating or seeking enlightenment on a higher plain. My brief excursion into yoga, for example, turned out to be a total bust. Was

◉ ◉ ◉

Tai Chi Classes at the Sally Griffin Center

Andrea Fuerst, Associate Executive Director of Meals on Wheels of the Monterey Peninsula and Director of the Sally Griffin Active Living Center since 2006, says programs get started there with an idea that can come from outside the center or be generated internally. "We have to assess the potential for the program. Is there a demand for it? Room for it? We're open to a wide variety of ideas. We had a mahjong group for a few months, but it faded away. We've had tai chi classes since 1999. In all, we have twenty or so fitness and health classes a week. We're considering adding some sort of theater programs now and maybe a Scrabble group. First we have to determine the interest level."

The free classes at the Griffin Center are open to everyone, but participants are encouraged to become members. At $35 for a single membership and $50 for a family membership, the yearly fees are a bargain. For example, a person with a single membership who takes the twice-a-week free tai chi classes for a year would contribute less than 35¢ per class. Plus they'd get the myriad other benefits of the center.

The monthly *Griffin Bulletin* lists the times for all current classes and events and is available at the Griffin Center and online at https://www.mowmp.org/library.cfm?id=7

For more information: Phone: 831/375-4454, Web:mowmp.org/sally-griffin-active-living-center.htm; or drop by the Griffin Center: 700 Jewell Avenue, Pacific Grove, CA 93950

Tai Chi Teachers at the Sally Griffin Center

Liana Olson

"...the rewards of teaching tai chi are often intangible and come from those she teaches."

A Senior Trainer for the Tai Chi for Health Institute, Liana Olson teaches tai chi classes at the Sally Griffin Active Living Center in Pacific Grove.

While growing up with her brothers and sisters, Liana was active in sports: running, basketball, soccer, baseball—even football! She also has a background in modern dance and horseback riding.

In the spring of 2012, fresh from attending a Seido Bio-Energy training that focused on the body's meridians, she read a life-changing article in a local newspaper. It was announcing an upcoming tai chi workshop sponsored by the Arthritis Foundation, conducted by Master Trainers certified to teach Tai Chi for Arthritis, and held at the Peninsula Wellness Center (now Montage Wellness Center), a division of the Community Hospital of the Monterey Peninsula.

"You know how sometimes something lights up for you?" she said. "I was looking for something new in my life, and I felt this was it. Despite being in the middle of preparing my income taxes and getting the information to my accountant, I couldn't resist the opportunity. The workshop was a few weeks off, and I had to jump through hoops to get my paperwork to Alexandra Fallon of the Arthritis Foundation on time, learn the tai chi form from a CD, and find a facility where I could teach."

Despite the challenges, she took the workshop and was certified as a Tai Chi for Arthritis instructor. She soon went to work as an independent instructor at the Sally Griffin Active Living Center and has been conducting weekly classes there ever since. She has subsequently studied with Dr. Paul Lam, founder of the Tai Chi for Health Institute, and studied and assisted in the classes of local Tai Chi for Health Master Trainers Hei Takarabe and Dr. Stephanie Taylor.

In addition to her classes at the Sally Griffin Center, Liana teaches tai chi at Forest Hill Manor, Pacific Grove; the Alliance on Aging, Salinas; Villa Serra, Salinas; the Carmel Valley Community Chapel Hall, and the Carmel Foundation. For the past three summers, she has taught tai chi classes at Garland Park Visitors Center as part of the "Let's Go Outdoors" program of the Monterey Peninsula Regional Park District.

For Liana, the rewards of teaching tai chi are often intangible and come from those she teaches. "I emphasize balance and safety. I want them to understand how to work within their personal comfort zones. And I try to show them how tai chi applies to the practical areas of life. Recently a woman in her late sixties came to me after her third class. She told me, 'When I take a shower now, I no longer have to lean against the wall.' She was delighted—and so was I. It's just such a pleasure to help people learn how to get to that quiet, peaceful, harmonious place tai chi offers."

Contact information for Liana: 831/659-2305

◉ ◉ ◉

Jesse Richards

One of tai chi's principles is the close relationship between mind and body. That's a relationship Jesse Richards is familiar with. On the mind side, she worked in the mental health field for fourteen years and holds master's degrees in both clinical psychology and in marriage, family, and child therapy.

On the body side, she's now a devoted practitioner of hot yoga and for ten years practiced karate. "I finally stopped karate," she says, "when my goals—maintaining fitness and some self-defense—no longer matched my sensei's goals—ever-increasing fitness and increasingly punishing self-defense."

After trying some tai chi with a friend—a long-time practitioner of the art—Jesse knew she wanted to learn more. In April 2012 she studied the 24 Forms at Chautauqua Hall with Dr. Stephanie Taylor, a Tai Chi for Health Master Trainer.

By 2013 she knew she wanted to teach tai chi. After

learning the Tai Chi for Energy form (TCE) from Master Trainer Hei Takarabe, she attended a Tai Chi for Health workshop in Walnut Creek and was certified as a TCE instructor. At the time she was the bookkeeper for Meals on Wheels in Pacific Grove, and she arranged with Executive Director Viveca Lohr and Active Living Center Director Andrea Fuerst to teach TCE classes there as part of her job. (She went on to be certified in Tai Chi for Diabetes and Tai Chi for Arthritis.)

There'd been fee-based tai chi classes at the Sally Griffin Active Living Center since 1999, but Jesse's were the first free classes. Although she left her bookkeeping job at MOWMP in 2016, she continues her volunteer teaching there.

"I like teaching," she says. "I also really like the folks who come to class. And I love that they keep coming back. I like feeling appreciated. I do believe that tai chi is good for everybody, and I'm happy to encourage people to move in a meditative way. Even though we may not be able to define it, I think there's got to be something about tai chi that's truly real and good."

Besides her classes at the Sally Griffin Active Living Center, Jesse teaches Tai Chi for Beginners and an introduction to the 24 Forms at the Scholze Senior Center in New Monterey.

◉ ◉ ◉

Linda Goulet

"You don't need to actually move to benefit from it. By visualizing the movements, you stimulate neural pathways."

Linda Goulet began teaching tai chi through the Pacific Grove Adult School two years ago, first at their headquarters on Lighthouse Avenue, and now at the Sally Griffin Active Living Center on Jewell Avenue.

She's been involved in health-care and self-care since the late 1970s, when she became interested in herbal medicine. In the 1990s she began exploring Reiki—the Japanese system designed to reduce stress, increase relaxation, and promote healing—and in 2000 she became a Reiki Master.

There was a side benefit to her training. "My teacher would have us do a series of qigong exercises, which I absolutely loved. And because he knew I loved to dance, he thought I might enjoy tai chi. He suggested I look for tai chi classes to augment my exercise classes and because of tai chi's emphasis on internal healing."

Linda's first tai chi instructor didn't say a word for the first twelve classes. It was a traditional martial arts system in which the students learn by imitation. It didn't really suit her. But once she found Lydia Olsen, her second 24 Forms teacher, she was hooked.

Then she heard about Dr. Lam's Tai Chi for Health program from her physician, Dr. Stephanie Taylor, a long-time Tai Chi for Health Master Trainer.

"I really learned intricacies of the 24 Forms from her. As a teacher, I adore Dr. Lam's Stepwise Method. It makes sense to people. It's a task-analysis system that breaks down the specific movements so that students don't get overwhelmed. I find it really effective."

Since 1990 Linda has been on the faculty of the Pacific Grove Middle School, first as a special education teacher and now as a home economics teacher. She also conducts a weekly Tea Time Tai Chi Tuesday with her students. "We have a cup of tea and do a few tai chi and qigong exercises. We also talk about self-regulation, good health, stress management, and other helpful ways to deal with the complications of their adolescent lives."

Three years ago, Linda's mother mentioned she was having some problems with her balance. That inspired Linda to volunteer to teach tai chi at a nursing home. She was impressed with the quick improvements older people showed from doing tai chi, even those who did a seated version. "You don't need to actually move, to benefit from it. By visualizing the movements, you stimulate neural pathways."

"For older people, tai chi enhances longevity. And for young and old alike, it enhances the overall quality of life. It's such a rich experience, and it's never too late to begin."

Contact information: lagoulet@gmail.com

TAI CHI RESOURCES

BOOKS

The Harvard Medical Guide to Tai Chi, Peter M. Wayne, with Mark Fuerst, Shambhala Publications, Inc., 2013. A ton of information about the benefits of tai chi for health.

Tai Chi for Beginners and the 24 Forms, Dr. Paul Lam & Nancy Kaye, Limelight Press, 2006. A good introduction to Tai Chi for Health.

Teaching Tai Chi Effectively, Dr. Paul Lam with Maureen Miller, Tai Chi Productions, 2006 (revised 2011). A useful book for Tai Chi for Health students. An *essential* book for Tai Chi for Health instructors. It includes "Ethics of Tai Chi Teaching," an essay by Dr. Stephanie Taylor, a Master Trainer who teaches tai chi at Chautauqua Hall in Pacific Grove. She's taught the 24 Forms to all the tai chi instructors at the Sally Griffin Active Living Center. She's also been a demonstrator for Dr. Lam on the "Tai Chi for Health" DVDs.)

Born Strong: From Surviving the Great Famine to Teaching Tai Chi to Millions, Dr. Paul Lam with Julie Bawden-Davis. Tai Chi Productions, 2015. The title of Dr. Lam's autobiography sums up a remarkable tale of the grit, survival, and ultimate triumph of the founder of the Tai Chi for Health programs.

Tai Chi Essentials: The Simplified 24 Form. Andrew Townsend, Create Space Independent Publishing Platform, 2015. A step-by-step-guide to the tai chi form most widely practiced throughout the world. Also information about tai chi history, principles, and styles.

ON THE INTERNET

Dr. Paul Lam's Tai Chi for Health Institute website (https://taichiforhealthinstitute.org) offers a wealth of information about the tai chi forms taught at the Sally Griffin Active Living Center. It features books and DVDs, information about upcoming workshops, listings of instructors by area, a newsletter, articles, and more. The institute has recently added online lessons, available at https://www.onlinetaichilessons.com/

YOUTUBE

YouTube offers a diversity of tai chi videos. Jennifer Chung demonstrates several of Dr. Lam's Tai Chi for Health programs with subtitles for each move.

Coach Li Jing's YouTube instructional video on the 24-Form runs for almost an hour. In the first of three sections, she demonstrates the individual moves; in the second, she demonstrates how tai chi moves derive from the martial art of Taijiquan; in the third she runs through the entire form.

Photo Peter Mounteer

PERSONAL REMINISCENCES

Living Mindfully in Pacific Grove
Joe Neary

One of my favorite things to do in P.G. is to walk along the Rec Trail between the Hopkins Marine Lab and Lovers Point. I pull on a comfortable pair of pants, lace up my Brooks Ghost 10 walking shoes, tie my Red Sox sweatshirt around my waist, put on my wide-brimmed golf hat, and step out of our wee cottage onto Laurel Avenue. I walk down Eighth Street to the bay and begin to stroll along the Rec Trail toward Hopkins Lab.

As I turn my attention to the sights and sounds of the magnificent seascape before me, my concerns and distractions of the day begin to fade. I begin my 'ten, twenty, thirty' exercise routine. In the slow part, I see the large rocks below and wonder how they became striated. Approaching Hopkins Lab, loud barking sounds draw my attention to the harbor seals on the beach below and I am fascinated by a mama seal teaching her young pup to slide off a shallow rock into icy water. After a few nudges, the baby seal slips into the water, but turns around quickly to get back up on the rock with mama. The patient mom persists, and after a few tries, the little seal gets more comfortable in the water—and maybe being apart from mom for a little while.

As I turn around at the Hopkins gate and head toward Lovers Point, I feel the refreshing westerly sea breeze on my face. Continuing past the chain link fence, the view of the coastline comes more clearly into view. A little group of purple flowers are sticking up from a rock. I stop to take a picture of the coastline with the flowers in the foreground and make a mental note to post it on Facebook so my family and friends on the east coast can see how beautiful it is here.

After my 15-20 min walk, I find an open bench and sit down to rest and enjoy the view of the bay. I'm fascinated by a flock of birds flying by in formation—with a straggler or two—swooping down to near ocean level and rising again to continue their journey. I love the sounds of the waves crashing against the rocks. The swells come in quietly at first and then, after two or three times, the swells increase in size and crash into the rocks with louder and higher sprays. I follow the waves as they move from left to right along the rocky coastline, kicking up sprays along the way and finishing up with the biggest spray of all, at Hopkins Point. Sometimes, I see a little groundhog—or maybe it's one of our infamous P.G. gophers—venture out raised in the prayer position. The contemplative groundhogs of P.G.. All in all, a most enjoyable, mindful time!

Nearby Resources for Mindful Living

I first became aware of meditation as a means of living mindfully when I attended a talk in the early 1990s by Fr Basil Pennington, a Trappist monk. Fr Basil talked about and led us through a session of an ancient Christian style of meditation called Centering Prayer. I was intrigued by it because it made me aware of the nature of my wandering mind; that I am more than my thoughts and feelings.

I decided to make meditation a regular practice. I started by getting to my office at the Miami VA Medical Center about thirty minutes earlier than usual. I would sit quietly and focus on my diaphragm, as it moved in and out with my exhalations and inhalations. Silently saying a short word or phrase to return my attention to my breath, I noticed that my mind had wandered, and quite often did!

After a few months of meditating, I noticed that I was more tolerant of the behavior of others, and of myself. I was less quick to react to what others said or did. I also had developed a more balanced approach to juggling my research studies with all my other academic duties, with my family life, and with my passion for playing golf.

My research was on the mechanisms of traumatic brain injury, what molecules are released, what signaling pathways and genes are activated by these molecules, and whether this helps the healing process—or not. My molecular studies were far removed from consciousness, but because I was experiencing effects of meditation on my behavior, I was very curious about what was happening in my brain. I wanted to see if we can use our minds to enhance our health and well-being, but the demands of my work didn't allow time for me to look into these possibilities.

◎ ◎ ◎

When I retired in 2008, I began to research the effects of meditation on the brain in PubMed, a great source of peer reviewed research papers.

I quickly discovered that while this was a young field, quite a bit had been learned in a short time. The main findings are that meditation and other mindful practices change the activity of our brains, as well as the structure of our brains, and activate genes that can support our health and well-being. I started to give talks on this, first to the Monterey Meditation Group and then to the Palo Alto Area Bar Association.

The latter invitation came about as I was sitting on a

bench after my exercise walk along the Rec Trail. I noticed a young couple trying to take a selfie of themselves, and I offered to take a picture for them. We struck up a conversation that led to an invitation to give a talk to the young lawyer's group in Palo Alto.

Both talks seemed to be well received, and shortly thereafter Chris Moore, a fellow meditator and Laurel Ave. neighbor, asked if I was interested in teaching a course on the topic of meditation and well-being? I said I was but I didn't have any connections with the local colleges. He said his neighbor, Michele Crompton, was the director of the Osher Lifelong Learning Institute (OLLI) at CSUMB.

I contacted Michele, we met for coffee at the Juice and Java Cafe on Lighthouse Ave, she was very supportive and enthusiastic about my suggestion for a course. I wasn't so sure that it would be of interest to many people, but three days after registration opened Michele called to say my course was filled with forty-five people! She asked if I would be willing to offer a repeat course later in the semester, which I was very happy to do!

Over the last couple of years, I've offered courses at OLLI on the neuroscience of meditation, happiness, gratitude, compassion and equanimity and how these mindful living practices can enhance our health and well being. I am very grateful to Michele for giving me the opportunity to do something that I love—share what I've learned!

The practice of living mindfully means to be present to each moment, moment by moment in our daily lives. Research studies show that the benefits of mindful practices such as meditation, yoga, tai chi, and repetitive prayer, as well as pro-social behaviors such as gratitude and compassion, can enhance our happiness, health and well-being. Benefits include increased immune function and longevity and decreased levels of stress, chronic pain, anxiety and depression.

Courses on the Neuroscience of Mindful Living are offered in the Osher Lifelong Leaning Institute (OLLI) at CSUMB Ryan Ranch. OLLI is a community of 925 members 'fifty and better' interested in intellectual and personal growth. Such growth is possible at all ages because of our ability to re-wire our brains, a phenomenon known as neuroplasticity. Michele Crompton, the Director of OLLI (and a resident of Pacific Grove), has developed a broad curriculum that in the Fall '17/Spring '18 year, for example, was composed of 130 offerings by 78 notable instructors and covered a broad range of topics in the humanities and sciences. OLLI is a real treasure here on the Monterey Peninsula!

At Robert Down Elementary School, Principal Linda Williams (another P.G. resident) and her teachers have utilized a mindful approach with children by encouraging them to pay attention to their breath and their emotions and to treat each other - and themselves - with kindness and respect.

The practice of meditation is a well-established way to increase our awareness on a moment to moment basis in our daily lives. While one can practice meditation individually, it is also rewarding to meditate with other like-minded individuals. My wife, Judy, and I sit with the Monterey Meditation Group on Thursday nights, 7 PM for 1 hour, in the Fellowship Hall of the First Presbyterian Church, El Dorado St., Monterey. There is no charge, and novices as well as experienced meditators are always welcome!

P.G. STUDIOS: Pacific Grove Mindfulness Studios: Montereybaymeditation.com, 529 Central, 831-233-1411; Montereycenterformindfullnessandcompassion.com, 716 Lighthouse #E, meika.hamisch@gmail.com

Biosketch: Joe has held positions at Massachusetts General Hospital, Harvard Medical School, Marine Biological Laboratory, University of Miami School of Medicine and the VA Medical Center. He has published 100 research and review papers on the mechanisms of learning and memory, neuroendocrinology, and traumatic brain injury.

The Journey is the Destination
Joy Ann Fischer

Our 1955 beach house in Pacific Grove is a dream come true. This purchase of our coastal cottage has been a long time vision that my husband Richard and I have had since our honeymoon here in the summer of 1980.

We have mounted on a wall in our living room a wooden sign that says, "The Journey is the Destination," I had it for many years stored in a closet behind my many boxes of shoes I hardly ever wore.

One cool, misty morning I decided to declutter my closet and donate some items (including my shoes) to Saint Vincent de Paul Thrift Shop in Pacific Grove. I came across this rustic sign nestled behind the mess. It was plain, black, fairly big and very close to being given away. I pulled the sign out of the closet, laid it on the table and decided to think about the words a bit and ponder its meaning.

The dictionary states that the word 'journey' means a long and often difficult process of personal change or development. I thought, "Okay, that's called life and life is a journey." I still wasn't sure if it was worth keeping the sign. I glanced out our family room sliding glass doors to see our very old oak tree towering over the roof of our home. In amongst the branches were hundreds of little white butterflies happily fluttering beneath its canopy of life. The tree provides shade, shelter, beauty, and a story of its own. If only trees could talk. In the same area there are new oak seedlings starting their own life's journey, to hopefully be a very old tree like generations past. While I sip on my cup of warm peppermint tea, I passed by the sign with continued puzzlement of keeping it or not.

Then it hit me! We are walking a part of the same journey our ancestors did that led them to Pacific Grove by the sea. This magical place and pathway to coastal living was our destination. It was just meant to be.

I went to my closet and pulled out my boxes of shoes for others to wear. Yes, the sign stayed. I got my glue gun out with some seashells I had purchased and decorated my plain, black, fairly big sign with artistic flare. I now pass our sign on the wall with a smile and with its own story; our family's story. It's a keeper just like the towering old oak trees and fluttering butterflies.

It's true! It is not about the destination, it is about the journey! It is about life lessons learned, sharing moments in P.G. with our children and our chosen friends we call family.

You know, maybe trees can talk!?

I Had a Dream
Joy Ann Fischer

This 4th of July remembrance was not about magnificent fireworks, or excitement in the air. It was about a coastal barbecue invitation, connections, and thoughts of those past or in need of care and support.

I have had many profound dreams in my 60 years of life. The American civil rights activist Martin Luther King Jr. spoke on August 28, 1963 about his dream of freedom and jobs for all. His speech 'I Have a Dream' was a defining moment of the civil rights movement that many will never forget.

On June 18th we received an email invitation to a festive barbecue on the 4th of July by our friends and P.G. realtor Joe Smith and his wife Peggy. Get out the red, white and blue clothes because we're going to a party! After a lovely afternoon gathering with many coastal friends, good food, and a colorful dessert to die for, we had a quiet evening in Pacific Grove. Before dusk, we walked to Asilomar Beach to take in the sunset and all its glory. I always thought fireworks were a necessity on the fourth, but a P.G. sunset is the best by far!

In the early morning of July 5th I had a dream. I was sitting on a porch with my friend Lynette. We were connecting, sharing a hug and enjoying our time together. Up the walkway came her husband John. With his sweet smile on his face and looking as happy and healthy as he ever did, he said, "May I join you two beautiful ladies?" Lynette said with a shy excitement in her voice, "Sure." John sat down between us on the porch step and put his arms around us and patted our shoulders. He said gently and peacefully, "I am good, and everything is going to be just fine!"

I don't remember much more than that but I'll take it! That morning I woke up around 7 AM to blue jays squawking and woodpeckers pecking on an old oak tree branch outside my window. The hummingbirds were fluttering around and very happy that I made a new batch of sweet nectar water for them to drink. Life seemed to be at peace.

In Martin Luther King Jr.'s speech he states, "We can never be satisfied"; "With this faith"; "Let freedom ring" and "Free at last!"

The morning of July 5th around 8 AM I received a call from Lynette. Her name showed up on my cell phone screen and my heart skipped a beat. I answered the call by the end of the first ring and said, "Hi, how's it going?" Lynette quietly said she wanted me to know that her husband John had passed away early that morning. There was silence on the phone. It's like I knew inside but not really. He lost his battle to the ugly disease called cancer. He died at home with his wife nearby. He knew he was loved.

I too have a dream. A visitation from a friend, hope for beyond, and faith for a better place for all someday. I hold close those I love in my heart. I am grateful for P.G. connections, memories of laughter, music opportunities, and singing together. I am especially grateful for dreams.

I had a dream, I knew a man, and I am forever blessed.

Stone Cat Spirit Sculpture
Elizabeth Fisher

I came to Pacific Grove from the East Coast in 1971. I didn't settle here at the time but I fell in love with the town, visiting often over forty years before I returned six years ago to become a resident. I consider myself a mystic, transcendentalist, art enthusiast and natural philosopher who draws from a variety of traditions. In this regard, I have found Pacific Grove is filled with surprises and creations in yards and along roadways.

I walk the streets looking for these hidden treasures. There's shell art, colored glass bottles on tree branches and altar style images such as Buddha's, Kuan Yin's, and Ganesh's. There are gnomes and unicorns, St. Francis and Mary Magdalene. Impressive Little Free Libraries pop up delightfully, and glorious renditions of otters, whales and seals echo the real ones in the bay.

For me, both past and present residents communicate by what they choose to display. I've also been struck by the many tables and chairs set up as conversation spaces. Some are ornate cast iron, usually painted white or black, some are Adirondack chairs, and others are more utilitarian. It's as if the residents who lived here during different time periods are continually sharing points of views with one another.

At Lighthouse Avenue and Sixth Street there is one particularly captivating sculpture atop a fifteen foot wall, a crouching stone cat overlooking the sidewalk. Everything is colored by our experiences and perspectives. To me this cat is a "She." I am a cat person so I find Her comforting. I saw Her on my first visit to Pacific Grove decades ago. In some ways *She* called me back.

Now I live within a few blocks of Her presence which I admire frequently. Perched on the upper side of Lighthouse, She faces the Bay, next to an iron grill gate at the entrance to a stairway to the impressive home above. The magnificent stone wall is also a work of art. Each boulder speaks its own messages. I have heard Her called a Mountain Lion. I like this since mountain lions did once roam this area, contributing significantly to the balance of nature.

Local lore says She was sculpted by the writer Clark Ashton Smith who lived in P.G. in his later years, dying here in 1961. Clark Ashton Smith has been called a visionary. He wrote science fiction fantasies and poetry. The P.G. Library has an impressive collection of his stories for loan. He also produced many fantastic paintings, drawings, and sculptures. When he lived locally, writing poetry, walking along the bay, and gardening occupied his time. We are fortunate to have one of his stone creations in our town.

The contemporary novel written about Pacific Grove entitled *Doubletime: It Never Happened in Pacific Grove or So They Say…* by Julian Collingwood says: "The gargoyle has special powers. It is said to guard the entrance to the spirit world."

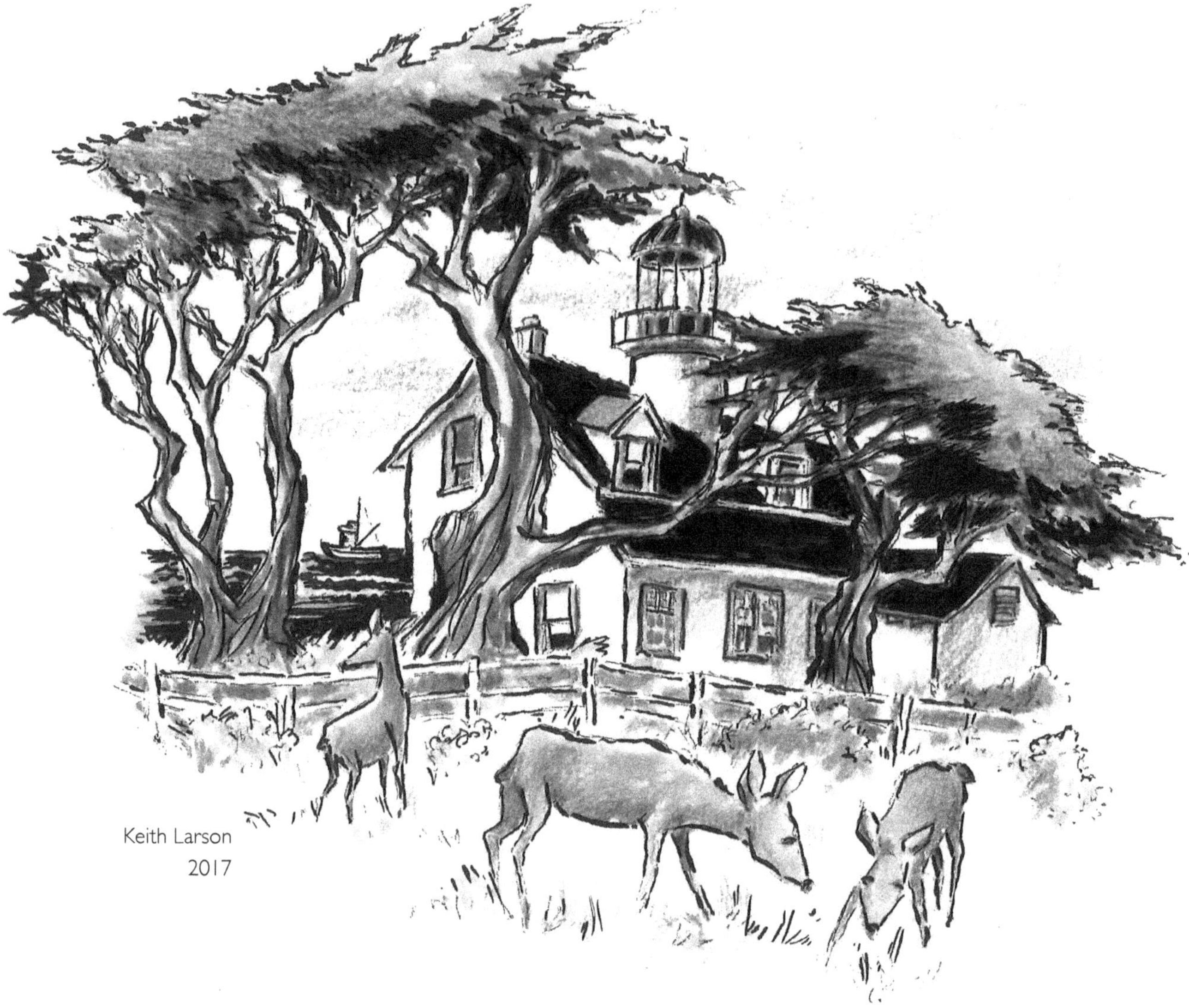
Keith Larson
2017

Keepers
of the Path
by Keith Larson
for Wesley

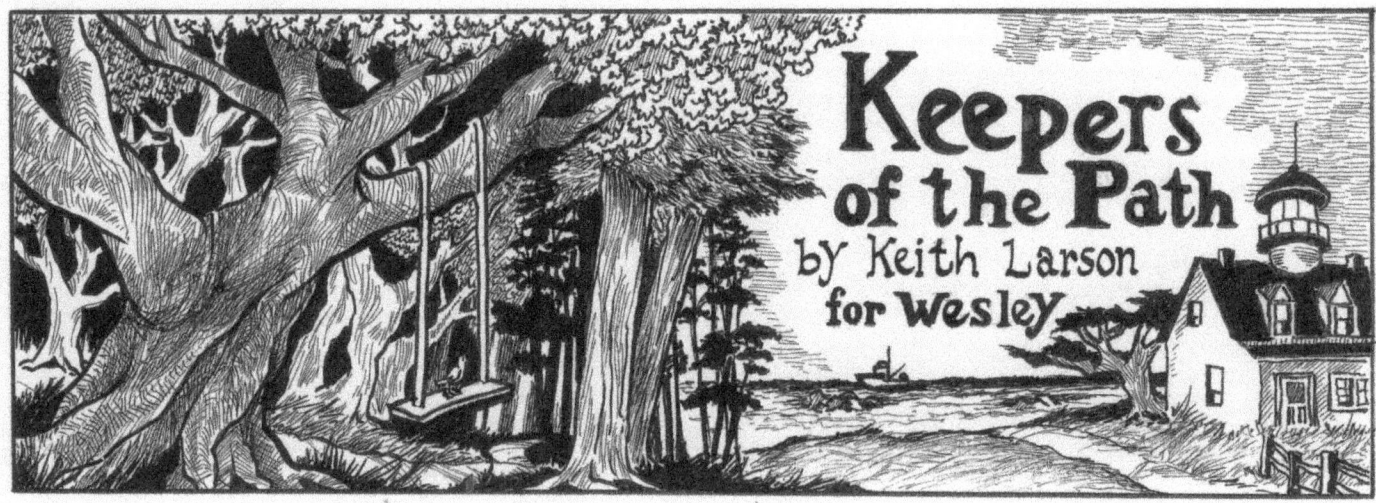

A Creative Journey to a True State of Being
Keith Larson

Every creative project I undertake is like a journey for me. I start out on a path, not sure where it will take me, I follow the art wherever it leads me. "Keepers of the Path" contains a lot of personal meaning and symbolism that only reveals itself as I continue to write and create the graphics.

A simple premise on the surface: two boys take a shortcut through the woods and meet some mystical characters on the way home from school. Some of us might remember a time when children had fewer structured activities after school. Left to our own imaginations, we enjoyed a few hours in the late afternoon to create pretend worlds to play in.

'Like Having a Dream'

Over the years I've carved a path of self-discovery from my writing, art, meditations and dream work. Using these creative tools as a way to get in touch with the intuitive aspects of myself, the interpretations of what I create help me see a larger view and deeper meaning for my life and the world around me. Writing and making art is like having a dream. After the work is finished I wake up and take a look at the gift in the form of a message that I have received. I try to give the highest interpretation I can to whatever I have created, hoping that through the creative process I become more open to endless possibilities.

In the very first panel of "Keepers of the Path," one of the characters is inviting his friend to take a different route home from school. This, to me, is an invitation to do something different, a new line of thinking perhaps, following a new path a little while to see if it is right, taking a chance on a new idea, breaking up a routine to try something new. The first panel sets the stage and my characters, Tim and Wesley, decide to answer the call to change their routine. Right away in the second panel the two boys meet a character called Kenpo who is the guardian of the forest path. In my story, I decided not to give the boys any big challenges, obstacles, goblins or ghouls to meet and overcome. Instead I highlight the building of trusting relationships with those who always seem to show up to guide us on a new path.

Paths take many forms and the journey may take varying amounts of time. We refer to career paths or taking the path of raising a family. Adversity means that at times we take a challenging or difficult path, defined sometimes as the dark night of the soul. What is true for any path is that we meet wise counsel and help that comes in many forms. I wanted to focus on and create characters who represent those that have our best interests in mind and want to see us succeed. The children in my story are learning to trust the path and their inner knowing.

Learning to play again is symbolized by the swing hanging from the big tree named Sylvia. When the children aren't sure which path to take, her advice is to swing awhile and maybe they'll see the answer. This is similar to my approach when I have a problem or am in a situation that doesn't seem to have a workable solution. For me, the answer often comes when I just take some art materials and play with them for a while. Oftentimes, something new opens up, the creative process being the catalyst for solutions and forward movement.

When the children in my story reach the lighthouse, they know where they are and can find their way home from there. They choose to stay and have cookies with Nana, the lighthouse keeper. Nana is based on some research I did, teaching me that not all lighthouse keepers were men. Keeping a lighthouse maintained was not an easy job in those days. For my story I decided it was best to show a nurturing side to this character, rather than the difficult aspects of the challenges she faced at her work.

Intuitive Gifts from Nature

Before they leave for home the two boys receive a gift from Nana: two special pine cones from Sylvia, the mother tree of the forest. Kenpo. Sylvia and Nana are connected in my story, as they represent the wisdom available to us on any path we take. Oftentimes this wisdom comes to us in the form of our own intuition rather than from an outer source. The pine cones, she explains, are like a ship's compass that guides us through the forest and to the light, so that we need never again lose our way completely. The pine cones can also be a symbol and reminder of the gifts available to us in the quiet and solitude of a forest retreat. The return to nature for a time is often the ideal solution to challenges in life.

In the final panels of my story, we discover that the journey being shared is actually being conveyed by a father telling his son a bedtime story. The story he has just told to his son represents cherished memories of afternoons long since passed, as the father recalls childhood days spending time with his friends and their collective imaginations. It is evident that at times the father has lost something that he would like to find again, something that he experienced in childhood but had to let go of later as he grew into an adult. This loss is difficult for many of us to put into words and sometimes is buried so completely we can't put meaning on the discomfort that is triggered from time-to-time. The old TV show *Twilight Zone* explored this common theme in a few very well-written episodes. And with all the inner-child work publications and processes, I believe the father in my story is not an unusual characterization.

The little boy in my story senses his father has lost his way and reminds him of the pine cone. Our children have a job and that is to teach us to play again. If we have children they will invite us to play and remember what it was like to just be in the moment playing and making up stories and games. So in the story, the pine cone is used as an invitation given to an adult by a child in hopes of forming a friendship through play. There is not a lot of time these days for play with the demands of work and keeping a household. I've realized looking back that it was not the amount of time spent, but the quality of attention I gave to my child. I believe total attention is the love children long for, and in giving this undivided attention we also feel the love our children have for us.

The final panel is a celebration. The father has received the special pine cone, the compass and catalyst for his return journey. He has heeded the call and done his inner work for however long and in whatever form it took to reconnect with the precious aspects of his innocent and true state of being.

The Basic Reminders of a Balanced Life

This final panel of my graphic journey looks like an arrival at a destination, and in some ways for me it is. I know this path very well now, but will need to be reminded of its main messages which for me are basic reminders of a balanced life. Take some chances without having to figure everything out. Use my tools of creativity, meditation and the wise counsel of those I respect to help me find my way if I become lost. Retreat to the silence and stillness of a forest for renewal, build trusting relationships, expect the unexpected good to manifest in some form, see every piece of art, every experience, every day as a private message just for me to be viewed with the highest interpretations possible at the time without blaming anyone for anything. Have strong intentions and goals for achieving my heart's deepest desires without trying to control what the path and circumstance should look like.

I recently went to a movie about the life of Mr. Rogers. One of the people being interviewed wondered if his television show, which I believe was done in the highest regard for the growth and welfare of childhood viewers, had really changed anything in a positive way. I think that would be very difficult to measure. I believe people like Mr. Rogers soften our experiences. Collectively it may look like we're not making much progress, but each of us, no matter what our work and circumstances, can soften another person's experience in this world through our intentions to practice compassion and kindness wherever we are called to be or whatever we are called to do. So now with the publication of this work I turn it over to you, the reader, in hopes that you will find some value in what I have expressed for your own journeys.

—*Kindest regards, Keith*

I'll Never Forget That Smile
As told by Engine No. 999
Keith Larson

I awoke one day in a place where men forged hot metal into ideas. Ideas born on slanted drawing boards and recorded on paper with rulers, T-squares and pencils. Dreams that came from a force to create something. I could have been made into anything. Only a few days earlier I had been ore sleeping in the earth. I was now destined for something, I felt important as plans were made and so much attention paid to me. For a brief moment I was no longer solid but a liquid of intense heat poured into a small mold.

When I emerged, I discovered I had been formed into a toy locomotive. I was then moved along an assembly line where I received a shiny black paint job. Men and women passed by in a blur, each one adding something to my metal frame: wheels, bells, lights and gears. At the end of this frantic but organized journey, I was placed on a track and began to move around and around in a circle. Then all of a sudden everything became still and dark again, like being back in the earth, as I was placed inside a box with other train cars, including a bright red caboose, all clean and neatly packed.

I didn't know what it would mean to be a toy locomotive, or what I would experience. One day the lid came off the box. A little boy of about six years old stared down at me with a look of complete joy. It was the most beautiful sight I could ever hope to see. His smile became even more intense as he and his dad took me out of the box, set up the track, and hooked up the big transformer that powered me and the other cars along the clackety-sounding rails.

I was built to last and I have outlasted and survived many situations that toy trains and toys in general succumb to. I've spent years packed away, and somehow got separated from the other train cars that I started out with. At one point a shoe box was my home instead of the beautiful packaging that I was first placed in. From flea market to antique store, it seemed like every few years I moved somewhere. Various new owners opened the boxes I was packed in, but I never again experienced the smile of a little boy looking down at me. Oh, but I had the memory, and I could remember that first time, and I could feel the joy of a father and son at the sight of me and the other train cars. No matter what, I have always tried to keep this memory fresh as if the moment had just happened.

My situation changed again and I found myself in an old building that had once been a sardine cannery in Monterey. Now it was an antique mall. I felt fortunate to be on a shelf next to a window where I could look out at the boats. I liked the fog even though it was hard on my metal frame. I hadn't run in years, but I was sure I still could with a little work. I worried that no one would find me, as I wasn't displayed prominently. My tag said fifteen dollars, "as is."

One day an old man started to poke around the shelf where I sat. He picked me up and closely examined my working parts. Then to my surprise, he carried me off. I was paid for and taken to his garage, where an old three-rail track was set up, the type I used to run on. I was placed on the track. The buzz of the 190-watt transformer sounded as it was plugged in. The old man moved the throttle slowly forward. My small driving wheels started to turn. I rounded the track once or twice, then I was taken to a work bench where I received a complete going-over: oil, grease, and electrical connections, even a brand-new paint job, I felt like a kid again and ran like one, too.

Then one day a little boy of about seven years old came into the garage. The old man let him take the throttle on the transformer and run me around the track. As the front of my engine rounded the curve I could see the boy's face, the same expression I had seen over eighty years ago when my box was opened for the first time—pure joy. I was not a computer game or a radio controlled car, but I still had it in me. I could still make a little boy smile.

Keith's grandson, Mattias Larson.

Keith's family: Son Wesley, daughter-in-law Kristen, granddaughter Kaia, and grandson Mattias Larson.

Dennis Trason
As in Life—So Too in Death
Deane Ramoni

I am Dennis Trason's last student. He was my significant sweetheart and soul mate for 25 years. Dennis, a 64 year resident of Pacific Grove, by profession was a beloved teacher and soccer and tennis coach at Monterey and Seaside High Schools. Even in his death, which occurred on March 31, 2018, he left an educational lesson for all of us on the Monterey Peninsula.

Dennis had two separate and distinct strokes this year with end results that were as different as night and day. The first happened on January 4, 2018. It was around 9:00 p.m. while we were talking together that I noticed a slight droop at the corner of his left lip and a little slurring of his words. When Dennis started to get up from his chair but couldn't, I tried to help him. We both ended up sliding down to the floor. Fortunately, he didn't hit his head or lose consciousness. He immediately begged me not to call 911, which I did anyway. Help came immediately. Yes, Dennis was having a stroke.

We live only five minutes away from CHOMP. The paramedics quickly took him there by ambulance. Dr. Centurion, a neurologist, met me at CHOMP's ER. He immediately started to explain about the pros and cons of giving Dennis a risky medication called TPA: Tissue Plasminogen Activator. This would either bust up Dennis' clot or could cause death. What a choice! I opted for the TPA and began to pray. In 48 hours the miracle occurred. Dennis was able to move his left hand and leg. In time, he was admitted into CHOMP's state-of-the-art, world class Inpatient Rehabilitation Unit. I can't say enough good things about this part of the story.

After 3 weeks, Dennis came home. His recovery was progressing along until Good Friday morning, March 30, when Dennis suffered his second stroke. This time the stroke, which occurred around 9:00 a.m., affected his right side. At ER the TPA was given immediately. Within 1 hour he was already moving his right side. I was elated and ready to call CHOMP's IRU to have them save Dennis a bed in rehab.

Soon after, I was given the bad news that this time Dennis' clot was in his neck. CHOMP did not have the doctors, radiologists or equipment to help. He would need to be transported to Stanford Hospital by helicopter.

Since CHOMP does not have a heliport, the helicopter had to land at the Monterey Airport and the flight nurses with all their equipment taken by ambulance to CHOMP, prepare, pickup and transport Dennis to the airport by ambulance.

Precious time was wasted. It took nearly 4 hours before Dennis arrived at Stanford Hospital and was given a brain scan. The result was that all the tissue in his head was gone and there was nothing that could be done for him except to ventilate and call for the next of kin to come to say goodbye. Dennis passed away the next day when the ventilator was removed.

There could have been a different ending to this story, if CHOMP had a heliport or was a Thrombectomy capable Stroke Center. Dennis has given me a crusade. I am in touch with representatives of CHOMP and have been told that a heliport is not in their next 5 year plan, and to become a TSC hospital is under consideration with no guarantees.

My grassroots effort to bring this issue to the people of Monterey County begins with a **Dennis Trason Charity Golf Tournament**, October 14, 2018, at Pacific Grove Golf Links. For more information about how you can help CHOMP become a TSC hospital, please contact me: Deane Ramon, ideane.ramoni@sothebyshomes.com 831-917-6080 Cell or 831-649-0591 Home.

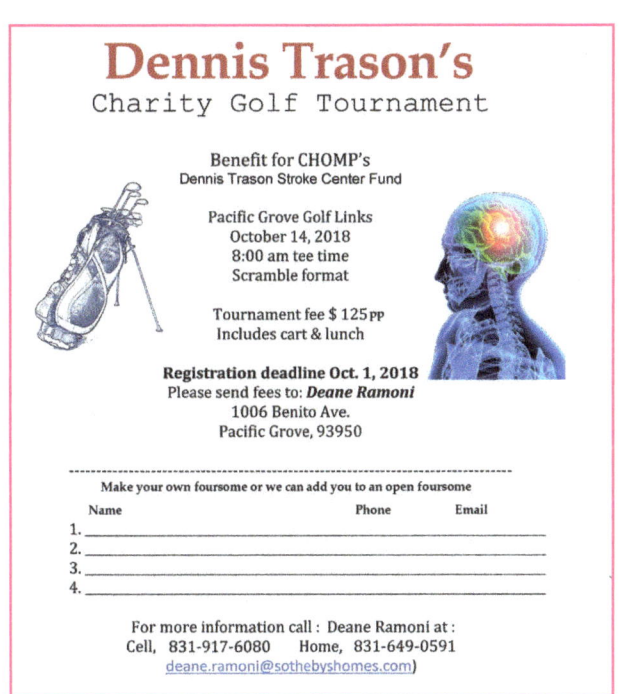

More than 20 people attended, including local Native Americans from around the peninsula. We were invited to watch and help Louis and Vincent prepare the dishes - and that alone was eye-opening. No foods from Charlie's Deli for them! I can't begin to describe the blend of natural flavors, because I had never tasted anything so truly alive and wonderful. I do recommend you cater your Thanksgiving with them, if you reserve early.

Bioneers Decolonize Thanksgiving Program

3:00-4:00 Drinks and Cultural Activities

Ohlone Yerba Buena Tea, Manzanita Cider
California Indian games and demonstrations

4:00-4:30 Welcome
Ohlone Blessing and Introduction to Indigenous Monterey
Welcome and opening remarks by Joshua Fouts and Alexis Bunten (Aleut)

4:30-5:00 Cultural Foods Presentation
Presentation of Ohlone traditional foods and description of the menu, with Louis Trevino (Rumsen Ohlone) and Vincent Medina (Chochenyo Ohlone)

5:00-6:00 Meal Service
Dinner is served during a Thanksgiving reading
Premier viewing from the 2017 Bioneers Indigenous Forum panels

6:00-7:00 Responses Talking Circle

"What Indigenous Thanksgiving means to me,"
Closing perspectives from special guest presenters

7:00-8:00 Dessert
Table Talk
Alexis Bunten presents "Future Visions from Bioneers Indigeneity"
Closing Prayer

"Indigenous Thanksgiving"
Patricia Hamilton with Alexis Bunten

November 2017

Dear Friends,

You are invited to "Indigenous Thanksgiving," an eye-opening evening of learning, incredible foods, and forging new friendships that I am hosting with my friend Alexis Bunten, with the Bioneers Indigeneity Program.

Alexis co-hosted the first Indigenous Thanksgiving with Heather Henson of the Jim Henson Company last year in New York City, and the event was such a success, she decided to bring it home to Monterey, and invited me to be this year's co-host.

This year's feast will be held at the Pacific Grove Youth Center on the Monterey Bay Peninsula, on Sunday, November 19, 2017, from 3-8 pm.

The modern take on traditional Ohlone foods served at this event may be the first time that California Native cuisine has been served on the Peninsula in over 150 years!

To learn more about the event, please read the "Official Invitation" below, and see the attached Program and Menu.

OFFICIAL INVITATION

At Bioneers, we are committed to honoring all peoples' connection to this beautiful planet through the experience of indigeneity. To do this, we are guided by a vision of social and ecological justice that must address the wounds of the past in order to collectively shape a flourishing future for all of life, for the generations to come.

In this spirit, I am writing to cordially invite you to the second annual "Decolonize Thanksgiving" feast co-hosted by the **Bioneers Indigeneity Program** and "**Keepers of Our Culture**," to be held at the **Pacific Grove Youth Center** on the Monterey Bay Peninsula, Sunday, November 19, 2017, from 3-8 pm.

This year's feast will feature traditional, California Native foods, locally-harvested by contemporary Ohlone caterers, **Mak-amham**, which means "Our Food" in the Chochenyo Language. Together, chefs Vincent Medina (Chochenyo Ohlone) and Louis Trevino (Rumsen Ohlone) have revitalized their ancestral food ways for healing and well-being. You will notice sweet and savory food combinations from simple pairings of 6 ingredients or less that make up the signature, pre-contact Ohlone palate.

True to the Indigeneity Program's mission, the evening program will share the real story of California to a diverse and family-friendly group through expressive and interactive dialogue. (Children are very welcome! We're bringing ours.) Together, we will celebrate people from many different backgrounds coming together to experience the revitalization of Indigenous traditions. This is a time for intercultural dialogue, and to make new friends of all generations and backgrounds. This is the REAL spirit of Thanksgiving.

Sincerely,
Alexis Celeste Bunten (Aleut/Yup'ik), Ph.D.
Bioneers Indigeneity Program

From the Caterers—Vincent and Louis:

"All our food is rooted in the values of our Indigenous communities and all our food is free of gluten, refined sugar, corn, soy, dairy, alcohol, or anything artificial. It is our hope to create beautiful Ohlone cuisine that allows us to be a little closer to those before us, and to honor the legacy we inherit from them. Our primary goal is always the wellness and decolonization of our Ohlone communities. We also hope to educate non-Indian people about who we are, as the Indigenous people of the East Bay and Carmel Valley. We hope to dispel negative stereotypes through actively demonstrating the vibrancy and beauty of Ohlone culture, and especially the deep + living connections we have to our homelands. We hope to raise awareness to people who are not indigenous to California what the true culture and cuisine of this beautiful and ancient place really is."

A True Christmas Story
Kristina Kringle

My name is Kristina Kringle. I am 19 years old. I came into being in December 1987. I am the happy ending to a woman's journey of transformation.

I first saw the woman 49 days before Christmas. She was in extreme pain. The kind that permeates from one's center to every cell of one's body. It is terrifying to be in that much pain. One wonders if it can even be survived.

How she got there is immaterial. We know that she is not the only one who experienced it, nor will she be the last. We just pray that people who experience deep core pain recover to wholeness.

Over the 19 years, I have watched this woman do exactly that. Not only has she done it for herself—for brief moments she offers others the opportunity to lighten their hearts.

This is our story. In that dreadful December the woman was invited to a Christmas party. She was in so much pain she couldn't fathom being gay or cheerful even for a moment.

Although she was very responsible at her job—arrived on time, did what was expected—when her shift ended, as she walked out of the building her eyes welled up in tears. She would tell herself, "Please not now, give me five or ten minutes—just don't come while I am around people that I know. You must wait."

At the bus stop—less than a five minute walk—she would cry, sob, and through her jolts, she managed to pull out a notebook. In that notebook, she would write letters. Sometimes they were addressed to herself, other letters would be addressed to the people who hurt her, other times they would be addressed to God or to a being greater than herself.

These letters were so horrifying, they were on fire. The woman literally thought that some were so hot, she expected them to spontaneously combust. (The letters were never mailed.) They weren't supposed to be. The woman was scared, she was angry, she was enraged. She must write her way through the pain.

It was during this time that she was invited to the Christmas party. She so badly wanted to decline. Her friends thought of every means possible for her to say yes. They offered to pick her up, they offered her to stay the night, they offered to make her breakfast the following day. They offered her the opportunity to be out of her pain.

As she listened to all that they offered, she accepted on one condition. She must wear a green pinafore apron with white ruffles and a Santa hat. She refused to attend the party in her so-called "street clothes." Let me clarify that she was not a lady of the night. This is where I, Kristina Kringle, come in; however, the woman doesn't know me yet. As a matter of fact, I am a secret to her for many years.

She puts on the green pinafore apron with white ruffles, and a Santa hat. Looks in the mirror, and asks her reflection straight in the puffy cried-out eyes, "how can i be sad, knowing that i look like this?"

For that one evening the woman makes conversation, people compliment her, she is in the group photos, she is a part of the party, she is in hope.

A week later, it is Christmas Eve. The woman is dreading going to work. Christmas is a time of romance, joy, and laughter. The woman is in her grief. She receives permission from her boss to don her elf costume (the green pinafore apron with white ruffles and a Santa hat). Her pockets are lined with candy canes to give to children and their parents as she sees them.

She sees me, Kristina Kringle, simply as Santa's elf

She dons herself as an elf with each passing year only as the situation presents itself. Such as the days her family or friends decorate their Christmas trees and she goes to help out. One year she decorated four trees in a week. It was fun. She always dresses as me, Kristina Kringle, on Christmas Eve and Christmas Day. Yet the woman continues to have no recognition of me.

We see the years pass by, the woman returns to school, graduates from college, falls in love and is married. She continues to celebrate the holidays in her elf costume—only it has grown. One year she purchased a pair of red sequined slip-on shoes with Santa faces on the tops. Another year, it was a pair of white polar fleece mittens; another year it was a snowman purse she calls "Snowden." The purchase of all purchases was a pair of red and white striped Raggedy Ann-type tights. The woman bought two packages just in case. I am pleased to report that both pairs are in excellent condition.

Her husband even bought a bracelet for the elf costume followed by a necklace. And yet, the woman and her husband still do not know me.

Over these five or six years of donning her elf clothes, she meets Santa and his wife. Upon occasion, she would make an appearance with them, yet I was not known to her. Until one magical, memorable evening. After meeting with Santa, the woman attended a neighborhood party, dressed as me, from head to toe. She looked radiant. The host and hostess provided a traditional English Christmas dinner with Yorkshire pudding and all of the works.

After the dinner was eaten, the guests were seated at the table enjoying dessert. The host looks straight into the woman's eyes and tells her, "I KNOW WHO YOU ARE!"

She replies, "Yes, I know that you know me."

He answers, "That's not what I mean." After a pause, he claims, "You're Kristina Kringle."

The woman looks back at his eyes, ponders the name, continues looking not at him but looking back at all of the years of donning her elf clothes and what it had meant for her over the years: REPRIEVE FROM HER PAIN. . . and joy to others.

Moments later she acknowledges the name, *my* name, Kristina Kringle. The woman likes it—LOVES IT.

She says to herself, "I am Kristina Kringle!" Ponders more upon my name. The woman is elated. She is named, I am named, I have a title. The woman embraced me, Kristina Kringle.

She informs the host that she cannot be referred to as Mrs. Claus because Mrs. Claus has been around for centuries, just like Santa. So the woman decides that Kristina Kringle must be Santa's young cousin. That works.

I don't know how old I was when I finally got named. I presume I was about 10 years old. Now I am 19.

I share my story with you because this has been one of my best years ever. The woman and her husband traveled a lot this year, they studied a foreign language. While they were away, they thought of me and bought me a new apron. It's a red plaid lightweight cotton pinafore. Imagine, buying Kristina Kringle a present in May.

They thought about me again in September. The woman makes quilts and sometimes dolls. I now have 24 pairs of Christmas socks, all unique in design and color. The woman made me a Sock Advent Calendar. It has 24 pockets. Each pocket is 12 inches by 12 inches, lined with white fabric and a white ruffle. The pockets are children playing in the snow. The colors are all bright red, green, white, and blue. It's happy and reminds the woman and her husband of me, Kristina Kringle. The piece is 7 feet tall by 43 inches wide. It is brilliant.

In November, the calendar gets hung and the pockets are filled. From December 1 on, a pair of socks are removed. I, Kristina Kringle, come out to play. This year, I appeared with Santa four times, I've gone to church, and I even went to work and was gainfully employed for three days. I received a handsome paycheck just for being me, Kristina Kringle.

I almost forgot, while the woman was shopping in December, she bought me a jewelry box. This is not an ordinary box with drawers and compartments for rings, necklaces, and bracelets. This jewelry box is a red wire mesh sleigh. Inside the sleigh stores my three little purses and two pairs of gloves. The outside mesh is adorned with my earrings, Christmas pins, hairclips, and necklaces. In front of the sleigh are three special pipe cleaner bracelets (red, green, and white) all braided by a special little girl.

My 19th year has been truly the best. I've been thought about many more times this year than usual.

A couple of years ago, the woman's husband asked her, "Why do you do it, you know, dress as Kristina Kringle?"

The woman thoughtfully, lovingly responded, "Do you remember the woman we saw this morning? She looked so sad, when she looked up and saw me as Kristina Kringle, her face broke into a smile?…"

The woman ended, "That's why I do it."

– AKA Kimberly Brown

Parade of Lights 2016. Photos Peter Mounteer.

My 2018 "Memoir Movie Method"–A Story Writing Technique: "It's All In Your Head"

You may believe you can't remember much from your childhood … or any other time in your life. Consider this: the sensory details of all your life's experiences are categorized and stored in your brain, and are available for recall. This retrieval/viewing/writing method will guide you in accessing even the deepest buried memories. *Follow this technique for easy recall and writing of your precious life stories—then share them with someone who loves you.*

— Prepare a quiet place for yourself, where you won't be disturbed. Turn off all electronics, and sit quietly in a comfortable chair or sofa. You'll need to sit upright because you will be typing or writing.

— Assemble what you will need for writing. I sit in a recliner with my iPad placed on a laptop desk—available at stationery stores and online.

— If you prefer to write longhand, I recommend a letter size, yellow lined tablet. You can fill up a page and quickly flip it over for a new one without looking. Have two or more writing implements at hand, your choice.

— Decide what story you want to tell and make an intention. For instance: "I want to write about the time my brother Bob and I traveled to Mexico on his 35th birthday."

— Now, you've made a quiet and comfortable place for yourself; you've set your intention to write about something, and you're sitting comfortably, with your writing tools in front of you and your hand poised to begin.

— Gently close your eyes and breathe deeply in and out as you relax into your chair or sofa. Give thanks for taking this time to write your story. Continue breathing naturally as you feel your body relax.

— Repeat your intention in your head and wait. Allow the memory to surface. Keep your eyes closed. Your mind will look here and there for something to grab onto. A movie begins to play in your mind's eye. As it plays across the screen behind your eyes, your hands type exactly what you see there inside your head. No editing, no stopping to check the spelling, just steady writing as images make their way across the screen in your head.

— Stay with your eyes closed, your hand recording what you see, until the movie is over—you'll know when that is.

— Open your eyes and look at what you've written. You are going to be very surprised by all the memories that surfaced—without trying to recall anything. In essence, you relived the experience and images flashed by of what you saw, where you went, what the weather was like, the food you ate, people you met, any sudden joys or irritations. And especially all the feelings you had as everything played across the screen inside your head. It's a wonderful thing that just happened to you.

Consider this your best first draft ever! You bypassed your inner critique and allowed free association in its most productive form to take place. You're excited now! The hardest part of writing—that first draft—never happened. Congratulate yourself. You'll be motivated to stay with the story and start adding little details here and there that you saw but didn't have time to write before the next picture flashed across your mind.

☉☉☉

Below is the first story I wrote using this technique. My writing prompt was, *"What about my visit to Alamos, Mexico, still enriches my life today?"* I sat with that question in my mind, eyes closed, and as images began to appear, I quickly typed each one, then the next one, and so on. I was standing at the entrance to a new nature park and knew this was the experience I wanted to write about. Below is what I typed (unedited) as I was transported back in time and relived a wonderful time I had in Mexico.

Closing my eyes here in California my mind goes back to Alamos, Mexico, reaching for enriching experiences which flood in quickly one after another: *I see smiling brown faces, sweet young girls and boys, smell shrimp tacos being fried and catch iguanas darting down drainpipes. Then my mind wanders to the new park in town—Palo Colorado. I ask directions and almost miss the tree limb and wire entrance but the sign leads me in and opens to brush and sandy hills and scrub trees. I follow a wide dirt path and fully enter the forest of mesquite, yucca, cholla, amapa, and saguaro. The path is smooth and wanders with care, decorated here and there with rocks to remind me humans have created this safe way into mother nature. Further along the few neighborhood noises of car and jeep fade away and there I hear only the crunch of my shoes and the occasional squawk of an overflying bird—magpie, cardinal, hawk. The natural world calms me completely and I search for a place to sit and meditate. Later I emerge back on the cobblestone streets and believe I have entered a different world, greeting people, strangers with a renewed calm. Yes, the nature of Palo Colorado enriches me still.*

☉☉☉

That was fun! I just sat down with my iPad and my intention, opened an email and typed blindly as I watched my movie. Now I'll add photos and details, then read it to my grandkids.- *Happy writing and sharing!*

~ *Patricia Hamilton, 2018*

INDEX TO WRITERS AND OTHER CONTRIBUTORS

Aeschliman, Robin 245
Anderson, Flora 239
Arcanin, Geva 194
Armstrong, Dawn 34
Avila, Judy 231
Azevedo, Elayne 184
Baley, Gary 270
Bell, Nancy 241-243
Bukowski, Wolf 154
Bunten, Alexis 311
Coleman, Kaye 50, 52
Corcoran, Annette 244
Countz, Stan 241-3
Cuneo, Ken 212
Dee, Ann 233
DeSmit, Becky 34
Edwards, Phyllis 129
Edwards, Rosi 236
Fischer, Joy Ann 152, 297-8
Fischer, Rudy 211, 213, 260,
Fisher, Bob 36
Fisher, Elizabeth 299
Flanigan, Patrick 153
Gianelli, Jim and Barbara 238
Goldbeck, Susan 264
Goulet, Linda 294
Greenfield, David W. 193
Guthrie, Cynthia B. 237
Hamilton, Patricia vii, 250, 311
Herzog, Brad 120
Higuera, Charlie 246
Howard, Sherry L
Hyler, Joanie 56
Jacobs, Nancy 43

Jarvis, Edward E. 262
Jenson, Richard 235
Joyce, Susie 152
Kahan, Evelyn 152, 263
Kraus, Barbara 232
Kraus, Kaito 232
Krieg, Joyce 94, 110
Kringle, Kristina 312
Larson, Keith 40, 300, 306-7
Laws, David A. 102, 104, 148, 226
Layne, Dixie 22, 27, 56
Livermore, Donald 220
Mason, Maureen 224
McCleary, John 72
Meuse, Joyce Day 66
Miller, Emily 260
Minor, Bill 90
Nattress, Joan 243
Neary, Joe 296
Neish, William 200
Ogden, Helen 232
Olson, Liana 293
Pagnella, Linda 243
Panarello, Tania 235
Peake, Bill 211
Pearse, John 192
Pearse, Vicki B. 224
Pierce, Frank 153
Piotrkowski, Terry 231
Ramoni, Deane 309
Reinstedt, Randall A. 3
Richards, Jesse 293
Riddell, Rebecca 162-171
Rockefeller, Ken 250,

Sailer, Bonnie 266
Selby, Vic 94
Shain, Katie 246
Sheridan, Mimi 105, 222,
Sproule, Betty A. 265
Stark, Devora 230
Stewart, LeeAnn 258-260
Sunshine, Russell 172
Swing, Nancy 158
Thompson, Alyce 31
Trason, Dennis 309
Tucker, Sharon Law 261
Tyrrel, Diane 136, 143, 146
Vucina, Anne (Allen) 35
Whitmore, Jeffrey 288-294
Willoughby, Jim 264
Wills, Judy 230
Ybarra, Dionne 210
Young, Betty Lou 197

PACIFIC GROVE BOOKS

Keith Larson, Pacific Grove writer, illustrator and painter.
Indie Author Day 2018 at Ketcham's Barn.
Photo Donna Kiernan.

www.ingramcontent.com/pod-product-compliance
Lightning Source LLC
Chambersburg PA
CBHW051346110526
44591CB00025B/2926